Reflections on Task-Based Language Teaching

MIX
Paper from
responsible sources
FSC® C014540

FSC
www.fsc.org

SECOND LANGUAGE ACQUISITION

Series Editors: Professor David Singleton, *University of Pannonia, Hungary and Fellow Emeritus, Trinity College, Dublin, Ireland* and Associate Professor Simone E. Pfenninger, *University of Salzburg, Austria*

This series brings together titles dealing with a variety of aspects of language acquisition and processing in situations where a language or languages other than the native language is involved. Second language is thus interpreted in its broadest possible sense. The volumes included in the series all offer in their different ways, on the one hand, exposition and discussion of empirical findings and, on the other, some degree of theoretical reflection. In this latter connection, no particular theoretical stance is privileged in the series; nor is any relevant perspective – sociolinguistic, psycholinguistic, neurolinguistic, etc. – deemed out of place. The intended readership of the series includes final-year undergraduates working on second language acquisition projects, postgraduate students involved in second language acquisition research, and researchers, teachers and policy-makers in general whose interests include a second language acquisition component.

All books in this series are externally peer-reviewed.

Full details of all the books in this series and of all our other publications can be found on http://www.multilingual-matters.com, or by writing to Multilingual Matters, St Nicholas House, 31–34 High Street, Bristol BS1 2AW, UK.

SECOND LANGUAGE ACQUISITION: 125

Reflections on Task-Based Language Teaching

Rod Ellis

MULTILINGUAL MATTERS
Bristol • Blue Ridge Summit

DOI https://doi.org/10.21832/ELLIS0131
Library of Congress Cataloging in Publication Data
A catalog record for this book is available from the Library of Congress.

Library of Congress Control Number: 2018001662

British Library Cataloguing in Publication Data
A catalogue entry for this book is available from the British Library.

ISBN-13: 978-1-78892-013-1 (hbk)
ISBN-13: 978-1-78892-012-4 (pbk)

Multilingual Matters
UK: St Nicholas House, 31–34 High Street, Bristol BS1 2AW, UK.
USA: NBN, Blue Ridge Summit, PA, USA.

Website: www.multilingual-matters.com
Twitter: Multi_Ling_Mat
Facebook: https://www.facebook.com/multilingualmatters
Blog: www.channelviewpublications.wordpress.com

The policy of Multilingual Matters/Channel View Publications is to use papers that are natural, renewable and recyclable products, made from wood grown in sustainable forests. In the manufacturing process of our books, and to further support our policy, preference is given to printers that have FSC and PEFC Chain of Custody certification. The FSC and/or PEFC logos will appear on those books where full certification has been granted to the printer concerned.

Typeset by Nova Techset Private Limited, Bengaluru and Chennai, India.
Printed and bound in the UK by Short Run Press Ltd.
Printed and bound in the US by Edwards Brothers Malloy, Inc.

Contents

Acknowledgements

My thanks to go the publishers of the articles and chapters listed below for permission to reprint them in this book.

Ellis, R. (2000) Task-based research and language pedagogy. *Language Teaching Research* 4, 193–220.

Ellis, R. (2001) Non-reciprocal tasks, comprehension and second language acquisition. In M. Bygate, P. Skehan and M. Swain (eds) *Researching Pedagogic Tasks Second Language Learning, Teaching and Testing* (pp. 49–74). Harlow: Longman Pearson.

Ellis, R. (2009) Task-based language teaching: Sorting out the misunderstandings. *International Journal of Applied Linguistics* 19 (3), 222–246.

Ellis, R. (2012) An options-based approach to doing task-based language teaching. In M. Eisenmann and T. Summer (eds) *Basic Issues in EFL Teaching* (pp. 19–33). Heidelberg: Winter.

Ellis, R. (2015) Teachers evaluating tasks. In M. Bygate (ed.) *Domains and Directions in the Development of TBLT* (pp. 247–270). Amsterdam: John Benjamins.

Ellis, R. (2016) Focus on form: A critical review. *Language Teaching Research* 20, 405–428.

Ellis, R. (2018) Preparing learners to perform tasks. In Z. Wen and M. Ahmadian (eds) *Researching Second Language Task Performance and Pedagogy: Essays in Honor of Peter Skehan*. Amsterdam: John Benjamins.

Ellis, R. (2017) Moving task-based language teaching forward. *Language Teaching* 50 (4), 441–482.

Ellis, R. (2017) Towards a modular curriculum. *Language Teaching Research*. DOI: 10.1177/1362168818765315

Preface

My interest in task-based language teaching (TBLT) dates back to the late 1970s when communicative tasks began to figure in language teaching. At that time, tasks were seen as a means of providing second language (L2) learners with opportunity for free oral practice in order to develop fluency. As such they were adjuncts to the 'serious' work involved in teaching language in traditional ways. Around the same time, researchers began to use tasks to investigate the strategies that speakers used to manage communication. It was not until a little later – the mid-1980s – that the first proposals for designing complete instructional programmes based on tasks appeared. A little later, researchers began to treat tasks not just as data-elicitation instruments but as objects worthy of study in their own right.

From these beginnings, TBLT has evolved into an 'approach' – in a sense a 'movement'. Countless articles on tasks and TBLT have been published in leading journals. There is a long list of books dealing with TBLT – some theoretical and research-oriented, others more practical. One publisher (John Benjamins) has a whole series devoted to TBLT. An international association has been formed which sponsors a bi-annual conference. Not surprisingly, perhaps, TBLT has also spawned its critics. Some of these critics view TBLT as foisted on the teaching community by researchers. Others argue that TBLT is impractical in cultural contexts very different from North America and Europe where it originated.

My own work more or less spans the history of TBLT. In the late 1970s I used information-gap tasks in my early teacher-education work to illustrate how teachers could motivate spontaneous communication in the classroom. As I turned more to research, I used tasks to collect the data I needed to investigate L2 use and learning. As time passed I became immersed in the issues facing the design and implementation of task-based programmes. I wrote a full-length book on task-based language learning and teaching. I tried (and failed) to get a leading publisher interested in publishing a task-based course. I gave talks on TBLT in different parts of the world. I ran full postgraduate courses for teachers. On one occasion I responded to an invitation to demonstrate how to do task-based teaching in a large junior high school class of low-proficiency learners in Japan.

I also continued to research task-based lessons, focusing (among other issues) on the role that corrective feedback plays in making linguistic forms salient to learners and facilitating acquisition. I supervised doctoral theses on different aspects TBLT. In other words, TBLT has figured in a very major way in my professional life. This book can be seen as a record of my involvement in and commitment to TBLT.

TBLT is where my interest in research and my concern for the practical business of language teaching coalesce. I am, however, a little wary of 'movements' and of the danger of being swept into the growing community of TBLT advocates. Movements can have a religious fervour that I shy away from. I find myself becoming hostile to the view that there is just one way of doing task-based teaching – identify the target tasks that learners need to perform, design pedagogic tasks based on these target tasks and then implement them, making sure to include focus-on-form. This is certainly one version of TBLT and it is undoubtedly well suited to groups of learners who have clearly identifiable needs, but it does not seem to me well suited to the contexts that I have had most contact with in recent years – classrooms in state schools in Asia. These call out for a different version of TBLT, one where it may be helpful to include elements of more traditional language teaching. So, I have another reason for writing this book. I want to present TBLT as an approach that can be adopted in and adapted to different instructional contexts.

I have one last aim in writing this book. I want to argue that the research focus should shift away from 'tasks' onto 'task-based teaching'. The case for focusing on task design rests on the need to develop a theory of task complexity that can be used to select and sequence tasks in task-based courses. But tasks in the real world of the classroom do not occur in isolation – they are mediated by the teachers and students and they figure in sequences of activities, which will inevitably affect how they are performed. It is surely much more important to investigate how tasks can be used effectively in complete lessons and whole courses rather than how particular design features influence the difficulty of specific tasks. So I would like to propose that researchers should focus more on the implementation of tasks in actual classrooms rather than on the design of tasks in carefully controlled experiments.

A word on the contents of this book. The chapters cover both research and pedagogy and, in particular, the relationship between them. There are chapters that are clearly research-focused but these address research related to pedagogic issues. There are other chapters that tackle pedagogic issues head-on but do so by drawing on relevant research. Most of the chapters are previously published articles, but some have been specially written for this book. The chapters do build on each other sequentially so it would help to read the book from beginning to end, but each chapter is also self-contained so readers could dip into those chapters that are of special interest to them.

All the chapters were authored solely by myself. However, this does not mean that I do not owe a debt to the many students, teachers and fellow researchers who have helped to shape my thinking about TBLT over the years.

Rod Ellis
Perth, 2018

Part 1

Introduction

The two chapters in this part of the book are intended to provide a foundation for the subsequent parts.

Chapter 1 is written for this book. In it I provide a brief historical sketch of how task-based language teaching (TBLT) has developed, tracing its origins in a strong version of communicative language teaching and in early second language acquisition research that pointed to the existence of natural orders and sequences of acquisition that are to a large extent impermeable to the influence of direct language instruction. I then consider how the early version of TBLT evolved over time, as it drew increasingly on general educational principles as well as second language acquisition (SLA). I emphasize that TBLT is not to be seen as monolithic but as quite varied, reflecting differences in how its advocates view the design of syllabuses and the ways in which tasks can be most effectively implemented to facilitate acquisition. Underlying these differences, however, is the common assumption that instruction should aim at facilitating rather than controlling and directing acquisition, which can be best achieved by using tasks.

Chapter 2 was first published in 2000. It introduces the theoretical underpinnings of TBLT. It contrasts two theoretical inputs. Cognitive theories point to the need to design and implement tasks in ways that connect with the cognitive processes involved in L2 production and acquisition. Sociocultural theory points to the need to acknowledge the difference between task-as-workplan and task-as-process and that how learners perform a task (i.e. the task-as-process) will always be – to some extent at least – unpredictable. Although these theoretical perspectives are often seen as oppositional and incommensurate, I argue that they are in fact complementary with research based on cognitive theory especially helpful for the planning of task-based courses and lessons and sociocultural theory serving as a valuable source for addressing the methodology of task-based teaching (i.e. how tasks can be constructively performed). Over time, however, I have become more sanguine regarding the value of research in helping to grade and sequence tasks for purposes of planning task-based courses. My doubts are explained in Chapter 9.

1 A Brief History of Task-based Language Teaching

Introduction

The first edition of Richards and Rogers *Approaches and Methods in Language Teaching* was published in 1986. It included 'Communicative Language Teaching (CLT)' but not 'Task-based Language Teaching (TBLT)' in the list of methods/approaches it considered. However, in the second edition, published in 2001, 'Task-based Language Teaching' was now listed under the general heading 'Current Communicative Approaches'.[1] Between 1986 and 2001, TBLT emerged as a sufficiently well-defined approach to warrant separate treatment by Richards and Rogers.

In this chapter, I will first consider the major influences on the emergence of TBLT followed by an account of the proposals for a task-based approach that appeared in the 1980s. I then examine how TBLT subsequently developed, focusing on key issues relating to the design of a task-based syllabus and the methodology for implementing tasks. I will also briefly consider how TBLT has been adapted to computer-mediated environments and take a look at task-based assessment. The chapter concludes with an account of what evaluations of task-based programmes have shown about the effectiveness of TBLT.

Background to the Emergence of TBLT

The importance of including tasks in a language curriculum was affirmed in the CLT movement of the 1970s and 1980s. TBLT grew out of this movement with further inputs from early research in second language acquisition (SLA).

Communicative language teaching

CLT drew on theories of language that viewed language not just as a set of formal structures but as a means of communication. Hymes (1971) outlined a theory of communicative competence that accounted for both what is formally possible in a language (i.e. grammatical) and what is feasible and acceptable in terms of performance. Halliday's (1973) model of language took as its starting point the functions that language served rather than the formal properties of a language. He distinguished three broad functions (the ideational, interpersonal and textual), each of which was elaborated into a series of semantic networks which were then related to their linguistic exponents. Hymes and Halliday's theories fed directly into the recognition that 'there is more to the business of communicating than the ability to produce grammatically correct utterances' (Johnson, 1982) and to proposals for teaching language as communication.

Wilkins (1976), drawing on Halliday's theory of language, proposed replacing the traditional structural syllabus with a notional syllabus consisting of an inventory of language functions (e.g. expressing agreement or disagreement), semantico-grammatical categories (e.g. expressing time, quantity and space) and modal-meaning categories (e.g. expressing certainty and commitment). He argued that a notional syllabus provided a basis for an 'analytic' way of learning. That is, learners pass through a series of approximations to the target language, gradually accumulating the linguistic resources required to perform the various notions. In this respect it differed radically from the traditional 'synthetic' approach where linguistic items are taught and mastered incrementally and not synthesized until the final stages. A notional approach was seen as having high 'surrender value' as it helped learners to communicate from the start. It also afforded an ideal means for defining learners' communicative needs and therefore appealed to course designers concerned with specific purpose teaching (e.g. Swales, 1987). Wilkin's ideas informed the work of the Council of Europe's unit/credit system for teaching foreign languages at different levels of proficiency (e.g. the *Threshold Level* and *Waystage Level*), where each level was specified in terms of notions and the linguistic exponents for expressing them. This led ultimately into the Common European Framework (Council of Europe, 2011) in which different levels of proficiency are described in functional (i.e. 'can do') rather than linguistic terms.

First attempts at developing teaching materials based on a notional syllabus (e.g. Abbs & Freebairn, 1982) utilized the existing techniques and procedures of structural courses. That is, the linguistic forms for expressing each notion were presented in situations and then practised in mainly controlled exercises. Thus, although the organizational framework of a language course had changed, the methodology had not. It was still what White (1988) called 'Type A' – it was 'other directed'. There was, however, a growing recognition of the need for a communicative methodology reflecting White's 'Type B' approach, where the emphasis is on the process of communicating and on 'doing things with or for the learner'. Johnson (1982), for example, advocated what he called the deep-end strategy, where 'the student is placed in a situation where he may need to use language not yet taught' so as to activate 'the ability to search for circumlocutions when the appropriate language item is not known' (1982: 193).

Publications began to appear with ideas for communicative tasks (e.g. Klippel, 1984). Describe and Draw, for example, involved students working in pairs with Student A attempting to draw a picture or diagram described by Student B. These tasks were to be judged not in terms of whether learners used language correctly but in terms of whether the communicative outcome was achieved (i.e. whether Student A succeeded in drawing the picture/diagram accurately). Tasks had arrived as a major tool for language teachers.

At this time, it was common to distinguish two types of language work depending on whether the focus was on 'accuracy' or 'fluency', with both seen as important (Brumfit, 1984). Providing opportunities for students to use their linguistic resources freely by performing communicative tasks in small group work catered to 'fluency', which Brumfit defined as 'the maximally effective operation of the language system acquired by the student so far' (1984: 57). However, Brumfit also stressed the importance of accuracy work involving more traditional types of instruction. The question that then arose was how to combine fluency and accuracy work in a language curriculum. Johnson (1982) suggested the answer lay in a 'communicative procedure' consisting of three stages. In Stage 1 the students perform a communicative task using whatever resources they have available (i.e. the deep-end strategy). In Stage 2, the teacher presents those linguistic items which the students' performance of the task showed they had not yet mastered. In Stage 3, these items are drilled if necessary. Brumfit went a step further by proposing an integrated language curriculum consisting of separate accuracy and fluency components, with accuracy dominant initially and fluency gradually taking over. Brumfit's ideas about an integrated curriculum are considered further in Chapter 10.

CLT was an 'approach' rather than a well-defined 'method'. Howatt (1984) distinguished a weak and strong version. In the weak version teaching content was defined in terms of the linguistic realizations of notions and functions but the methodology remained essentially the same as in the traditional structural approach – a Type A approach. In the strong version, the content of a language programme was specified in terms of communicative tasks and the methodological focus was on fluency – a Type B approach. There were also proposals for combining the two approaches as in Johnson's 'communicative procedure' and Brumfit's modular curriculum. As we will see, this attempt to encourage fluency while not neglecting accuracy figures too in TBLT.

CLT has had a major impact throughout the world. Nunan (2003), for example, reported that the educational policies of seven countries in the Asian region mandated the use of CLT. Its influence in Europe has been even greater with the European Common Language framework providing the basis for the teaching and assessment of languages throughout the region. Just about every course book emanating from major publishers today lays claim to being 'communicative'. As its influence has spread, however, CLT has become increasingly less well defined. Littlewood (2014) noted its vagueness, commenting 'the most common understanding has been that it means teachers including communicative activities in their repertoire' (2014: 350). Today even approaches based on a structural syllabus and a presentation–practice–production (PPP) methodology lay claim to being 'communicative' on the grounds they include a communicative task in the final production stage. Clearly, such an interpretation represents an even weaker version of CLT than Howatt's 'weak version', creating the space for TBLT to take over the reins of the 'strong version'.

Second language acquisition research

SLA research also contributed to the emergence of TBLT. The 1960s and 1970s saw a number of cross-sectional and longitudinal studies of learners acquiring an L2 naturalistically (e.g. Cancino *et al.*, 1978; Dulay & Burt, 1973). The cross-sectional studies examined the accuracy with which a set of English grammatical morphemes (e.g. Ving, plural-s, Ved, 3rd person-s) were produced by different groups of learners. They resulted in the claim that there was an acquisition order that was common to all learners irrespective of their first Languages (L1) or their age. Furthermore, a very similar order was found in classroom learners suggesting that instruction did not have a major impact on the developmental route learners followed. The longitudinal studies focused on individual learners' acquisition of specific grammatical structures (e.g. negatives, interrogatives and relative clauses). They showed that learners did not progress directly from zero knowledge of these structures to target-like use but instead passed through a series of stages involving 'transitional constructions' *en route* to the target form. Progress was gradual and often very slow and at any one stage of development considerable variability was evident in the use of those constructions that had been acquired up to that point. Furthermore, it was clear that learners did not set about achieving target-like use of one structure before embarking on another. Rather they worked on several structures concurrently. This research led to the claim that learners might have their own 'built-in syllabus' for learning an L2 (Corder, 1967).

Drawing on these studies, Krashen (1981, 1985) proposed a theory consisting of five hypotheses. The central hypothesis was the Acquisition-Learning Hypothesis. This proposed a distinction between 'acquisition', defined as the 'subconscious process identical in all important ways to the process children utilize in acquiring their first language' and 'learning', defined as 'the conscious process that results in "knowing about" language' (Krashen, 1985: 1). Krashen argued that true proficiency in an L2 depended on 'acquisition' and that the 'natural order' reported in studies of L2 learners was a manifestation of 'acquisition'. 'Learning' had some value for monitoring output derived from the acquired language system but only in a very limited way. Krashen attached most importance to the fourth of his hypotheses – the Input Hypothesis – which stated that 'humans acquire language in only one way – by understanding messages or by receiving "comprehensible input"' (1985: 2). The hypothesis had two corollaries. The first was that 'speaking is the result of acquisition, and not its cause'. In other words, Krashen saw acquisition as entirely input-driven and claimed that 'speech cannot be taught'. The second corollary was that 'if input is understood, and there is enough of it, the necessary grammar is automatically provided' and thus there was no need to teach the grammar of a language.

At the same time that Krashen was developing his theory of L2 acquisition, Terrell was experimenting with a new way of teaching Spanish as a foreign language in the United States that did not involve the presentation and practice of discrete grammatical structures.[2] Krashen's hypotheses provided the theoretical rationale for this approach. In 1983 Krashen and Terrell published a book called *The Natural Approach*. The book outlined both the theoretical basis of the approach and a curriculum for implementing it. The stated goal was to develop the ability to communicate in the target language. Objectives were specified in terms of the topics the teacher and students would communicate about (e.g. clothing; sports and games; work activities). In accordance with the Input Hypothesis, the instructional activities for the early stages were comprehension-based and even later 'the great majority of class time is devoted to activities that provide input for acquisition' (1983: 58). Emphasis was placed on ensuring a constant flow of comprehensible input through teacher talk. Early production activities were an extension of the input-based activities, requiring simple one-word utterances from the students. As learners progressed, a greater variety of 'acquisition activities' figured, including dialogues, interviews, preference ranking activities, personal charts and tables, and 'tasks' where the teacher or students chose a specific activity such as 'washing a car' and then described the components of the activity. The emphasis throughout was on activities that cater to 'acquisition' but there were also suggestions for teaching monitor use. These included both direct grammar explanation and traditional practice exercises (e.g. blank-filling, sentence combination; substitution) aimed at 'learning'. However, Krashen and Terrell recommended that learning activities should be delayed until students were spontaneously producing short sentences and should focus on simpler grammatical rules such as inflections and simple word order changes. They commented 'learning activities will be used judiciously and in some cases not at all' (1983: 148).

The Natural Approach is based on the principle that L2 development does not require intentional learning on the part of learners. It emphasizes activities that focus learners' primary attention on meaning and thereby cater to incidental acquisition. TBLT is based on the same principle. However, in some other important respects The Natural Approach differs from TBLT. It was premised on the assumption that acquisition is an entirely subconscious process and it gave little recognition to the important role that production plays in language learning. However, the research on order and sequence in L2 acquisition along with Krashen's claim that 'acquisition' could not be taught fed into the early proposals for TBLT.

First Proposals for TBLT

'Tasks' figured in both early CLT and The Natural Approach but in neither were they conceived of as the units around which a complete language course could be built. In CLT they served either as the means for identifying which specific properties of language needed to be taught as in Johnson's (1982) 'communicative procedure' or as an adjunct to a traditional structural approach to cater for the development of 'fluency' as in Brumfit's (1984) integrated curriculum. In *The Natural Approach*, course content was specified in terms of topics and situations with tasks serving as one type of activity for generating comprehensible input.

It was not until the mid to late 1980s that the first proposals for a task-based approach appeared. These early proposals (Breen, 1989; Candlin, 1987; Long, 1985) were largely programmatic in nature. They focused on the rationale for a task-based syllabus and outlined how to design and evaluate a task-based curriculum. Prabhu (1987) provided the first complete account of a task-based course,[3] whereas Nunan (1989) gave practical advice about how to design tasks along with examples of actual tasks.

Rationale for TBLT

From the start, therefore, there were multiple inputs into the rationale for TBLT. Long's (1985) advocacy of TBLT was premised on the need for any approach to teaching to be 'psycholinguistically based'. Drawing on research in SLA, he argued that 'there is no reason to assume that presenting the target language as a series of discrete linguistic or sociolinguistic teaching points is the best, or even *a* way to get learners to synthesize the parts into a coherent whole' (1985: 79). He saw an approach based on tasks as providing an 'integrated solution to both syllabus and methodological issues' (1985: 89).

Candlin (1987) critiqued traditional approaches from an educational standpoint. He argued that they failed to 'emphasize educational goals … in their pursuit of cost-effective training' (1987: 16). Along with Breen (1989) he emphasized the importance of teachers and students jointly negotiating the content of a course and argued that tasks provided the best means for achieving this.

Prabhu's (1987) starting point was dissatisfaction with the Structural-Oral Situational Method which was dominant in his particular teaching context (India) at that time. Drawing on his own and others' experience of this method, he concluded that even after several years of instruction students were unable to deploy the language they had been taught either accurately or appropriately outside the classroom. He argued that 'the development of competence in a second language requires not systematization of language input or maximization of planned practice, but rather the creation of conditions in which learners engage in an effort to cope with communication' (1987: 1). This could be best achieved by having students perform tasks.

Nunan (1989) was more concerned with providing teachers with a practical introduction to the design and use of tasks, which he viewed as essential in communicative language teaching. He claimed that basing teaching on tasks avoided the traditional distinction between syllabus and methodology. Traditional syllabuses did have a role, but as checklists rather than as directives about what to teach. Thus the starting point was the selection of the task(s) for a particular lesson, which he suggested is how teachers typically set about planning their teaching.

Defining 'task'

Task is the basic organization unit of a task-based course. It was therefore important to have a clear understanding of what a task consists of. The early proposals for task-based teaching all provided definitions, but these varied in a number of ways. Breen's (1989) definition was the most encompassing. A task is 'a structured plan for the provision of opportunities for the refinement of knowledge and capabilities entailed in a new language and its use during communication' (1989: 187). According to this definition, a task could be both a brief practice exercise and 'a more complex workplan that requires spontaneous communication'.

Other definitions emphasized four important aspects of a task:

- A task is a meaning-focused activity. That is, 'learners are occupied with understanding, extending (through reasoning) or conveying meaning' and 'have to cope with language forms as defined by that process' (Prabhu, 1987: 27). A task requires learners to focus on meaning rather than form (Nunan, 1989).
- A task does not specify the exact meaning-content to be addressed as this will be subject to modification when it is performed. The language needed to perform a task is negotiable as the task is performed.
- A task should bear some resemblance to a task that people perform in real life. Long (1985) defined tasks as 'the hundred and one things people do in everyday life, at work, at play and in between' (1985: 89).
- A task should have 'a sense of completeness' and 'stand alone as a communicative act in its own right' (Nunan, 1989: 10).

One of the problems with these early definitions is that they conflated two senses of 'task' – task-as-workplan and task-as-process

(Breen, 1989). It was the failure to make this crucial distinction that led to the claim that the traditional distinction between 'syllabus' and 'methodology' loses relevance. I will argue later, that it only makes sense to define task as a workplan and that the process that results from the performance of a task depends not just on its design but also on how it is implemented.

Classifying tasks

We find a mixed bag of suggestions for distinguishing different types of tasks in these early proposals. Candlin (1987) commented that it is not possible to 'offer anything other than implicit suggestions that tasks might be catalogued under several distinct types' (1987: 14) and that as a result 'a typology is bound to be fuzzy-edged and at most a managerial convenience' (1987: 15). Long distinguished 'target tasks' (i.e. real-life tasks such as 'selling an airline ticket'), 'task types' (i.e. general tasks such as 'selling an item') and 'pedagogic tasks' (i.e. the actual tasks that teachers and students work with). Long proposed first conducting a needs analysis to identify the target tasks relevant to a specific group of learners, classifying them into target types, and finally designing pedagogic tasks. Nunan presented a number of task typologies drawn from different sources, the most useful of which was Prabhu's, which distinguished three types of tasks.

(1) Information-gap tasks involving 'a transfer of given information from one person to another – or from one form to another, or from one place to another'.
(2) Reasoning gap tasks involving 'deriving some new information from given information through the processes of inference, deduction, practical reasoning, or a perception of relationships or patterns'.
(3) Opinion-gap tasks involving 'identifying and articulating a personal preference, feeling, or attitude in response to a given situation'. (Nunan, 1989: 46–47).

Grading and sequencing tasks

The development of a syllabus requires procedures for grading and sequencing tasks in terms of their difficulty. The early proposals for TBLT identified a number of criteria for determining the difficulty of pedagogical tasks:

• the linguistic complexity of the input provided by a task;
• the amount of input provided in the task;
• the number of steps involved in the execution of a task;
• the degree of structure in the information presented or required by the task;

- the number of objects, events or people that need to be distinguished when performing the task;
- the extent to which the task requires reference to present or past/future events;
- the extent to which reasons for actions or decisions need to be given;
- the intellectual challenge posed;
- the learners' familiarity with the topic of the task.

It should be immediately clear, however, that although such factors clearly can influence the difficulty of individual tasks, they do not provide a clear basis for grading and sequencing a series of tasks. Prabhu found that grading was more a matter of intuition that precise measurement. He proposed that teachers should be guided by the general principle of what constitutes a 'reasonable challenge' for a particular group of learners and noted that 'the working rule for reasonable challenge was the outcome of experience' (Prabhu, 1987: 57). In other words, grading and sequencing was to a considerable extent a matter of trial and error.[4]

Subsequent Developments

I will now consider how the issues raised in the early proposals were built on and how new issues emerged in later developments of TBLT.

Broadening the rationale for TBLT

As we have seen, the underpinnings of TBLT lay in CLT (the 'strong version') and in SLA research and theory. With the exception of Candlin (1987) little attention was initially paid to broader educational principles. One of the major developments that followed was an attempt to align TBLT with general theories of education.

Samuda and Bygate (2008) drew on Dewey's (1938) critique of the traditional classroom, where learning entailed the mastery of ready-made products, and on his emphasis on the importance of learning that connects with experience of the real world. They pointed to Bruner's (1960) emphasis on 'learning for use' where the learner is positioned not just as a 'student' but as a 'practitioner'. Long (2015) aligned his version of TBLT with philosophies of education that emphasize 'integrated, whole person, mind-and-body education' (2015: 66). He claimed that 'a synergistic relationship exists between the philosophical principles and TBLT's psycholinguistic underpinnings' (2015: 82).

Defining 'task'

Definitions of tasks have proliferated over the years. Van den Branden (2006b) reviewed a total of 17 different definitions which he divided into

Table 1.1 Criteria for defining a task-as-workplan (based on Ellis & Shintani, 2014)

Criteria	Description
The primary focus is on meaning	The workplan is intended to ensure that learners are primarily concerned with comprehending or/and producing messages for a communicative purpose.
There is some kind of gap	The workplan is designed in such a way as to incorporate a gap that will need to be closed when the task is performed. The gap creates a need to convey information, to reason or to express an opinion.
Learners rely mainly on their own linguistic and non-linguistic resources	The workplan does not include any presentation of the language needed to perform the task, although it may supply input that can be 'borrowed' during the performance of the task. Learners need to draw on their existing linguistic resources (potentially both L1 and L2) and their non-linguistic resources (e.g. gesture; facial expressions) for comprehension and/or production.
There is a clearly defined communicative outcome	The workplan specifies the communicative outcome of the task. Thus task accomplishment is to be assessed not in terms of whether learners use language correctly but in terms of whether the communicative outcome is achieved.

two groups depending on whether they viewed tasks in terms of language learning goals or educational activity. Arguably, this proliferation of definitions is not helpful. There is continued failure to distinguish task-as-workplan and task-as-process as is evident in the meaning attached to the word 'activity,' which figures in many of the different definitions. This term is ambiguous as it can refer to both the actual materials that constitute a task (i.e. the workplan) and to the language use resulting from the performance of the task (i.e. the process). I argue that a task cannot be defined in terms of process as this is to some extent at least unpredictable. Also, from the perspective of course design, language testing and research, the starting point needs to be the task-as-workplan, which embodies the attempt to create a context for the communicative and purposive use of the L2. In Ellis (2003), I offered a definition in terms of four criteria that can distinguish a 'task' from an 'exercise'. Over time I have refined these. Table 1.1 shows the definition in Ellis and Shintani (2014). This allows for the possibility that an instructional activity may satisfy some but not all the criteria and thus that activities can be more or less task-like.

Issues relating to task design

Task types

There is still no generally accepted way of classifying tasks. By and large pedagogical accounts of tasks have continued to distinguish tasks in terms of the operations learners are required to carry out when they perform them. Willis (1996), for example, distinguished six types – listing, ordering and sequencing, comparing, problem solving, sharing personal experiences and creative. Other ways of classifying tasks have emerged from research that has investigated the communicative and cognitive processes involved in performing different tasks. This has led to a set of features such as whether a task requires one-way or two-way communication and whether the outcome is closed or open. For example, 'Spot the Difference' (a task where students have to work together to identify the differences in two similar pictures) is a two-way, closed task. A jigsaw task where information is split among a number of learners is a two-way, open task.

There are a number of other pedagogically useful ways of classifying tasks. An important distinction is between *real-world* and *pedagogic tasks*. The former are tasks that have situational authenticity; that is, they are based on tasks that can be found in real life (i.e. target tasks). An example might be a task where two students take on the roles of hotel receptionist and prospective guest where the latter has to make a booking for a room based on the information provided by the former. A pedagogic task lacks situational authenticity but must still display interactional authenticity (i.e. results in the kind of natural language use found in the world outside the classroom). An example is the Spot the Difference task. It is very unlikely that two people would engage in talk aimed at identifying the differences in two pictures but this task can result in patterns of turn taking and repair of misunderstandings that are typical of everyday talk and thus achieve interactional authenticity. Real-world tasks are required in specific purpose language courses but in general-purpose courses it is likely that many of the tasks will be pedagogic in nature.

A task can be *input-based* requiring learners to simply process the oral or written information provided and demonstrate their understanding of it (for example by drawing a picture or making a model) or it can be *output-based*, requiring the learner to speak or write to achieve the task outcome. This distinction is important because, as Prabhu (1987) noted, beginner learners cannot be expected to use the L2 productively so task-based learning must initially be input-driven.

Tasks can also be unfocused or focused (Ellis, 2003). An *unfocused task* is intended to elicit general samples of language. A *focused task* must satisfy the general criteria for a task but is designed in such a way as to orientate learners to the use of a particular linguistic feature (typically but not necessarily a grammatical structure). This possibility was explored by Loschky and Bley-Vroman (1993). They suggested that a task could be designed in such a way that it made the processing of a particular grammatical structure 'natural' (i.e. the task lends itself, in some natural way, to the frequent use of the structure' (1993: 132), 'useful' (i.e. the use of the structure is very helpful for performing the task) or 'essential' (i.e. successful performance of the task is only possible if the structure is used).[5] Advocates of TBLT differ in their views about the inclusion of focused tasks. I will argue they have a role to play (see Chapter 6). However, both Skehan (1998) and Long (2015) favour a curriculum consisting only of unfocused tasks.

Task selection

Long (1985) proposed that the tasks to be included in a course should be needs-based. That is, the starting point is the identification of the target tasks that a specific group of learners need to be able to perform to 'function adequately in a particular target domain' (1985: 91). Long (2015) has continued to emphasize the importance of needs analysis as a basis for task selection. There is an obvious advantage in such an approach as it helps to ensure the relevance of the content of a task-based course. It is, however, very difficult to identify target tasks for some groups of learners. In the case of second language learners living in a country where they will need to use the target language for daily survival and work purposes, a needs analysis may make sense. However, in an instructional context where the target language plays no significant role in the wider society, identifying target tasks is clearly more problematic and can only be conducted on the basis of speculation about possible future uses of the target language. Cameron (2001), for example argued that for young foreign language learners a needs-based syllabus is not feasible.[6]

If task-selection is not based on a needs analysis some other basis is needed. Estaire and Zanon (1994) in one of the earliest attempts to provide practical guidance in how to plan a task-based course, suggested that task selection should be based on 'themes', which they classified in terms of how close or remote they are to the lives of the learners – the students themselves, their homes, their school, the world around them and fantasy and imagination. Which themes are chosen depends in part on the learners' proficiency level, with themes closer to their everyday lives more appropriate for beginner-level learners and more remote themes for more advanced learners.

Task complexity

I pointed out that the early proposals identified a number of factors that influence the complexity of a task but gave no guidance as to how these factors were to be applied in the practical business of grading tasks. Subsequently, theories of task complexity have been proposed with the aim of providing a principled basis for grading tasks. Robinson's (2011a) Cognition Hypothesis, for example, identifies a set of factors that influence the complexity of a task.

Robinson (2001) distinguished 'resource-directing' variables and 'resourced dispersing' variables of a task. The former affect the demands the task can make on the learner's attention and, in so doing, cause the learner to focus on specific linguistic forms (i.e. accuracy and complexity) and thus potentially promote interlanguage development. Task variables that are resource-directing include whether the task requires reference to events happening in the 'here-and-now' or to events that took place in the past elsewhere (in the 'there-and-then'), and whether or not the task requires giving reasons for intentions, beliefs, or relations. Resource-dispersing variables affect the demands on the learners' attentional and memory resources Examples are providing strategic planning time, and whether or not a task has a clear structure. The complexity of a task is determined by the resource-directing and resource-dispersing variables. For example, a task (+ reasons) is more complex than task (− reasons), whereas a task (+ reasons/ − strategic planning) is more complex than a task (+ reasons/ + strategic planning). However, it is difficult to see how Robinson's theory can be used to systematically grade tasks. Tasks are clusters of variables and the theory does not address how different clusters affect complexity. Also, as Skehan and Foster (2001) have pointed out, there is no single, general measure of task performance that can be used to determine whether one task is more complex than another. It is not surprising, therefore that pedagogical accounts of task-based teaching continue to conclude that teachers will have to rely on their own intuitions. Willis and Willis (2007), for example, commented 'teachers would be able to tell simply by looking at a task whether it is appropriate for a particular group of students' and that a list of variables serves only as 'a useful way of sharpening and focusing teachers' intuitions'.

Perhaps also the idea of grading tasks-as-workplans is problematic as complexity depends as much if not more on how a task is implemented. The same task will vary in difficulty depending on the nature and extent of the pre-task activity and the level of support provided by the teacher as the task is performed. Also, the same task may be easy for a learner who possesses background content knowledge but difficult for a learner who does not. What is arguably more crucial than task design and selection is the methodology of TBLT (i.e. how tasks are implemented in the classroom).[7] This issue is addressed in Chapter 2 and again in Chapter 9.

Methodological issues

The early proposals had little to say about how a task should be implemented and, with the exception of Prahbu, even less about how to plan a task-based lesson. Subsequently, however, greater attention has been paid to methodological issues in TBLT.

The task-based lesson

Prabhu's Communicational Language Project, a task-based lesson consisted of a 'pre-task', which served as a preparation for a 'task' of the same kind. The pre-task was performed publicly in a whole-class context, whereas the 'task' was completed by the students working individually. In other words, there was no small group work in this project. In the pre-task the teacher guided learners' performance of the task by simplifying, repeating and paraphrasing input to make it comprehensible and where necessary by reformulating the learners' own attempts to use the L2 in a target-like way.

Willis (1996) proposed a very different framework for a task-based lesson, one that prioritized learner–learner interaction. Willis' framework established the standard format for a task-based lesson, namely a pre-task stage, a main-task stage and a post-task stage. Willis prioritized small group work in the main task phase (called the 'task cycle') but allowed for teacher-centred activity in the pre-task and language focus stages. She aimed to cater for 'fluency' in the task cycle and to 'accuracy' in the post-task ('language focus') stage of the lesson.

Focus on form

In the task-cycle stage Willis (1996) advised teachers to 'stand back and let the learners get on with the task on their own' (1996: 54). In this respect, however, Willis differed from other educators. Long (1991) argued that there was a need to draw learners' attention to form *during* the performance of a task (i.e. in the main task phase of a lesson). He distinguished 'focus on forms' (traditional language teaching based on a structural syllabus) and 'focus on form' which 'overtly draws students' attention to linguistic elements as they arise incidentally in lessons whose overriding focus is on meaning or communication' (1991: 45–46). The recognition that task-based teaching does not require an exclusive focus on meaning but also allows for (indeed requires in the opinion of many commentators) attention to form during the performance of a task constitutes one of the major developments in TBLT. Nevertheless, the belief that teachers should not intervene in a 'fluency' activity still holds sway in popular teacher guides. Hedge (2000), for example, observed that the teacher guides accompanying course books frequently instruct teachers to avoid correcting learners until the end of a fluency activity.

There are also opportunities to focus on form in the pre-task and post-task stages of a lesson. Willis (1996) saw the primary purpose of the pre-stage as introducing the topic of the main task and helping students with the vocabulary they would need. In general, educators adhere to the general principle of task-based teaching, namely that there should be no direct teaching of the language to be used for performing a task – even when the task is of the focused kind. However, this does not exclude the possibility of introducing a focus on form in the pre-task phase. One possibility is to give learners the opportunity to plan before they perform a task. This will involve them in both conceptualizing what they wish to communicate and in formulating the language they will need. The advantage of pre-task planning is that it places the burden of working out how to perform the task squarely on the learner and thus is compatible with a key principle of TBLT, namely that the learners should not be directed which linguistic forms to use but be allowed to choose from their own linguistic repertoires.

The post-task stage offers the clearest opportunities for form-focused activities including traditional ones. Willis and Willis (2007) suggest that when the task cycle is complete the teacher is free to isolate specific linguistic forms for study and work on these forms outside the context of the communicative activity. In this respect, TBLT closely resembles Johnson's (1982) 'deep-end strategy', where teachers only address form if the learners' performance of task shows this to be necessary.

The methodology of TBLT is now well-articulated but there is no consensus about which methodological procedures are appropriate. Although there is a growing consensus that attention to linguistic form is needed, there are differences in opinion regarding when the focus on form should take place and the teaching strategies needed to achieve it. TBLT, like any 'approach', is not monolithic. Variants exist.

Focus-on-form is considered in detail in Chapter 4.

Technology-mediated TBLT

Computer-mediated language learning (CALL) appeared on the scene in the 1980s at much the same time as the early proposals for TBLT. Thus, although the initial proposals for TBLT had the face-to face classroom very much in mind, it was not long before suggestions appeared for computer-mediated task-based teaching. Developments in CALL mirrored those in general language pedagogy. That is, there was a structural/behaviourist phase that gave way to a communicative phase and finally to a more integrative stage with the 'centrality of task-based authentic learning moving increasingly into the foreground' (Thomas & Reinders, 2010: 6).

Commentators have claimed that technology-mediated TBLT has several advantages over face-to-face TBLT. Lai and Li (2011), for example, claimed that it expands the range of resources available to the learner, enhances learners' motivation to undertake tasks, increases learners' agency and sense of ownership of tasks, and it facilitates the provision of follow-up work in the post-task stage. Technology affords multi-modal (i.e. aural, written and visual) opportunities for presenting complex workplans and for performing them synchronously and/or asynchronously. Appel and Gilabert (2002) described a task, which involved planning a route and budget for a one-night trip that required email exchanges, the use of webpages, and synchronous communication. Technology allows the input materials for a task to be fed into the performance of the task in steps. This is also possible in the face-to-face classroom but is much easier in a technologically mediated environment. In short, technology makes possible tasks with complex outcomes and it can make rich, multi-layered input available for achieving them.

However, there are also problems and challenges with technologically mediated TBLT. Skehan (2003) noted that technologically-mediated tasks can lead to learners prioritizing meaning at the expense of form when they perform tasks. Learners may also lack the necessary technical skills to exploit the multi-modal resources made available to them. Teachers often

lack training in how to handle tasks in a technologically-mediated environment. Despite these problems, there is growing interest in technologically-
mediated TBLT as reflected in the expanding literature on this topic (e.g.
Gonzalez-Lloret & Ortega, 2014; Thomas & Reinders, 2010) and in the
appearance of online TBLT courses (e.g. Duran & Ramault, 2006).

Task-based Language Assessment

Tasks provide the means for integrated, direct performance assessment of L2 learners' abilities (Norris *et al.*, 1998). Such assessment contrasts with the more traditional discrete-point, indirect testing. Task-based
assessment can be undertaken in two ways. If tasks are used to assess L2
general proficiency, the assessor makes a judgment of the learner's performance of a task based on a rating scale that specifies the different abilities
being assessed and the level achieved. Popular tests such as TOEFL and
IELTS assess proficiency in this way. However, more compatible with the
principles of TBLT is the second way, where task performance is assessed
in terms of task accomplishment. This can be achieved by seeing if learners are able to achieve the task outcome. This is, however, only possible if
the task outcome is a closed one. For open tasks it will be necessary to rate
learners' performance of a task using criteria derived from the performance of the target task by members of the target language community.

For Long and Norris (2000) – in line with Long's (1985) views about
TBLT – the tasks used for assessment should reflect target tasks (i.e. real-
life tasks). They proposed a needs analysis be conducted to identify the
specific target tasks relevant to a particular group of learners and authentic assessment tasks be derived from these. Douglas (2000) developed a
framework for analysing target tasks as communicative events. This was
designed to provide a specification of both the external context in which
a particular target task was performed and the nature of the interactions
that the task elicited. The aim was to ensure a high level of correspondence between the target task and the assessment task. There are, however, problems with such an approach (see Bachman, 2002). As we have
already pointed out, a needs-based approach is not appropriate for all
learners. Situational authenticity is clearly important if the purpose of the
test is to assess learners' ability to perform the tasks in a specific target
domain but it is less relevant when the purpose is to assess the communicative abilities of general-purpose learners for whom there is no clearly
defined target domain. For such learners the aim should assessment tasks
that achieve interactional authenticity.

Formative assessment is an essential part of TBLT. It involves obtain-
ing information about how learners perform tasks. The information
needed is both product-based (i.e. Did the students succeed in achieving
the outcome of the task?) and process-based (i.e. Did the students engage

actively when they performed the task?). Formative assessment can shed light not just on the students' abilities and the teacher's contribution to their development but also on how the task itself might be improved for future use. In other words, formative assessment involves assessing the students (i.e. what they have learned and still need to learn), the task itself, and the activity that results from the performance of the task. It is multi-purposeful.

Evaluating TBLT

There is plenty of evidence of the uptake of TBLT. A number of countries have officially mandated TBLT. In 1999 the Education Department of Hong Kong launched the Target Oriented Curriculum which was underwritten by a task-based approach. In Belgium task-based syllabuses and materials were developed for teaching Dutch both as a first and second language at the primary, secondary and adult education levels (see Van den Branden, 2006a). The new English curriculum in China does not specify any particular teaching approach but recommends the use of task-based teaching as the means for achieving integrated skills development, problem solving abilities and cooperative learning (Wang, 2007). There have also been countless small-scale implementations of TBLT in contexts where teachers are free to choose their own approach – see, for example, Leaver and Willis (2004) and Edwards and Willis (2005). It is clear, then, that TBLT has progressed well beyond theory into actual practice, raising the important question of whether and to what extent it has been successfully implemented in different instructional contexts.

There have been a number of evaluations of TBLT programmes – e.g. Beretta and Davies' (1985) evaluation of the Communicational Language Teaching Project in Bangalore; Carless' (2004) evaluation of task-based teaching in Hong Kong elementary schools; Watson-Todd's (2006) evaluation of a task-based course for university students in Thailand; Gonzalez-Lloret and Nielson's (2015) evaluation of a specific-purposes programme for US Border Patrol Agents. In general, these evaluations point to the successful implementation of TBLT in a variety of contexts. But they also indicate that the teachers experienced a number of difficulties in implementing TBLT. Teachers do not always have a clear idea of what a task is, they are uncertain of their oral proficiency, they may overuse the students' L1, they face problems of implementing tasks in large classes, they are concerned that task-based teaching will not adequately prepare students for the traditional examinations they will be required to take, and they are uncertain about how grammar should be handled in TBLT. Some of these problems are likely to arise no matter what the teaching approach is but others are specific to TBLT. They are indicative of the need for training teachers to cope with the demands of TBLT.

Conclusion

We have seen that TBLT grew out disillusionment with the structural approach. CLT established the need for tasks to develop fluency in an L2. Theory and research in SLA pointed to the difficulty of intervening directly in the process of L2 acquisition. Educational theories challenged the traditional transmission-style teaching and emphasized the need for holistic, experiential instructional activities. From its starting point in the 1980s it has developed into fully fledged proposals for using tasks as the basic tools for teaching and assessment. There are now accounts and evaluations of complete task-based programmes. There are books that detail how teachers can set about implementing TBLT in their classrooms. Starting in 2005, there has been a biennial TBLT conference where task-based educational ideas are investigated and a journal devoted to TBLT is being planned.

The advocacy of TBLT has to a large extent been driven top-down by teacher educators with a background in applied linguistics, in particular second language acquisition theory and research. For this reason, perhaps, TBLT has met with considerable resistance and is the subject of a number of critiques. I address these critiques in Chapter 8, pointing out that in many cases they derive from a misunderstanding of TBLT.

There are, however, a number of issues that do need addressing (see Chapter 13). One is whether TBLT is appropriate for all instructional contexts[8] – in particular those where the cultures of teaching and learning are very different from those in Western settings. Littlewood (2007) argued the case for task-supported language teaching, where tasks provide communicative practice for language items taught in accordance with a traditional structural syllabus. This raises an important question. To what extent should the choice of teaching approach be determined by psycholinguistic or by cultural factors? To a very considerable extent the advocacy of TBLT has been based on the former. Opposition to TBLT has been based on the need to acknowledge the cultural realities of classroom life. If the goal is to achieve the ability to use an L2 for real-life purposes then traditional approaches do not have a good record of success. If, however, the alternative to these approaches – TBLT – proves difficult to implement, then, it too is unlikely to be successful. I grapple with this issue in later chapters of this book where I address such issues as the role of explicit instruction in TBLT (Chapter 6) and the case for a modular curriculum that combines TBLT and traditional approaches (see Chapter 10).

Notes

(1) In the most recent edition of Richards and Rogers' book, published in 2014, TBLT is no longer listed under 'communicative methods and approaches' but is dealt with separately under the rubric 'current approaches and methods' reflecting its emergence as a separate approach no longer so clearly tied to CLT.

(2) Rejection of structural approaches and the linear, bit-by-bit approach to teaching can be found much earlier in an article by Newmark (1966) entitled 'how not to interfere with language learning'.

(3) Perhaps the earliest programme that could lay claim to be being task-based was in Malaysia. The Malaysian Language Syllabus (see Richards, 1984) specified objectives in task-like terms and suggested 'procedures' for realizing them.

(4) As a result of experience with the Communicational Teaching Project, Prabhu offered some quite concrete suggestions for grading and sequencing tasks. Beginning tasks needed to be input rather than output-based. Information-gap tasks were easier than reason-gap tasks which in turn were easier than opinion-gap tasks.

(5) Loschky and Bley-Vroman (1993) acknowledged that it is very difficult to design a structure-based task that makes the production of a predetermined linguistic feature essential given that the choice of what linguistic resources to use when performing the task lies with the learner. Achieving task-essentialness is much easier with input-based tasks that learners can only perform successfully if they are able to process the target structure.

(6) Long (2005), however, claimed that 'every language course should be considered a course for specific purposes, varying only (and considerably, to be sure) in the precision with which learner needs can be specified' (2005: 1).

(7) The view I have expressed here regarding the difficulty in determining the complexity of tasks is not shared by all task-based commentators and researchers. An alternative view is that task complexity can be established empirically by conducting studies that compare the effects of different design features on L2 performance – see, for example, Sasayama (2016). I continue to have major doubts about whether such a research programme will provide a basis for task selection and grading.

(8) Richards and Rodgers (2014) also concluded that TBLT was unlikely to provide a basis for national teaching programs and but suggested it could constitute a 'partial approach' alongside a traditional language-based syllabus.

2 Task-based Research and Language Pedagogy[1]

Introduction

Recent years have seen an enormous growth of interest in task-based language learning and teaching (see, for example, Bygate *et al.*, 2001a; Skehan, 1998b; Willis, 1996). This interest has been motivated to a considerable extent by the fact that 'task' is seen as a construct of equal importance to second language acquisition (SLA) researchers and to language teachers (Pica, 1997). 'Task' is both a means of clinically eliciting samples of learner language for purposes of research (Corder, 1981) and a device for organizing the content and methodology of language teaching (Prabhu, 1987). However, as Bygate *et al.* (2001b) point out, 'task' is viewed differently depending on whether the perspective is that of research or pedagogy. Researchers, for example, may view a task in terms of a set of variables that impact on performance and language acquisition whereas teachers see it as a unit of work in an overall scheme of work. Of course, there are also points of contact between the two views – for example, information about significant task variables acquired through research can assist teachers in deciding what tasks to use and when.

The purpose of this chapter is to examine theoretical views of language use, learning and teaching that underlie the work on tasks that has taken place to date. Two broad and disparate views will be identified and discussed. The first of these draws on what Lantolf (1996) has referred to as computational models of second language (L2) acquisition, which treat acquisition as the product of processing input and output. In accordance with this model, researchers have sought to identify 'psycholinguistically motivated dimensions' of tasks (Long & Crookes, 1987) – that is, to establish the task features that have a significant impact on the way learners process language in performance and, therefore, potentially, on how they acquire an L2. The identification of such dimensions can be used to select and grade tasks for teaching and learning. The second view is sociocultural in orientation, drawing on the work of Vygotsky, as this has been applied to L2 learning (see, for example, Lantolf & Appel, 1994; Lantolf, 2000a). This approach views language learning as socially constructed through interaction of one kind or another and, thus, treats 'tasks' as workplans that are enacted in accordance with the personal dispositions and goals of individual learners in particular settings, making it difficult to predict the nature of the activity that arises out of a task. This socio-cultural perspective, I will argue, has important implications for how tasks are conceptualized for both research and language pedagogy. In particular, it can contribute to the development of a methodology for task-based teaching and learning.

The chapter begins with a brief definition of 'task'. The two theoretical views are then outlined and examples of the research based on each discussed. The chapter concludes by arguing that language pedagogy needs to take account of both views in order to accommodate what Van Lier (1991) has advanced as the two essential dimensions of teaching – 'planning' and 'improvising'.

Defining 'Task'

As Bygate *et al.* (2001b) point out, definitions of tasks are generally 'context-free' and for that reason alone run into problems. Nevertheless, it would seem to me that to operate without some clear idea of the 'signification' of 'task' and to argue instead that 'task' can only be defined in terms of 'value'[2] is not helpful. I shall attempt, therefore, a context-free definition. In so doing, of course, I recognize that 'task' will indeed have somewhat different meanings in different contexts of use.

A task is a 'workplan'; that is, it takes the form of materials for researching or teaching language. A workplan typically involves the following: (1) some input (i.e. information that learners are required to process and use); and (2) some instructions relating to what outcome the learners are supposed to achieve. As Breen (1989) has pointed out, the task-as-workplan is to be distinguished from the task-as-process (i.e. the activity that transpires when particular learners in a particular setting perform the task). As we will see, the activity predicted by the task-as-workplan may or may not accord with the activity that arises from the task-as-process. Definitions of 'task' typically relate to task-as-workplan.

At the level of workplan, then, what distinguishes a 'task' from an 'exercise'? Skehan (1998a), reflecting a broad consensus among researchers and educators, suggests four defining criteria.

(1) Meaning is primary.
(2) There is a goal which needs to be worked towards.
(3) The activity is outcome-evaluated.
(4) There is a real-world relationship. (1998a: 268)

Thus, in a 'task' such as Same-or-Different[3] the learners are primarily engaged in trying to communicate content (meaning is primary), they work towards the goal of determining whether the picture they hold is the same as or different to the picture held by their partner, the outcome is evaluated in terms of whether they are successful in this goal, and there is a relationship with the real world in the sense that the kind of discourse that arises from this task is intended to resemble that which occurs naturally. In contrast, in an 'exercise' such as a fill-in-the-blank grammar exercise, the learners are primarily engaged in producing correct linguistic forms, there is no obvious communicative goal to be achieved, the outcome is evaluated in terms of whether the learners' answers are grammatically correct or not, and no direct relationship between the type of language activity involved and naturally occurring discourse is intended.

Widdowson (1998a) is critical of such a definition of 'task', arguing that the 'criteria do not in themselves distinguish the linguistic exercise and the communicative task' (1998a: 328). He argued that 'exercise' and 'task' differ with regard to the kind of meaning, goal and outcome they are directed towards. Thus, an exercise is premised on the need to develop linguistic skills as a prerequisite for the learning of communicative abilities, whereas a task is based on the assumption that linguistic abilities are developed through communicative activity. Widdowson suggested that what constitutes the primary focus of attention, the goal, the way in which the outcome is evaluated and the relationship to the real world are all interpreted differently in accordance with this basic difference in orientation. In effect, however, Widdowson is not so much disagreeing with Skehan's definition as, with his customary elegance, refining it. Table 2.1 is an attempt to incorporate Widdowson's insight into Skehan's definition.[4]

A possible objection to this conceptualization of 'exercise' and 'task' is that teachers and learners in a classroom context are unlikely to forget the overarching reason for any activity they engage in, namely, to learn the

Table 2.1 Distinguishing 'exercise' and 'task' (based on Skehan, 1998a, 1998b)

Aspects	Exercise	Task
Orientation	Linguistic skills viewed as pre-requisite for learning communicative abilities.	Linguistic skills are developed while engaging in communicative activity.
Focus	Linguistic form and semantic meaning (i.e. primary focus on form).	Propositional content and pragmatic communicative meaning (primary focus on meaning).[5]
Goal	Manifestation of code knowledge.	Achievement of a communicative goal.
Outcome evaluation	Performance evaluated in terms of conformity to the code.	Performance evaluated in terms of whether the communicative goal has been achieved.
Real-world relationship	Internalization of linguistic skills serves as an investment for future use.	There is a relationship between the activity that arises from the task and the way language is used in the real world.

language. In other words, it can be claimed that the achievement of a communicative goal will always be subservient to a learning agenda. Such a claim, reasonable as it seems, needs to be subjected to empirical investigation. But irrespective of whether it is valid or not, it does not preclude the need for the kind of theoretical distinction between 'exercise' and 'task' outlined in Table 2.1. No matter what the actual behaviour that arises when teachers and learners perform an exercise or task is, there is a need to distinguish 'exercise' and 'task' at the level of workplan. The extent to which workplans and actual behaviour are matched remains an issue of obvious importance but cannot be studied unless clearly defined categories of workplan are established.

Task from a Psycholinguistic Perspective

From a psycholinguistic[6] perspective a task is a device that guides learners to engage in certain types of information-processing that are claimed to be important for effective language use and/or for language acquisition from some theoretical standpoint. This perspective is predictive, and, in some cases, deterministic. That is, it assumes that there are properties in a task that will predispose, even induce, learners to engage in certain types of language use and mental processing that are beneficial to acquisition. As Skehan *et al*. (1998) put it 'task properties have a significant impact on the nature of performance' (1998: 245). The claim is, therefore, that there is a close correlation between the task-as-workplan and the task-as-process because the activity that results from the task-as-workplan is predictable from the design features of the task. As I will later argue, such a view constitutes both a strength and a weakness where language pedagogy is concerned. I believe, therefore, that it needs to be acknowledged but also challenged, not least because of its dominance in task-based research and pedagogy.

The underlying theoretical position adopted by task-based researchers who work in this tradition derives from what Lantolf (1996) called the 'computational metaphor'. Lantolf saw Chomsky as the person most responsible for the dominance of this metaphor in linguistics and applied linguistics since the 1960s but recognized that it is evident in cognitive as well as nativist accounts of language learning. He commented:

> It quickly became regularized as theory within the cognitive science of the 1970s and 1980s. Mainstream cognitive science so strongly believes in the metaphor – in effect, to be in mainstream cognitive science means that many people find it difficult to conceive of neural computation as a theory, it must surely be a fact. (1996: 724–725)

It is not surprising, therefore, that this metaphor underlies the work on task-based learning/teaching of Long (1989), Skehan (1996b) and Yule (1997), among others, all of whom view tasks as devices for manipulating how learners process language. Tasks, in other words, are seen as the external means by which we can influence the mental computations that learners make. These computations determine how effectively they communicate and how they acquire language.

Within this basic metaphor, it is possible to distinguish a number of different theoretical positions. I will briefly consider three here. The first, which was prominent in research in the 1980s and continues to attract attention, albeit in somewhat revised form, is Long's Interaction Hypothesis. The second is Skehan's 'cognitive approach', based on the distinction between two types of processing that learners can engage in (lexical processing and rule-based processing). Skehan's theoretical position has informed a number of studies carried out in the 1990s and since. The third is Yule's model of communicative effectiveness, which has attracted less attention, but is of obvious promise where language pedagogy is concerned.

The Interaction Hypothesis

In its early form (Long, 1983), the Interaction Hypothesis claimed that acquisition is facilitated when learners obtain comprehensible input as a result of the opportunity to negotiate meaning when communication breakdown occurs. In its later form (Long, 1996), the theory has been extended to take account of other ways in which meaning negotiation can contribute to L2 acquisition, namely through the feedback that learners receive on their own production when they attempt to communicate and through the modified output that arises when learners are pushed to reformulate their productions to make them comprehensible. In the later version, then, meaning negotiation serves to draw learners' attention to linguistic form in the context of a primary focus-on-meaning and in so doing induces the 'noticing' that has been claimed necessary for acquisition to take place (Schmidt, 1990).

It follows from the Interaction Hypothesis, whether in its early or late form, that what is important for acquisition is the opportunity for learners to engage in meaning negotiation. Meaning negotiation serves as the means by which learners' 'data needs' (Pica, 1996) can be effectively met. It should be noted, however, that, with the exception of a few studies (e.g. Ellis *et al.*, 1994; Ellis & He, 1999; Mackey, 1999), researchers have focused more on which task characteristics induce negotiation than on whether the negotiation that results from performing the task promotes acquisition.

A question that has attracted the attention of research informed by the Interaction Hypothesis is how opportunities for meaning negotiation can be provided. Clearly, there are many factors that can bear on this question, including those relating to the setting, the learner and the tasks that learners are asked to perform. We will be concerned only with research that has investigated the latter set of factors. This research has sought to identify the task dimensions that impact on meaning negotiation and thereby to establish a psycholinguistic basis for the classification of tasks (e.g. Pica *et al.*, 1993).

Drawing on research to date, Table 2.2 below indicates somewhat crudely, which task characteristics are likely to have a 'more positive' and a 'less positive' effect on the quantity of meaning negotiation likely to take place. It suggests that the kinds of interactional modifications hypothesized to contribute to L2 acquisition are likely to be more frequent in tasks that: (1) have a required information exchange; (2) involve a two-way (as opposed to one-way) exchange of information; (3) have a closed outcome; (4) have topics that are not familiar to the interactants; (5) involve a human/ethical type problem; (6) involve a narrative discourse mode; and (7) are context-free (in the sense that the task does not provide contextual support for communication) and involve considerable detail. This summary is based on a detailed survey of the research (see Ellis, 2003). One problem with this research, however, is that it provides little information relating to how the different dimensions shown in Table 2.2 interact in the impact they have on meaning negotiation. Typically, the research has compared tasks that differ with regard to a single task dimension (e.g. the effect of a two-way as opposed to a one-way information gap). It is likely, of course, that the various dimensions interact in complex ways, with some combinations having a greater influence on negotiation than others.

A somewhat different but related approach to investigating tasks is that followed by Swain. She based her approach on the role that output can play in L2 acquisition, a role which Long (1996) also incorporated into his revised Interaction Hypothesis. Swain (1985, 1995) suggested that output serves to help learners notice gaps in their linguistic knowledge and thus triggers both analysis of input and of their own existing internal resources. In addition, it provides a means by which learners

Table 2.2 Task dimensions hypothesized to promote meaning negotiation (from Ellis, 2003: 96)

Task features	More positive	Less positive
Information exchange	Required (information- gap)	Optional (opinion-gap)
Information gap	Two-way	One-way
Outcome	Closed	Open
Topic	Human/ethical	Objective/spatial
	Familiar	Less familiar
Discourse domain	Narrative;	Description;
	Collaborative	Expository
Cognitive complexity	Context-free;	Context-dependent;
	Detailed information	Less-detailed information

can test hypotheses about the L2 and reflect on their own and the interlocutors' use of language. In accordance with this theoretical position, Swain and her co-researchers examined how tasks impact on 'language-related episodes' (i.e. occasions where linguistic form is explicitly discussed by learners). Such episodes arise when learners temporarily attend to form in the context of performing a task. They involve what might be called the 'negotiation of form' – an attempt to determine collaboratively which form to use in order to express meaning accurately and coherently. Such negotiation is directed at the achievement of a communicative goal, not at conformity to the code for its own sake, and, therefore, lies within the kind of behaviour a 'task' is intended to elicit (see Table 2.1). However, Swain and Lapkin (2001) found no major task differences in the degree of attention that L2 learners paid to form.[7]

A 'cognitive approach' to tasks

Skehan (1998a) developed what he called a 'cognitive approach' to support his empirical investigations of tasks. This approach is based on a distinction in the way in which learners are believed to represent L2 knowledge. Learners (like native speakers) construct both an exemplar-based system and a rule-based system. The former is lexical in nature and includes both discrete lexical items and, importantly, ready-made formulaic chunks of language. The linguistic knowledge contained in this system can be easily and quickly accessed and thus is ideally suited for occasions calling for fluent language performance. The rule-based system consists of abstract representations of the underlying patterns of the language. They require more processing and thus are best suited for more controlled, less fluent language performance. They are needed when learners have to creatively construct utterances to express meaning precisely or in sociolinguistically appropriate ways. The distinction between these two types of linguistic knowledge is broadly acknowledged in cognitive psychology (see, for example, N. Ellis, 1996).

Whereas the task-based research originating from the Interaction Hypothesis has focused on meaning negotiation, Skehan's research has examined individual learners' production. Skehan distinguished three aspects of production: (1) fluency (i.e. the capacity of the learner to mobilize his/her system to communicate in real time); (2) accuracy (i.e. the ability of the learner to perform in accordance with target language norms); and (3) complexity (i.e. the utilization of interlanguage structures that are 'cutting edge', elaborate and structured). Skehan suggested that language users vary in the extent to which they emphasize fluency, accuracy or complexity, with some tasks predisposing them to focus on fluency, others on accuracy and yet others on complexity. These different aspects of production draw on different systems of language. Fluency requires learners to draw on their memory-based system, accessing and deploying ready-made chunks of language, and, when problems arise, using communication strategies to get by. In contrast, accuracy and, in particular, complexity are achieved by learners drawing on their rule-based system and thus require syntactic processing. Skehan argued that it may be possible to influence different aspects of language acquisition (i.e. fluency, accuracy and complexity) by providing opportunities for learners to engage in different types of production.

The research based on Skehan's 'cognitive account' has been directed at discovering what task variables predispose learners to emphasize fluency, accuracy or complexity in their production. These task variables can be divided into two broad groups: (1) task features and (2) task implementation. Table 2.3 summarizes the results of the early research. Skehan (1998b), in a review of task-based research, acknowledged that the various task variables referred to in Table 2.3 can potentially interact in complex ways to influence learner production and that currently little is known about these interactions. However, he was optimistic that with further research, 'greater precision of influence' could be established.[8]

Skehan's research assumes that learners possess a limited processing capacity such that trade-offs between fluency, accuracy and complexity are likely to occur. However, other cognitive models are premised on a multiple-resources view of processing – that is, that learners, like native speakers, have the capacity to attend to more than one aspect of language

Table 2.3 Effects of task variables on the fluency, accuracy and complexity of learner production

Task variables	Main findings
A. Task features	
1. Extent to which task involves well-structured information	Promotes fluency
2. Number of elements to be manipulated	More elements result in greater complexity
3. Decision-making tasks requiring differentiated responses	Greater differentiation results in greater complexity
B. Task variables	
1. Planning time	Planning time results in greater complexity and, sometimes, greater accuracy; different types and amounts of planning time differentially affect complexity and accuracy
2. Task repetition	Asking learners to repeat a task results in more complex language production
3. Simultaneous vs subsequent task performance	Accuracy and complexity greater in subsequent task performance
4. Knowledge of subsequent public task performance	In some tasks, this resulted in greater accuracy

and language processing at the same time. Such models have also informed task-based research. Robinson (see Robinson, 1995b; Robinson *et al.*, 1996), for example, made use of a multiple-resources view of processing to try to identify the differential complexity of tasks.

One of the design features he investigated is the availability of contextual support in the performance of a task, the hypothesis being that tasks that do not provide such support will be more complex than those that do because they make parallel attention to form and message more difficult. The results, however, are inconclusive. The problem, as Skehan and Foster (2001) have pointed out, is that there is no single, general measure of task performance that can be used to determine whether one task is more complex than another. As Skehan's own research shows and as Robinson's research seems to bear out, a task may be difficult in terms of one aspect of language use (e.g. a measure of linguistic accuracy) but relatively easy in terms of another (e.g. a measure of fluency). This finding, then, is more supportive of a limited processing view of capacity than of a multiple-resources view.

Communicative effectiveness

Whereas research based on both the Interaction/Output Hypothesis and Skehan's 'cognitive approach' is oriented towards identifying those task features that result in learner production of potential importance for L2 acquisition, Yule's research is directed at examining task-processes that contribute to communicative effectiveness. The extent to which task design and implementation impacts on the skilfulness of L2 learners' performance (as opposed to their linguistic competence) is seen, quite legitimately, as an important target for research in its own right.

We have seen that a defining feature of a 'task' is that it is outcome-evaluated in the sense that the success or failure of the task is determined by whether the learners achieve the goal of the task (e.g. establishing whether two pictures are the same or different). Building on this feature, Yule proposed a theory of communicative effectiveness for referential tasks of the Same-or-Different kind. Yule (1997) distinguishes two broad dimensions of communicative effectiveness: (1) the identification-of-referent dimension and (2) the role-taking dimension. Learners need to be able to encode the referents they have to communicate about. They require the perceptual ability to notice specific attributes of the referent, the comparison ability to distinguish one referent from another, and the linguistic ability needed to encode the referent in such a way that it is sufficiently distinguished from other referents.

The role-taking dimension concerns the ability of the participants to take account of their communicative partners in order to achieve intersubjectivity. They must be able to recognize the importance of the other speaker's perspective, to make inferences about the other speaker's perspective, to take these inferences into account when encoding a message and to attend to the feedback provided by the other speakers in order to monitor output accordingly.

Yule based his study of communicative effectiveness on an analysis of communicative outcomes. This goes beyond simply identifying whether the task participants have successfully accomplished a task. Yule and Powers (1994) proposed a framework for the micro-analysis of communicative outcomes based on how specific referential problems are solved (see Table 2.4). The advantage of this framework is that it provides information about how participants set about dealing with the various referential problems that arise in performing a task.

This framework was used in research aimed at identifying the impact of task variables on communicative outcomes. Yule *et al*. (1992), for example, used the framework to compare learners' performance on two similar map tasks in each of which one learner had to describe a route drawn on a map to a second learner whose map did not show the route. The tasks contained built-in referential problems in that the maps the learners used were not identical. The study showed that the learners favoured non-negotiated solutions in the first task but negotiated solutions in the second task. This study, then, indicates that repeating a task not only results in greater communicative efficiency but also affects the kind of strategies learners use to tackle referential problems. It is also likely that tasks vary in terms of the ease with which participants achieve communicative effectiveness and that this may serve as a way of measuring task complexity. Brown (1995), for example, reports that native speakers of English found it easier to perform a task that required the participants to simply 'utilize an interpretation', as was the case in the kind of map task used in Yule's research, than a task where the participants had to 'construct an interpretation', as in a storytelling task involving events that were capable of more than one interpretation.

As should be clear from this brief account of Yule's theory, communicative effectiveness is determined not just by the nature of the task but also by learner factors, such as personality and cognitive style. The content of a task impacts on the identification-of-referent dimension, whereas learner factors are involved in the role-taking dimension. In acknowledging the importance of the learner's contribution to the activity that arises from a task, and given that the first dimension can only be communicated through the second dimension, Yule's theory of task performance goes beyond that of both the Interaction/Output Hypothesis and Skehan's cognitive approach. However, to date, there have been few studies examining the impact of task design and implementation on communicative effectiveness. Also, the question of how task performance might contribute to the development of communicative effectiveness has not been addressed. As it stands, therefore, Yule's model may be of greater applicability to performance testing than to task-based teaching.

Table 2.4 A framework for describing communicative outcomes

1. No problem: A referential problem exists but is not identified.

2. Non-negotiated solutions:
  a. Unacknowledged problem: a problem is identified by the receiver but not acknowledged by the sender.
  b. Abandon responsibility: a problem is acknowledged by the sender, but responsibility is not taken for solving it.
  c. Arbitrary solution: a problem is acknowledged by the sender who solves it arbitrarily, ignoring the receiver's contribution.

3. Negotiated solutions
  a. Other-centred solution: the sender tries to solve the problem based on the receiver's (and the sender's) perspective.
  b. Self-centred solution: the sender tries to solve the problem by making the receiver's perspective fit the sender's.

Source: Yule and Powers (1994).

Evaluating the psycholinguistic perspective

The strength of the psycholinguistic perspective is that it has served to identify features of task design and task implementation that can impact on L2 performance and L2 acquisition. The approach adopted has been as follows.

(1) Determine what effect task variables have on task performance.
(2) Draw on a theory of L2 acquisition/communicative effectiveness to make claims regarding the relationship between specific types of language performance and L2 acquisition/communicative effectiveness.
(3) Infer which kinds of tasks will work best for promoting L2 acquisition/communicative effectiveness.

As Skehan (1998a) pointed out, the inherent weakness of this approach lies in the failure to show a direct relationship between task-design and L2 acquisition (or, I would add, between task-design and the development of communicative efficiency). This arises because the research to date has been invariably cross-sectional in design. Skehan's solution is to examine the relationship between task and L2 acquisition longitudinally. However, this solution ignores the problem of controlling for the myriad factors that impact on acquisition/communicative efficiency over and above those involved in the design and implementation of the tasks the learners are asked to perform. The extent to which it is possible to identify empirically which kinds of tasks work best for acquisition/communicative efficiency is clearly problematic. One solution is to design tasks that incorporate specific linguistic features which learners have not yet acquired, as in Ellis *et al.* (1994) – see Chapter 3. This will make it possible to determine what effect the design of a task has on the acquisition of these features.

The psycholinguistic perspective suffers from another drawback. There is an inherent problem in examining tasks without any consideration of other general factors that are bound to influence task performance. For one thing, task performance, as Yule acknowledged, depends not just on the nature of the task but also on learner factors (such as those involved in the role-taking dimension of task performance). Another dimension that researchers in the psycholinguistic tradition have paid scant attention to is the setting. For example, it cannot be assumed that tasks performed in a pseudo-laboratory-type setting (as has been the case with much of the research to date) will be performed in the same way as tasks performed in the classroom (see Foster, 1998). Also, the same task performed with the whole class can result in a very different kind of activity to the activity that arises when the task is performed in pairs or small groups (see Ellis & He, 1999). Similarly, the same task might also result in very different kinds of activity depending on the role that the teacher plays in the interactions that arise at various stages of a lesson (see Samuda, 2001). Further, the nature of the activities learners engage in before they perform a task can impact on their performance (see note 5). In short, a psycholinguistic approach to investigating tasks needs to take account of these other factors. It needs to demonstrate how task factors interact with them. Given the complexity of these interactions it may prove very difficult to arrive at ecologically valid generalizations about the effect task variables have on learner performance. In the view of some (e.g. Coughlan & Duff, 1994; Platt & Brooks, 1994), this invalidates the psycholinguistic perspective on tasks. I will take a different view but first we will explore an alternative paradigm for examining the relationship between tasks and acquisition, one that views the activity that arises when learners perform a task from a constructivist perspective.

Task from a Sociocultural Perspective

The perspective on tasks I shall now explore draws on sociocultural theory, as this has grown out of the work of Vygotsky (1978) and Leont'ev (1981), among others. I shall not attempt to present this complex theory in detail here – readers are referred to summaries provided by Lantolf (2000b), Lantolf and Appel (1994) and in two full-length books (Lantolf & Poehner, 2014; Lantolf & Thorne, 2006). Sociocultural theory has relatively to say about task design. Storch (2017) noted that tasks need to challenge learners but she offered no suggestions for how to select challenging tasks. In contrast, sociocultural theory has been applied to investigating how learners make sense of the tasks they are asked to perform and how they learn from them and thus provides valuable insights into how tasks can be implanted to promote learning.

One of the central claims of socio-cultural theory is that participants always co-construct the activity they engage in, in accordance with their own socio-history and locally determined goals. As Appel and Lantolf (1994) pointed out 'performance depends crucially on the interaction of individual and task' rather than on the inherent properties of the task itself. Implicit in sociocultural accounts of tasks is the view that the same task can result in very different kinds of activity when performed by the same learners at different times. Coughlan and Duff (1994) distinguished what they called 'task' (i.e. the workplan) and 'activity' (i.e. the actual language that occurs when learners perform the task). In a study of one Cambodian ESL learner, they were able to demonstrate that the same task (a picture description task) was performed very differently on two separate occasions. They also showed that the way another type of learner – EFL students in a Hungarian secondary school – performed the task was, again, entirely different. Coughlan and Duff showed how an entire range of discourse types arose from this task reflecting their subjects' multiple interpretations of it. They concluded that 'task' cannot be treated as a constant in research as 'the activity it generates will be unique' (1994: 191). Other studies (e.g. Foster, 1998; Platt & Brooks, 1994) lend support to such a conclusion.

In order to perform a task, the learners have to 'interpret' it. This is reflected in the effort that learners put into orientating to the task and establishing their goals for performing it. Brooks and Donato (1994), for example, showed that even though the teacher carefully explained the task goals to third-year high school learners of L2 Spanish, the participants engaged in extensive metatalk about the task (typically in the L1) to establish the goals and to orient themselves to how they might accomplish them. Brooks and Donato showed that particular students hit on quite unique ways of performing the task (e.g. numbering the squares on a matrix sheet to enable them to identify where specific objects needed to be placed on it). Other studies indicate how learners' orientation can change during the performance of a task. Appel and Lantolf (1994), for example, showed how learners re-orientated themselves from 'recalling' to 'retelling' at a certain stage in an oral narrative task.

According to sociocultural theory, learning arises not *through* interaction but *in* interaction. Learners first succeed in performing a new function with the assistance of another person and then internalize this function so that they can perform it unassisted. In this way, social interaction mediates learning. The theory has gone some way to specifying the kinds of interactions that most successfully mediate learning. They are those in which the new functions are 'scaffolded' by the participants. Scaffolding[9] is the dialogic process by which one speaker assists another to perform a new function. According to Wood et al. (1976), it can involve recruiting interest in the task, simplifying the task as necessary, maintaining pursuit of the goal of the task, marking critical features and discrepancies between what has been produced and the ideal solution, controlling frustration during problem solving and demonstrating an idealized version of the act to be performed.

Task-based research in the sociocultural tradition has been directed at demonstrating how scaffolding helps learners achieve a successful task outcome. Donato (1994), for example, described the collective scaffolding employed by groups of university students performing an oral task. He showed how one group of learners was able to produce a particular grammatical construction jointly even though none of the students individually knew it. He also provided evidence to suggest that language acquisition was taking place. The performance of new grammatical constructions on one occasion was frequently followed by the independent use of them by individual learners on a later occasion. Studies by Swain (e.g. Swain & Lapkin, 1998) also testify to learners' ability to internalize grammatical features that they initially constructed collaboratively through dialogue when performing a task. Samuda (2001) showed how a teacher created the conditions for students to uptake a new grammatical feature (the modal verb 'may') through implicit scaffolding but also, interestingly, that the students did not in fact use the new feature in their own speech until the teacher provided a much more explicit scaffold. Both the teacher's implicit and explicit focus occurred in the context of performing the same communicative task. Samuda does not discuss her study from a sociocultural perspective. However, her insistence on the need to view tasks in relation to how teachers shape opportunities for learning rather than as objective instruments for providing opportunities for learning is reflective of such a perspective.

Sociocultural theory, then, offers a very different perspective on tasks. Whereas researchers in the psycholinguistic tradition have emphasized the role of the inherent task properties on performance and acquisition, sociocultural researchers have focused on how tasks are accomplished by learners and teachers and how the process of accomplishing them might contribute to language acquisition. They view the learners, the teacher and the setting in which they interact as just as important as the task itself. They reject attempts to externally define and classify tasks on the grounds that the 'activity' that derives from a task cannot be predicted from the task itself. They focus instead on how task participants achieve intersubjectivity with regard to goals and procedures and on how they collaborate to scaffold each other's attempt to perform functions that lie outside their individual abilities. Such a perspective is both persuasive and informative, as is reflected in Swain's recent adoption of sociocultural theory in her own research. Swain (2000) argued that a constructionist account of tasks is needed to understand how learning arises out of performance.

Clearly, if there is no close correspondence between 'task' and 'activity' as sociocultural theory claims, a traditional needs analysis of the kind that Long (2005, 2015) recommends makes little sense. Mochizuki (2017), however, showed how a 'contingent needs analysis' can be derived from a socioculturally informed study of learners' performing tasks. Mochizuki's idea was that an analysis of how learners perform a task can help to identify the contradictions and tensions that arise and this information can be fed back into what teachers need to do to ensure the effective mediation of subsequent tasks. Mochizuki used Activity Theory to examine how two different groups of learners participated in feedback sessions on doctoral students' writing. The 'needs' she identified included the importance of the facilitators equipping students with the strategies required for giving and receiving feedback and of addressing the power relations that suppress some students' participation in giving and receiving feedback.

There are some noteworthy limitations of sociocultural research on tasks. As in psycholinguistically oriented research on tasks, researchers in the sociocultural tradition have concentrated on describing the social interactions that arise when learners perform tasks and have made little attempt to demonstrate if these interactions contribute to acquisition.[10] In part this is a product of equating 'use' with 'acquisition' (i.e. what learners have been shown to do in interaction is taken as evidence of learning). In part, it is the result of the same problem facing psycholinguistic task-based research – the lack of a longitudinal dimension. Also, in rejecting the deterministic view of tasks that underlies some of the research in the psycholinguistic tradition (see, for example, Long, 1989), sociocultural researchers fail to acknowledge that task features and variables do have an impact on task performance, albeit in ways that may defy precise specification. It should be noted, however, that sociocultural theory does not preclude recognizing the role played by task variables. Variation in task design is equivalent to variation in the task-as-artefact, which, according to sociocultural theory impacts on how the artefact is deployed. This problem, then, is not inherent in the theory but rather reflects the way the theory has been taken up in task-based research. It could be argued that Samuda (2001), in the study referred to above, shows how a sociocultural perspective might accommodate attention to the design of tasks. Samuda acknowledged the importance of examining the task and teacher 'in action' but also illustrated how a task can be designed to create a 'semantic space' so as to provide opportunities for learners to use a specifically targeted grammatical feature. In accepting that learners co-construct task-based activity, it is not necessary to reject entirely the claim that the design of a task impacts on that activity.

Tasks in Language Pedagogy

I would now like to turn to how these different conceptualizations of 'task' can inform task-based language pedagogy. I shall attempt this by making two distinctions. The first concerns the 'goal' of task-based instruction, namely whether this is 'communicative effectiveness' or 'L2 acquisition'. I shall argue that task-based language pedagogy has paid insufficient attention to this distinction. The second concerns the two dimensions of teaching identified by Van Lier (1991) – 'planning' and 'improvising'. I shall argue that the two perspectives on tasks discussed in the preceding sections of this paper are differentially relevant to these dimensions.

Task-based language instruction has a number of purposes. Willis (1996: 35–6) identifies eight.

(1) To give learners confidence in trying out whatever language they know.
(2) To give learners experience of spontaneous interaction.
(3) To give learners the chance to benefit from noticing how others express similar meanings.
(4) To give learners chances for negotiating turns to speak.
(5) To engage learners in using language purposefully and cooperatively.
(6) To make learners participate in a complete interaction, not just one-off sentences.
(7) To give learners chances to try out communication strategies.
(8) To develop learners' confidence that they can achieve communicative goals.

These purposes relate to two general goals: communicative effectiveness and L2 acquisition. Interestingly, seven of Willis' purposes relate primarily to communicative effectiveness; only one, (3), relates specifically to L2 acquisition. This reflects, perhaps, the general perception among language teachers and educators that task-based instruction is mainly directed at improving students' abilities to use the target language rather than at enabling them to acquire new linguistic skills (see Samuda, 2000). This contrasts with the orientation of SLA researchers such as Long *et al.* whose primary concern is how tasks can contribute to language acquisition.

The theoretical perspectives that have been discussed in the previous section suggest that there is a need to distinguish between task-based performance that contributes to effective language use and that which facilitates L2 acquisition. That is, it cannot be assumed that achieving communicative effectiveness in the performance of a task will involve the interactive conditions that promote L2 acquisition. Students may succeed in performing a task successfully without the need to participate in much meaning negotiation or the need to attend to linguistic form. In so doing, they may emphasize fluency over accuracy or complexity by drawing on their lexicalized system, thus failing to stretch their interlanguage systems. The task may not confront them with the need to collaborate in the joint construction of new knowledge. Similarly, tasks that are directed at improving students' communicative abilities – for example, by promoting confidence in using language or by providing opportunities for trying out communication strategies – may fail to develop their linguistic skills. It follows that teachers and language educators need to give more attention to the properties of tasks that respectively aim to promote communicative efficiency and L2 acquisition. In this respect, Skehan's cognitive approach and Yule's theory of communicative effectiveness appear most promising. Yule's theory provides a basis for evaluating the kinds of tasks that contribute to developing communicative effectiveness, whereas Skehan's work suggests the kinds of tasks that are needed to promote accuracy/ complexity and, thereby, potentially to influence language acquisition.

Implicit in this argument, however, is the assumption that it is possible to predict with some degree of certainty what kind of language performance will result from specific tasks. It is precisely, this claim, however, that research based on sociocultural theory has challenged. If it is not possible to establish how students will behave when asked to perform particular tasks, then, clearly it is not possible to design a task-based syllabus based on such constructs as meaning negotiation, fluency, accuracy and complexity or communicative effectiveness. Put simply, if the position adopted by some sociocultural researchers is accepted, there is no basis for the selection or grading of tasks other, perhaps, than the very general idea that a task should afford opportunities for students to construct linguistic forms collaboratively that they have not yet fully internalized (i.e. functions that lie within their zone of proximal development).

There, are, however, good reasons for dismissing this argument. First, while acknowledging that task performances are necessarily always constructed rather than determined, recognition can still be given to the propensity of certain tasks to lead to particular types of language behaviour. As I pointed out above, such a position is not, in fact, incompatible with sociocultural theory. There is sufficient research to demonstrate that such variables as the inherent structure of a task, the availability of planning time and the opportunity to repeat a task have certain probabilistic process outcomes. Second, given the strong theoretical rationale for task-based courses, teachers need to be able to design such courses. Thus, they need to take principled decisions about what kinds of tasks to include in the course, the balance of the different types of task, and the sequencing of the tasks. As Corder (1980) pointed out long ago, teachers cannot wait until researchers have resolved their differences – they must get on with the practical task of teaching. It is reasonable to suggest, therefore, that they should draw on the available research to help them in their planning decisions.

Van Lier (1991, 1996) suggested that 'planning' is one of two dimensions of teaching, the other being 'improvisation' (i.e. the actual behaviours that arise during the process of a lesson which have not been planned for). He sees both as important for a teacher's professionalism. Any lesson needs to achieve a balance between these two dimensions. He commented:

> The term 'balanced' suggests that in most cases a lesson which is so tightly planned (and implemented) that there is no room at all for improvisation, and conversely, a lesson which is not planned at all and therefore entirely improvised, would generally be considered unbalanced and perhaps not entirely effective. (Van Lier, 1996: 200)

'Balanced' teaching involves teachers moving back and forwards between planned and improvised decision-making in the course of a lesson. Van

Lier, of course, is talking about teaching in general but the distinction is of obvious relevance to task-based language pedagogy.

Research in the psycholinguistic tradition of Long, Skehan and Yule has an obvious role to play in the 'planning' dimension of language teaching. It provides information that can be used to select and grade tasks – to suit the tasks to particular groups of learners. In other words, it can assist in the design of task-based courses. It can also help guide general methodological decisions, such as when and when not to provide learners with opportunities to plan before performing a task, what kind of planning to require of them or whether to repeat a task. In contrast, research in the sociocultural tradition can make teachers aware that the activity that arises from a task may not be exactly what was planned and that this is not a consequence of poor planning or bad teaching but of the participants adapting the task to their own purposes. It can also help to illuminate how teachers can improvise in order to construct activity from tasks in ways that promote the development of linguistic abilities and skills. In particular, it illustrates the processes involved in determining task goals, establishing intersubjectivity and scaffolding learners' attempts to perform beyond their current level. Such illustrations can serve an awareness-raising function, enabling teachers (and learners) to see the kind of strategies that can be exploited to co-construct activity relevant to their goals. For example, it might help teachers to see when to provide an 'implicit' and 'explicit' focus on form in the performance of a task (see Samuda, 2001).

From a pedagogic perspective, then, the two research traditions need not be seen as incompatible. Rather they mutually inform task-based instruction. Van Lier argued that teachers need to develop a 'dual vision' – to keep in mind both a long-term sense of direction and the need to make on-line decisions that take account of the exigencies of the moment. Such a vision will need to draw on a variety of theoretical perspectives and the research they give rise to. The goal of a pedagogically relevant programme of task-based research must be to address both the planning and improvising dimensions of teaching. This can be achieved if researchers eschew the temptation to promote their own preferred approach to researching tasks at the expense of other approaches – a clear tendency in some sociocultural researchers such as Platt and Brooks (1994) – and, instead, accept the need for a pluralistic research agenda capable of addressing the multifaceted nature of task-based instruction.

Notes

(1)   This chapter is based on a paper that was given at the AILA Conference in Tokyo, Japan in 1999. I would like to thank Martin Bygate, Jim Lantolf and two anonymous reviewers for comments on this paper, many of which were incorporated into the present chapter.

(2)   Widdowson (1978) drew a distinction between 'signification' and 'value'. 'Signification' relates to 'usage', as this is represented in a dictionary or a reference

grammar. 'Value' relates to the actual meaning a linguistic item takes on when it is used in communication.

(3)   A Same-or-Different task typically consists of one or more pairs of pictures. Working in pairs, learners are asked to describe the picture they are holding, which their partner cannot see, in order to decide whether it is the same as or different from their partner's.

(4)   In Chapter 1 I offered a definition of a 'task' that addresses some of the problems that Widdowson identified with Skehan's definition.

(5)   Widdowson (1998b) also took issue with the widely used distinction between a 'focus on form' and a 'focus on meaning', arguing that it is fundamentally mistaken because 'meaning' (at least 'semantic meaning') has always been a part of what SLA researchers refer to as a 'focus on form'. However, the contrast SLA researchers wish to make is between a 'focus on form' defined as attention to linguistic forms and the semantic meanings they can potentially realize, and a 'focus on meaning' defined as attempts to use language pragmatically to convey messages in context. This, of course, is precisely the distinction Widdowson himself makes when he talks of 'usage' and 'use'.

(6)   The use of the term 'psycholinguistic' here refers to the computational view of language acquisition. In fact, as Lantolf pointed out to me (personal correspondence), sociocultural theory is also 'psycholinguistic' in that it purports to account for mental activity. However, sociocultural theory is not concerned solely with mental activity but rather views social and mental activity as seamlessly related. It would seem appropriate, therefore, to reserve the term 'psycholinguistic' to refer to 'black box' models of learning of the kind referred to in this section and to look for other terms to describe models that emphasize the role of social activity in learning.

(7)   Swain and Lapkin's (2001) study compared the language-related episodes that resulted from a jigsaw task and a dictogloss task (where students listened to a text, took notes, and then tried to reconstruct it). Both tasks were preceded by a mini-lesson on the targeted grammatical structure and both tasks involved the production of a written text. Swain and Lapkin suggested that these commonalities may explain why the tasks did not result in any differences in attention to form. In this respect, the study is illustrative of a general problem with research directed at investigating the effects of task type on language performance; the sequence of activities that tasks are embedded in may have a more significant effect on performance than the design of the tasks themselves. Later Swain (2000) switched paradigms. Adopting a sociocultural perspective on tasks, she argued that collaboratively solving linguistic problems enabled learners to produce linguistic forms that they were incapable of producing independently. In other words, learning occurred not in the minds of learners but in flight as they interacted.

(8)   Later, Skehan (2016) argued that it is task conditions rather than task design features that have the greater impact on learner production.

(9)   The term 'scaffolding' also figures in research based on the Interaction Hypothesis. However, it is used in a much more limited sense to refer to the way in which learners build syntactic constructions vertically over several turns. In sociocultural theory, 'scaffolding' is used to refer to the interactional, social and affective support that one interactant gives another.

(10) In this respect, Swain's recent research is an exception. Swain has attempted to show how learners' dialogic construction of a task can lead to acquisition of new L2 forms.

Part 2

Researching Task-based Teaching

Over the years I have conducted a number of studies of task-based teaching. One of my earliest studies (Nobuyoshi & Ellis, 1993) used a narrative task to investigate what effect prompting learners to self-correct their past tense errors had on their accuracy in the use of this tense in a subsequent narrative task. The study was motivated by Swain's (1985) claims about the importance of 'pushed output' for language learning. It pre-dated Lyster's later research (Lyster, 2004) on prompts. Subsequently, I turned my attention to input-based tasks – in part because I wanted to conduct a classroom-based study with students who had very limited speaking abilities and in part because input-based tasks were convenient for investigating Long's (1983) Interaction Hypothesis. In Ellis *et al.* (1994) we used a listen-and-do task where students had to listen to the teacher's description of where different objects were located and note their location on a picture of a kitchen. We found that when learners had the opportunity to request clarification if they could not understand the teacher's description, they both performed the task better (i.e. they were successful in locating the objects in the kitchen picture) and they also learned more of the difficult words we had embedded in the description than if they had no opportunity to negotiate their understanding. Later, in Ellis and He (1999), we used another listen-and-do task (the students listened to descriptions of where to locate different objects in a diagram of an apartment) to investigate the relative effects of simplified input, interactionally modified input and pushed output, reporting that the output condition led to more new words being acquired. These (and other studies) are described and discussed in Chapter 3. All of the studies considered in this chapter were theoretically motivated but they were also designed with practical concerns in mind. In particular, I was interested in listen-and-do tasks because it struck me that they provided a practical way of introducing task-based language teaching into classrooms where the students were used to treating English as an object. Quite apart from the theoretical issues these

41

studies tackled, they showed how task-based language teaching could be effectively implemented in the Japanese school context.

The research discussed in the following chapters was likewise directed at theoretical issues but at the same time addressed practical matters relating to the implementation of task-based language teaching (TBLT). In Chapter 4 I review research about 'focus-on-form' (i.e. the various ways in which learners' attention can be attracted to form as they perform a task when their primary focus is on meaning). I note that this construct – first introduced by Long (1991) – has evolved considerably over time, making it problematic for newcomers to TBLT to have a clear understanding of what it involves. I try to spell out the different ways of achieving a focus-on-form and in so doing expand the construct well-beyond what Long had in mind and probably still does (see Long, 2015).

My interest in pre-task planning – the focus of Chapter 5 – has quite a long history. It started with an article I published in 1987 where I investigated the effects of having learners write out a story before performing it orally and compared their performance with a task performed without any written preparation. I did not intend this to be a study of tasks as I was interested in interlanguage variability at that time. But it was subsequently interpreted as such by Crookes (1989) and Skehan (1996b). It produced clear evidence that pre-task planning can have an effect on the accuracy of use of a specific grammatical structure (regular past tense). Subsequently I published a study that investigated the effect of pre-task and within-task planning conditions on the complexity, accuracy and fluency of learners' oral and written production (Ellis & Yuan, 2004; Yuan & Ellis, 2003). Then in 2005 I edited a book of studies involving different kinds of planning. In Chapter 5, however, I view planning as just one of several different ways in which learners can be prepared to perform a task, reflecting my current view that planning needs to be considered alongside other pre-task activities. Investigating task-preparation activities allows for theoretical claims to be tested but it is also of obvious practical value. Teachers need to make informed decisions whether they want to give their students the opportunity to prepare for a task and, if so, how to do this.

In Chapter 6 I look at what I have come to think is one of the key issues in TBLT – namely whether or not to explicitly pre-teach the language that students will need to use when they perform the task. In effect, this chapter looks at the merits of task-supported instruction (where explicit pre-teaching of language occurs) and task-based instruction (where it does not occur). I point out that to investigate the effects pre-task explicit instruction it is necessary to examine both what effect the explicit instruction has on how learners perform a task and on whether it enhances the learning that results from performing it. Surprisingly though there are relatively few studies that have compared how learners perform a task and what they learn with and without a priori explicit instruction. This is surely an area in need of further research.

All of these chapters focus on research but also address issues of pedagogic significance. The final chapter in this section, however, is really just for researchers. In any research study it will be necessary to consider how to measure learners' performance of a task. In fact, there are many different ways in which researchers have done this, each way drawing on a different theoretical base. In this chapter I examine the types of measurement corresponding to the cognitive-interactionist, sociocultural, cognitive and personal identity approaches to investigating tasks. I see strengths and weaknesses in each of these approaches. Hopefully, this chapter will be of use to researchers in deciding how to measure the learner production that results from performing a task.

3 Non-Reciprocal Tasks, Comprehension and Second Language Acquisition

Introduction

Tasks can involve varying degrees of reciprocity. Reciprocal tasks are tasks that require a two-way flow of information between a speaker and a listener; they are speaking tasks. Non-reciprocal tasks require only a one-way flow of information from a speaker to a listener. This distinction, however, is best viewed as reflecting a continuum rather than a dichotomy as the extent to which the participants in a task are required to interact can vary. At one end of the continuum are tasks that are entirely non-reciprocal in that they do not permit learners any opportunity to interject whatsoever even if they do not understand (e.g. a non-interactive lecture), whereas at the other end are reciprocal tasks that can only be successfully accomplished if the participants interact to ensure mutual understanding (e.g. an information-gap task where the information has been split among the learners). In between, there are tasks that provide the learners with some negotiation rights but these are restricted (e.g. an interactive lecture where students have the opportunity to interrupt the lecturer occasionally). This chapter is concerned with tasks that are either entirely non-reciprocal or that allow relatively limited opportunities for two-way interaction. Where the learner is the addressee, such tasks are, in fact, listening tasks. Where the learner is responsible for communicating the information, they are speaking tasks.

There are two good reasons for examining non-reciprocal tasks. The first is that, in general, they have been somewhat neglected in the pedagogic literature on tasks. For example, the tasks described in Klippel (1984) or in Nunan (1989) are all reciprocal tasks. So too are the tasks typically referred to in the task-based research literature (e.g. Crookes & Gass, 1993; Skehan, 1998b). It would appear, therefore, that both teachers and researchers assume that a 'task' must involve speaking. Such an assumption, however, is not warranted by common definitions of a 'task' such as Ellis and Shintani's (2014) definition presented in Chapter 1 Such a definition is as applicable to listening tasks as it is to speaking tasks.

The second reason is that, from the second language acquisition (SLA) researcher's perspective, non-reciprocal tasks have an enormous advantage; they make it possible to investigate not only the kind of processing that results from performing a listening task but also what learners actually acquire from the performance. There is now a very considerable literature examining the kinds of language learners produce when they undertake different kinds of tasks under different conditions. However, this literature has not addressed directly what effect learner performance has on acquisition. There are good reasons for this. First, it is unlikely that a single task (or even a short series of tasks) will result in measurable *changes* in general language skill (e.g. fluency). Second, it is extremely difficult to devise focused tasks that make the use of some specific linguistic feature obligatory. Loschky and Bley-Vroman (1993) pointed out that, although it may be possible to construct tasks that make it 'natural' or 'useful' for learners to employ a specific feature, it is almost impossible to ensure that the feature is 'essential'. As a result, researchers such as Skehan (1998a), who are interested in the relationship between production on a task and language acquisition, have not been able to examine the relationship empirically (i.e. they have not investigated what effect performing a task has on a learner's interlanguage system). Instead, they have invoked theoretical arguments to make claims about the possible effects that certain types of task-derived production might have on learners' interlanguage development without examining whether these effects actually occur. Non-reciprocal tasks, in contrast, do provide a means by which researchers can directly investigate the relationship between task performance and acquisition. As Loschky and Bley-Vroman observed, comprehension tasks allow for the input to be scripted in such a way that it contains particular linguistic features, the learners' acquisition of which can be tested on completion of the task.

This chapter, then, differs from mainstream task-based research in that it examines tasks that are essentially non-reciprocal and also by examining the relationship between task-design on the one hand and acquisition/comprehension on the other. It also differs in the theoretical basis of the research reported. For while researchers such as Skehan have drawn on output theories of one kind or another, the research presented in this chapter is based mainly on input theories.

In the following section an example of the kind of non-reciprocal task used in the research is provided and discussed. Then, the theoretical basis of the research is outlined. A summary of the findings of a series of studies is then given. Finally, some implications for task-based teaching are considered.

An Example of a Non-reciprocal Task

Like the task in Pica *et al*. (1987), the tasks used in the research consisted of:

(a) structured input (i.e. input that had been specially designed to include specific linguistic features – vocabulary items);
(b) a non-verbal device (i.e. a diagram).

In each task, the structured input took the form of a series of directives requesting the learners to carry out a series of actions. These actions involved them in identifying the referents referred to in the directives and shown in an array of pictures, and then indicating the correct position of the referents in a matrix diagram. Such tasks are examples of what Widdowson (1978) has called information-transfer tasks, in that they require learners to transfer information from one modality (linguistic) to another (diagrammatic). They are also examples of what Pica *et al*. (1993) have called one-way information-gap tasks.

The pictorial materials for the task used in Ellis *et al*. (1994) are shown in Figure 3.1. In this task, the directives consisted of instructions about where to place a series of objects in a diagram of a kitchen. Here is an example of one of the directives:

> Can you find the scouring pad? Take the scouring pad and put it on top of the counter by the sink – the right side of the sink.

For this directive, the students had to identify the scouring pad among a series of small pictures and then write the number of the picture in the correct position in the matrix diagram of the kitchen.

This kind of task has a number of advantages. First, as pointed out above, it enables the researcher to incorporate specific linguistic features into the input (hence the term 'structured input'). In the research to be summarized below, the linguistic features were lexical items (such as 'scouring pad') which prior testing had shown the learners did not know. Second, it is possible to manipulate the input in different ways in order to test what effect various input modifications have on comprehension and acquisition. For example, the directive shown above is an example of 'baseline input' (i.e. the kind of input that native speakers provide when they talk to other native speakers). In another version of the same task, the directive consisted of 'premodified input'. That is, the baseline input was modified prior to the learners performing the task in accordance with how native speakers typically address learners. The premodified directive took this form:

> Can you find the scouring pad? A scouring pad – *scour* means to clean a dish. A scouring pad is a small thing you hold in your hand and you clean a dish with it. Take the scouring pad and put it on top of the counter by the sink – on the right side of the sink.

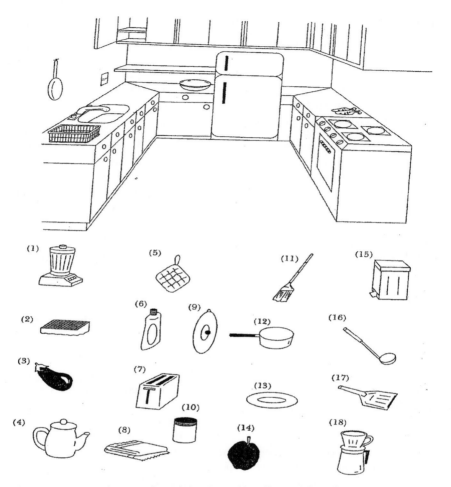

Figure 3.1 Pictorial materials in the task used by Ellis *et al.* (1994)

A third advantage of this kind of task is that it contains a built-in measure of learners' comprehension. Comprehension is demonstrated if a learner can indicate the position of the correct object on the matrix picture. This obviates the need for a separate test to ascertain whether learners have understood the directives.

The tasks used in the studies varied in a number of ways. First, the *content* of the tasks differed. The content of the above task was 'kitchen objects'; that of the task in Ellis and Heimbach (1997) was 'bugs and birds'; in Ellis and He (1999) it was 'furniture'. Another difference concerned the *response manner*. In Ellis *et al.* (1994) and Ellis and He (1999) the learners were adolescents or adults, who were able to respond to the directives by writing the numbers of the pictures in the matrix picture. In Ellis and Heimbach (1997), however, the learners were young children, for whom such a response might have been problematic. In this case, therefore, the learners were provided with separate cards which they picked up and placed manually on the matrix diagram. More significantly from a theoretical point of view, the tasks differed with regard to their *interactivity*. In all the studies, some learners were not allowed to interact when they listened to the directives, even if they did not understand them, whereas other learners were allowed (indeed, encouraged) to interact by requesting clarification. One of the purposes of the study was to compare comprehension and acquisition under these two conditions. Finally, the tasks differed in terms of the *input source*. In Ellis *et al.* (1994) and in Ellis and Heimbach (1997) the source of input was the classroom teacher (i.e. the learners functioned as listeners). However, in one of the conditions studied in Ellis and He (1999), the source of the input was the learners (i.e. learners addressed the directives to each other). As we will see later, where there was interactivity and, in particular, where the learners acted as the source of the input, the tasks became more reciprocal in nature. However, because the degree of interactivity was still restricted by the design of the tasks, they remained essentially non-reciprocal in type. Table 3.1 summarizes the main design features of the tasks. The tasks were designed to test specific hypotheses relating to L2 comprehension and acquisition. In the next section, the theoretical basis of these hypotheses is discussed.

Table 3.1 Main design features of the non-reciprocal tasks used in the studies

Study	Content	Response manner	Interactivity	Input source
Ellis *et al.* (1994)	Kitchen; objects found in a kitchen	Students write numbers of pictures of kitchen objects in a matrix picture of a kitchen.	Students permitted to signal non-comprehension in one of the task conditions but not in the other two.	Teacher
Ellis and Heimbach (1997)	Bugs and birds; cages.	Students place small cards with with pictures in a diagram of coloured cages.	Students interact teacher in pairs and in small groups.	Teacher
Ellis and He (1999)	Furniture; apartment	Students write in numbers of pictures of furniture in a plan of an apartment.	Students permitted to signal non-comprehension in two of the task conditions but not in the other.	Teacher in two of the conditions; fellow students in the third condition

Input, Interaction and Language Acquisition: The Theoretical Background

A number of researchers have argued that acquisition occurs incidentally when learners are able to comprehend the input they are exposed to. Krashen (1985, 1994) argued that the 'fundamental principle' of L2 acquisition is that 'acquisition', which he defines as the subconscious process of internalizing new linguistic forms and their meanings, will occur automatically if learners receive comprehensible input. According to Krashen's Input Hypothesis, learners need (1) access to comprehensible input and (2) a low affective filter that makes them open to the input in order to acquire. Krashen identifies two primary ways in which input is made comprehensible. Firstly, speakers employ 'simplified registers' when speaking to learners. These registers provide learners with the kind of 'modified input' illustrated in the previous section. They involve what Krashen (1981) refers to as 'rough tuning', i.e. pitching the input at a level that enables the learner to understand, but also containing some linguistic forms that the learner has not yet acquired. Secondly, listeners can use contextual information to help them decode input containing unknown linguistic forms and thereby comprehend and acquire them.

The idea that comprehension is crucial for acquisition also underlies Long's Interaction Hypothesis (Long, 1983), according to which:

(a) comprehensible input is necessary for acquisition; and
(b) modifications to the interactional structure of conversations which take place in the process of negotiating solutions to communication problems help to make input comprehensible to the learner and, thereby, potentially enable learners to process linguistic forms that are problematic to them.[1]

Interactional modifications can be triggered in a number of ways – see, for example, Varonis and Gass (1985). In the case of the interactions arising from the kind of task described above, the trigger was a directive, which a learner failed to understand often because (s)he did not know a key lexical item. The indicator of non-understanding took the form of a clarification request and the teacher's response usually involved some attempt to define the meaning of the key lexical item. Here is an example, taken from Ellis *et al.* (1994):

> T: We have an apple. And I'd like you to put the apple in the sink. (Trigger)
> S: What is the sink? (Indicator)
> T: Sink is a place to wash dishes. It's a hole where you wash dishes. (Response)

Such negotiation provides the learners with information that may help them to acquire new language. For example, in the above exchange, learners are given the opportunity to learn the meaning of 'sink'. Such interactions, assuming they engage the learner in message-oriented communication, involve *incidental* rather than *intentional* acquisition (Schmidt, 1990). Of course, they may also result in some kind of deliberate attempt on the part of the learner to memorize the new items.

There are a number of objections to the central claim that acquisition will occur naturally if learners understand what is said to them. One obvious objection is that neither Krashen nor Long specify what they mean by 'comprehension'. As Anderson and Lynch (1988) point out, comprehension involves degrees of understanding. At one end of the continuum is total non-comprehension (i.e. the listener does not even hear what is said), whereas at the other is successful comprehension (i.e. the listener has attended to the message fully and is able to construct a coherent interpretation). Intermediate levels of comprehension arise when the listener can hear words but cannot fully understand them, or can hear them but only has an imprecise idea of what they mean, or is able to hear and understand what has been said but has 'switched off', so the input goes in one ear and out of the other. A key question, not addressed by either Krashen or Long, is what degree of comprehension is necessary for acquisition to take place.

Other applied linguists have pointed out that there is a theoretical need to distinguish input that functions as intake for comprehension and input that functions as intake for learning. White (1987), for example, argued that the kind of simplified input that works well for comprehension may be of little value for acquisition because it deprives learners of essential information about the target language. This is not a strong argument, however, because it views simplified registers as static. In fact, research has shown that such registers are progressively complexified in accordance with the language proficiency of the learners (see, for example, Henzl, 1979). It would seem likely, then, that simplified input does not totally deprive learners of the input that is crucial to acquisition but rather systematically supplies them with input that is more and more linguistically complex. If one assumes that this input is one step ahead of learner, then, it may serve as the ideal source of input that Krashen claims it can be.

A stronger criticism of the Input and Interaction Hypotheses can be found in Sharwood-Smith's (1986) argument that there are two ways of processing input, one involving comprehension and the other acquisition. He argued that acquisition only occurs when learners discover that their original surface structure representation of the input does not match the semantic representation required by the situation. It will not occur if learners rely purely on top-down processing by utilizing non-linguistic input to infer what is meant; extensive bottom-up processing is also needed. In other words, comprehension is necessary but not sufficient for acquisition to take place. Faerch and Kasper (1986) offered a similar view, arguing that interactional input modifications will only lead to acquisition if learners recognize that a 'gap' in understanding is the result, not of the interlocutor's failure to make herself understood, but of the learner's own lack of linguistic knowledge. They also pointed out that not all communication problems, even when fully negotiated, will contribute to acquisition.

A further challenge to the position adopted by Krashen comes from research on the role of consciousness in language acquisition. Krashen consistently argued that acquisition is a subconscious process (i.e. learners are not aware of what they attend to in the input or of what they acquire). Schmidt (1990, 1994), however, argued persuasively that what he calls 'noticing' is a conscious process. Furthermore, he claimed that 'noticing' and 'noticing-the-gap' (i.e. identifying how the input to which the learner is exposed differs from the output the learner is able to generate) are essential processes in L2 acquisition. He referred to a diary study of his own learning of Portuguese in Brazil to demonstrate that in nearly every case new forms that appeared in his spontaneous speech were consciously attended to previously in the input (see Schmidt & Frota, 1986). Schmidt's position is clearly incompatible with Krashen's Input Hypothesis. However, a role for consciousness would seem to be implicit in Long's Interaction Hypothesis if it is assumed that one of principal functions of interactional modifications is to draw the learners' conscious attention to the linguistic properties of the input and how these differ from those of the learners' output (Ellis, 1994). In fact, Long (1996), is explicit in acknowledging the consciousness-raising function of meaning negotiation.

Information processing models of L2 acquisition also distinguish the processes responsible for comprehension and acquisition. Robinson (1995a), in a review of these models, identified two general types. Filter models view information as being processed serially and attention as selective. Capacity models allow for the parallel processing of information with the possibility of allocating attention to two tasks simultaneously. The research considered in the next section is based on a capacity model. That is, the listener is credited with being able to attend simultaneously to both message and to code and thus to be capable of engaging in both processing for comprehension and processing for acquisition. However, such dual processing only becomes possible when learners can draw on automatized knowledge of the L2. As VanPatten (1989) pointed out, tremendous demands are placed on learners' information processing systems when listening. The controlled processing required to extract meaning from input may prevent learners from attending to form or, conversely, the effort expended in attending to form may make the extraction of meaning problematic. Less proficient learners, therefore, may be faced with a choice – to attend to message content or to focus on the linguistic code. However, as they become more proficient and are able to engage in automatic processing, dual attention becomes more possible.

The assumption that language acquisition is entirely input-driven has also been challenged. Swain (1985, 1995) suggested that learner output also has a role to play. Like others, she noted that learners can comprehend input by means of 'semantic processing' and thus avoid having to attend to linguistic form. She argued that when learners are 'pushed' to produce output that is concise and appropriate, they are forced into making use of the kind 'syntactic processing' needed for acquisition. In this way, they may come to 'notice the gap' between the forms they use in their output and the forms present in input. In other words, output works together with input, the former serving as a cognitive trigger for the kind of input processing needed for acquisition. It would follow from Swain's position, that when learners have the opportunity to produce target items they are more likely to acquire them.

This theoretical background suggests a number of key questions which can be investigated by means of non-reciprocal tasks.

(1) What kind of input (simplified or interactionally modified) works best for comprehension?
(2) What kind of input (simplified or interactionally modified) works best for acquisition?
(3) What is the relationship between comprehension and acquisition? For example, are learners more likely to acquire new words if they understand the directives in which they are embedded?
(4) What are the features of modified input that promote comprehension and acquisition?
(5) Does the opportunity to produce target forms promote their acquisition?

In the following section, these questions are examined in relation to the comprehension and acquisition of word meanings. Vocabulary, rather than grammar, was chosen for study because it is reasonable to assume that measurable acquisition of lexical items can occur as the result of completing a single task. It is less likely that learners will acquire grammatical structures in the course of a single task.[2]

Modified Input and Comprehension

Two of the studies investigated the relative effects of simplified and interactionally modified input on the comprehension of directives containing new lexical items. In Ellis *et al.* (1994), two groups of high Japanese high school students (N = 79 and N = 129) completed the kitchen task (see above) under three conditions; (1) baseline (i.e. the directives were based on the kind of language native speakers use when addressing each other), (2) pre-modified (i.e. the directives were simplified by the task designer in accordance with the kind of language native speakers use when addressing language learners and (3) interactionally modified (i.e. the students had the opportunity to negotiate meaning when they did not understand a baseline directive). Examples of these three kinds of input have been provided above. The results were clear cut where interactionally modified input was concerned. In both groups, the students comprehended the interactionally modified directives better (means = 9.91 out of 15 and 10.69 out of 16) than both the students who heard baseline directives (means = 2.32 and 1.2) and the students who heard the premodified directives (means = 4.0 and 6.79). The results were less clear cut in the case of premodified input. In one group, the students receiving the premodified input comprehended better than the students receiving the baseline input but in the other group the difference was not statistically significant. This study, then, supports that part of the Interaction Hypothesis which claims that interactionally modified input enhances comprehension. It lends somewhat less support to Krashen's claim that simplified input facilitates comprehension.

It is important to note, however, that no attempt was made to control for the time taken to complete the tasks under the different conditions in the study. In fact, as might be expected, the tasks differed in time, with the learners receiving interactionally modified input enjoying a considerable advantage over the learners receiving both the premodified and baseline input. It is possible, therefore, that it was the additional processing time rather than the interactional modifications per se that was important for comprehension. In this respect, it is interesting to note that the two groups differed in the time they took to complete the task in the premodified input condition (20 minutes in the case of one group and 10 minutes in the other) and that it was the students who took the longer time that demonstrated a comprehension advantage over the students receiving baseline input. In other words, premodified input may work well for comprehension when it is accompanied with adequate processing time.

In the second study, Ellis and He (1999), the time taken to complete the task under the premodified and interactionally modified conditions was carefully controlled. All the students (N = 50) took the same amount of time. This was achieved by having the teacher repeat the premodified directions to use up the same amount of time taken by the students receiving the interactionally modified input. In this study, the difference between the comprehension of the students listening to the two kinds of modified input was not statistically different (mean for premodified = 6.67 out of 10; mean for interactionally modified group = 7.13). It would seem, therefore, that what is crucial for comprehension is not so much the *type* of modified input as the time available for learners to process it.

However, this conclusion, should not be seen as dismissive of the need for interactionally modified input for in many real-life situations it may constitute the main way in which L2 learners can obtain the time they need to process input for comprehension. As Loschky (1994) pointed out, 'increased time is an inherent difference between negotiated and unnegotiated interaction' (1994: 313). Nevertheless, it does appear that premodified input can serve just as well as interactionally modified input provided that learners have sufficient time to process it. Repeating premodified directions can assist comprehension as effectively as providing opportunities for learners to negotiate.

It is also possible that certain kinds of learners may experience difficulty in negotiating input. Individual variation in the ability to negotiate for meaning is a potential intervening variable in these studies. In Ellis *et al.* (1994) for example, relatively few of the classroom learners made any attempt to indicate problems in understanding (e.g. only 7 out of 42 in one group). Most of the learners preferred to remain silent. This may reflect Japanese students' dislike of initiating discourse in classroom contexts. Young children, in particular, may find it difficult to negotiate meaning as they often fail to signal when they have not understood a message (see Patterson & Kister, 1981). Such was the finding of Ellis and Heimbach (1997) in a study which investigated the effects of giving young children aged five to six years (N = 10) the opportunity to negotiate for meaning. The task in this study involved asking the children to locate a picture depicting a bug or a bird and then place it in the correct position on a board. Different versions of the same task were performed with the same children performing in pairs and then in groups, with their teacher giving the descriptions of the bugs and birds in both settings. In the pair setting, only three children made any attempt to negotiate, even though none of them knew the names of the bugs and birds. In the group setting, there was considerably more negotiation, but four of the children still declined to say anything. This difference was reflected in the comprehension levels (a mean of 28% for the pairs and 68% for the groups). In the pair work setting, the extent to which individual children engaged in negotiation was significantly correlated with their comprehension scores ($r = 0.819$; $p < 0\ 01$). However, in the group work setting, the relationship was not statistically significant ($r = -0.142$), presumably because those children who did not negotiate were able to benefit from the interactional work of those children who did. This study, then, suggests that meaning negotiation is less important for children than adolescent learners (see also Scarcella & Higa, 1981) but also that when children do negotiate it helps comprehension.

Another issue of importance in considering the effect of meaning negotiation on comprehension concerns whether those learners who actively participate in signalling a problem in understanding benefit more from the ensuing modified input than learners who just 'eavesdrop'. We have already seen that Ellis and Heimbach found that children who interacted did not comprehend any better than children who remained silent in the group work setting. Ellis *et al.* also found no relationship between the number of times individual students interacted with the teacher and their comprehension scores. These results, then, support Pica's (1992) finding that there was no difference in comprehension levels among negotiators and observers in a study that experimentally manipulated the two conditions. Clearly, though, further research is needed to identify the relative contributions of participation in and observation of meaning negotiation to learners' comprehension of different learning targets and in different settings.

To sum up, there is clear evidence that providing learners with the opportunity to negotiate meaning aids comprehension. However, interactionally modified input may only work better for comprehension than premodified input because it affords learners more time to process the input. Premodified input can prove as effective as interactionally modified input when learners have the same amount of time to process it. Also, interactionally modified input may not be beneficial for some learners, such as young children who have not learned to signal non-understanding. Finally, it appears that learners may not need to actively negotiate themselves to understand but can benefit from the modified input obtained through the interactional work of other learners.

Modified Input and Acquisition

All the studies examined only vocabulary acquisition. Therefore, the results cannot address the relationship between modified input and grammar acquisition. Also, only one aspect of vocabulary acquisition was studied – word meaning; these studies did not address the role of modified input in the acquisition of other aspects of vocabulary such as collocation. Limiting the research to the acquisition of word meanings is justified, however, on a number of grounds. First, there have been very few studies that have explored the effects of different kinds of oral input on any aspect of L2 acquisition. Second, it is reasonable to suppose that exposure to input in the context of a single task will have some measurable effect on learners' knowledge of word meanings whereas it may be less reasonable to expect it would do so on learners' knowledge of grammar or of word collocation. Third, according to some theoretical accounts of L2 acquisition, (see, for example, N. Ellis, 1996) acquisition commences with the kind of item learning that these studies investigated. It should also be noted that both the Input and the Interactional Hypotheses encompass all aspects of L2 acquisition, including vocabulary acquisition.

The methodology for investigating the effects of modified input on the acquisition of word meanings was the same in all the studies. The learners were pre-tested a week or so before they performed the task in order to identify a set of items drawn from a single semantic field (e.g. the kitchen) that they did not know. The pre-tests included distractor items so that the learners were not be forewarned about the items that were to be targeted. The items found to be 'new' to the learners were then embedded in the directives that comprised the task.[3] After performing the task the learners were tested on their knowledge of the new items. In Ellis *et al.* (1994) and Ellis and He (1999) there was both an immediate and a delayed post-test.

In Ellis and Heimbach (1997) there was one post-test administered seven days after the task. The nature of the tests differed somewhat from study to study. Ellis *et al.* used a translation test and a picture matching test (i.e. the learners were given a written list of the target items and asked to match each item with a picture). Ellis and Heimbach used a picture labelling test (i.e. the learners were asked to name the bugs/birds shown in a series of flash cards) and a picture matching test (i.e. they were given the name of a bug/bird orally and asked to choose the matching picture from a set of six pictures). Ellis and He used a picture-matching test (i.e. as in Ellis *et al.*, 1994) and a picture-labelling production test (i.e. the learners were asked to label pictures without being shown a list of the target items).

Two of the studies found that giving learners the opportunity to signal non-understanding resulted in them acquiring more new words than exposing them to baseline or premodified input. Ellis *et al.* found that high school Japanese students receiving interactionally modified input (e.g. mean for Tokyo group = 5.55 out of 19 items) outscored both the learners receiving baseline (e.g. mean = 2.02) and premodified input (e.g. mean = 4.02) on the immediate post-test.[4] On the follow-up test, however, the advantage noted for interactionally modified input over the premodified input was no longer apparent in the Tokyo group, possibly because the learners had made conscious efforts to learn the target words between the post-test and follow-up test. Ellis *et al.* also found that premodified input led to more words being acquired and retained than the baseline input. All these differences were statistically significant. This study only investigated receptive vocabulary knowledge. Ellis and Heimbach, however, investigated both receptive and productive knowledge. They found that in the case of young children given the opportunity to signal non-understanding a reasonable level of receptive vocabulary was achieved (a mean of 28.3% in the pair work task and 25% in the group work task) but very little productive vocabulary (6.7% and 0% respectively). As in Ellis *et al.* (1994) there was no relationship between the frequency with which individual learners signalled non-understanding and their receptive vocabulary learning in either the pair or group work condition. Finally, He and Ellis found that, in general, adult learners receiving interactionally modified input scored higher in tests of both receptive and productive knowledge of the targeted words (e.g. means = 7.0 and 5.75 out of 10 respectively) than learners receiving premodified input (e.g. means = 6.17 and 5.6). However, in contrast to the other studies, the differences were not statistically significant in this study.

One way of comparing the relative efficiency of premodified and interactionally modified input for vocabulary acquisition is by examining the number of words acquired per minute of exposure. Ellis (1995) undertook such an analysis using the data for one of the studies reported in Ellis *et al.* (1994). Table 3.2 gives the mean vocabulary acquisition scores for the premodified and interactionally modified groups of learners. It shows that

Table 3.2 Mean vocabulary acquisition scores for the premodified and interactionally modified groups (Ellis, 1995: 418)

	Post-test 1	Post-test 2	Post-test 3
Premodified Group (N = 27)			
Mean score	2.52	2.59	4.70
Mean wpm	0.25	0.26	0.47
Interactionally Modified Group (N = 24)			
Mean score	6.00	4.75	7.08
Mean wpm	0.13	0.11	0.16

whereas the mean acquisition scores for the interactionally modified group were higher than those for the premodified group the opposite was true for the mean words per minute scores. In other words, although the premodified group acquired fewer words overall, they acquired them in less time, suggesting that if they had had the same amount of time as the interactionally modified group they might have acquired more words.

To sum up, the studies lend some support to the principal claim of the Input and Interaction Hypotheses, namely that premodified and interactionally modified input facilitate acquisition. Premodified input in the context of non-reciprocal task promotes vocabulary acquisition, particularly of receptive knowledge. Interactionally modified input results in more words being acquired. However, this advantage largely reflects the additional time learners obtain for processing the input when they are given the opportunity to signal non-comprehension. In Ellis and He (1999), when the time taken to complete the tasks under the different conditions was the same, the differences between the premodified and interactionally modified input groups' acquisition scores were statistically non-significant. In some cases, as shown in Table 3.2, learners acquire new words more rapidly from premodified than from interactionally modified input, the explanation for which will become clear later. Finally, any advantage for interactionally modified input does not appear to be dependent on learners actively participating in the task; learners who just listened learned just as many new words as those that participated.

Comprehension and Language Acquisition

The studies also provide data for examining the extent to which there is a relationship between comprehension and language acquisition. This relationship is central to both the Input and Interaction Hypotheses as both claim that acquisition occurs when learners are able to comprehend input. However, as we noted earlier, there are theoretical grounds for disputing such a relationship, namely that the processes of comprehension and language acquisition are not isomorphic and that they only co-occur to the extent that learners engage in bottom-up processing and thus 'notice' input features that are not yet part of their interlanguage systems. It is possible, then, that the strength of the relationship between comprehension and acquisition will depend on the kind of processing learners engage in, which, in turn, may be influenced by the kind of input they are exposed to. Modified input, for example, may make it easier for learners to engage in bottom-up processing both because it makes certain linguistic features more salient and because it allows learners more time to process than unmodified input. The key questions, therefore, are:

(a) How closely are comprehension and acquisition scores related?
(b) To what extent is the relationship between comprehension and acquisition scores dependent on the type of input?

These questions were addressed by correlating comprehension and acquisition scores.

Ellis (1995) reports the Pearson Product Moment Correlation coefficients for one of the two groups investigated by Ellis *et al*. (1994). These are shown in Table 3.3. Three points are worth making. The first is that the relationship between the comprehension of the directives and the acquisition of word meanings is not a strong one. Ellis and Heimbach (1997) also found the relationship between the children's comprehension scores and word acquisition scores to be weak (r = 0.459 in the pair work task and 0.215 in the group work task). The second point about Table 3.3 is that the relationship is much stronger in the case of the picture-matching test (the follow-up test) than in the translation tests (post-test 1 and post-test 2). In fact, the coefficient for the follow-up test is statistically significant (p < 0.05), although it still accounts for only a relatively small portion of the variance in the comprehension and vocabulary acquisition scores. The third point is that the coefficients are very similar for both the premodified and interactionally modified input; in other words, the strength of the relationship was not affected by the nature of the input.

In general, then, these results support the view that comprehension and acquisition may not necessarily be closely related, a view that follows logically from the earlier claim that input functioning as intake for comprehension and acquisition need to be distinguished. There were

Table 3.3 Simple correlations between comprehension and vocabulary acquisition (Ellis, 1995)

Comprehension	Post-test 1	Post-test 2	Follow-up test
Premodified input	0.33	0.40	0.59**
Interactionally modified	0.42	0.43	0.51*

N = 18; *p < 0.05; **p < 0.01
Note: In this analysis the mean comprehension and acquisition scores for each directive were correlated. Hence the N size is 18, corresponding to the number of directions in each condition.

occasions in these studies where learners comprehended a directive containing a new word but failed to acquire the word and also where they failed to comprehend a directive and yet acquired the new word. The former situation is not surprising for clearly there are many factors impinging on whether a comprehended word is stored in long-term memory (e.g. whether it is, in fact, 'noticed', and, if so, whether it is deemed valuable enough to store). The latter situation is more puzzling. One possibility is that the learners sometimes understood a new item but still failed to understand the directive as a whole. As I pointed out in Ellis (1995), this raises the important question as to what is meant by 'comprehensible input', in particular the unit of discourse (word, utterance, text) to which this notion should be applied.

There is a fairly obvious reason why comprehension was found to be more strongly related to acquisition when this was measured by a picture-matching test than by the translation tests. The picture-matching test used the same materials as the treatment task. In effect, then, the picture-matching task constituted a very similar situational context to that in which the words were first encountered and thus may have triggered memory. It should be noted that the word acquisition scores for the picture-matching test were much higher than for the translation tests even though it was completed several weeks later.

There is no evidence in these studies that the kind of modified input affects the strength of the relationship between comprehension and acquisition. Thus, although, the comprehension and acquisition scores of the learners receiving the interactionally modified input were higher than those of the learners receiving premodified input, this was not reflected in a stronger relationship between comprehension and acquisition. This again suggests that the advantages conferred by the interactionally modified input in the original study (Ellis *et al.*, 1994) are best explained in terms of time rather than the inherent properties of this type of input.

Qualitative Aspects of Modified Input and Acquisition

So far we have focused very generally on the relative effects of baseline, premodified and interactionally modified input on vocabulary acquisition. However, potentially of greater theoretical and practical importance, is what features of modified input are important. This is this question that I addressed in Ellis (1995). It is useful to consider two sets of input properties – those features inherent in the specific linguistic items and those that derive from the linguistic contexts in which the items were encountered. Both sets of features can be potentially manipulated in the design of reciprocal tasks.

Two item-inherent properties were examined: (1) word length and (2) prototypicality. The choice of the first was motivated by evidence suggesting that longer words are generally more difficult to comprehend and learn than shorter words – see, for example, Harrison's (1980) discussion of word length in relation to readability and Meara's (1980) observation about the effect of word length on Chinese learners' acquisition of English vocabulary. In Ellis (1995) word length was measured in terms of number of syllables. The choice of prototypicality as the second property was informed by Rosch's (1975) research, which has shown that native speakers have intuitions regarding which words in a semantic field (such as 'birds') are more basic (i.e. more 'bird-like') than others. It seemed possible that learners would be more likely to remember the more prototypical items. As a measure of the prototypicality of the lexical items, I asked 20 native speakers of American English to rate the 'kitcheness' of each target item in the kitchen task on a five-point scale and then averaged the scores for each word.

Word length scores were weakly and non-significantly related to acquisition scores for both premodified and interactionally modified input (e.g. $r = 0.03$; $r = -0.25$) in the immediate post-test). Where the words in this study were concerned, therefore, length was not a factor. In contrast, prototypicality was significant. Learners were much more likely to remember 'basic' kitchen terms such as *stove, plate,* and *sink* than less basic terms such as *lid* and *shelf*. Interestingly the effect for protoypicality was stronger for premodified ($r = 0.64$) input than for interactionally modified input (i.e. $r = 0.49$) in the follow-up test, suggesting that one of the effects of interaction might be to modify the inherent learnability of words (i.e. negotiating the meaning on non-prototypical items helps learners learn them). The effects of prototypicality on vocabulary acquisition warrant further study.

A number of linguistic context factors were investigated. The factors found to be most important were (1) frequency, (2) range and (3) length of directive. Frequency refers to the number of times a particular targeted item occurred in all the directives addressed to the learners. Range refers to the number of different directives a target item appeared in. Length of directive was calculated by the counting the number of words said by the teacher in performing each directive; in the case of the premodified input this was determined in advance whereas in the interactionally modified input it depended on the amount of negotiation that occurred.

As might be expected, learners were more likely to remember those words that occurred more frequently. However, range proved a more important factor overall than frequency and constituted the single most important factor for learners receiving the interactionally modified input. Together frequency and range accounted for half of the variance in vocabulary acquisition scores in both sets of learners. This result bears out the general finding of vocabulary acquisition studies (see Nation, 1990). The most interesting result, however, involved length of directive. In the case of premodified input, length increased the likelihood a word would be acquired (e.g. in the case of the follow-up test $r = 0.59$; $p < 0.05$), but in the interactionally modified input, the effect was reversed; the longer the directive, the least likely the learners were to remember the target word ($r = -0.47$; $p < 0.05$). This is illustrated in the interactionally modified input sequences below. In the case of 'stove' the directive is short, providing succinct and relevant definitional information whereas in the case of 'lid' it is lengthy and contains definitional information that the learners might have found difficult to process. This is reflected in the acquisition scores for these two words. Thus, whereas elaborative simplification may help acquisition, over-elaborated input of the kind that can arise through meaning negotiation may have a deleterious effect – see also Chaudron (1982) and Ehrlich *et al.* (1989).

'stove'
> **Student:**   What is a stove?
> **Teacher:**   Stove is a hot place for cooking.
> Acquisition scores: Post-test 1 83%, Post-test 2 46%, Picture-matching test 96%.

'lid'
> **Student:**   What is a lid?
> **Teacher:**   Lid? A lid is round. It's round like a circle, and you put it on top of a pan and it's like a hat for a pan and it keeps the food inside. You understand?
> **Student:**   One more time.
> **Teacher:**   OK. There's a lid. OK? And take the lid and hang it over the sink. On the left side of the frying pan.
> **Student:**   What is a lid?
> **Teacher:**   Lid? A lid is round, it's a circle, round, and you put it on top of a pan. It's like a hat, it's like a hat for a pan, for cooking.
> Acquisition scores: Post-test 10%; Post-test 20%; Picture-matching test 13%.

These results again cast doubts on the kinds of claims that have been made for interactionally modified input. Earlier we saw that when time is carefully controlled interactionally modified input may prove less efficient in promoting acquisition than *premodified* input (see Table 3.2). One of the reasons should now be clear. Meaning negotiation takes up time and, on occasions, can result in input that overloads the processing capacities of learners and thus impedes rather than facilitates acquisition. In contrast, *premodified* input is economical with time and, providing learners are given sufficient clues to the meanings of new words, it can promote acquisition more efficiently. Learners, it seems, need input that is elaborated (the length of the *premodified* directives was *positively* and significantly related to acquisition scores) but not over-elaborated (the length of the interactionally modified directives was *negatively* and significantly related to acquisition scores). This is not to say that negotiation does not work; it does, but clearly it is the *quality* that matters. This casts some doubt on the large number of studies investigating tasks that have been based on counts of the kinds of topic-incorporation features associated with meaning negotiation (e.g. comprehension checks; requests for clarification; requests for confirmation). Tasks that induce lots of negotiation are not necessarily the ones that work best for acquisition.

There is, of course, much more work that needs to be done to investigate what modified input properties are important for acquisition. The amount of input data analysed in Ellis (1995) was relatively small. Also, relatively few properties of the input were studied. Nor, of course, can it be assumed that the input properties found to be important in one task for one group of learners will prove significant in other tasks and for other groups of learners.

Modified Output and Comprehension/Acquisition

So far we have focused on those studies that made use of non-reciprocal tasks involving premodified and interactionally modified input. A theoretically important question, however, is whether, as Krashen (1994) claimed, acquisition is entirely input-driven, or whether learner output also plays a role as Swain (1995) argued. The study reported in Ellis and He (1999) addressed this issue, allowing for a direct comparison of the relative effects of modified input and modified output on both comprehension and acquisition.

In this study, the non-reciprocal task was redesigned to afford opportunities for learners to produce the target items in directives as well as to receive input. Learners were given a matrix picture of an apartment and a set of small pictures depicting pieces of furniture. The teacher read out the words labelling the small pictures and the subjects wrote them down next to each picture. The teacher then gave an example of how to make up a directive about using the words and asked the learners to write directives about where to place the pieces of furniture in the apartment, one directive for each word.[5] The learners worked in pairs giving their directions orally and negotiating meaning whenever they did not understand. The interactions afforded opportunities for the learners to modify their own output. The resulting task, although still primarily non reciprocal in so far as it required only a one-way flow of information (i.e. from the student performing the directives), clearly corresponds more closely to the kinds of tasks discussed in the task-based research literature as it required the learners to engage in speaking as well as listening.

The study, therefore, allowed comparisons to be made between the groups of learners receiving premodified and interactionally modified

Table 3.4 Mean vocabulary acquisition scores for the premodified, interactionally modified and modified output groups in Ellis and He (1999)

Group	Vocabulary post tests (N = 10)				
	1	**2**	**3**	**4**	**5**
Premodified	6.17	5.6	6.33	6.22	6.72
Interactionally modified	7.0	5.75	7.56	6.44	7.31
Modified output	8.19	7.55	9.0	8.19	8.63

Post tests 1, 3 and 5 = recognition tests: Post tests 2 and 4 = production tests.

input on the one hand and a group which was required to speak the directives. As in the previous studies, the comparisons involved both comprehension and vocabulary acquisition. The results were quite conclusive. Giving the learners the opportunity to produce and negotiate the directives in pairs resulted in significantly higher levels of comprehension than exposing them to premodified directives or giving them the opportunity to negotiate the teacher's baseline directives (i.e. a mean of 8.13 out of a total of 10 as opposed to means of 6.67 and 7.13). Also, the speaking task produced higher vocabulary acquisition scores on the receptive and productive vocabulary tests administered immediately after the task was completed and on all subsequent tests (see Table 3.4). In short, the speaking task proved more effective than the listening tasks with regard to both comprehension and vocabulary acquisition. It should be noted all the tasks in the Ellis and He study took the same length of time.

A simple explanation of these results is that giving learners the chance to produce new words (in both writing and speech) helped them to process them more deeply – whether for comprehension or for acquisition – than simply hearing them. This is very plausible. It should be noted, however, that the speaking task involved not just production but production in the context of interaction. One possibility, then, is that the interactions that occurred when the learners where interacting in pairs were qualitatively different from those that occurred when the students interacted with the teacher.[6] This seems to have been the case. To illustrate the differences, consider these two examples.

Example 1

T: Here is a rocker. Please put the rocker next to the sofa in the living room.
S: What is the rocker?
T: A rocker is a chair that can be rocked back and forth.
S: One more time.
T: A rocker is a chair which can be rocked back and forth.
S: Please repeat.
T: A rocker is a chair that can rocked back and forth.

Example 2

S1:   Please put the rocker on the living room.

S2:   What is rocker?

S1:   Rocker is like chair. You can sit and move. Look at the picture. You know now?

S2:   Yes. Put rocker where?

S1:   In the living room. There are three rooms in your big picture. Put rocker in the room in the middle of the picture.

S2:   OK.

The interactionally modified group's comprehension score for this directive was 75%, whereas the production group's was 93%.[7] Similar differences were evident in the various vocabulary tests. It is not difficult to see why the production group outscored the interactionally modified group. The interaction in the first example is qualitatively different from that in the second in a number of respects. First, the definitional information provided by S1 is couched in vocabulary ('chair', 'sit and move') that is likely to be familiar to S2. In contrast, the definition supplied by the teacher in the first example uses a low-frequency item ('rock') that the students may not have known. Second, the learners in the second example tackle the task systematically by breaking it into two parts; they begin by locating the correct picture of the rocking chair, dealing with the meaning of the unknown lexical item in the process, and then they work out where this piece of furniture is to be placed in the matrix picture of the apartment. S1 scaffolds the task for S2 by encouraging her to relate the definitional information he supplies to the picture and he then checks whether she has successfully accomplished this ('You know now?'). This kind of scaffolding does not occur in in the teacher-directed interaction. Of course, in the learner-learner interaction one learner's output is another learner's input. Thus, we cannot be sure whether it was opportunity to modify output or to access high-quality input (or both) that was beneficial. All we can say on the basis of this study is that giving learners the opportunity to produce and negotiate the directives created conditions that were especially favourable to comprehension and vocabulary acquisition.

Implications for Language Teaching

The studies reviewed in the previous sections have shown that it is possible to use non-reciprocal tasks as a tool for teaching specific linguistic items by embedding them in the text of the task. Because these tasks require a primary focus on message rather than code (i.e. the learners have to understand and act on a series of directives) they provide a pedagogic means for integrating what White (1988) referred to as the Type A and the Type B traditions in language teaching. The tasks allow the teacher to focus on linguistic content and thus to attempt to intervene directly in the process of learning (Type A), while at the same time creating conditions that will foster the natural processes of language acquisition (Type B). In other words, the tasks foster the *incidental acquisition* of pre-selected target items as the students engage in communicative activity. This is achieved by 'hiding' the linguistic focus of the tasks from the learners.[8] Nevertheless, the tasks do promote 'noticing' of the targeted items, as they complete the task. The noticing takes place 'under real operating conditions' (Johnson, 1988) – that is, the students are required to attend to form while grappling with the process of making sense of what they hear.

The main purpose of the various studies was to discover the particular conditions relating to the design of non-reciprocal tasks that promote acquisition of lexical items. Some of the conditions that the studies indicate may be important are given below.

(1) *Simplified input*: Giving students the opportunity to listen to simplified input promotes both comprehension and language acquisition. It constitutes a time-effective way of ensuring that learners obtain the kind of input they need. Simplified text appears to work best for acquisition when it contains sufficient redundancy to aid processing, when the targeted items embedded within it occur frequently, and when they appear in a range of contexts.

(2) *Interactionally modified input*: Giving students the opportunity to signal their non-understanding of input can also prove effective for both comprehension and acquisition. However, there are a number of important provisos. Young children may not be able to benefit from such an opportunity because they have not yet developed the necessary interactional skills. There is a danger of interactionally modified input becoming over-elaborated with consequent negative effects for learners' comprehension and acquisition. A lot depends on the quality of the meaning negotiation (e.g. on how a teacher handles a problem when it arises). Teachers need to be skilled at ensuring that the input at the right level for their students.

(3) *Modified output*: Allowing learners the opportunity to clarify their own output has a qualitative effect on the interaction that facilitates both comprehension and language acquisition.

(4) *Comprehension*: Although comprehending input is obviously important for successfully completing a task, it does not guarantee acquisition of the targeted items. Acquisition can occur even if the input has not been fully comprehended. It does not follow, therefore, where acquisition is concerned, that a task has to be carried out in such a way that students achieve full comprehension.

The studies involved child, adolescent and adult learners of English as a foreign/second language. However, as in many other L2 classroom studies of this kind, the groups investigated were relatively small (between 10 and 43). The studies have involved just one type of non-reciprocal task where students listen to or speak directives and demonstrate their understanding by locating objects on some kind of visual display. Given the enormous diversity in instructional settings, in types of learners and the kinds of tasks now available, it is obviously necessary to 'apply with caution' (Hatch, 1978). The findings outlined above, therefore, should be treated as 'provisional specifications' (Stenhouse, 1975).

Conclusion

The studies reviewed in this chapter were carried out with the dual purpose of testing various hypotheses drawn from theories of L2 acquisition and also investigating the potential pedagogical uses of a particular kind of task (non-reciprocal tasks). As such, they reflect much of the task-based research that has taken place to date. For as Pica (1997) has pointed out, the use of communicative tasks constitutes 'a growing area of compatibility between the fields of L2 teaching and research' (1997: 61). Non-reciprocal tasks warrant careful study because they provide a context for investigating the Input, Interaction and Modified Output Hypotheses which have assumed such importance in mainstream SLA and because they constitute a powerful device for integrating interventionist and non-interventionist teaching. They serve as an effective way of directing learners' attention to the linguistic code while communicating for meaning. In this respect, they are of value to both researchers and teachers.

There is, however, a general limitation of task-based research that is reflected in the studies I have examined here. The theoretical framework which informed the studies was drawn from a computational model of L2 acquisition. This assumes that acquisition occurs when learners have the opportunity to process input and output. In this framework, tasks provide the means for studying the roles of input and output in acquisition. However, tasks are in actuality devices for creating social contexts as the 'activity' that arises from a them can vary in accordance with the culturally and socially constituted goals of the participants (Coughlan & Duff, 1994) as discussed in Chapter 2 of this book. For example, in Ellis and He (1999) the teacher and the students appear to have interpreted the task differently. The teacher saw it as a kind of 'test' designed to measure how well the students could understand the directions and learn the new words whereas the students treated it more as a collaborative problem-solving activity. This suggests the need to examine tasks from a sociocultural perspective by investigating how task participants come to perform a task in the way they do and how this impacts on acquisition. Such a perspective may also have the advantage of corresponding more closely to how teachers and students, as social agents, orientate to tasks. Future research, then, also needs to consider how opportunities for processing language arise out of the choices that the participants in a task make as social agents; it ideally requires attention to both the psycholinguistic and social contexts that are created when different learners perform different tasks under different conditions.

Notes

(1) Long (1996) has revised and expanded the Interaction Hypothesis. While earlier versions, as summarized here, refer only to comprehensible input, the later version also recognizes that interaction can contribute to language acquisition by providing negative feedback and opportunities for learners to modify their output.

(2) Of course, much depends on what is meant by the term 'acquire' a grammatical structure. It is quite possible that learners will 'notice' a new grammatical feature while performing a task and perhaps also store this feature in long-term memory. It is much less likely, however, that they will 'acquire' it in the sense of being able to use in accurately in their own subsequent production. Tasks involving structured input can also provide a basis for investigating the 'noticing' of grammatical features (see, for example, Alanen, 1995).

(3) In some of the studies, not all the targeted items were 'new' to the learners (i.e. some of the learners already knew some of the items). This was because it proved impossible to identify sufficient items that were entirely new to all the learners. However, at least 80% of the items were unknown by all learners in each study.

(4) In one of the groups studied by Ellis *et al.* (1994) no scores were available for the learners receiving baseline input. However, the learners in this group who received interactionally modified input outscored those receiving premodified input.

(5) It should be noted that, although the learners were instructed to use the words they were given to write their directives, they were nevertheless primarily focused on meaning rather than form in this task. Their task was to prepare, say and negotiate directives about where to place the pieces of furniture. The interactions that took place were quite clearly message-oriented.

(6) Ellis and He's study does not make it possible to decide between these two explanations of the beneficial effects of the output condition as the learners had both the opportunity to orally produce the directives and to negotiate them when they did not understand. It should be noted, however, that this confounding of variables (output and interaction) is inevitable when the output occurs in the context of conversation.

(7) The premodified groups' comprehension and vocabulary acquisition scores were very close to those of the interactionally modified group.

(8) Of course, it is always possible that the learners will become aware of the linguistic focus in which case they are more likely to engage in *intentional acquisition*. In such a case, it might be argued that the 'activity' that results from the 'task' is more like that which might be expected from an 'exercise'. In the studies reported in this chapter, the teachers did not feel that this happened (i.e. the learners did not attempt to deliberately memorize the target items while they were performing the tasks).

4 Focus on Form

Introduction

Applied Linguistics is a relatively new academic discipline and, as such, is characterized by the invention of a large number of technical terms to label constructs of importance to the field. These constructs are, however, not stable, evolving as a result of research and accompanying theory development. However, even though the constructs themselves are not stable, the original labels stick. The result is uncertainty as to the reference of a specific term. There is perhaps no term in Applied Linguistics that this applies to more than 'focus on form', whose meaning has morphed quite remarkably since it was first introduced.

In this chapter I will use the terms 'focus on form', 'focus on forms', 'FonF', 'and 'FonFs'. I will use the terms FonF and FonFs to refer to general *approaches* to teaching and 'focus on form' and 'focus on forms' to refer to specific instructional *procedures*.

I will begin by considering the early use of 'focus on form' by Michael Long and how his definition of it has stretched over time. I will then offer my own definition of the construct, at the same time presenting a classification of different types of focus on form. In the next two sections I will examine the psycholinguistic and discoursal dimensions of focus on form. This will prepare the way for a review of the research that has investigated different realizations of focus on form. Next, I take a look at the criticisms that have been levelled against focus on form followed by a review of studies that have compared FonF and FonFs. Finally, I draw the various threads of this review together in the conclusion section and argue that little is to be gained by disputing the relative merits of FonF and FonFs as what is important is to examine how 'focus on form' procedures can occur in both approaches and what effect these have on acquisition.

Focus-on-form According to Long

'Focus on form' was first used by Michael Long but has been borrowed (and extended) by countless scholars and researchers since. A good starting point, however, is to examine how Long's own use of this term has changed over time. To the best of my knowledge, Long first used the term in 1988 in a review of research of instructed interlanguage development. He concluded this article as follows:

> … a focus on *form* is probably a key feature of second language instruction because of the salience it brings to targeted features in classroom input, and also in input outside the classroom, where this is available. I do not think, on the other hand, that there is any evidence that an instructional programme built around a series (or even a sequence) of isolated *forms* is any more supportable now, either theoretically, empirically, or logically than it was when Krashen and others attacked it several years ago. (p. 136: italics in original)

Here Long views FonF and FonFs as 'programmes' or 'approaches'. In a later article ('Focus on form: A design feature in language teaching methodology'), Long (1991) elaborated on the differences between these two approaches. FonF 'overtly draws students' attention to linguistic elements as they arise incidentally in lessons whose overriding focus is on meaning or communication' (1991: 45–46). In contrast, FonFs involves traditional language teaching consisting of the presentation and practice of items drawn from a structural syllabus. Later Long (1997) also sought to distinguish 'FonF' from 'focus on meaning' (FonM) – an approach to teaching that emphasized incidental and implicit language learning through content-based instruction or immersion programmes where the learners' focus was more or less entirely on meaning.[1]

In a series of articles (Long, 1996, 1997; Long & Robinson, 1998), Long drew extensively on research and theory in second language acquisition (SLA) – in particular Schmidt's views about the importance of 'noticing' – to point out the problems with the FonFs and FonM approaches and the strengths of FonF. I have summarized his main points in Table 4.1. Given that the focus on form needs to occur in a communicative context, it requires the use of 'tasks' that focus learners' primary attention on meaning but also provide periodic attention to form by the teacher and/or students when this is triggered by communicative need. In other words, focus on form lies at the heart of Long's advocacy of task-based language teaching (TBLT) (see Long & Crookes, 1992). Initially Long conceived of focus on form as providing learners with input (see the quotation from his 1988 article) but by this time focus on form clearly involves production as well as input.

At this point, then, Long's views about FonF can be characterized as entailing a focus on form that:

- arises in interaction involving the L2 learner;
- is reactive (i.e. occurs in response to a communication problem);
- is incidental (i.e. it is not pre-planned);
- is brief (i.e. it does not interfere with the primary focus on meaning);

Table 4.1 Summary of Long's views about three approaches to language teaching

FonFs	FonM	FonF
No needs analysis.	Usually no needs analysis.	A needs analysis of the target tasks learners need to perform provides the basis of a task-based syllabus.
No realistic models of language.	Older learners cannot fully acquire an L2 'naturally' and thus FonM cannot succeed in enabling such learners to achieve high levels of L2 proficiency.	Attracts attention to forms that otherwise learners might not notice.
Ignores the fact that learning a new word or rule is a slow and gradual process.	Even prolonged exposure to the L2 does not ensure that learners will acquire non-salient linguistic features.	Allows for the slow and gradual process involved in the learning of L2 linguistic features.
Fails to recognize that the teachability of grammatical forms is constrained by their learnability.	Learners need negative evidence because positive evidence is insufficient to guarantee acquisition of some grammatical features.	Respects the learner's internal syllabus.
Tends to result in boring lessons.	FonM is inefficient because it results in only slow progress.	Is under learner control because it only occurs in response to the learner's communication problems.
Results in more false beginners than finishers.	Can result in confidence and fluency in the use of the L2 but limited accuracy in use of the target language system.	Assists the development of form-function mapping and so promotes both fluency and accuracy.

- is typically implicit (e.g. it does not involve any metalinguistic explanation);
- induces 'noticing' (i.e. conscious attention to target linguistic forms);
- induces form-function mapping;
- constitutes an 'approach' to teaching (i.e. FonF) contrasting with a traditional form-centred approach (i.e. FonFs).

This characterization of focus on form clearly reflects Long's continuing work on the role of the negotiation of meaning in L2 acquisition and his advocacy of task-based language teaching (TBLT). Initially, Long (1983) emphasized how the negotiation of meaning makes input comprehensible to learners but later, drawing on work by Pica (1992), Long (1996) recognized that negotiation can also provide learners with negative feedback and push them to modify their utterances by making them more target-like. For Long, then, the negotiation of meaning was the primary means for achieving a focus on form.

As we will see in the next section, as other researchers and teacher educators have seized on the importance of incorporating attention to form in a communicative curriculum, the scope of the term 'focus on form' has expanded considerably. This is reflected in part in Long's latest definition taken from his 2015 book *Second Language Acquisition and Task-based Language Teaching*:

> Focus on form involves reactive use of a wide variety of pedagogic procedures to draw learners' attention to linguistic problems in context, as they arise during communication in TBLT, typically as students work on problem-solving tasks, thereby increasing the likelihood that attention to code features will be synchronized with the learner's internal syllabus, developmental stage and processing ability. (2015: 317)

The essential theoretical foundation remains intact – attention to linguistic form needs to occur in ways that are compatible with how an L2 is acquired by learners. So too is Long's insistence that the focus must be *reactive* and *brief*. But it would seem that 'focus on form' is no longer seen as an 'approach' (i.e. FonF) but as a set of procedures. Nor is it just an interactive phenomenon. Also – and in this respect there is major shift – focus on form need not be implicit. Long acknowledged that it can even include provision of an explicit grammar rule as long as this is provided in response to a problem that arises during a communicative exchange. Nor did Long see focus on form as catering just to incidental learning; rather 'intentional learning is brought to the aid of incidental learning, thereby improving the likelihood that a new form-meaning association will be perceived or perceived more quickly' (2015: 317). Clearly, focus on form now involves much more than the negotiation of meaning.

This account of the how 'focus on form' has been construed in Long's work is not intended as a critique of Long. The development I have described is quite natural, reflecting Long's response to continuing research and theory development. It does, however, serve as a warning to readers. The term has a long life and lives on but the construct it refers to has changed in quite major ways. In the following section I will attempt my own definition of this construct.

Defining Pedagogic Focus on Form

'Form' is often misunderstood as referring solely to grammatical form. In fact, 'form' can refer to lexical (both phonological and orthographic), grammatical and pragmalinguistic features. However, in this review I will mainly address grammar. Also the term 'focus on form' is somewhat misleading as the desired focus is not just on form but on form-meaning mapping (e.g. the use of the *–ed* morpheme to denote past time or the pronunciation of a word like *alibi* so that its meaning can be understand by listeners) as Long made clear.

We have seen that Long defined FonFs as involving the explicit teaching of linguistic forms based on a structural syllabus. The problem here is that explicit language teaching can also include activities designed to focus learners' attention on form in communicative activities. For example, the final stage of presentation–practice–produce (PPP) involves such activities. To address this difficulty, Doughty and Williams (1998a) emphasized that FonF and FonFs 'are *not* polar opposites' and that the essential difference is that FonF '*entails* a focus on formal elements of language, whereas focus on forms is *limited* to such a focus' (1998a: 4; italics as in original). Thus, whereas PPP might initially be viewed as a FonFs approach as it is based on a structural syllabus and involves the explicit presentation and controlled practice of discrete linguistic features, it can be seen as including focus on form as it is not limited to a focus on purely formal linguistic elements. Indeed, the collection of articles on focus on form that Doughty and Williams (1998b) edited includes one by DeKeyser (1998) that draws on skill learning theory to promote PPP. Thus PPP can also incorporate focus of form.

This, however, is quite clearly incompatible with both Long's early and later accounts of focus on form. He emphasizes the fundamental difference between a synthetic approach involving the linear teaching of discrete linguistic features and an analytical approach where attention to form only emerges out of the efforts to comprehend and produce meaningful texts in the L2. The problem here lies in trying to characterize FonF and FonFs as *approaches*. As I have argued elsewhere (Ellis, 2015), focus on form is best understood not as an approach (i.e. as FonF) but as involving different kinds of instructional *procedures*. That is, focus on form entails various techniques designed to *attract* learners' attention to form while they are using the L2 as a *tool* for communicating. In contrast, focus on forms entails various devices (such as 'exercises') designed to *direct* learners' attention to specific forms that are to be studied and learned as *objects*.

Treating focus on form as procedures also avoids another problem, namely whether it can only take place incidentally (as Long initially envisaged) or can be pre-planned. Clearly, in PPP the focus on form in the production activity must be planned. This can be achieved by designing focused tasks (Ellis, 2003) intended to elicit the use of a pre-planned target feature(s) in a context that is communicative. The activities in which focus on form occurs, then, can be either *unfocused* (i.e. designed to simply elicit general samples of the L2) leading to incidental attention to a variety of forms) or they can be *focused* leading to a pre-determined and intensive focus on a specific form(s). In the case of the latter a focus-on-form activity can be incorporated into a synthetic approach such as PPP, which some commentators (e.g. Fotos, 1998; Littlewood, 2007) have argued is needed in contexts where the L2 is a foreign rather than a second language and where there is an expectancy that the language will be taught explicitly.

I noted that Long initially viewed focus on form as an interactional phenomenon. That is, it occurred when a communication problem arose and was addressed while learners were interacting with the teacher or other learners and negotiation of meaning occurred. Other researchers (e.g. Ellis *et al.*, 2001; Lyster, 2001), however, have noted that the same kinds of interactional sequences can occur in a classroom where there is negotiation of form (i.e. negotiation occurs even though there is no communication problem).

Long also insists that focus on form occurs as a *response* to a problem. This also seems far too narrow. As Ellis *et al.* (2001) noted in their study of focus on form episodes in communicative ESL classes, there are occasions when teachers pre-empt a problem, for example, by reminding students they need to pay attention to a particular grammatical feature when they perform a task and learners also sometimes pre-empt as when they ask questions about linguistic forms. These focus on form episodes are designed to avoid rather than repair a linguistic problem but they are clearly still problem-oriented. Interactive focus on form, then, can be defined as the pre-emptive or responsive attention to form that occurs during an activity that is primarily meaning-focused and that addresses either a communicative or linguistic problem.

Interactive focus on form certainly allows for relatively implicit ways of focusing on form, which was initially seen as a defining feature of focus on form. However, as Long (2015) later came to recognize, focus on form can at times be quite explicit and even involve metalinguistic comments. When learners are engaged in a communicative activity they often participate in 'language-related episodes' (LREs), defined by Swain (1998) as 'any part of a dialogue in which students talk about the language they are producing, question their language use, or other- or self-correct' (1998: 70). LREs are clearly instances of focus on form and typically involve explicit attention to form.

However, as Long (2015) came to recognize, focus on form can also be non-interactive when learners are asked to process oral or written input seeded with specific target features that have been highlighted (i.e. enhanced input). In this case the primary focus is on comprehending the input but learners' attention is also attracted to the target feature(s). Non-interactive focus on form has also attracted considerable research.

Focus on form – both interactive and non-interactive – can vary in how obtrusive it is (i.e. how much it interferes with communication). Doughty and Williams (1998c), for example, offered a taxonomy of focus-on-form techniques that vary in terms of the extent they interrupt the flow of communication. For example, 'input flood' is viewed as minimally obtrusive, corrective recasts as more obtrusive, whereas 'input processing' involving structured input (VanPatten, 1996) is very clearly obtrusive. The more obtrusive techniques, however, might be better classified as focus-on-forms techniques as arguably they *direct* rather than *attract* attention to form. Perhaps, though, focus on form and focus on forms activities should be seen as poles on a continuum with different strategies varying in the extent to which they cater to intentional or incidental language learning.

Central to all these senses of focus on form is that learners' attention is attracted to form-meaning mapping while they are engaged in an activity where the primary focus is on meaning. Skehan (1996b), however, proposed that a focus on form can be induced *outside* of the performance of a communicative activity by providing time for pre-task planning. As Ortega (1999) put it, 'the provision of time for learners to plan is a pedagogical manipulation assumed to induce learners to focus on whatever formal and systemic aspects of the language are needed to accomplish a particular task' (1996: 110). This manipulation may also lead to enhanced attention to form when learners perform the task. Asking learners to repeat a task can also lead to enhanced focus on form (Bygate, 1996).

Figure 4.1 schematizes the various ways in which a focus on form, as pedagogical activity, can take place. Clearly an expanded definition of focus on form is needed. Drawing on the definition proposed by Nassaji and Fotos (2010), I propose the following:

> Focus on form occurs in activities where meaning is primary but attempts are made to attract attention to form. Thus it is not an approach but rather a set of techniques deployed in a communicative context by the teacher and/or the learners to draw attention implicitly or explicitly and often briefly to linguistic forms that are problematic for the learners. The focus on form may be pre-planned and thus address a pre-determined linguistic feature(s) or it can be incidental as a response to whatever communicative or linguistic problems arise. Focus on form activities can be interactive or non-interactive and involve both production and reception. They can be found in both explicit and implicit approaches to language teaching. They can also occur before a communicative task is performed or while it is being performed.[2]

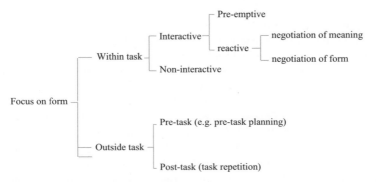

Figure 4.1 Types of focus on form activities

The Psycholinguistic Dimension of Focus on Form

Focus on form can also be viewed from a psycholinguistic perspective by considering 'the cognitive correlates of the components of focus on form' (Doughty, 2001: 211) as these relate to both language use and learning. Two key cognitive constructs (selective attention and cognitive comparison) along with the memory systems (working memory and long-term memory) that support the functioning of these constructs underlie psycholinguistic accounts of focus on form.

Selective attention

Selective attention refers to the act of purposively focusing conscious attention on some particular object or goal while ignoring extraneous information that may be present in the situational context. In the case of language, attention may be selectively focused on meaning or on form. In focus on forms activities attention is intended to be selectively focused on linguistic form. In focus on form activities attention is selectively focused on meaning but may also from time to time be voluntarily or involuntarily focused on specific linguistic forms that occur in the input or that the learner needs to express a particular meaning. This can occur when learners become aware of a 'hole' in their existing L2 knowledge (Swain, 1998), which prevents them from expressing what they want to say. As a result, they are sensitized to attend to input containing the linguistic forms they need or to request assistance from the teacher or another learner (a pre-emptive type of focus on form).

A key issue – one that continues to be debated in SLA circles – is whether the attention to form that occurs while learners are primarily focused on meaning necessarily involves conscious awareness. Schmidt (1994, 2001) considered that, in general, learning is only possible if attention to form is conscious, i.e. 'noticing' occurs. In contrast, Tomlin and Villa (1993) argued that what they called 'detection' can occur without conscious awareness. N. Ellis (2005) suggested that conscious attention is needed in order to establish a new form in long-term memory but that subsequent attention to this form in the input can occur subconsciously, strengthening and modifying the initial neural connections. Irrespective of whether focus on form involves conscious noticing or subconscious attention it caters to incidental learning, that is, learning that takes place without intention, whereas selective attention switches briefly from meaning to form.

There is now sufficient evidence to show that purely implicit learning is possible (see J. Williams, 2009). However, there is also evidence to suggest that when focus on form leads to learners consciously attending to linguistic forms they are more likely to learn what they have attended to (Mackey, 2006). Whether noticing of form is needed is likely to depend on the salience of the linguistic feature. Features that are salient and communicatively functional in context (e.g. lexical items or grammatical features such as plural-s) may be acquired implicitly whereas features that are non-salient and communicatively redundant (e.g. 3rd person-s) may only be acquired if they are explicitly noticed. This raises the likelihood that different kinds of focus on form may be needed to facilitate the acquisition of different linguistic features. For example, recasts (generally considered an implicit type of focus on form) may facilitate the acquisition of salient/non-redundant features but explicit focus on form may be needed for non-salient/communicatively redundant features.

Cognitive comparison

The learning of new forms can take place when learners simply attend to linguistic forms in the input but it can also take place when erroneous linguistic forms receive corrective feedback (i.e. reactive focus on form). In these ways focus on form can help learners to compare the current state of their L2 knowledge with the input they are provided with. As Doughty (2001) pointed out, this involves establishing a link between input held in a temporary perceptual store and already-stored L2 knowledge.

The importance of making cognitive comparisons for L2 acquisition was first recognized in Schmidt and Frota's (1986) study of the first author's acquisition of L2 Portuguese. Schmidt became aware that he frequently engaged in 'noticing-the-gap' between his own output and the input he was exposed to as in this example: 'I often say *dois anos ante* for two years ago. I think it should be *anos atras*. I have been hearing it that way in conversation …'. The cognitive comparison in this example is clearly a very conscious process but interactive focus-on-form episodes may lead to 'detection' without any conscious awareness. In the example below, the teacher recasts the learner's utterance:

> **Learner:**   No go disco this Saturday.
> **Teacher:**   Oh so you're not going to the disco this Saturday.

This affords the learner an overt comparison between his erroneous utterance and the target form and an opportunity for the learner to carry out the kind of the mental comparison hypothesized to assist the restructuring of the L2 system. However, for such restructuring to take place, the learner would need to engage in some analysis of the recast. That is, the learner needs to compare not just 'no go' with 'you're not going' but rather the underlying negative patterns (i.e. 'no + verb' and 'auxiliary + not + verb'). Only then can the learner recognize that the target version of his utterance is 'I'm not going'. In other words, carrying out a cognitive comparison may often involve more than just attending to the surface differences between the learner's own utterance and the target language input.

Doughty and Williams (1998a) proposed that there is a 'cognitive window' for carrying out cognitive comparisons and suggested that this can last up to 40 seconds if learners are able to rehearse what they have just heard in their perceptual memory. However, Doughty and Williams clearly had interactive focus on form in mind. Non-interactive focus on form involving enhanced input potentially allows the learner much longer to carry out the comparison as it does not occur in online processing.

The timing of focus on form

A key issue is the timing of focus-on-form. Doughty (2001) discussed four possibilities.

(1) Simultaneous processing (i.e. attention to form and meaning occur conjointly).
(2) Focus on form in advance (i.e. priming the learner to attend to specific forms, for example by pre-teaching the forms, prior to their engagement in a communicative task).
(3) Shifts of attention during processing (i.e. selective attention is temporarily switched to form).
(4) Immediately contingent focus on form (i.e. attracting learners' attention to a specific form in the previous utterance, for example by means of a recast).

There are doubts about L2 learners' ability to engage in simultaneous processing of meaning and form. Especially when learners' proficiency is weak, the difficulty experienced in decoding and encoding meaning may inhibit attention to form (see VanPatten, 1990). Pre-teaching the target form may help learners to attend to it while communicating and may also facilitate learning – see, for example, studies by Lyster (2004) and Cintron-Valentin and Ellis (2015). Pre-task planning can also be seen as a pre-emptive focus-on-form strategy that helps learners attend to form while performing a communicative task. Temporary shifts in attention can occur as a result of both pre-emptive and reactive focus on form. Studies by J. Williams (2001) and Loewen (2005) provide evidence that this happens with some frequency in task-based interactions and can lead to learning. Immediately contingent focus on form through recasting is favoured by both Long (1996, 2006) and Doughty (2001) on the grounds it brings together input, learners' internal cognitive processes (such as noticing and noticing-the-gap) and output and thus facilitates cognitive comparison without interrupting the flow of communication. In this way, so it is claimed, recasts create the ideal conditions for implicit learning. There is now substantial evidence to show that recasts do facilitate attention and learning (see, for example, Goo & Mackey, 2013) but as several commentators have pointed out (Ellis & Sheen, 2006; Nicholas *et al.*, 2001) recasts vary in terms of how implicit and explicit they are and learners are more likely to benefit if the recasts are intensive and explicit as in Doughty and Varela's (1998) study of corrective recasts (i.e. recasts preceded by a repetition of the learner's erroneous utterance with the incorrect elements highlighted). There are also other ways of achieving an immediately contingent focus on form by prompting learners to self-correct. Some researchers (e.g. Lyster (2004); Kartchava & Ammar (2014)) argue that prompts such as requests for clarification and elicitations are more likely to bring about changes in the learners' L2 system than recasts because they induce learners to produce the target forms whereas recasts frequently to not lead to self-correction.

From a psycholinguistic and pedagogic standpoint, it is important to investigate these different ways of timing a focus on form. In the classroom, opportunities will exist for the simultaneous processing of form and meaning, focusing on form in advance of a communicative activity (for example, by means of direct instruction), temporary shifts of attention from meaning to form, and immediately contingent focus on form. If what is important is that learners' attention to form takes place while they are primarily engaged in meaning-making (either receptively or productively), then, all four ways of timing have merit. To date, however, we have no understanding of whether some of these ways are more effective for learning than others.

Working memory and focus on form

In order to explain how focus on form can contribute to acquisition researchers are increasingly drawing on models of working memory on the grounds that the processing of focus-on-form interventions must necessarily involve (1) temporary storage of input and output and (2) establishing links with long-term memory. Although there are a number of different models of working memory (see Wen, 2015), they all acknowledge that working memory is limited in capacity and functions as a site where information can be (1) temporarily stored, (2) rehearsed to prolong activation and (3) processed by establishing links with long-term procedural and declarative memories. In terms familiar to SLA researchers, the functioning of working memory enables 'intake' that may be incorporated into the learner's interlanguage system either as implicit knowledge in procedural memory or as explicit knowledge in declarative memory.

We noted earlier that learners may have difficulty in attending simultaneously to both meaning and form. This can be explained by the limited capacity of working memory. Skehan's (1998, 2009) Trade-Off Hypothesis proposes that learners will prioritize one aspect of language use over others – for example, meaning over form or, in the case of form, complexity over accuracy. Skehan is less concerned with how instructional interventions can attract learners' attention to *specific* linguistic forms (as in mainstream accounts of focus on form) than with how the particular focus-on-form strategy he is most interested in (pre-task planning) can orientate learners *generally* to form as opposed to meaning and to complexity as opposed to accuracy. Drawing on Levelt's (1989) model of speaking, he suggests that pre-task planning aids conceptualization (i.e. deciding what to say) thus enabling learners to pay greater attention to formulation (i.e. accessing the lexical and grammatical features needed to encode what is to be said) during actual production when performing a task. Also, as Ortega (1999) showed, planning may enable learners to activate their existing linguistic resources in working memory thus enabling ready access to these resources again when they perform the task.

Models of working memory also provide a basis for addressing whether focus on form results in changes in procedural memory (i.e. implicit knowledge) or declarative memory (i.e. explicit knowledge). This is another key issue for focus-on-form researchers. One reason why Doughty (2001) favoured immediate contingent focus on form was because she considered it assists the development of true linguistic competence (i.e. implicit knowledge). This is arguably most likely to occur if the focus on form leads to temporary storage of the targeted features in learners' phonological short-term memory. In contrast, if there is time for analysis of the input, deeper processing involving declarative memory may take place resulting in explicit knowledge. Révész's (2012) study lends support to such a possibility. She investigated the relationship between gains in grammatical accuracy following recasting. She reported that differences in the learners' phonological working memories were related to accuracy gains in an oral description task, whereas differences in their complex working memory were related to gains in a written test. She then interpreted these results as showing that how the learners processed the recasts in working memory affected whether development led to procedural or declarative knowledge.

It is becoming clear that the role of working memory in processing focus-on-form interventions is complex. Simplistic notions that learners with larger working memories will benefit more from focus on form are giving way to more nuanced positions that distinguish how different aspects of working memory are involved in processing different types of focus-on-form interventions.

The Discoursal Dimension of Focus on Form

In a task-based approach focus on form can be achieved interactively by means of the negotiation of meaning or form and non-interactively (see Figure 4.1). It is the interactive focus-on-form, however, that has attracted the greatest attention of SLA researchers such as Long, Doughty, Mackey and R. Ellis as they view interaction playing a central role in acquisition.

Ellis *et al.* (2002) identified a set of 'options' for 'doing focus-on-form'. They distinguished two basic types of focus on form: reactive and pre-emptive focus on form. These two types of can be realized by means of a number of discoursal strategies. Reactive focus-on-form can be conversational or didactic. Conversational focus-on-form occurs when the attention to form arises in the course of dealing with a communication problem resulting in the negotiation of meaning. Didactic focus-on-form occurs when attention to form arises even though no communication problem has occurred. In this case, negotiation of form rather than negotiation of meaning takes place. Pre-emptive focus-on-form can also take a number of forms. It can be student-initiated as when a student asks a question about a linguistic form or it can be teacher-initiated. In this latter case the teacher may pre-empt by means of a query to check whether students know a particular linguistic form or the teacher may directly advise students to take care that they use a particular linguistic feature correctly as, for example, by reminding them to use the past tense in an activity involving the reporting of an accident.

There is now a substantial body of descriptive classroom-based research that has investigated the discoursal aspects of focus-on-form. A full review of the descriptive studies of focus on form is not possible in the space of this chapter so instead I will summarize the main findings and cite studies that are illustrative of these.

(1)   In lessons where there is a primary focus on meaning, focus on form occurs frequently (Ellis *et al.*, 2001; Nassaji, 2010). Often, however, teachers are not aware of the extent to which they engage in focus in form (Basturkmen *et al.*, 2004).

(2)   Both teachers and learners vary in the extent to which they engage in focus on form (Loewen, 2003).

(3)   Both learners and teachers sometimes make effective use of the learner's L1 to address linguistic problems in the L2 when performing communicative tasks (Nakatsukasa & Loewen, 2015; Storch & Wigglesworth, 2003).

(4)   By and large, focus on form episodes are triggered by lexical or grammatical problems. In a classroom context, relatively few episodes concern pragmatic aspects of language (Ellis *et al.*, 2001).

(5)   The instructional context affects the frequency with which different focus on form options occur and also the extent to which they result in uptake with repair (Sheen, 2004).[3] In part this depends on the extent to which the learners' general orientation is to meaning or form.

(6)   The extent to which learners notice those forms that are focused on during communicative interactions varies according to a number of factors such as whether the form receiving the focus is relevant to the learners' communicative needs (J. Williams, 2001) and the discoursal

characteristics of specific focus on form strategies in particular the level of explicitness (Egi, 2007).

(7) Although uptake-with-repair cannot be taken as evidence of learning, in some studies it has been found to be facilitative of learning (Loewen & Philp, 2006). Nassaji (2011) showed that the relationship between uptake/repair with learning depended on the type of repair with a stronger relationship between the two when the repair involved incorporation of the target form into new utterance than when it just involved repetition of the feedback.

(8) Both focus on form initiated by learners in learner-learner interaction and by teachers in whole-class interaction benefit acquisition (Loewen, 2005; J. Williams, 2001).

(9) In interactions involving the teacher there is evidence that pre-emptive focus on form is more effective than reactive focus on form especially if it is the learner who pre-empts (Nassaji, 2013).

(10) The effectiveness of focus on form also differs according to the participatory structure in the classroom, with a stronger effect evident when the teacher participates in small group work than in whole-class interaction (Nassaji, 2013).

(11) The extent to which learners participate in and benefit from focus on form depends on their L2 proficiency with higher proficiency learners focusing on form more and benefitting more from it than lower proficiency learners (J. Williams, 2001). Nassaji (2010) found that the effectiveness of reactive and pre-emptive focus on form also differed depending on learners' language proficiency and class level, with advanced-level learners benefiting more from reactive focus on form than less advanced learners.

The Effects of Different Types of Focus on Form

In this section I will review research which has investigated the different types of focus on form shown in Figure 4.1.

Text-enhancement

The research on text-enhancement suggests that text-enhancement is effective in helping learners to notice the target feature but not always so (Lee & Huang, 2008). There are a number of factors that influence whether noticing occurs. In part it depends on the nature of the target structure. Some structures are more salient than others. Learners may also be more likely to attend to a grammatical form if they have already partially acquired it and/or have explicit knowledge of it than if it is a completely new form. The main constraint, however, is the learner's level of proficiency. Less proficient learners may struggle to engage in dual processing – comprehending the meaning of the text and consciously attending to linguistic form – and are likely to prioritize meaning over form. Studies (e.g. Shook, 1999) have shown that if learners engage in the top-down processing required for comprehension, less noticing of specific forms occurs.

Even if learners do notice the target feature, they may not acquire it. Noticing affects intake but not everything that is taken into working memory passes into long term memory. Lee and Huang's (2008) meta-analysis examined 20 text-enhancement studies. They reported an overall positive effect in tests administered shortly after the learners had completed reading the enhanced texts but acknowledged that this was quite small and also that there were marked differences in the results of individual studies. Lee and Huang also reported that the benefits of the exposure tended to wear off over time.

Overall, text-enhancement does not emerge as a very effective type of focus on form unless it is combined with other instructional techniques that encourage intentional learning. When performing a task that prioritizes comprehension, learners may rely on top-down processing and pay little attention to the enhanced elements.

Corrective feedback

Corrective feedback (CF) constitutes a reactive type of focus on form that occurs in both the negotiation of meaning and of form and in FonFs instruction. It involves a number of different strategies that can be classified in terms of whether they are (1) implicit/explicit and (2) input-providing/ output-prompting strategies (see Table 4.2).

No type of focus-on-form has received more attention than corrective feedback. In addition to a number of descriptive studies (e.g. Chaudron, 1977; Lyster & Ranta, 1997; Sheen, 2004), there are now numerous experimental studies. A number of meta-analyses of CF studies are now available (Li, 2010; Lyster & Saito, 2010; Mackey & Goo, 2007; Russell & Spada, 2006).[4] All these meta-analyses reported that CF has a sizable positive effect on L2 learning. In general, explicit types of feedback are more effective than implicit. Ellis *et al.* (2006), for example, reported that

Table 4.2 Types of corrective feedback (adapted from Lyster *et al.*, 2013: 3)

	Implicit	Explicit
Input-providing	Conversational recasts	Didactic recasts Explicit correction Explicit correction + metalinguistic explanation
Output-prompting	Repetition Clarification requests	Metalinguistic comments Elicitation Paralinguistic signal

repetition followed by metalinguistic feedback led to greater gains in tests designed to measure both implicit and explicit knowledge of the target structure (past tense –ed) than recasts. However, Li's (2010) meta-analysis found that implicit CF proved to be more effective in post-tests completed a long time after the instruction. Perhaps, then, the effects of implicit CF, like a good wine, need time to mature.

Lyster and Saito's (2010) meta-analysis, which focused exclusively on classroom studies of corrective feedback, compared the relative effects of input-providing CF (recasts) and output-prompting CF. They reported that both recasts and prompts are effective in promoting acquisition but the effect size for prompts (0.83) was appreciably larger than that for recasts (0.53). However, the relative effectiveness of recasts and prompts has continued to be debated – see, for example, Goo and Mackey (2013) and Lyster and Ranta (2013). Perhaps it is fundamentally mistaken to look for the most effective type of corrective strategy. Different strategies may prove effective for learners at different developmental levels as claimed by sociocultural theorists such as Aljaafreh and Lantolf (1994). Also, individual differences in language aptitude or working memory may affect learners' ability to process the different strategies as suggested by Révész's (2012) study, which I considered earlier.

Researchers have also investigated whether the corrections that learners receive are noticed and whether noticing promotes learning. There is clear evidence that learners do notice the corrections they receive even in implicit types of CF such as recasts (Egi, 2007) but to date there is little evidence to show a consistent direct effect of such noticing on acquisition – see, for example, Mackey (2006).

A few studies have also investigated whether learner-generated CF results in learning. Adams (2007) recorded interactions while learners were performing tasks in pairs, identified corrective feedback sequences, and then administered tailor made tests to assess whether learning had taken place. She reported that over 60% of the feedback episodes led to learning. McDonough (2004) investigated learner-learner corrections directed at conditionals when performing a focused task designed to elicit the use of this structure. She reported that those learners who experienced the corrective feedback more frequently were the ones who showed significant improvement in oral tests that elicited use of conditionals.

The results of the CF research provide the clearest support for focus on form. Correcting learners' errors while they are communicating is a highly effective way of drawing their attention to form and there is clear evidence that CF facilitates acquisition. On balance CF is more effective if it is explicit, presumably because it is more likely to guarantee a switch in selective attention to form. But implicit forms of CF such as recasts have also been found to be effective and may even have a greater long-term effect. CF is likely to be more intensive when it is in the hands of the teacher but it also occurs in learner-learner interactions and contributes to learning.

Pre-task planning

As noted earlier, pre-task planning serves to alleviate the problems that learners face in L2 production due to the limited capacity of their working memories. It facilitates 'planned language use', which, as Ochs (1979) noted, is characterized by more complex, target-like forms than unplanned language use.

The bulk of the research has investigated what effect pre-task planning has on the complexity, accuracy and fluency of learners' language when they perform the task. Pre-task planning studies distinguish 'guided planning' where learners are directed to pay attention to some specific aspect of language (i.e. form or meaning) or even some specific grammatical feature and 'unguided planning' where they left to decide for themselves what aspects they plan. In a survey of planning studies, R. Ellis (2009) found that both had a positive overall effect on fluency except if the task was performed in a testing (as opposed to teaching) context. Interestingly, however, in one study of guided planning where learners were asked to focus their planning on a single grammatical structure (Mochizuki & Ortega, 2008), fluency did not benefit. Pre-task planning also benefited complexity (especially grammatical complexity) in 13 of the 19 studies Ellis included in his review. A similar number of studies also reported it had an effect on accuracy. Some studies reported that pre-task planning aided complexity but not accuracy and vice-versa, lending support to Skehan's (2009) Trade-off Hypothesis. Subsequent studies have also found that pre-task planning affects complexity or accuracy but not both. Hsu (2017), for example, investigated the effects of 10 minutes of pre-task planning on L2 learners' performance of a narrative task in text-based computer-mediated communication and reported that it resulted in greater accuracy of verb forms but it did not enhance complexity more than a no pre-task planning condition. Exactly what factors mediate the impact of pre-task planning on accuracy and complexity remain uncertain. As Ellis' review showed, factors such as the nature of the task, the length of the planning time, the type of planning required, and the learners' level of L2 proficiency can influence the effects on L2 production.

The effect that pre-task planning has on task performance will obviously depend on what learners do while they plan. Some studies have investigated this (e.g. Mochizuki & Ortega, 2008; Ortega, 1999, 2005; Pang & Skehan, 2014). The guided planning in Mochizuki and Ortega led to more accurate uses of the target structure (relative clauses) than did unguided planning but, importantly, it also resulted in similar levels of global complexity and fluency. Pang and Skehan attempted to relate coded features of the learners' unguided planning to measures of complexity, accuracy and fluency derived from their performance of the task. They reported that a general focus on grammar had a negative impact on complexity and fluency without enhancing accuracy and concluded 'focusing on grammar confers only disadvantages and no advantages' (2014: 120). Clearly, more work is needed on how specific planning strategies and foci affect performance of a task but if these two studies are indicative, it is the guided planning that focuses on a specific linguistic feature that is needed to achieve an effect on accuracy.

Task-repetition

When learners are asked to repeat the same task, the first performance functions in much the same way as pre-task planning – it enables learners to both conceptualize what to say and select the language needed to say it. Potentially, then, it enables learners to focus attention more closely on linguistic form in the repeat performance. It can be expected then that task repetition will have a similar effect on complexity, accuracy and fluency as pre-task planning.

However, the results of task-repetition studies have produced somewhat mixed results along with evidence of trade-off effects in the repeated task. Bygate (1996, 2001), for example reported that fluency and complexity increased in the repeated task but not accuracy. Lynch and McLean (2000) found that repetition led to increased accuracy in low-proficiency learners but to more complex language in higher proficiency learners. Gass *et al.* (1999) found an effect for repetition on the accurate use of a specific grammatical feature. However, none of these studies found evidence of any transfer-effects to a new task. Bygate (2001) suggested that 'massed' repetition practice may be needed for such transfer effects to occur. Perhaps, though, what is needed is some kind of intervention between performances of the same task to induce attention to form. Sheppard (2006) tried providing learners with input and feedback between performances and found that both led to improvements in complexity, accuracy and fluency in the repeat performance and also in complexity (but not in accuracy or fluency) in the performance of a new task.

Critiques of Focus on Form

Focus on form is a crucial feature of task-based language teaching, which has attracted considerable criticism from advocates of more traditional approaches to teaching such as FonFs. The main objections to TBLT and FonF (as an approach) are as follows:

- FonF is based entirely on theoretical hypotheses (e.g. Schmidt's Noticing Hypothesis) that are themselves lacking in empirical support (Swan, 2005a);

- focus on form consists only of quick feedback on learners' errors while they are performing a communicative task (Sheen, 2003);
- advocates of FonF present it as the only theoretically sound way of teaching an L2, rejecting FonFs entirely (Swan, 2005);
- there is no report of any successful long-term implementation of FonF (Sheen, 2005a, 2005b);
- there is no evidence to show that FonF results in superior L2 learning than FonFs (Sheen, 1994);
- FonF is an experiential approach to language teaching that is ill-suited to cultures of teaching and learning that are different from those of Western settings (Littlewood, 2007, 2015).

Most of these objections are entirely misplaced reflecting fundamental misunderstandings about task-based language teaching and the role of focus on form (see Chapter 8). There is ample evidence to support theoretical hypotheses such as the Noticing Hypothesis and also to show that focus on form results in learning (see previous sections). Focus on form involves much more than quick feedback on learner errors – as defined in this article it includes, for example, text-enhancement, pre-task planning and task- repetition. Not all advocates of TBLT reject FonFs; R. Ellis, for example, suggests that a modular system that includes both a FonFs and a TBLT component might be best suited to some instructional contexts (see Chapter 10). Also, if focus on form is viewed as a set of procedures rather than as an approach – as I have argued it should be – then clearly it has a place in any approach that includes communicative tasks, including PPP. There is also evidence that a task-based approach that incorporates focus on form can be successfully implemented and is effective (e.g. Prabhu, 1987; chapters in Van den Branden, 2006a). The cultural inappropriateness of a FonF approach, however, is a weightier criticism, which I will return to in the conclusion section of this paper.

Comparative Studies of FonF and FonFs

There are no global comparative method studies that have investigated the relative effectiveness of FonF and FonFs in developing general L2 proficiency, reflecting the difficulty of achieving internal and external validity in the design of such studies (see R. Ellis, 2012). However, there are a number of 'local' comparative studies, which have investigated these two approaches in terms of their effect on the acquisition of specific target language features. Sheen (2003, 2005) has argued that such studies are needed.

Several studies examined their relative effectiveness of FonF and FonFs on the acquisition of vocabulary but, for reasons of space, I will only consider those studies that investigated grammar. Sheen (2006) found that FonFs instruction led to greater learning than FonF but this study was seriously flawed. Sheen admitted that the FonF instruction in his study was not properly implemented as the teacher failed to correct the learners' errors consistently while they were performing the communicative tasks (i.e. in other words there was very little focus on form). Also the tests in his study all involved controlled production of the target features and so favoured the FonFs group.

Shintani (2015) investigated the incidental acquisition of grammar in FonF and FonFs instruction. The instructional materials in both approaches exposed the learners to exemplars of grammatical structures, whereas the instructional target was vocabulary. Shintani reported that FonF led to greater incidental learning, which was attributed to the fact that it created a greater functional need to attend to the target structures and afforded more opportunities for noticing them. However, this was only true for one of the structures – the meaning-bearing grammatical morpheme (plural-s) – and not for the non-meaning bearing structure (copula be). This is a still noteworthy finding, however, as any kind of instruction affords opportunities for incidental learning and it is helpful to know what kind of instruction promotes it most effectively.

These studies only go some way to addressing Sheen's (2006) call for comparative studies of FonF and FonFs and they certainly do not allow any clear conclusions to be reached. They demonstrate the problems of designing such comparative studies and also the importance of examining the classroom processes associated with the two types of instruction in order to understand how these shape opportunities for learning and can help to explain the test results. However, as I will argue below, a better approach might be to focus on how specific options of both the focus-on-form and focus-on-forms kinds direct or attract learners' attention to form and what their impact on learning is.

Conclusion

This review of focus on form has raised a number of points.

(1) 'Focus-on-form' refers not just to form but to form-function mapping.

(2) Focus on form was first introduced as a pedagogic approach (FonF) that was seen as an alternative to a structural-based approach (i.e. FonFs). Subsequently, however, focus on form came to be viewed as a set of procedures for attracting attention to form that can figure in both approaches.

(3) The scope of pedagogic focus on form has expanded considerably over the years. Initially, it referred to the interventions designed to attract learners' attention to form while they performed a communicative task. Later it was expanded to include interactive and

non-interactive ways of drawing attention to form both prior to and after performance of a task.

(4) Central to all kinds of focus on form instruction, however, is some kind of meaning-focused task that provides the context for the focus on form. Thus focus on form is integral to task-based language teaching.

(5) There is well-defined psycholinguistic dimension to focus on form. To understand this, it is necessary to consider, in particular, the role of selective attention and cognitive comparison in language learning as these occur when learners process language in their working memories. The limited capacity of working memory (WM) constrains what learners can attend to while communicating and thus influences what they can focus on and learn.

(6) There is also an important discoursal dimension to interactive focus-on-form. Descriptive research has identified a number of pre-emptive and reactive strategies that can be used to address form and how these strategies impact on learner production (for example, uptake with repair) and learning.

(7) Experimental studies of focus-on-form have shown that it facilitates L2 acquisition although this depends on a number of factors such as the salience of the focus on form and the learners' L2 proficiency. Reactive focus-on-form (i.e. corrective feedback) is especially facilitative although focus on form undertaken pre-emptively can also aid learning as does non-interactive enhanced input.

(8) Pre-task planning and task-repetition have been shown to influence how learners orientate to the performance of a communicative task and impact on the complexity of the language involved.

(9) FonF as a pedagogic approach has been the subject of considerable criticism. Many of the objections are spurious resting on misconceptions about task-based teaching.

(10) Calls for comparative studies of FonF and FonFs have been answered but the research to date does not allow a clear answer as to their relative effectiveness. There is some evidence that FonF results in richer types of classroom interaction that benefit the incidental acquisition of non-targeted features.

I have dismissed many of the criticisms of FonF as an approach but I acknowledge that there can be problems in implementing it as discussed in Chapter 1. A number of teacher educators (e.g. Bax, 2003) have argued it is necessary to take account of the particular instructional context before deciding which approach to use. In contexts where the teachers are unfamiliar with focus on form, the learners are concerned with language as an object rather than as a tool for communicating, and the educational system requires students to take traditional type tests to progress academically formidable obstacles in implementing an approach that prioritizes focus on form rather than focus on forms can occur.

Perhaps, though, as I have argued, it is time to stop treating FonF and FonFs as approaches and instead view focus on form as a set of procedures for attracting attention to form while learners are engaged in meaning-making. Such procedures belong naturally to task-based teaching but they can also be found in more traditional approaches providing there is some opportunity for free production in the L2. There are current studies (e.g. Cintron-Valentin & Ellis, 2015) that claim to investigate 'focus on form' but also include explicit instruction of a target feature prior to the focus on form activity. We need studies that compare focus on form treatments that include and exclude explicit instruction with care taken to measure the effects on the acquisition of both explicit and implicit knowledge.

In Chapter 6 that follows I examine studies that have investigated the effects of explicit instruction on task performance. First though, in Chapter 5, I look more generally at how learners can be prepared to perform tasks and what effect this has on task performance.

Notes

(1) In fact, it is doubtful whether any instructional approach is totally devoid of a focus on form. In immersion classrooms, for example, corrective feedback of various kinds still occurs (Lyster & Ranta, 1997).

(2) Post-task activities can also involve focus on form activities as, for example, when learners are asked to present a report of the outcome of the task they have just completed. Post-task activities can also be of the focus on forms kind (e.g. grammar exercises).

(3) Sheen (2006) found that uptake-with-repair was more likely following corrective feedback in a Korean-as-a-foreign-language context than in the immersion classrooms investigated by Lyster and Ranta (1997).

(4) Of these meta-analyses only Lyster and Saito (2010) focuses exclusively on classroom-based studies of corrective feedback. The other meta-analyses also included laboratory-based studies.

5 Preparing Learners to Perform Tasks

Introduction

There are two principal types of planning – pre-task planning and within-task planning. The former consists of rehearsal or task repetition, where the performance of a task at one time serves as a preparation for the performance of the same task later, and strategic planning, where learners are given time to consider what they want to say and how to say it. Within-task planning varies according to whether it is pressured or unpressured, which constitutes a continuum rather than a dichotomy. This taxonomy, which I introduced in Ellis (2005b) needs refining and extending. Bui (2014), for example, pointed out that it might be useful to distinguish 'rehearsal' when learners are made aware they will have to repeat the task and 'repetition' when there is no such warning. Strategic planning can be guided or unguided and in the case of the former there are a number of possibilities. Finally, if planning is viewed as just one way of preparing learners to perform a task, then it will be helpful to distinguish what Bui called 'internal readiness' which arises from topic familiarity, schematic familiarity or task familiarity from 'external readiness' involving the various types of planning. In this chapter I will review research that has investigated different types of 'task preparedness'.

Studies that have investigated preparedness variables have primarily been concerned with the effect that these variables have on how a task is performed. The great majority of these studies have analysed task performance in terms of complexity, accuracy and fluency but some have also used other ways, for example language-related episodes (LREs) (e.g. Kim, 2013) or the use of specific target structures (Van de Guchte et al., 2016). Relatively few studies have investigated what effect preparedness variables have on the language learning that results from performing tasks. This constitutes a major limitation of the research to date. It has led researchers – such as Skehan –to make the link between task performance and learning theoretically.

In this chapter, I will attempt to review the research on task preparedness. However, I will not aim to be comprehensive. Instead, I will focus on conceptual issues and construct definition, selecting studies that illustrate these. In so doing I hope to provide a framework that can inform both a meta-analysis of extant research and guide future research. I begin with a few comments about the importance of distinguishing task-design and implementation variables. I will then move on consider the research that has investigated task rehearsal (repetition), pre-task planning, online planning, and other forms of task preparedness.

Design versus Implementation Variables

Ways of preparing students to perform a task belong to what I call 'implementation' options. In a recent article, Skehan (2016) ventured a discussion of the relative effects of design and implementation variables on task performance. He commented 'some insights have been achieved about task qualities that have systematic connections with performance, but not much more than that' (2016: 44–45) and then went on to suggest 'in contrast, if we switch to methodology the claims are much more encouraging' (2016: 45). In other words, he acknowledged that implementation variables are likely to have much greater impact on task performance than design variables and he also suggested that they were of greater significance for achieving the balance between complexity, accuracy and fluency which he sees as the goal of task-based language teaching. Of the various implementation options that Skehan and his co-researchers have investigated (see Skehan, 2014a), task-preparedness is arguably the most interesting and clearly the most researched. The preparedness options are also of pedagogical importance because they can be easily acted on by teachers. If there is one area of task-based research that teachers can definitely benefit from it is the research on task preparedness.

Rehearsal

Bui's (2014) suggestion that we should distinguish 'rehearsal' and 'repetition' has not been acted on to date. Studies that have investigated rehearsal often do not make it clear whether learners are told they will have to repeat the task. Of course, in some studies such as Lambert *et al.* (2017a), where the same task is repeated multiple times, it will become evident to learners that they will perform the task again. But if a task is repeated only once the question of whether or not they are told that they will have to repeat the task becomes relevant. It seems likely that if they are told, they will pay greater attention to the linguistic encoding of what they want to say. That is, they will engage more extensively in what Levelt (1989) called formulation and this will impact on how they perform the task a second time. However, we await a study that compares 'rehearsal' and 'repetition'.

Ignoring Bui's potentially important distinction, it has now become clear there are different types of rehearsal. Pattansorn (2010) distinguished the following types.

(1) Procedural repetition – 'refers to carrying out several tasks that require the same procedure to accomplish the communicative goal but require different content knowledge':
(2) Content repetition – 'refers to carrying out the same tasks that require different procedures to accomplish the communicative goal but require the same content knowledge':
(3) Task repetition – 'refers to carrying out the same task repeatedly, using the same procedure to accomplish the communicative goal and requiring the same content knowledge'. (Pattansorn, 2010: 13)

Pattansorn's own study compared the effects of these different types of repetition in terms of complexity, accuracy and fluency. The tasks were repeated three times. She reported that those learners who engaged in procedural repetition improved in accuracy of past tense, those learners who repeated tasks with the same content improved in global fluency but declined in accuracy, and those learners who repeated exactly the same task failed to show any changes. The result for task repetition (Type 3) is surprising given that most studies report gains in at least fluency and complexity when the same task is repeated. Kim and Tracy-Ventura (2013) compared the effects of procedural repetition and task repetition and found some positive effects for both (e.g. improvement in accuracy of past tense). They concluded, however, that their findings did not provide support for one type of task rehearsal over the other.

Distinguishing procedural, content and task repetition may prove useful but the results of these two studies do not seem encouraging. There is a fundamental difference between repeating the same task and performing different tasks with either the same procedure or the same content. Only the former makes it possible for learners to draw on both the conceptualization and formulation involved in the first performance of a task. The bulk of the repetition studies to date have examined what Pattansorn called 'task repetition', which I will now focus on.

Task repetition studies differ in a number of ways.

- Whether the study was carried out in a classroom context (Lambert *et al.*, 2017b), in a laboratory (most studies) or in a chat room (Hsu, 2017).
- The type of task that is repeated. Many studies have used monologic narrative tasks but some have used dialogic tasks.
- They number of times the task is repeated. This varies between one in Wang (2014) and five in Lambert *et al.* (2017a).

- The time interval between repetitions of the task. This can vary from immediate repetition to several days.
- Whether the performance of the task involves some other methodological manipulation such as within-task planning as in Hsu (2017), corrective feedback as in Van de Guchte *et al.* (2016), or audio input as in Lambert *et al.* (2017a).
- Whether there is any pedagogic intervention between performances of the same task as in Hawkes (2012) and Sheppard and Ellis (2018).
- Investigating whether task repetition leads to language development by either including a new task after the task repetition(s) (Bygate, 2001) or embedding the task repetition into a pre-test/post-test design sequence as in Van de Guchte *et al.* (2016).
- Whether the participants' opinions about task repetition are investigated.

This diversity of designs in investigating a single (but clearly complex) construct is, if course, a feature of second language acquisition (SLA) research in general but it makes it dangerous to try to reach any conclusions about the effects of task repetition. The general conclusion I reached in my 2009 review of rehearsal studies was:

> Task repetition … results in greater fluency and complexity (and to a lesser extent accuracy) but these effects do not transfer to the performance of a new task unless there is some kind of additional intervention, suggesting that simply repeating a task may not have a measurable impact on acquisition. (Ellis, 2009b: 501)

However, although there was little evidence of any transfer of learning (i.e. language development) resulting from task repetition in the studies included in my 2009 review, subsequent research is more promising.

Wang's (2014) study found that immediate task repetition[1] was the only preparedness condition out of those she investigated (the others being strategic and online planning) that had a positive effect on all three aspects of performance – complexity, accuracy and fluency. Wang's study, then differs from many of the earlier studies in that there was an effect on accuracy. She argued that task repetition impacted on accuracy because it led to the learners monitoring when they performed the task a second time. This might also be the reason for the positive effects that task repetition has on accuracy when it is supported by some other type of preparedness. Two studies have shown that repeating a task when the online planning is unpressured produces favourable results. Hsu (2017) reported that rehearsal together with pre-task planning and unpressured online planning resulted in greater accuracy in the performance of a new task. Ahmadian and Tavakoli (2010) found that task repetition in conjunction with careful online planning benefitted complexity, accuracy and fluency and was more beneficial that either careful planning or task repetition when the online planning was pressured. De Jong and Perfetti (2011) compared two groups of L2 learners, one of which repeated the same task (i.e. 'task repetition') three times and the other three tasks which had different topics but the same procedures (i.e. procedural repetition). They reported that fluency improved in both groups over time but was only maintained in post-tests in the exact repetition group. Thai and Boers (2015) compared the effects of repeating the same task with and without increasing time pressure. They found that increasing time pressure led to more fluent production but did not result in more complex or accurate language. In contrast, those learners who performed the task three times without any increase in time pressure manifested small gains in fluency along with modest gains in complexity and accuracy. These studies strongly suggest that repeating a task (exactly or procedurally) is likely to lead to greater fluency and perhaps complexity but it may have no effect on accuracy unless learners can also engage in careful online planning when they repeat the task.

Several studies have investigated the effect of task repetition in conjunction with some kind of pedagogic intervention. Van de Guchte *et al.* (2016) investigated the effects of task repetition in conjunction with corrective feedback consisting of both metalinguistic comments and prompts directed at two grammatical structures when they performed the task for the first time. They found that those learners who underwent this treatment scored higher on a post-test measuring controlled use of the target structure (but not on an oral production test) than those learners who received corrective feedback but did not have the opportunity to repeat the task. Other studies investigated some kind of intervention between performances of the task. Hawkes (2012) investigated the effect of inducing a focus on form by practising specific structures and vocabulary relevant to the tasks. Results showed an increase in the number of lexical and grammatical corrections in the repeat performances of the tasks. In Fukuta (2016) relatively high-proficiency L2 learners took part in a stimulated recall session following the first performance of a narrative task. They demonstrated gains in accuracy and lexical variety when the task was repeated one week later but no gains in fluency or complexity. However, not all interventions have proved so effective. Sheppard and Ellis (2018) found little effect for the same kind of stimulated recall activity as in Fukuta's study. Relatively low-proficiency learners listened to their original performance of the task and commented on occasions where they had made pauses. However, Sheppard and Ellis found that this did not lead to the learners focusing on form. What appears to be crucial, then, is whether learners focus on form in subsequent performances of the task and that this may depend on whether there is opportunity for unpressured planning or there is some between-performance pedagogic intervention that explicitly draws attention to form.

Tentatively, then, building on my earlier summary, I suggest that task repetition by itself is beneficial in enhancing fluency and complexity – especially if the task is repeated several times, However, for it to have a marked effect on accuracy on either the repeated task or in the performance of a new task something more is needed – the opportunity for unpressured online planning and/or some kind of form-focused intervention. Skehan (2014b) concluded that repetition has a lot going for it as a pedagogic intervention but the recent research suggests that the full value of task repetition may only be realized if it is combined with some other implementation option.

Several studies investigated participant's views about task repetition. These appear to be quite varied. Aubrey (2015) reported that a group of Japanese university students indicated boredom with having to repeat a series of tasks with a Japanese interlocutor although not when they repeated the task with an international student at their university. In other words, in the case of dialogic tasks, who the learners' interlocutors are may be a crucial factor. Kim (2013) also reported that the participants in her study found task repetition not very helpful although they did feel that procedural repetition was useful for improving language skills. The learners in Lambert *et al.* (2017a) (also Japanese university students) were positive about being asked to repeat the tasks but felt that repeating them five times was unnecessary. They indicated that three or four repetitions were optimal. Interestingly, the quantitative analyses of fluency gains from repeating the tasks in this study also indicated that three or four repetitions were ideal. There was no increase in the fifth repetition. Participants' views about task repetition are likely to vary – as these studies show – depending on various factors such as whether task repetition or procedural repetition is involved and whether the task generates intrinsic motivation. Future studies should obtain information about participants' attitudes to task repetition and also investigate whether there is any difference in the complexity, accuracy and fluency of the repeated performance(s) between participants with favourable and unfavourable attitudes.

Strategic Planning

Of the various types of preparedness options strategic planning has received the greatest attention. I reviewed 19 studies in Ellis (2009). My overall conclusion was as follows:

> Strategic planning clearly benefits fluency but results are more mixed where complexity and accuracy are concerned, possibly because there is a trade-off in these two aspects (i.e. learners will tend to prioritize either complexity or accuracy). A number of variables have been shown to have an impact on the effect that strategic planning has, in particular the learners' proficiency (the effects are less evident in very advanced learners), the

degree of structure of the information in the task (planning is of greater benefit with less well-structured tasks), and, in one study, working memory. However, different types of strategic planning seem to have a negligible effect on production. (2009: 501–502)

In the 2009 article I examined a number of parameters in the strategic planning studies – whether the participants were second or foreign language learners, the proficiency of the participants, whether the studies were carried out in a laboratory or testing setting, the nature of the task (simple or complex; interactive or monologic), and the nature of the planning (the time allocated; guided versus unguided; form vs meaning focused). These same parameters also figure in more recent studies.

Second vs foreign language learners

We find new studies conducted with both ESL learners (e.g. Hsu, 2012; Nielson, 2014) and EFL learners (e.g. Bui, 2014; Kim, 2012; Li et al., 2015; Mehrang & Rahimpour, 2010; Saeedi, 2015; Wang, 2014). Up to 2009 the studies were fairly evenly divided between second and foreign language learners. Subsequently, EFL studies have predominated, in part because of the contributions of Skehan and his co-researchers in Hong Kong and in part because Iranian researchers seem to have latched onto to strategic planning as a productive research area. The combined results of the various studies indicate that strategic planning has positive effects on task performance irrespective of setting. However, as was the case prior to 2009, there is no study that has directly compared the effects of strategic planning in different language settings.[2]

Interactive vs monologic tasks

Unlike the earlier studies, the majority of which investigated the effects of strategic planning on interactive tasks, most of the recent studies involved monologic tasks (Bui; Li, Chen and Sun; Mehrang & Rahimpor; Nielson; Saeedi; Wang) and only two studies looked at interactive tasks (Hsu; Kim). The monologic studies generally involved narrating a story. Nearly all these new studies were carried out in a laboratory setting. Hsu's (2012) study was located in a chat room, one-on-one with the researcher, and, interestingly is the only study to report no impact for strategic planning. Hsu compared a group that experienced both time to plan and unpressured online planning and a group that experienced unpressured online planning but with no opportunity to plan. There were no group differences in any of the complexity, accuracy and fluency (CAF) measures, which Hsu suggested might have been because the students were not used to performing an interactive task in a chat environment. It is perhaps unfortunate that laboratory-based studies involving mainly monologic tasks have become the norm. Some doubts must always exist as to whether laboratory-based findings can be generalized to classrooms and teachers might have more confidence in research involving interactive tasks given their central role in task-based language teaching.

Learners' proficiency level

Understandably perhaps, the recent studies, like the earlier studies, investigated learners of intermediate-level L2 proficiency. Only one of the recent studies included proficiency as a design variable in order to investigate whether strategic planning had different effects on intermediate- and advanced-level learners. Bui (2014) reported that strategic planning had the same effects on learners of both proficiency levels – that is, like many other studies, strategic planning led to greater complexity and fluency but not to increased accuracy. More studies like Bui's are needed. The relevance of the different preparedness conditions to language pedagogy needs to be demonstrated for learners of different proficiency levels including low-proficiency students, who have been neglected in the research to date.[3]

Task structure

One of the task-design variables of interest is whether the information in a task is tightly structured or loosely structured. Early studies (e.g. Foster & Skehan, 1996; Skehan & Foster, 1997) indicated that this task design variable interacted with strategic planning. This possibility has been further explored in some of the recent studies. Mehrang and Rahimour (2010) reported that, although neither planning nor task structure had any effect on accuracy, fluency was greater with the structured task in the planned condition and complexity greater with the unstructured task in the planned condition. Saeedi (2015) compared the effects of strategic planning and no planning on the performance of structured and unstructured tasks. Contrary to the findings of the earlier studies, he reported that learners who performed the structured task in the strategic planning condition produced language that was more complex, accurate and fluent than learners who performed the unstructured task with no strategic planning. But he also noted that planning had positive effects on complexity irrespective of whether the task was structured or unstructured. These studies bear out Skehan and Foster's (1996) early claim that planning time interacts with task structure to influence CAF – although not in consistent ways.

More studies that investigate the combined effect of design and implementation variables are sorely needed. Tasks are bundles of characteristics (Skehan, 2014c) and if we are to understand how tasks impact on performance it is essential that we look at the effect of combinations of variables – starting with those variables, such as pre-task planning and task structure, which have been shown to have a powerful impact singly.

Strategic planning is complex activity. It can vary in a number of ways – how much time is allocated to it, whether it is guided or unguided (and there are many different ways of providing guidance), and whether it is combined with some other way of helping learners to perform a task.

Time allocated to strategic planning

There is an obvious need to investigate whether the time allocated affects the performance of a task. Mehnert (1998) was the first to undertake this, reporting that different lengths impacted variably on complexity, accuracy and fluency. For example, in the case of accuracy in the performance of an unstructured task, one minute was sufficient to result in a significant difference from the no planning condition. Of the new studies, only Li *et al.* (2015) followed up on Mehnert's study. The learners in this study performed six monologic opinion-gap tasks after different lengths of planning time (0, 0.6, 1, 2, 3 and 5 minutes). The general finding was:

> More fluency, accuracy and lexical complexity were attained under planned conditions than unplanned condition, and increasing amount of planning time produced gradually more accurate but not steadily more fluent or complex utterances. (Li *et al.*, 2015: 56)

In fact, there was no effect for any length of planning on syntactical complexity. Like Mehnert they found that 1 minute of planning time was sufficient for a significant effect on accuracy. Li *et al.* concluded that the optimal planning time was between 1 and 3 minutes suggesting that the 10 minutes allocated in many strategic planning studies might be unnecessarily long.

One problem with both Mehnert's and Li *et al.*'s studies is that no attempt was made to control within-task planning or to examine to what extent the learners were engaging in within-task planning by recording the time taken to perform the tasks. It would seem very possible that there is trade-off between strategic and within-task planning. That is, the shorter the time available for strategic planning, the more time will be needed for within-task planning.

Guided planning

From a pedagogic perspective, it is clearly important to consider which type of strategic planning will yield the best results. It was this consideration that motivated a number of the earlier studies to investigate different types of planning activities. Foster and Skehan (1996), for example, compared the effects of unguided and guided planning, whereas in another study (Skehan & Foster, 1999) they compared the effects of planning carried out individually, in groups, or with the teacher. Somewhat surprisingly, the more recent studies have not continued this line of research, opting for unguided strategic planning carried out by individual learners. The exception is Kim (2012). In this study one group watched a task modelling video in their 10 minutes of planning time, whereas another group just planned individually for the 10 minutes. The modelling video illustrated how the learners could pay attention to the linguistic code and how to perform a task collaboratively by sharing ideas, asking ideas and providing feedback. The dependent variables in this study were the LREs that the learners produced when they performed the tasks and development in question formation measured in a post-test. Those learners who watched the videos produced more LREs focusing on question formation when they performed the tasks and also were more likely to manifest development. Previous guided planning studies have simply instructed learners on what to focus on as they plan (e.g. on content or on language). Kim's study is unique in showing the learners how the planning can be carried out. Her task modelling video constitutes an additional preparedness option and the results of her study suggest that it is effective in both improving the quality of learners' planning and task performance. It would be interesting to see a follow-up study that compared groups that just watched the video (with no time for planning) with another group that both watched and planned to see whether the video alone can successfully prepare learners to perform a task.

Working memory

Another line of research on pre-task planning examines whether learner factors mediate its effect on task performance. One learner factor that is of obvious importance is working memory. The often-stated rationale for strategic planning is that it helps learners to overcome the limitations in attention that arise because of the pressure on their working memory when they perform a task. Because working memory is limited learners experience problems in carrying out conceptualization, formulation and articulation in parallel. Strategic planning eases these problems because learners will already have an idea of what they want to say and how to say it and thus do not have to conceptualize and formulate from scratch.

In 2009 I was only able to locate one study that investigated the role of working memory in mediating the effect that strategic planning has on task performance. Guara-Tavares (2008) reported that working memory correlated with measures of task fluency and complexity in a planning group but with accuracy in a no-planning group. Interest in working memory in relation to strategic planning is clearly on the increase. Nielson (2014) measured working memory using a new test (Shapebuilder) to overcome the problem of the verbal test in

Guara-Tavares' study where proficiency and working memory were conflated. Intermediate ESL learners performed two tasks in both a planned and unplanned condition. Working memory was found to correlate significantly with fluency and complexity (but not consistently with accuracy) scores but, contrary to expectations, Nielson found that planning time did not help low working memory participants more than high working memory participants. She suggested that this was because the task may not have been complex enough. Wen (2016), however, did find an interaction between phonological working memory and planning conditions on fluency scores. Learners with low working memory benefitted from the opportunity to plan for 10 minutes. Interestingly, though, the high working memory learners were actually less fluent in the planning than in the no-planning condition. Similarly, only learners with low executive working memory were able to take advantage of the planning time to use more diversified lexis when they performed the task.

The results of these studies to date are very mixed, making it impossible to reach any conclusions. There are many possible reasons for this – how working memory is measured, the nature of the task, the proficiency levels of the learners, and, of course, the length and nature of the planning condition – pointing to the difficulty in designing studies to examine how working memory mediates the effects of planning.

Learners' use of strategic planning time

It is of course not the opportunity to plan itself that produces the effects described in the previous paragraphs but what learners make of this opportunity. Thus, arguably, for research on strategic planning studies to advance, greater efforts are needed to investigate how learners use their planning time. There are still very few studies that have done this. The only study I identified attempting this in my 2009 survey was Ortega (2005). There are several later studies. Kim (2012) used think-aloud protocols to investigate the effects of her two planning conditions (see above). She reported that the task-modelling condition produced significantly more LREs during planning. In Pang and Skehan (2014) learners planned and then performed two narrative retelling tasks. They were then interviewed to investigate what they did when they planned and whether they found planning helpful. The interviews were recorded, transcribed and analysed qualitatively resulting in a taxonomy of planning strategies. Pang and Skehan then correlated the frequency with which individual learners made use of the different strategies with CAF scores derived from their performance of the tasks. As a result of this analysis, they were able to identify which planning approaches were beneficial (e.g. 'build your own story structure') and which ones were not (e.g. 'focus on grammar'). Commenting on this study, Skehan (2014b) observed that it revealed more about what learners should not do when they planned (i.e. focus on grammar) than what they should do.

All of these studies all used some type of self-report to investigate planning but Markee and Kumitz (2013) questioned the validity of this method and instead proposed an 'ethnomethodological respecification' of planning work that locates planning in turn-taking, repair and sequencing organizing practices. However, such an approach is only viable if the planning is collaborative and thus cannot address the individual planning that most researchers have employed.

Summary

Table 5.1 summarizes the main results of the new batch of studies. The results largely bear out those of the earlier studies reviewed in Ellis (2009). Six out of the eight studies found that strategic planning enhanced fluency. The only two studies that reported no positive effect on fluency were Hsu (2012) and Mehrang and Rahimpour (2010). The new batch of studies are more consistent in reporting an effect on complexity (only Hsu's study failing to do so) than the studies reviewed in Ellis (2009) where six out of 19 studies failed to find this effect. The new studies are also consistent in failing to find that strategic planning led to increased accuracy with only two studies reporting a benefit (Li *et al.* (2015) and Saeedi (2015) in a structured task). This again contrasts with the results of Ellis (2009) where 13 out of the 19 studies reviewed reported an effect on accuracy. Clearly further research is needed to tease out the conditions that influence when and how strategic planning assists accuracy. In Ellis (2009) there was evidence of a trade-off between complexity and accuracy (i.e. often pre-task planning benefited one but not the other). In the new studies, however, there is no consistent evidence of any such trade-off.

Table 5.1 Effects of strategic planning on CAF

Study	Fluency	Complexity	Accuracy
Ahangari and Abdi (2011)	Not investigated	Yes	No
Bui (2014)	Yes	Yes	No
Hsu (2012)	No	No	No
Li *et al.* (2015)	Yes	Yes	Yes
Mehrang and Rahimpour (2010) Structured task	No	No	No
Unstructured task	No	Yes	No
Nielson (2014)	Yes	Yes	No
Saeedi (2015) Structured task	Yes	Yes	Yes
Unstructured task	Yes	Yes	No
Wang (2014)	Yes	Yes	No

Explaining the differences in the results obtained for strategic planning is problematic because the measures of CAF vary from study to study. In this section I have attempted to identify some of the factors that appear to be important but more research is clearly needed.

Within-task Planning

Within-task planning is not in itself a task-preparedness option. However, researchers and teachers need to decide whether to pressurize learners to perform a task rapidly or to allow them to perform it in their own time. Also, importantly the opportunity for within-task planning interacts with task preparedness conditions. Table 5.2, for example, shows the combinations of strategic and within-task planning that are possible. However, although there has been continuing interest in within-task planning my suggestion in the 2009 article that the impact of these different conditions be systematically investigated has not been taken up.

Yuan and Ellis (2003) was the first study to investigate the relative effects of strategic and within-task planning. This study compared the effects of condition 4 (the control condition) with those of condition 2 (strategic planning with pressured online planning) and condition 3 (no strategic planning with unpressured online planning). The main findings were that that strategic planning benefited fluency and complexity, whereas unpressured online planning led to increases in both complexity and accuracy.

Studies that have investigated within-task planning have adopted quite different approaches. In Yuan and Ellis (2003) unpressured within-task planning was operationalized in two ways: by (1) allowing learners ample time to finish the task and (2) requiring them to produce at least four sentences for every picture in the picture story task. Ahmadian (2011, 2012) and Nakakubo (2011) operationalized it in terms of (1) only. Wang (2014), however, followed a very different approach. For the pressured online planning condition, she asked the learners to watch a video and say what was happened as they watched. In one of Nakakubo's unpressured within-task condition the learners first performed a familiarization task where they were reminded every 30 seconds to take time to plan what they were going to say. Skehan and Foster (2005) suggested that ideally

Table 5.2 Planning conditions (Ellis, 2005: 5)

	Strategic planning	Unpressured within-task planning
Condition 1	Yes	Yes
Condition 2	Yes	No
Condition 3	No	Yes
Condition 4	No	No

evidence is needed to show that online planning is taking place and suggested examining false starts, mid-clause pausing, filled pauses and reformulations. However, this idea has not as yet been acted upon.

Ahmadian (2011) compared conditions 3 and 4 in Table 5.2. For condition 3, one group received prior guidance in the form of a handout explaining the rules for English articles and the other no guidance. Learners watched a video and afterwards narrated it. In the pressured online condition, they were told to complete narrating the story in eight minutes.[4] The results largely replicated those of Yuan and Ellis. Unguided unpressured within-task planning – the same condition as in Yuan and Ellis – benefited both complexity and accuracy but had a detrimental effect on fluency. Guided unpressured within task planning resulted in greater accuracy in use of the target structure (articles) than the unguided condition but it did not have any greater effect on complexity. This study, then, adds to Yuan and Ellis by indicating that providing learners with *a priori* explicit instruction can enhance the effect of unpressured within task planning.

Wang's (2014) study also investigated condition 3 but found that it had no overall effect on enhancing accuracy. However, this study differed from Yuan and Ellis' because, as noted above, Wang's learners were required to narrate a story while they watched a video with no opportunity to preview the video. In Yuan and Ellis and in the other within-task planning studies discussed here the learners had an opportunity to look over the task materials (e.g. the picture story) before they began narrating. In fact, one of Wang's other conditions, where the learners first watched the video and then narrated it without time pressure while watching it again, corresponded more closely to Ellis and Yuan's unpressured online condition. Wang reported that in this condition both complexity and accuracy benefited and also monitoring increased, results that were in line with Yuan and Ellis' results.

Nakakubo's (2011) unpublished doctoral thesis involving high-intermediate learners of L2 Japanese investigated all four conditions in Table 5.2. A particular strength of this study is that the participants were interviewed after they had finished performing the task to gain an understanding of what uses they had made of the planning conditions while performing the task. Nakakubo reported that the pressured within-task planners spoke more fluently than the unpressured planners but there was no difference in lexical or syntactical complexity or in specific or global measures of accuracy. Interestingly, the interviews indicated that performing a task under time pressure led some learners to modify the plan they had developed during pre-task planning. In other words, pressured online planning may have negated the potential benefits gained from pre-task planning. There was evidence of a trade-off between lexical complexity and global grammatical accuracy in the whole sample of learners. The main results of this study differ from those of the other studies involving within-task planning, which Nakakubo suggested may have been because the narrative task he used was too easy so that even in the pressured condition the learners were able to access their linguistic resources without difficulty.

Ahmadian and Tavakoli (2010) investigated the combined effects of repetition and unpressured (i.e. careful) online planning in intermediate-level EFL (Iranian) learners' performance of a narrative task. There were four conditions: (1) + careful online planning/ − task repetition, (2) pressured online planning/ + task repetition, (3) careful online planning/ + task repetition and (4) pressured online planning/ − task repetition. They reported that careful online planning improved accuracy (replicating Yuan & Ellis, 2003) but that there was no additional advantage for task repetition.

Finally, one study examined the mediating role of working memory on the effects of unpressured within task planning. Ahmadian (2012) hypothesized that in the unpressured online condition learners with higher working memory (WM) would be better able to cope with the overloading on WM resulting from limited L2 proficiency when they monitored and that also they would be better able to inhibit use of their L1. Correlational analyses between working memory scores derived from an L1 version of the listening span test and CAF measures obtained from the performance of a narrative task showed no relationship between WM and complexity but statistically significant correlations with measures of accuracy and fluency. Ahmadian speculated that because working memory capacity is unrelated to risk-taking and cutting edge grammatical knowledge it cannot be expected to be involved in complexity.

These studies provide convincing evidence that online planning conditions have a powerful effect on how a task is performed. When learners have the opportunity to engage in careful online planning, accuracy is likely to be enhanced and often complexity as well. In other words, time to plan while performing a task helps learners to handle the pressure on their WM and thereby to overcome the trade-off between accuracy and complexity evident in many of the strategic planning studies. With time on task learners can access cutting edge linguistic knowledge and also carry out the monitoring that aids accuracy.

Other Forms of Preparation

Skehan (2014a) included planning, repetition and topic familiarity under the general heading of 'preparedness'. There are, of course, other options that are possible. A broad distinction can be made between form-focused options, as in Mochizuki and Ortega (2008) and Ahmadian (2011), and the readiness-type options that Skehan had in mind. This distinction raises a key issue for pedagogy, namely whether the pre-task stage of a lesson should include pre-teaching of language useful to the performance of the task (as in task-supported language teaching) or whether it should involve options that leave it up to the learner to select what language to use as advocates of pure-language teaching such as Skehan propose.

Bui's (2014) study explored the relative contributions of what he called 'internal' and 'external readiness' – options that left formulation entirely up to the learners. We have already seen that the strategic planning (external readiness) in Bui's study led to greater complexity and fluency but lower breakdown and repair fluency. Internal readiness was operationalized in terms of topic familiarity, with one group of learners performing a task with a familiar topic and another group a similar task with an unfamiliar topic. Bui reported that topic familiarity had little effect on complexity but resulted in a slightly higher level of accuracy and greater overall fluency. Of interest here is that topic familiarity benefitted the one aspect that strategic planning did not benefit – accuracy. Overall, however, topic familiarity had a lesser overall effect on task performance than strategic planning.

We have already seen in Ahmadian (2011) that the pre-task teaching of a grammatical structure led to accurate use of it when a task was performed in an unpressured within-task condition. A number of other studies have investigated the effect of *a priori* grammar teaching on the performance of a task. However, as these are examined in detail in the next chapter (Chapter 6), they will not be considered here.

Conclusion: Moving Forward

This review of recent studies that have investigated the effects of different ways of preparing learners to perform tasks has revealed the rich range of pre-task and within task options available to teachers. These options can be operationalized and combined in different ways. Repetition of a task can occur once or many times. It can be carried out immediately after the first performance of the task or later. There can be some kind of intervention to focus learners' attention on form between task performances. Repetition can also be combined with different within-task conditions. Strategic planning varies according to the time allocated and whether it is guided or unguided. It also can be combined with different within-task conditions. Strategic planning can have different effects depending on the design of task (e.g. whether it is tightly or loosely structured). Within-task planning is a continuous not dichotomous variable but the effects of varying the time for within-task planning have not yet been investigated. Within-task planning can also be unguided or guided depending on whether learners are directed to attend to specific linguistic features. Various other preparation options are available which can be combined with one or more of the main options.

In short, the construct of pre-task preparedness is a highly complex one and its effects on task performance inevitably varied – not least because, in addition to the factors listed above, they will depend on the type of task, the learners' L2 proficiency, and various individual learner factors such as working memory. It is not surprising, therefore that the results of studies investigating the various kinds of pre-task preparedness are quite mixed. For this reason, care must be taken in advancing general conclusions. Nevertheless, I will grasp the nettle and suggest that the research to date provides support for the claims below about the contributions of different types of task-preparedness to task-performance. I do so with some confidence as the results of the more recent batch of studies I have considered in this chapter broadly support those of the earlier studies that I reviewed in 2009.

The main conclusions are outlined below.

(1) Task repetition is more likely to benefit fluency and complexity than accuracy. Some kind of form-focused intervention between performances of a task may be needed for repetition to enhance accuracy.
(2) In general, strategic planning leads to increased fluency and complexity but not usually to greater accuracy. However, guided planning that draws learners' attention to the linguistic code can impact positively on accuracy. Task structure mediates the effects of strategic planning.
(3) Careful online planning when there is no time pressure results in higher levels of both complexity and accuracy but may lower fluency.
(4) There is some evidence that working memory capacity mediates the effects of these different types of preparedness but more research is needed to conclusively demonstrate this.
(5) There is growing evidence that focusing learners' attention on form can enhance the effects of all these types of preparedness on accuracy.

Skehan (2014a) doubted whether we are ready to advance a theory of task performance and suggested that researchers should aim to (1) investigate neighbouring disciplines (Skehan has himself consistently drawn on Levelt's (1989) model of L1 speaking), (2) explore how attentional and working memory limitations can account for differences between speaking in an L1 and L2 and (3) build a data base by gaining an understanding of how key variables affect L2 use. My aim in this chapter has been to focus on (3). I make no suggestions for a theory of task performance. However, I would like to propose ways for gathering a 'data base' by suggesting how future research on task preparedness might proceed.

(1) The cognitive and affective processes associated with the different kinds of preparedness activities need to be investigated. To date, researchers have focused on the product of preparedness (i.e. the

complexity, accuracy and fluency of the performance of a task). Clearly, though, we need to know what mental processes and emotional responses are activated when learners repeat a task or when they perform a task after strategic planning or during careful online planning. Some progress has been made in this direction in studies such as Pang and Skehan (2014), which have investigated what learners do when the plan strategically, but more research is needed. Constructs such as repetition, strategic planning, within-task planning and internal-readiness have only been defined notionally. To demonstrate their validity, it is necessary to obtain evidence of the cognitive operations and affective responses that potentially distinguish them. We cannot carry on just inferring what these operations and responses are from the products of their task performances.

(2) It is clearly important to pay close attention to the kind of tasks that researchers ask learners to perform. The early planning studies reviewed in Ellis (2009) involved a mixture of tasks (dialogic as well as monologic) but the studies I have considered here were mainly monologic. I have two reasons for questioning this. First, it limits extrapolation of results to language pedagogy where interactive tasks are the norm. Second, it is surely very possible that the effects of pre-paredness activities will differ for monologic and dialogic tasks. Linked to my doubts about studies of monologic tasks is the fact that they have generally been carried out in a laboratory setting, further limiting their ecological validity. Researchers also need to give thought to the specific design features of tasks. There are several studies considered in this chapter that indicate the effects of preparedness options vary with structured and unstructured tasks. Researchers should always provide explicit reasons for the particular tasks they have chosen to investigate. Some researchers of course do this but others do not.

(3) The CAF measures chosen to investigate task performance need to be theoretically justified. Again, there has been progress in this direction. In the case of fluency, Skehan and Foster (2005) distinguished three types – speech fluency, breakdown fluency and repair fluency – and studies are now including measures of each of these. Lambert *et al.* (2017a) found that multiple repetitions of a task led to staged gains in these different types of fluency. Clause final pausing decreased between the first two performances, mid-clause pausing decreased in stepwise fashion in the five performances but changes on overt self-repair were only evident in the later performances. The choice of these fluency measures enabled Lambert *et al.* to show that the task exerted a differential effect on the linguistic encoding processes associated with these different types of fluency over a series of repetitions. Suggestions have also been advanced for improving measures of complexity – see, for example, Norris and Ortega (2009) – in order to align measures

with developmental level. In particular it is the measures of accuracy that need further thought. There is, to my mind, too much reliance on global measures (e.g. error-free clauses) and not enough consideration given to developmentally sensitive measures – but see Foster and Wigglesworth's (2016) attempt in the direction. What is becoming clear is that different measures of fluency, complexity and accuracy produce different results and that it is dangerous to talk holistically about the effects of this and that kind of preparedness on task performance. I am, of course, guilty of just this in this chapter. In Chapter 7 I take a detailed look at different ways of measuring learners' performance of tasks.

(4) Finally, I would like to see more studies that investigate the effects of different kinds of preparedness in a pre-test/post-test design. We have seen that some studies have done this (e.g. Kim, 2012; Van de Gucghte *et al.*, 2016). Skehan (2014b) suggested that the three aspects of task performance that he and others have traditionally examined constitute an 'acquisitional dynamic' (2014b: 2). That is, there is an ongoing cycle involving complexity (new language), accuracy (greater control over the new language) and fluency (proceduralization of the new language). This is Skehan's attempt to suggest how these general aspects of language figure in actual L2 development. But we cannot be sure that this is what happens unless we can show that preparedness activities actually result in the acquisition of new language and/ or greater control and proceduralization. This calls for either a time series design involving the longitudinal study of tasks or for pre- and post-tests.

Finally, it is worth noting, however, that the research to date has focused on the effects of preparedness activities on production and has more or less been exclusively concerned with speaking tasks. Work is also needed on how preparedness activities influence learners' processing in non-reciprocal listening tasks (i.e. their comprehension and the level of 'noticing') and also on the acquisition that results from performing this kind of task.

Notes

(1) Skehan (2014a) noted that Wang's repetition condition differed from Bygate's (2001) because it was immediate rather than delayed. It is possible, therefore, that the timing of the task repetition affects what aspects of performance benefit with only immediate repetition fostering improvement in all three aspects. However, to the best of my knowledge there is no study that has compared the effects of immediate and delayed task repetition.

(2) The only study I am aware of that compared the effect of setting on the performance of tasks was Tavakoli and Foster (2011). This study, however, only investigated the effects of two task design variables – task structure and the inclusion of background events in narratives.

(3)   Kawauchi (2005) is the only other study I am aware of that included low-proficiency learners. He reported that strategic planning helped accuracy in the low-proficiency learners to a greater extent than in more proficient learners.

(4)   Eight minutes does seem rather long to ensure planning is pressured. There are no guidelines for deciding the length of time to allocate to the performance of a task in the pressured online planning condition. Some studies piloted the task and recorded the time learners took the complete it. Then they set a time based on this.

6 Is There a Role for Explicit Instruction in Task-based Language Teaching?

Introduction

All language instruction aims to intervene in the process of learning a second language in one way or another. Intervention can be direct or indirect. Direct instruction specifies what it is that learners are supposed to learn and sets out to help them by explicitly informing them of the learning targets and through practice activities that cater to intentional learning. Indirect instruction, in contrast, aims to set up opportunities for learners to learn without specifying the specific learning targets. In this way, it caters to incidental acquisition by exposing learners to input and engaging them in the meaningful use of the L2. Examples of direct instruction are traditional language teaching based on a structural syllabus – what Long (1981) called 'focus-on-forms' (FonFs). Examples of completely indirect instruction are immersion language programmes and content-based language teaching where the focus is entirely on meaning (FonM) and there is no attempt to induce learners' attention to form. Task-based language teaching is also primarily an indirect form of acquisition – what Long called FonF. It differs from FonM types of indirect instruction in that it incorporates various ways of attracting learners' attention to form as they are communicating.

Task-based language teaching, therefore, is best characterized as a hybrid form of language instruction. Its primary goal is to facilitate incidental language learning through the performance of tasks where learners are primarily engaged with the effort to communicate. In this respect it is clearly a type of indirect instruction. However, as we saw in Chapter 4, an essential feature of task-based language teaching (TBLT) is 'focus on form' where learners' attention is attracted to form either before they perform a task (as with the kinds of task-preparation activities considered in Chapter 5) or by means of pre-emptive and reactive strategies while the task is being performed. Where the focus on form is implicit in nature (i.e. it occurs spontaneously and unobtrusively) it can be seen as indirect. But there is also the possibility for more explicit interventions where learners' attention is focused on pre-determined linguistic forms in quite obtrusive ways. When this happens TBLT incorporates aspects of direct language instruction.

An issue of considerable debate among advocates of TBLT is the extent to which intervention should be entirely of the implicit kind or whether more explicit types of intervention are also possible, and, if the latter, exactly what forms these explicit interventions can legitimately take. As we saw in Chapter 4, Long initially saw focus-on-form as taking place implicitly but later acknowledged that more explicit types of corrective feedback are useful and indeed sometimes needed. However, he continues to maintain that focus-on-form must be reactive in nature – that is, it should occur while a task is being performed. Skehan (1998), however, sees task preparation activities – in particular strategic planning – as providing opportunities for learners to focus on form. Skehan, though, does not envisage explicit instruction playing a role.[1] He sees attention to form arising naturally and incidentally as learners perform a task with the learner-generated attention to form that occurs during strategic planning facilitating online performance. In contrast, some advocates (e.g. Shehadeh, 2005) propose – especially for foreign language teaching contexts – that explicit instruction directed at specific target features is desirable before learners perform a task. Others (e.g. Samuda, 2001) see value in explicit instruction occurring in the middle of a task if more implicit strategies have failed to elicit use of a target feature.

In this chapter I will examine research that has investigated the effects of explicit instruction in the pre-task stage of a lesson involving tasks.[2] I will consider both the effect that explicit instruction has on the performance of tasks and on acquisition of target structures. I will also consider studies that have embedded explicit instruction into the performance of a task. Finally, I will look at studies that have investigated the effects of delaying explicit instruction until after the completion of a task. First, though, I will briefly consider what is meant by 'explicit instruction'.

Explicit Instruction

The term 'explicit instruction' refers to attempts to intervene directly in the process of acquisition. It can take a number of forms including the kind of inductive presentation of a target feature through examples that many teacher educators (e.g. Scrivener, 2005) recommend. In this chapter, however, I am principally concerned with deductive forms of explicit instruction, in particular instruction that includes the provision of meta-linguistic information about a target language feature.

A key pedagogic issue is how detailed grammatical explanation needs to be. By and large teacher educators (e.g. Swan, 1994; Ur, 1996) prefer simplified, pedagogic descriptions involving limited use of metalanguage rather than full linguistic descriptions. A different view is taken by Lantolf and Thorne (2006). They draw on Systemic-Theoretical Instruction (Galperin, 1989) to argue that technical descriptions that reflect 'scientific concepts' are essential for ensuring that learners develop a full understanding of a target feature. Whether deductive explicit instruction should utilize simple, pedagogical accounts or full linguistic accounts is clearly and important issue. However, I know of no research that has compared the effectiveness of these two types of metalinguistic explanation. All the studies I will now consider have followed normal pedagogic practice in utilizing simplified pedagogic descriptions. It would, however, be interesting to investigate what effect the kind of explanations Lantolf and Thorne favour have on the performance of a task and the acquisition that results from it.

Explicit Instruction in the Pre-task Phase

As I noted in Chapter 1, the pedagogic literature (e.g. Bohlke, 2014; Scrivener, 2005) makes a distinction between accuracy work and fluency work. In accuracy work, explicit instruction is seen as necessary. In fluency work, however, some teacher educators argue that no attempt should be made to direct learners' attention to form through explicit instruction. They claim that if the aim is to promote fluency, communication should be unfettered. Some advocates of TBLT very clearly reject explicit instruction in the pre-task stage of a task-based lesson. Willis and Willis (2007), for example commented:

> We should not allow form-focused activities to detract from a focus on meaning. If we have spent time presenting and practising specific forms immediately before introducing a task, then it is likely that the learners will be concerned to display the target forms rather than concentrate on getting the message across. The task is likely to become a 'further practice' of form activity. (2007: 113)

Somewhat surprisingly, however, there has been very little research that has investigated the effects of *a priori* explicit instruction on either the performance of a task or on learning. Research is needed to establish whether explicit instruction followed by a task leads to acquisition of the target feature(s) and also whether the explicit instruction impacts on how the task is performed. Does it just result in 'further practice' of the target feature as Willis and Willis suggest? I will first consider the effect that explicit instruction has on how learners perform a task and then on whether explicit instruction preceding a task results in more effective learning than performing the task without such instruction.

What effect does explicit instruction have on the performance of a task?

There are two ways of answering this question. We could simply ask whether prior explicit instruction directed at a target feature facilitates the use of that feature when the task is performed. We can also consider whether explicit instruction impacts on the global complexity, accuracy and fluency of learners' production. In both cases, we will need to look at studies that have made use of focused tasks (i.e. tasks specifically designed to elicit some predetermined feature – see Chapter 1).

There have been a number of studies that have investigated whether focused tasks are successful in eliciting the use of the target structure when there is no explicit presentation of the structure. These studies have reported mixed results. In some studies (e.g. Doughty & Varela, 1998; Mackey, 1999) the focused tasks elicited both attempted and target-like use of the targeted features. Samuda (2001), however, found that learners avoided using epistemic modal verbs when performing a task designed to create a semantic space for their use. Only after an explicit presentation of the modal verbs later in the lesson did the students begin to start trying to use them. Boston (2010) reported that the focused task he used – an opinion-gap narrative task – did not result in attempted use of the target structure (passive voice).[3] These failures reflect the difficulty of ensuring that focused tasks – by themselves – make the use of the targeted structures 'essential' as opposed to just 'useful' or 'natural' (Loschky & Bley-Vroman, 1993; see Chapter 1). If the target structure lies well beyond the learners' developmental stage, avoidance is likely.

Other studies have investigated whether providing prior explicit instruction encourages learners to produce the target features when they subsequently perform a task. De la Fuente (2006) investigated a lesson where the students received explicit explanation of 15 Spanish words, engaged in controlled practice exercises, and then performed a free meaning-based production task where they were reminded to use the target words. She reported that, in general, this task-supported instruction did not result in the use of the target words in the free-production stage of the lesson and suggested that this was probably because the task did not make the use of the words essential. Kowal and Swain (1997) reported a study where learners performed a dictogloss task after prior explanation of the target structure. The task resulted in minimal use of the target structure, leading Kowal and Swain to conclude that 'the dictogloss approach might be better suited to promoting syntactic processing skills in general than as a means for drawing attention to a particular grammar form' (1997: 300). The research to date is limited but it is clear that focused tasks are often not successful in eliciting use of the target even when explicit instruction has been provided.

I know of very few studies that have compared the performance of a task with and without *a priori* explicit instruction in terms of use of the target structure. In Mochizuki and Ortega (2008) there were three treatment conditions – a no-planning condition, an unguided planning condition and the condition of greatest interest here – a guided planning condition, where the participants (first-year high school students in Japan) were given a handout about English relative clauses, listened to a pre-recording of the task performance, and then had five minutes to plan before they performed the task. The performance of the task, which was designed to create opportunities for use of relative clauses, was analysed in terms of amount of relative clause use and the quality of relative clause use. The guided planning group produced more than twice as many relative clauses as the other two groups and also their relative clauses were more target-like. This study then suggests that providing explicit instruction is beneficial in prompting learners to use the target structure and in using it accurately.

The second study – Li *et al.* (forthcoming) – produced somewhat different results. In this study low-proficiency Chinese high school students performed two dictogloss tasks. The students listened to the teacher read each narrative three times. On the second occasion the learners listened and read as the teacher displayed the stories on power point one or two sentences at a time along with vocabulary annotations. The students then worked in pairs to reproduce the stories. Finally, each pair reported the stories to the whole class. One group of students received explicit instruction before performing the task. This consisted of a 15-minute explanation of the meaning, form and use of the target structure (past passive verbs) followed by a short grammaticality judgement exercise. Another group just performed the task. The group that received the explicit instruction made more attempts at producing the target structure when they performed the task than the task-only group but there was no difference in the two groups' accurate use of passive verbs, which in both cases was very low.

Both of these studies also investigated whether explicit instruction had any effect on the general quality of the learners' production when they performed the tasks. Mochizuki and Ortega compared the fluency and complexity of the two groups' speech reporting that there was no difference. In other words, in this study the explicit instruction had no effect on the quality of the learners' production. Li *et al.*, however, did find that the explicit instruction in their study impacted negatively on the overall performance of the tasks. The task-only group produced more complex, accurate and fluent speech than the group that received explicit instruction.

These two studies offer a number of interesting findings. The first is that the focused tasks were successful in eliciting attempted use of the target structures in the task-only condition even though both structures are complex and typically late acquired. One reason for this success was the nature of the tasks. In both studies, the tasks provided learners with input containing exemplars of the target structure. In Mochizuki and Ortega both groups listened to a pre-recorded description of the picture story. In Li *et al.* they heard the teacher reading the narrative three times and also had the opportunity to read the sentences presented by power point. Perhaps, then, structure-based production tasks can work well if input containing the target structure is included in their design. Second, explicit instruction does increase learners' use of the target structures. This is not surprising. It is a key assumption of task-supported language teaching. If learners are aware of the need to use a specific structure they will try to do so when they perform a task. Third, explicit instruction does not necessarily result in greater accuracy of the target structure. It did in Mochizuki and Ortega but it did not in Li *et al.*'s study. Fourth, explicit instruction may or may not impact on learners' overall production when they perform the task. In Mochizuki and Ortega it had no effect on overall complexity and fluency but in Li *et al.* it did, with the task only group producing language that was more complex, accurate and fluent. This is the crucial issue. We have seen that some educators (e.g. Willis & Willis, 2007) argue against explicit instruction if the aim is to encourage communicative fluency. Li *et al.*'s study lends some support to this position. When the aim is to facilitate the development of general proficiency (i.e. complex, accurate and fluent L2 use) it might be best to avoid pre-task explicit instruction and opt for a task-based approach. However, if the aim is to elicit use of a specific target structure, then pre-task explicit instruction may help although it may not result in greater accuracy of the target structure.

There are a number of explanations for the different results of these two studies. The explicit instruction in Mochizuki and Ortega's study was delivered by means of a handout whereas in Li *et al.* it was teacher-led, lasted 15 minutes, and was followed by a practice exercise. The learners in the explicit instruction group in this study may have focused more on producing the target structure when they performed the tasks with consequential effects on global aspects of production. Mochizuki and Ortega also allocated five minutes of individual planning time which, as research has shown (see Chapter 5), can benefit complexity and fluency. The target structures also differed – relative clauses involve subordination, whereas passive verbs are morphological. There was also a difference in the proficiency levels of the learners – those in Mochizuki and Ortega were higher. Clearly, more research is needed to tease out what factors influence the impact that explicit instruction can have on task performance.

What effect does explicit instruction have on acquisition?

Even if learners are successful in producing the target structure accurately when they perform the task, they may not acquire it. Thus, it is important to investigate whether *a priori* explicit instruction followed by a task results in acquisition. There is now ample evidence that explicit instruction is effective in enabling learners to use targeted features more accurately in post-tests. A key finding of Norris and Ortega's (2000) meta-analysis of form-focused instruction studies was that explicit instruction is more effective than implicit instruction:

> The average observed effect for explicit treatments ($d = 1.13$) differed by more than half a standard deviation unit from the average effect for implicit treatments ($d = 0.54$, and 95% confidence intervals around these two observed effect sizes did not overlap, indicating a trustworthy observed difference.

Similar findings emerged from by Spada and Tomita's (2010) meta-analysis. However, not all the explicit treatments in the studies included in these meta-analyses were task-based and also many of the studies did not examine the effects of the instruction on spontaneous free production and thus did not show whether the explicit instruction resulted in changes in the learners' implicit/procedural knowledge.

The issue that concerns us here is whether explicit instruction followed by the performance of a task is *more* effective in enabling learners to acquire a linguistic feature than just performing the task by itself. Theoretical perspectives offer differ predictions. According to a dual memory system (N. Ellis, 1994; R. Ellis, 1994; Reber & Squire, 1998), explicit instruction can help learners develop an initial conscious representation of a linguistic feature but implicit learning processes automatically take over, catering to the gradual development of implicit knowledge. Also, explicit instruction may be unnecessary as learners appear to automatically form their own initial explicit representation without assistance (see Morgan-Short *et al.*, 2014, 2015). In contrast, a single or integrated model of memory (Cleermans & Jimenez, 2002; Shanks, 2005) assigns greater importance to explicit instruction. According to this model, declarative (explicit) knowledge is proceduralized through practice. As DeKeyser (1998) put it, 'proceduralization is achieved by engaging in the target behaviour – or procedure – while temporarily leaning on declarative crutches' (1998: 49). Thus, whereas the dual model supports a task-based approach where explicit training is not needed, the single, integrated model points do the advantage of a task-supported approach that includes *a priori* explicit instruction.[4]

Support for the dual memory system comes from a psychological study by Sanchez and Reber (2013). They investigated 'whether explicit knowledge information contributes directly to learning to perform or whether it reflects concomitant knowledge in a separate representational system that is epiphenomenal to task performance' (Sanchez & Reber, 2013: 3). This is the key issue regarding the claims of the dual model vs the single-integrated model. Using an implicit perceptual-motor sequence learning task, Sanchez and Reber compared a group that received explicit pre-training instruction with a group that simply performed the perceptual learning task. Both groups had no explicit knowledge of the sequence at the beginning of the study. The key finding was that all the participants developed robust explicit knowledge irrespective of whether or not they received explicit training and that the training did not lead to better performance or better learning. Sanchez and Reber concluded that explicit knowledge can play a role in guiding performance initially but that it is not necessary as implicit learning takes place separately and automatically during practice.

There are plenty of language studies that have compared implicit and explicit language instruction but these studies typically involved other form-focused instruction options, such as within-task explicit instruction in the form of 'exercises' (as in Andringa *et al.*, 2011), integrated explicit instruction (as in Spada *et al.*, 2014), corrective feedback while performing a task (Lyster, 2004; Sanz & Morgan-Short, 2004) or explicit instruction on completion of a task (Murunoi, 2000) and/or they did not involve tasks as I have defined 'task' in this book. To the best of my knowledge there are only three studies that have directly addressed the effect of prior explicit instruction in conjunction with a task on the acquisition of implicit L2 knowledge of the target feature.

Williams and Evans (1998) compared groups of university ESL learners who were exposed to an input flood providing frequent exposure to the target structures (participial adjectives of emotive verbs and passive construction) with another group that received the same input preceded by explicit instruction. There was also a control group that completed just the pre- and post-tests. Both groups outperformed the control group in use of the passive on both a sentence-completion and a written narrative task but there were no differences between the two experimental groups. In other words, *a priori* explicit instruction conferred no advantage. However, the target structure in this study was not entirely 'new' as the learners already had some explicit knowledge of passives at the start of the study. Also, the study only investigated the effects of explicit instruction followed by input exposure – there was no production task.

In Li *et al.* (2016), the effects of performing a task with and without prior explicit instruction on learners' acquisition of passive verbs were compared. In this study, the learners had no or very little explicit knowledge of the target structure at the start of the study. The explicit instruction and the tasks were the same as in Li *et al.* (forthcoming) – see previous section in this chapter. Acquisition was measured by means of a grammaticality judgment test (GJT) and an oral elicited imitation test (EIT), designed to provide measures of explicit and implicit knowledge respectively as claimed by R. Ellis (2005c). The control group just completed the pre-test, immediate post-test and delayed post-test. On the GJT, the group that received explicit instruction and then performed the dictogloss tasks scored significantly higher than the control group on both post-tests with large effect sizes ($d = 1.11$ and 1.21). The differences in GJT scores between the group that just performed the task and the control group were not statistically significant and the effect sizes notably smaller ($d = 0.58$ and 0.63). The explicit instruction + task group also outperformed the task-only group on both post-tests ($d = 63$ and 0.60), although the differences only approached statistical significance ($p = 0.06$ and $p = 0.09$). On the EIT, there was very limited improvement for either experimental group with none of the comparisons reaching statistical significance. This study, then, indicates that just performing the task had minimal effects on both explicit and implicit knowledge. Performing the task following explicit instruction resulted in the development of explicit knowledge but not implicit knowledge. In other words, although the task-supported instruction helped the development of explicit knowledge, it was no more effective than the task-based instruction in developing implicit knowledge. Li *et al.* suggested that the learners' failure to acquire implicit knowledge of past-passive verbs may have been because they were not developmentally ready for this late-acquired structure and/or because the tasks provided insufficient practice opportunities. This study is important because it examined the effects of task-based and task-supported instruction[5] on the acquisition of a new structure.

The third study (Shintani, 2018) is interesting because it also included a group that only received explicit instruction (i.e. did not perform any task). In this study, two groups of Japanese university students (one receiving explicit instruction and the other not) performed four oral story reconstruction tasks after listening to an audio narration of the stories. Another group just received the explicit instruction and the control group just completed the pre-test and a delayed post-test. The target structure was hypothetical conditionals. The explicit instruction took the form of a handout explaining the target structure, which the learners read before they performed each task but could not refer to as they performed the tasks. The effects of the instruction were measured by means of an error correction test (EC test), measuring explicit knowledge, and a story reconstruction test (SR test) of the same type as the treatment tasks, which Shintani suggested provided a measure of proceduralized production.[6] The EC scores of all three experimental groups improved significantly from pre- to post-test, with the explicit instruction + task group improving the most. Only this group outperformed the control group. The results for the SR test were similar. Again, all three groups improved in oral production accuracy but only the group performing the tasks after receiving explicit instruction differed significantly from the control group. This study, then, indicates that just providing explicit instruction by itself or performing tasks without any explicit instruction can help the development of explicit knowledge and, to a lesser extent, oral production accuracy. However, it was the task-supported condition (i.e. explicit instruction + tasks) that proved the most effective.

To understand what these studies tell us about the relative merits of task-based and task-supported language instruction it is necessary to take account of the differences in their design and procedures. The studies differ in the age and context of their participants, the target structures, the extent to which the participants had prior knowledge of the target structures, how the explicit instruction was provided, the kinds of tasks they experienced, the length of the instruction and how acquisition was measured. Any conclusions that follow must necessarily be tentative.

Regarding the effects on explicit knowledge, the results of the studies suggest the following:

(1) Explicit instruction by itself can result in gains in explicit knowledge as in Shintani's study.
(2) The task-based condition (where learners just perform the tasks) can result in gains in explicit knowledge but only if learners already have some existing knowledge of the target structure as in Williams and Evans' and in Shintani's studies. Performing tasks by themselves may result in insignificant gains in explicit knowledge if learners have no pre-existing knowledge as in Li *et al.*'s study.
(3) The task-supported condition (where learners receive explicit instruction and then perform the tasks) leads to gains in explicit knowledge. All three studies report this. They also indicate that this condition leads to greater gains in explicit knowledge than the task-only condition and, in Shintani's study, greater gains than the explicit instruction alone condition.

These findings are unsurprising as they replicate the results of meta-analyses (Norris & Ortega, 2000; Spada & Tomita, 2010). Instruction involving the explicit presentation of metalinguistic knowledge results in learners' ability to use what they learned in tests likely to measure explicit knowledge.

Regarding the effects on implicit/proceduralized knowledge, the studies suggest the following:

(1) Explicit instruction by itself can result in gains in accuracy in guided oral production if learners have some prior knowledge of the target structure (as in Shintani's study).
(2) Both task-based and task-supported instruction can help the development of implicit/proceduralized knowledge if the learners have some prior explicit knowledge as in Shintani's and Williams and Evans' studies.
(3) However, neither task-based nor task-supported instruction lead to implicit knowledge if learners have no prior explicit knowledge of the target structure as in Li *et al.*'s study.
(4) Task-supported instruction may be more effective than task-based instruction in advancing learners' procedural knowledge of the target

structure if the instruction is short-term (Shintani) but if it is long-term when learners have ample exposure to the target structure, task-based instruction may be equally effective (Williams & Evans).

What may be crucial, then, regarding the effectiveness of task-based instruction relative to task-supported instruction for the development of implicit/proceduralized knowledge is whether the learners have some prior knowledge of the target structure, their readiness to acquire it, and also the extent to which they are exposed to the target structure. Clearly, though, these tentative findings need to be tested in further research.

Explicit Instruction in the Main-task Phase

The Transfer Appropriate Processing (TAP) Hypothesis provides a theoretical justification for integrating explicit instruction in the performance of task rather than providing it before the task. TAP claims 'that we can use what we have learned if the cognitive processes that are active during learning are similar to those that are active during retrieval' (Lightbown, 2008: 27). It would follow that explicit instruction provided while learners are performing a task may help them to utilize this information in the performance of the task more effectively than if it is provided prior to the task and, also, that it would be more effective in developing implicit/proceduralized knowledge. There are, however, few studies that have investigated this.

In Samuda (2001), the task-based lesson began by performing a focused task designed to provide learners with communicative opportunities for using and learning epistemic modals (e.g. *might* and *must*). The learners were told the contents of a mystery person's pocket and were asked to work together in groups, completing a table speculating about the person's possible identity. However, the students failed to use the target modal forms in this stage of the lesson. In the following class discussion, the teacher attempted to shift the students' focus from meaning to form by interweaving the target forms into the interaction by means of recasts. However, the students still failed to use the target structures. The teacher then resorted to explicit explanation – for example:

> When you when you're NOT 100% certain, you can use must. OK? Not he *is* a business man but he *must* be a businessman.

The students now began to use the target forms and informal tests administered at the end of the lesson indicated gains in their procedural knowledge of the target structure. This study, then, points to the problems of using focused tasks referred to above – they may not result in attempted use of the target task. It also suggests that intervening in the performance of the task with explicit instruction can lead to its use and may assist acquisition. However, this study did not compare *a priori* and embedded explicit instruction.

Spada and Lightbown (2008) contrasted isolated and integrated form-focused instruction. They defined isolated instruction as instruction where 'the focus on language form is separated from the communicative or content-based activity' (2008: 186) and integrated instruction as instruction 'where ... the learners' attention is drawn to language form during communicative or content-based instruction' (2008: 186). In integrated instruction 'feedback or brief explanations are offered to help students express meaning more effectively or more accurately within the communicative interaction' (2008: 187). In some ways integrated instruction is analogous to Long's 'focus on form', especially as this has been defined in his later work (see Chapter 4).

In Spada et al.'s (2014) study, both types of instruction drew on the same topics and themes (e.g. medical practices, famous places) and both involved providing learners with explicit information about the target structure (English passive). In the isolated instruction, the target structure was first explained to the learners who then engaged in communicative/content-based activities without any further explicit focus on the passive. In the integrated instruction, a specific theme was first introduced focusing purely on content. Then the learners performed the communicative activities during which the teacher provided brief interventions by means of quick explanations and corrective feedback. Learning was assessed by means of a written error-correction test and a picture-cued oral production task. Both types of instruction proved effective and there were no significant group differences. However, the group receiving the isolated instruction gained higher scores for passive on the error-correction test, whereas the integrated instruction group did better on the oral production task. The researchers suggested that the isolated instruction benefited the development of explicit knowledge, whereas the integrated instruction benefited implicit/proceduralized knowledge.

These two studies provide evidence to suggest that when explicit instruction (especially when combined with corrective feedback) is integrated into the performance of a task it can have a beneficial effect on learners' procedural use of the target structure as they perform the task (Samuda) and also on acquisition (both studies). Shintani's study (2018) considered in the previous section of this chapter can also be re-interpreted as providing further support for the positive effect of integrated instruction on acquisition as her learners studied the metalinguistic handout before starting each task (i.e. the explicit instruction was embedded into the series of four tasks they completed). Nevertheless, it is not possible to conclude that integrated instruction is superior to isolated form-focused instruction. Shintani's study was not a comparative study. Spada et al.'s study found no statistically significant differences in the effects of the two types of instruction. Also, as Spada and Lightbown (2008) pointed out there are moderating factors (e.g. learners' language aptitude and their developmental level) that might affect the relative effectiveness of the two types of instruction. One can, however, point to one clear advantage of integrated explicit instruction – it only needs to be provided if learners fail to use the target structure accurately as they perform a task.

Explicit Instruction in the Post-task Phase

In Chapter 1 I referred briefly to Johnson's (1982) 'deep-end strategy'. This entails learners first performing a task without any explicit instruction in either the pre-task or main task phase of a lesson and then, when the task, is over, explicitly teaching and practising just those grammatical structures that the learners either failed to use or used incorrectly. I also noted earlier in this chapter that some teacher educators recommend that if the purpose of a task is to develop fluency, explicit focus on linguistic form should be delayed until the task is completed.

There is, however, general acceptance by advocates of task-based teaching that explicit instruction is appropriate in the post-task stage of a lesson. In Willis' (1996) task-based framework, for example, it is only in the final stage of a lesson where specific language features from the task can be highlighted and worked on.

In Ellis (2003; Chap. 8) I considered various options for the post-task stage including explicit instruction. However, there has been little research that has investigated what effect explicit instruction in the post-task stage has on acquisition. I will consider two lines of enquiry – one investigating learners self-transcribing their performance of a task and the other delayed corrective feedback. I know of no study that has investigated what effect metalinguistic explanation of grammatical features in the post-task stage has on acquisition.

Learner self-transcribing

One way of inductively drawing learners' attention to linguistic form is by audio recording learners' performance of a task and then in the post-task stage asking them to listen to the recording, transcribe extracts of it, and then edit it (Lynch, 2001). The teacher then reformulates the edited transcripts and asks the learners to compare their own edited transcript with the teacher's reformulated version. Lynch reported that the learners made a number of changes when they edited their transcripts, most of which involved accurate corrections of linguistic form. Because the learners undertook the transcriptions collaboratively, there were plentiful instances of language-related episodes.

A number of studies have followed up on Lynch's self-transcribing procedure. Lynch (2005) reported a small-scale study where he compared the relative effects of learners' self-transcribing and teacher initiated feedback (i.e. the teacher transcribed and corrected the extracts) on learners' long-term progress in spoken English. He reported that the self-transcribing procedure resulted in higher levels of oral accuracy in a subsequent perfor-mance of the same task. An obvious limitation of self-transcribing, how-ever, is that learners will only be able to correct those errors that they become aware of and have knowledge of. That is, they will be able to cor-rect 'mistakes' resulting from non-automatized implicit/procedural knowl-edge but not 'errors' where they lack even explicit knowledge of the correct forms. Valdebento (2015) found that the learners he investigated only attended to 25% of the total errors they made when transcribing a three minutes' talk. Mennim (2012), however, showed that relatively advanced-level Japanese learners engaged in 'extensive deliberation' (2012: 60) when working collaboratively to notice problems in their transcriptions of an oral presentation. He argued that this revealed depth in cognitive process-ing that is likely to facilitate language development.

Delayed corrective feedback

It is possible to delay corrective feedback (CF) until the task is com-pleted – as teacher guides accompanying course textbooks typically pro-pose (Hedge, 2000). Delayed CF – in contrast to immediate feedback that is provided online as the task is performed – is inevitably very explicit. Some second language acquisition (SLA) theories (e.g. Long's (1983, 1996) Interaction Hypothesis) and the Transfer Appropriate Processing Hypothesis point to the advantage of immediate CF in activating those cognitive mechanisms responsible for the development of implicit knowl-edge. These theories suggest that delayed feedback may only aid the devel-opment of explicit knowledge. In contrast, theories from cognitive psychology (see Quinn, 2014) suggest that delayed CF may be preferable because it removes the need for concurrent attention to both meaning and form and because it can foster the processes of retrieval and reconsolida-tion in the development of both declarative and procedural memories.

Several studies have investigated the relative effects of immediate and delayed CF. In a descriptive study, Rolin-Ianzati (2010) identified two dif-ferent approaches corresponding to the input-providing and output-prompting types of feedback found in immediate CF (see Chapter 4). In one approach the teacher provided the corrections, whereas in the other the teacher elicited corrections from the students. Drawing on sociocul-tural theory, Rolin-Ianzati suggested that eliciting correction may be more effective but she did not investigate if this was the case. Quinn (2014) conducted a laboratory-based study involving 90 intermediate-level adult ESL learners who were randomly assigned to immediate, delayed and no CF conditions. The grammatical target was English passive constructions. In a pre-test, immediate post-test, delayed-post-test design involving an aural grammaticality judgement test, an oral written error correction test and a written error-correction test, the learners completed three commu-nicative tasks. The immediate and delayed feedback consisted of a prompt that pushed the learners to self-correct followed by a recast if needed. There were statistically significant improvements resulting from both feedback conditions but there were no statistically significant differences between the experimental and control conditions. In other words, not only was the timing of the feedback of no significance but, in this study, feedback itself conferred no learning advantage. Li *et al.* (2016) also compared the effects of immediate and delayed CF involving prompts followed by recasts using the same participants and design as in Li *et al.* (2016) mentioned earlier in this chapter. Both types of CF resulted in gains in GJT scores with some advantage for the immediate over the delayed feedback. No effect for either type of CF was found on the elicited imitation test, however. In other words, this study only found an effect for CF on learners' explicit/declarative knowledge. The slight advantage found for immediate feedback was explained in terms of the learners using the feedback progressively in the production of new past passive sentences as they performed the tasks.

These studies do not allow any clear conclusion to be reached about the relative effects of immediate and delayed CF. The difference in the results reported by Quinn and Li *et al.* may be due any number of factors. The studies point to the need for further research, including research that investigates the combined effect of immediate and delayed CF.

Conclusion

In this chapter I have reviewed research that has addressed different ways in which direct instruction can be included in a lesson built around a task. I have examined the potential contributions of direct instruction in the pre-task stage, the main-task stage and the post-task stage of a lesson. The place of explicit instruction in task-based teaching continues to be an issue of controversy both among educationalists and SLA researchers. Whereas some educationalists (e.g. Willis) and researchers (e.g. Long) reject explicit instruction in the pre-task of a lesson and favour a task-based approach, other educationalists (Shehadeh) and researchers (DeKeyser) consider pre-task explicit instruction in a task supported approach to be beneficial. It is not clear to me that the relative advantages of these two approaches can be decided purely on theoretical grounds. There is a need for empirical research that compares them both in terms of task performance and L2 acquisition.

The benefits of explicit instruction in the main-task phase are less contentious. Advocates of both task-based and task-supported instruction recognize that explicit instruction – in the form of metalinguistic explanation and explicit types of corrective feedback – is potentially helpful. But there is still a need to compare the relative effectiveness of explicit instruction in the pre-task stage (as in isolated instruction) and in the main-task stage (as in integrated instruction). To date few studies have attempted this.

The use of form-focused instruction in the post-task stage is uncontroversial as it cannot interfere with how a task is performed – one of the potential problems with pre-task explicit instruction in particular. But the relative effects of explicit instruction in the pre-task and post-task stages have not – to the best of my knowledge – been investigated.

It is perhaps disappointing to conclude a chapter whose purpose is to examine the research that has investigated the impact of explicit instruction in the different stages of a task-based lesson by just pointing out the need for such research. It would be preferable to be able to point to clear findings. However, at the moment, this is not possible. There are conflicting findings in studies that have investigated explicit instruction in all stages of a lesson. In this respect, however, the research I have reviewed is not so different from instructed second language acquisition research in general. The problem lies in the plethora of factors involved in the design of studies and the attendant difficulty of generalising from them. However, the studies have raised questions that are of real importance for TBLT. On balance they show that explicit instruction has a place in TBLT, including in the pre-task stage. Their real value, though, lies in showing the way forward. One way of resolving some of the conflicting findings might be to undertake exact and partial replications of some of the key studies mentioned in this chapter.[7]

Notes

(1) Skehan (1996), however, includes in his list of pre-task options 'an approach that simply sets up the relevant language for a task, in which case it is essentially dealing with some form of pre-teaching, whether explicit or implicit' (1996: 54). In effect, this blurs the distinction between task-based and task-supported instruction. In subsequent publications, however, Skehan makes no mention of the explicit pre-teaching of target language and appears to disfavour it.

(2) There is wide agreement among advocates of TBLT that explicit instruction – including quite traditional types – can have a place in the post-task stage of a lesson. This is uncontroversial because – by definition – it cannot have any impact on how the task is performed. I consider post-task activities in Chapter 11.

(3) In Boston's (2010) study there was no *a priori* explicit instruction but Boston did attempt to prime the use of the passive voice by providing exemplars of it before the learners performed the task.

(4) There is, however, another possibility; namely that explicit instruction can be provided while a task is being performed in what Spada and Lightbown (2008) called 'integrated' (as opposed to 'isolated') instruction. This is considered later in the chapter.

(5) In this chapter, I have opted for a narrow definition of task-supported instruction, namely one that consists of *a priori* explicit instruction followed by the performance of a task. Samuda and Bygate (2009) define task-supported instruction much more broadly – as any instruction where 'tasks themselves are not the central unit of activity within the overall programme' (2009: 213). In effect, my definition of task-supported instruction corresponds to what Samuda and Bygate call 'TSLT at the level of instructional sequence' as in presentation–practice–production (PPP).

(6) The tasks in Shintani (2018) did not involve totally free production. They required learners to produce the target structure by giving them key words and sentence prompts. It could be argued, therefore, that these were not tasks as defined by Ellis and Shintani (2014). However, they clearly did involve proceduralized production as they were oral.

(7) See Porte (2012) for information about conducting replication studies along with examples of such studies.

7 Measuring Second Language Learners' Oral Performance of Tasks

Introduction

In general, task-based researchers have not investigated the effect that performing tasks has on second language (L2) acquisition. Instead they have examined how task design features (e.g. a task with a tight or loose information structure) or implementation options (e.g. pre-task planning) impact on the way in which a task is performed. Researchers then theorize how task *performance* contributes to *acquisition* by, for example, suggesting that tasks that induce a focus-on-form (Long, 1991) promote the processes involved in acquisition (e.g. 'noticing'). Crucial to this line of research, then, is how the performance of tasks is measured and analysed. I shall consider four broad approaches to investigating task-based performance in this chapter.[1]

Early research drew on Long's (1983) Interaction Hypothesis to examine the negotiation of meaning that occurs when communication problems arise and attempts are made to resolve them. This research was premised on the claim that negotiation of meaning aids acquisition by helping to make input comprehensible, providing learners with feedback on their production, and pushing them to produce output that is more target-like (Pica, 1992). The continuation of this line of research has drawn on what Gass and Mackey (2007) call the Interaction Approach, which explores how interaction helps learners to connect the external processes arising from the performance of task to the internal processes involved in acquisition. It has also been extended to include the negotiation of form as the structure of negotiation sequences is the same when negotiation is focused solely on linguistic form (i.e. there is no linguistic breakdown). Discourse analysis has afforded a variety of measures to capture the discourse moves found in negotiation sequences.

An alternative approach to investigating dialogic tasks draws on sociocultural theory (SCT). SCT, like the Interaction Approach, views language learning as dialogically based. However, whereas the Interaction

Approach considers that interaction prompts the internal mechanisms responsible for learning, SCT sees acquisition occurring *within* interaction when learners act collaboratively to produce linguistic forms that they are not capable of producing independently. A key construct here is 'languaging' (Swain, 2006), talk about language, which serves to transform 'thinking' into 'an artefactual form' and thereby facilitates reflection on the form. 'Languaging' is investigated by identifying the 'language-related episodes' (LREs) that occur when a task is performed. Swain (1998) defines an LRE as 'any part of a dialogue in which students talk about the language they are producing, question their language use, or other- or self-correct' (1998: 70).[2] LREs include negotiation sequences but also other sequences where a linguistic difficulty is pre-empted – for example, when a learner seeks help about a vocabulary item or a grammatical structure.

The third approach focuses on individual learners' production rather than interactional sequences. It has been used to investigate what affect both dialogic and monologic tasks have on the complexity, accuracy and fluency (CAF) of learners' output. This approach is psycholinguistic in orientation. For example, Housen and Kuiken (2009) drew on Bialystok and Sharwood-Smith's (1985) distinction between 'representation' and 'control' to suggest that complexity and accuracy relate to L2 knowledge representation and fluency to the control that learners have over their knowledge. Fundamental to this approach is the assumption that the three aspects of production constitute indicators of learners' language proficiency. Researchers (e.g. Skehan, 1998b) have drawn on models of working memory to suggest that learners will struggle to address all three aspects of language at the same time and so will prioritize one aspect over another (for example complexity over accuracy). Skehan proposes varying the design of tasks and how they are implemented to induce a focus on different aspects of language at different times so as to ensure the development of a balanced proficiency in the long run. Considerable effort has been invested in identifying a range of measures of CAF (Ellis & Barkhuizen, 2003; Housen *et al.*, 2012b).

The fourth approach I will consider has drawn on educational research on engagement – in particular Maehr's (1984) theory of personal investment. Maehr's theory is a broad one as it acknowledges both external factors (e.g. the design of a task and how it is implemented) and internal factors (e.g. learners' beliefs, abilities, prior learning experiences and subjective appraisal of a task) that influence personal investment. It points to the importance of learners' motivation while performing a task and thus introduces a psychological element that is largely missing from research based on the other three approaches. Drawing on Maehr's theory, Philp and Duchesne (2016) defined engagement as 'a state of heightened attention and involvement, in which participation is reflected not only in the cognitive dimension, but in social, behavioural, and affective dimensions

Table 7.1 Four approaches to investigating task performance

Approach	Theoretical background	Key constructs
Interaction Approach	Tasks lead to interaction that provides comprehensible input, feedback and pushes output in ways that connect with internal mental processing and facilitate acquisition.	Negotiation of meaning; negotiation of form; interactionally modified input; interactionally modified output.
Sociocultural Approach	Learning occurs within the interaction resulting from the performance of a task when linguistic problems arise and learners engage collaboratively in solving them.	'Languaging'; language-related episodes.
Psycholinguistic approach; Representation and control of linguistic knowledge	Tasks can be designed and implemented to take account of learners' limited processing capacity by inducing a variable focus on complexity, accuracy and fluency, which ensures the development of a balanced L2 proficiency over time.	Complexity, accuracy and fluency.
Personal investment approach	Tasks that result in personal investment on the part of learners, as reflected in how they engage with the task, will promote L2 development.	Engagement; behavioural, cognitive, social and affective.

as well' (2016: 51). They proposed a variety of measures of oral production that provide evidence of engagement in terms of these dimensions. Researchers in this approach have also made of use learners' self-reports to capture their affective responses to tasks.

Table 7.1 summarizes these different approaches to investigating the oral performance of tasks. The approaches vary considerably in scope. The Interaction Approach and the Sociocultural Approach focus on specific aspects of interaction (i.e. those where a problem of some sort arises) whereas the Psycholinguistic Approach looks at the entirety of learners' production. Both the Interaction Approach and the Sociocultural Approach are social and cognitive in orientation but they do not address the affective level. The Psycholinguistic Approach only concerns the cognitive aspect. The Personal Investment Approach is the broadest in scope as it addresses the cognitive, social and affective aspects of task performance in terms of the general construct of 'engagement'.

With this background in mind, I now turn to examine how task performance has been measured in these three approaches. I will first describe the measures used in each approach and then comment on their usefulness for investigating task-based performances.

Measurement in the Interaction Approach

In the Interaction Approach measures are derived from the analysis of the negotiation sequences that arise in social interaction. First, the negotiation sequences resulting from the performance of dialogic tasks are identified. The macro structure of these sequences serves as a basis for distinguishing and labelling the individual moves that comprise them. The measures are based on these separate moves. This approach allows for quantification by determining the frequencies of the different moves and also for more qualitative analyses of specific sequences.

There are two ways of dealing with the communication difficulties that learners are likely to experience when they perform a task. The first involves discourse management. The aim here is to avoid communication break-down. A common strategy is a *Comprehension Check*, defined as a move by which one speaker attempts to determine whether the other speaker has understood a preceding message (Pica, 1992). If the addressee then indicates there is a comprehension problem, the speaker has a chance to paraphrase the problematic utterance to make it more comprehensible. Comprehension checks, therefore, help to make input comprehensible, which Krashen (1985) argued is the primary condition for acquisition to occur.

The second approach involves the discourse repair that in occurs addressing a communication problem. Varonis and Gass' (1985) model of the structure of 'non-understanding routines' (see Figure 7.1) provides a basis for identifying specific measures. The model distinguishes the turn that triggers non-understanding from the subsequent turns involving the resolution of the problem. One measure employed in some studies is simply *Number of Non-Understanding Routines*. This is of interest to task-based researchers as the Interaction Approach is premised on the assumption that frequent engagement in such routines is beneficial for language learning. In addition, specific measures have been developed to capture the different ways in which the Indicator of Misunderstanding and the Response are realized in interaction. These are considered below.

Trigger   Resolution

T   I   R   RR

T = trigger (i.e. the utterance which causes misunderstanding)
I = indicator (i.e. of misunderstanding)
R = response
RR = reaction to response

Example:

S1:   And your what is your mmm father's job?
S2:   My father now is retire.   T
S1:   retire?   I
S2:   yes   R
S1:   Oh, yes.   RR

Figure 7.1 Model of non-understanding routines (Varonis & Gass, 1985)

Indicator measures

Indicator moves can be distinguished in terms of whether they are input-providing (i.e. they provide the learner with linguistic input that resolves the problem) or output prompting (i.e. they push learners to find the linguistic solution to the problem themselves) and also whether they are implicit (i.e. they do not directly signal that there is a problem) or explicit (i.e. they clearly signal there is a problem). The specific measures described and illustrated below are classified in terms of these two dimensions. However, as will become clear, whereas the distinction between input-providing and output-prompting indicators is clear, that between implicit and explicit is fuzzier as it depends more on how a specific indicator is delivered than on the specific type of indicator.

These indicators also differ in the nature of the problem they are typically used to tackle. Some, such as confirmation checks and clarification requests, signal that there is a communication problem and thus relate to the negotiation of meaning. Others, such as metalinguistic comments and elicitation, signal that the problem is linguistic in nature; that is, they occur even when there is no actual communication problem and thus relate to the negotiation of form. Again, whether meaning or form is being negotiated is not always totally clear. However, some indicators (e.g. metalinguistic clue) occur only in negotiation of form sequences.

(1) *Repetition* (i.e. the addressee repeats the speaker's utterance to signal that there is a comprehension problem):

> **L1:** I felt really chuffed with the results of my exam.
> **L2:** *Chuffed.*
> **L1:** Yes, I did better than I expected.

This is relatively implicit and output-prompting. However, as Lyster (1998) pointed out repetitions are ambiguous as they can also signal understanding. Thus, they may or may not lead to a resolution of the problem.

(2) *Confirmation check* (i.e. are any expressions 'immediately following an utterance by the interlocutor which are designed to elicit confirmation that the utterance has been correctly heard or understood by the speaker' – Long, 1983: 137):

> **Learner 1:** ok it's in the it's in the corner the building
> **Learner 2:** *in the corner?*
> **Learner 1:** yeah
> (Gilabert *et al.*, 2009: 377)

Like a repetition, a confirmation check simply repeats the problematic utterance or part of an utterance but the rising intonation more clearly signals there is a problem (i.e. makes the move more functionally explicit) and thus may be more likely to lead to a successful resolution.

(3) *Clarification requests* (i.e. any expression that elicits clarification of the preceding utterance)

Learner 1: go walking it's two apples further two streets more it looks
Learner 2: *two what?*
Learner 1: two streets further
(Gilabert *et al.*, 2009: 376)

Clarification requests are output-prompting. They place the burden of resolving the problem on the speaker who created it. They are often viewed as implicit as they occur naturally in everyday conversation but they are in fact functionally explicit in so far as they signal that there is a communication problem.

(4) *Metalinguistic clue* (i.e. a move that provides a comment or questions some aspect of the preceding utterance signalling a linguistic problem)

S: There are influence person who
T: *Influential is an adjective*
S: Influential person (unintelligible) because of his power.
(Sheen, 2004: 278)

Metalinguistic clues are output-prompting (i.e. they do not provide learner with the remedy of the problem) and they are clearly very explicit as they respond to the form of the preceding utterance rather than its meaning. This type of indicator is more likely to be used by a teacher than by a learner.

(5) *Explicit correction* (i.e. a move that indicates an utterance is problematic and at the same time provides the solution to the problem):

S1: and three pear (sounds like 'beer')
S2: three beer
T: *Not beer. Pear.*

This type of indicator, as its label suggests, is explicit and input-providing. Like metalinguistic clues it is more likely to be performed by a teacher although learners have also been observed to correct each other explicitly on occasions.

(6) *Elicitation* (i.e. a move aimed at extracting the correct linguistic form from a speaker in order to repair the speaker's previous utterance). An elicitation can take the form of a question (e.g. How do we say x in English?), a statement requiring completion (e.g. You _) or a request to reformulate (e.g. Can you say it another way?) – Sheen (2004: 278). It is output prompting and explicitly corrective. It negotiates form rather than meaning and is used more or less exclusively by teachers.

(7) *Recast* (i.e. an utterance that rephrases an utterance 'by changing one or more of its sentence components (subject, verb or object) while still referring to its central meanings' – Long, 1996: 436):

S: I stand in the first row.
T: You stood in the first row.
S: Yes.
     (Sheen, 2006: 35)

Recasts are input-providing and are generally considered implicit. However, they can also be more explicit, especially if intonation is used to highlight the part of the utterance that has been reformulated. Various types and characteristics of recasts have been identified. Sheen (2006) developed a coding system that distinguished multi-move and single-move recasts and then went on to describe seven characteristics of single-move recasts. Her study suggested that it may be mistaken to treat recasts as a single type of indicator as they can vary in ways that affect the subsequent response move (see also Ellis & Sheen, 2006).

Response measures

Figure 7.2 shows the different response categories. Not all indicators require a response. Input-providing indicators such as recasts place no obligation on the addressee to respond. In contrast, output-prompting indicators do require a response in accordance with Grice's (1975) Cooperative Principle but even in this case learners may fail to respond if, for example, their linguistic resources are inadequate. So the first response option is *No Response*.

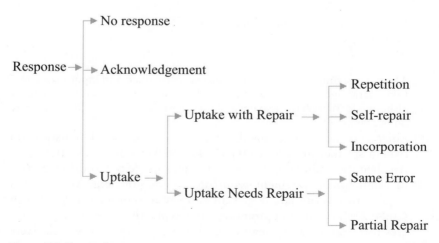

Figure 7.2 Types of response moves

Some indicators – a confirmation check for example – require no more than an *Acknowledgement*. This often takes the form of simply saying 'yes' followed by a topic-continuing move as in this example:

S: I was in pub
     (2.0)
S: I was in pub
T: in the pub?
S: **yeah** and I was drinking beer with my friend

Of greater interest to researchers is when learners respond to an indicator by echoing it or by modifying their output. Echoing and modifying output are examples of what has commonly been called 'uptake', which as Lyster and Ranta (1997) pointed can be of two kinds depending on whether the problem is repaired. The following example illustrates *Uptake with Repair*:

S: they looking the Glockenspiel today morning
T: today morning? This morning.
S: this morning.

In this example, Uptake with Repair takes the form of *Repetition* but when the indicator is a prompt it can lead to *Self-Repair*. Lyster and Ranta (1997) also suggested a third subcategory – *Incorporation* (i.e. the student incorporates repetition of the correct form in a longer utterance.

Here is an example of *Uptake Needs Repair*

S: I have an ali [bi]
T: **You have what?**
S: an ali [bi]

Uptake Needs Repair can involve a complete failure to address the problem (i.e. *Same Error*) as in this example or, in some cases, *Partial Repair* (i.e. the learner corrects part of an erroneous utterance).

Commentary

The Interaction Approach and the measures it has given rise to have proved enormously productive. The early research was descriptive in nature. It was based on the assumption that the modification of interaction that occurs in negotiation sequences is the necessary and sufficient condition for L2 acquisition (Long, 1981) and thus it aimed to identify which types of tasks resulted in high levels of negotiation. Pica *et al.*'s (1993) psycholinguistic classification of tasks was based on four key design features – the interactant relationship, the interaction requirement, the goal orientation and the outcome options. They concluded that the jigsaw tasks where the interactant relationship is two-way, the participants have to request and supply information, they need to converge on a solution to the task and the solution is a closed one had the greatest psycholinguistic validity because they resulted in the greatest negotiation. In general, research (e.g. Foster, 1998; Newton, 1991, 1995) supports such a conclusion. However, limitations in this line of research have also been noted. Much of the research was conducted in laboratory settings and it does not follow that what occurs in this setting will also occur in classroom settings. Foster, for example, reported that in a classroom setting even jigsaw tasks resulted in very little negotiation. Pica (1996) herself noted that negotiation was only a small part of interaction and that other aspects may be of equal importance for acquisition.

More recent research has moved on to investigating what effects different negotiating strategies have on learners' attention to form (i.e. noticing) and on language acquisition in experimentally designed studies. Mackey and Goo (2007) identified more than 40 published studies that had investigated the relationship between interaction and L2 learning. One line of research that has proved especially productive is studies that have investigated the effect of different kinds of corrective indicators on acquisition – input-providing versus output-prompting (e.g. Lyster, 2004) and implicit versus explicit (Yilmaz, 2012). The Interaction Approach is alive and well and continues to draw on negotiation as a key construct but it is currently less concerned with researching the effects of different types of tasks and more concerned with investigating how different features of interaction connect with internal processing and acquisition.

Sociocultural Theory Approach

Sociocultural theorists such as Swain and her co-researchers have focused on the genesis of language learning by examining the LREs that occur when tasks are performed. As noted above, LREs are instances of 'languaging' (Swain, 1998) where learners address the linguistic forms needed to the express specific meanings as they work towards achieving the task outcome. LREs arise in interaction but can also involve self-repair in monologic language use.

Types of LREs

Different types of LREs have been distinguished depending on whether the linguistic form addressed is phonological (or in the case of talk directed at a writing task, orthographical), lexical, grammatical or pragmatic and also whether an LRE results in a correct resolution (either by the speaker or an interlocutor), an incorrect resolution, or remains unresolved. Table 7.2 permutes the types of LREs possible in terms of these two dimensions. The following examples illustrate how LREs are coded in terms of this framework.

Table 7.2 Types of language-related episodes

Linguistic level	Resolution		
	Correct	Incorrect	Unresolved
Phonological/ orthographical			
Lexical			
Grammatical			
Pragmatic			

Example 1: Phonological/incorrectly resolved (interactional)

L1:   Is there any sand castle (/kaetl/)?
L2:   Castle (/kaetl/)? Let me see … I don't have
L1:   Yes. Castle (/kaetl/)
      (Kim, 2009: 259)

Example 2: Lexical/unresolved (interactional)

L1:   What is this?
L2:   Sea animal?
L1:   No … not sea animal.
L2:   I don't know.
      (Kim, 2009: 259)

Example 3: Grammatical/correctly resolved (interactional)

L1:   She find the money.
L2:   No … it should be … she found the money … past.
L1:   Ah … sorry … she found the money.
      (Kim, 2009: 258)

Example 4: Pragmatic/incorrectly resolved (self-repair)

L1:   Learner 1: In this fall, fall, picnic, fall picnic, picnic, is there any, is
      there any way that I could . . . that I could could . . . is there can
      could possibly possibly go to Everland . . . participate, possibly go
      to go to Everland?
      (Taguchi & Kim, 2016: 425)

Researching tasks in terms of LREs

A number of studies have investigated whether the type of task has
any effect on the LREs produced. Two examples of such studies illustrate the kind of research undertaken. Swain and Lapkin (2001) compared the LREs resulting from a jigsaw task and a dictogloss task. Both
tasks were similar in content and both involved students writing out a
narrative text. Swain and Lapkin compared the number of form-directed
LREs where the focus was on spelling or grammar with the number of
meaning-directed LREs where the focus was on lexis or pragmatics,

hypothesizing that the learners would focus more on form in the dicto-gloss task. However, there was no difference in either the total number or types of LREs although the dictogloss task did result in a smaller range of LREs than the jigsaw task. Kim (2009) compared versions of picture narration tasks that differed in cognitive complexity, drawing on Robinson's (2007) Cognition Hypothesis. Simple tasks were those that had few elements and did not require reasoning. Complex tasks were those that had more elements and required reasoning. The tasks were performed by groups of learners who differed in proficiency. Kim found an interactive effect for task type and learner proficiency. The low-proficiency learners produced more LREs during the simple task, whereas the high-proficiency learners produced more with the complex task. Most of the LREs were lexical but that the high-proficiency learn-ers were more likely to also produce successfully resolved grammatical LREs in the complex task.

As with the Interaction Approach, researchers have increasingly gone beyond examining how task types affect LREs to examining the effect that LREs have on learning. In particular, researchers have asked whether LREs that are successfully resolved are associated with learning as measured in post-tests. In such studies, the tasks were focused tasks – that is, they were designed to elicit the use of specific linguistic (usually grammatical) features. Swain and Lapkin's (2001) study was of this kind. They reported no significant differences in the accuracy of French pronominal verbs (the linguistic focus) in either the written stories or in the post-test of the two groups of learners who performed the tasks. In fact, in both groups there were no measurable gains. Other studies (e.g. Swain & Lapkin, 1998), however, have been able to show a relationship between successfully resolved LREs and gains in grammatical accu-racy.[3] Some studies (e.g. Eckerth, 2008b) have reported that LREs often involve linguistic features other than those specifically targeted by the tasks. These 'unexpected LREs' have also been found to be beneficial for learning.

Commentary

Like the negotiation measures, LREs lend themselves to quantification. A strength of LREs is that they constitute a broader measure than negotia-tion sequences as they include ways of addressing linguistic form not cov-ered by negotiation. However, they do not lend themselves to experimental manipulation in the same way as the different moves involved in negotia-tion sequences. That is, the difference between successfully resolved and unsuccessfully resolved or unresolved LREs can only be investigated *post hoc*. Arguably, the main strength of the research lies in the qualitative anal-ysis of specific LREs aimed at demonstrating how learning can take place on the fly as LREs are enacted in accordance with sociocultural theory.

Researchers provide copious examples of how learners collaborate and assist each other to resolve linguistic problems. Taguchi and Kim (2016), for example, show how the LREs produced by a collaborative group of learners led to the accurate production of requests (the target feature) and how a 'by-product of this process is likely the deeper level of processing of the form and consolidation of pragmatic knowledge' (2016: 430) – something that was not observed in a group that performed the same task individually.

The Psycholinguistic Approach

Measures of CAF as a means for investigating how task design features and implementation conditions impact task performance can be found in the earliest studies of tasks (e.g. Crookes, 1988) and have become increasingly popular over time. Lists and descriptions of the various measures can be found in Skehan (1998), Ellis and Barkhuizen (2003), articles in the Special Issue in *Applied Linguistics* 30/4 (2009) and Housen *et al.* (2012a).

Notional definitions of the three aspects are provided in Table 7.3. An assumption of research based on CAF is that the three aspects are separate. That is, each aspect is claimed to be independent of the others. This is important because it allows for the possibility – clearly attested in a number of studies (e.g. Foster & Skehan, 1996; Wang, 2014; Yuan & Ellis, 2003) – that learners can elect (or be led by the task design and conditions) to give priority to one aspect over the others. Skehan (2009) suggested that a fourth aspect needs to be added – lexis – resulting in the acronym CALF. He argued that whereas grammatical and lexical complexity are interdependent in native speakers (i.e. complexity of lexis and grammar correlate), this is not the case for L2 learners as their use of difficult words and grammatically complex sentences can compete with each other, leading to learners prioritizing one over the other. This is especially the case if the learners are of limited proficiency. The following sections examine typical measures of complexity, accuracy, fluency and lexis.

Table 7.3 Definitions of complexity accuracy and fluency (from Ellis, 2003)

Aspect	Definition
Complexity	The extent to which the language produced in performing a task is elaborate and varied. (2003: 340)
Accuracy	The extent to which the language produced in performing a task conforms to target language norms. (2003: 339)
Fluency	The extent to which the language produced in performing a task manifests pausing, hesitation or reformulation. (2003: 342)

Complexity

As Housen and Kuiken (2009) noted 'complexity is the most complex, ambiguous, and least understood dimension of the CAF triad' (2009: 463). They go on to point out that this is because L2 complexity has been interpreted in terms of both cognitive complexity and linguistic complexity, the former referring to 'the relative difficulty with which language features are processed in L2 performance and acquisition' and the latter to inherent characteristics of specific L2 features. Cognitive and linguistic complexity may be related but they need not be. For example, 3rd person English –s can be considered cognitively complex (i.e. it is late acquired) but linguistically it is a very simple feature. The measures I will now consider concern only linguistic complexity.

The most complete account of measures of complexity can be found in Bulté and Housen (2012). They proposed that three components of complexity need to be distinguished – propositional complexity, discourse-interactional complexity and linguistic complexity. They noted, however, that the first two of these components have received little attention and that measures of linguistic complexity predominate in the L2 literature. Bulté and Hosusen identified a total of 32 different quantitative measures of grammatical complexity[4] in 40 L2 studies. They found that most of these studies made use of very general measures that tapped global complexity. These involve calculating the mean length of some unit of production such as Analysis of Speech Unit (AS-unit), which Foster *et al.* (2000) defined as follows:

> ... a single speaker's utterance consisting of an *independent clause* or *subclausal unit*, together with *any subordinate clause(s)* associated with it. (2000: 365)

Typical complexity measures are mean length of AS unit and mean number of clauses in an AS unit.

Such global measures, however, may fail to capture how complexity evolves in learner production over time. Norris and Ortega (2009) argued that global measures cannot by themselves serve as indices of development and that finer-grained, intra-phrasal measures – such as mean length of nominal phrases – are needed to capture complexity in more advanced language learners. There have also been calls for specific measures of complexity focusing on the use of individual grammatical features. Yuan and Ellis (2003), for example, examined the number of different verb forms in learners' production as a measure of grammatical variety.

Linguistic complexity is a multi-layered construct that can be measured in different ways. There is an obvious danger in attempting to generalize about the effect that task design and conditions have on complexity based on studies that have employed different measures. It is also clear that the measurement of complexity cannot be effectively undertaken by a single metric, especially if this is of the global type. Multiple measures are needed and care taken to relate the measures chosen to an explicit model of L2 complexity and, ideally, to language development.[5]

Accuracy

Accuracy would seem to be a simpler construct than complexity. But there are problems here too. Perhaps the most serious is what is meant by 'target language norms' (see definition in Table 7.3). These vary to some extent even in standard varieties of the target language and much more in the non-standard dialects that serve as the reference grammars for many L2 learners. Accuracy is ultimately a relative not an absolute phenomenon and yet it has been treated as absolute in most task-based studies.

Just as there are global and specific measures of complexity, so too there are of accuracy. Global measures are calculated by dividing an oral text into segments and then calculating the error rate. Typical global measures are *proportion of error-free clauses, number of errors per 100 words, errors per AS unit* or *mean clause length free of error.* Specific measures determine the accuracy of particular grammatical structures – usually morphemes such as articles or past tense forms. There are pros and cons for each type of measurement. Skehan prefers global measures on the grounds they are more sensitive to task design and implementation variables than specific measures. However, identifying errors is no easy task as work in error analysis has shown (see Ellis, 2008: Chap. 2) and raises questions about how reliable such measures are. It is much easier to determine an error in a specific morphological feature by means of *obligatory occasion analysis.* This involves identifying the contexts for the required use of a particular morpheme, seeing whether it is supplied and then calculating the percentage of accurate suppliance. *Target-like use analysis* (Pica, 1984) takes this kind of analysis a step further by including over-suppliance of a morpheme using this formula:

$$\frac{\text{N correct suppliance in contexts}}{\text{N obligatory contexts} + \text{n suppliance in non-obligatory contexts}} \times 100$$

A problem with both general and specific measures of accuracy is that they are premised on the assumption that learners become more accurate as their interlanguages develop. Although this might be broadly true, it ignores well-attested U-shaped patterns of development where initial accuracy gives way to error before target-like use eventually emerges.

Another problem is that traditional measures of accuracy treat all errors as equal but clearly they are not. Some errors impede smooth communication more than others. It would be useful, then, to devise a metric that took account of the gravity of errors. Foster and Wigglesworth (2016) attempted this. They proposed a finely tuned weighted clause ratio measure that distinguishes errors at three levels. Level 1 consists of minor errors (e.g. in morphosyntax) that do not compromise meaning. Level 2 errors (e.g. in verb tense or word choice) are more serious; the meaning is recoverable but is not always obvious. Level 3 errors are very serious as they obfuscate meaning. Foster *et al.* weight errors at the clause level like this:

Entirely accurate 1.0
Level 1 error 0.80
Level 2 error 0.50
Level 3 error 0.10

This is superficially very attractive but there remains the problem of determining which level particular errors belong to. There is likely to be a considerable degree of subjectivity in determining the gravity of specific errors as the early studies investigating error gravity have shown (see Ellis, 2008: Chap. 2). Nevertheless, a metric of accuracy that takes account the impact that error has on comprehensibility has high face validity for task-based teaching where the emphasis is on the development of communicative competence.

Fluency

Like complexity, fluency is a multi-compositional construct. Skehan (2009) distinguished three dimensions of fluency. (1) Speed fluency refers to the speed at which speech is performed, (2) breakdown fluency refers to the pauses and silences that break the flow of speech and (3) repair fluency refers to hesitations, reformulations that are used to repair speech during the production process. Regarding breakdown fluency, a distinction has been made between pauses that occur at clause boundaries and those that occur within a clause. As fluency increases, within clause pauses, which signal breakdowns in lexical and syntactic coding, diminish with learners approximating more closely to native speakers, who more typically pause at the end of clauses.

Table 7.4 shows common measures of these different aspects of fluency. Measures of speed fluency and repair fluency are typically calculated

Table 7.4 Common measures of fluency

Dimension	Measures
Speed fluency	Number of pruned syllables per second
Breakdown fluency	Filled (or unfilled) pauses at clause end per number of syllables Filled (or unfilled) pauses in mid clause per number of syllables Length of run (i.e. the number of syllables between two pauses)
Repair fluency	Self-initiated and self-completed corrections per number of pruned syllables

after a text has been pruned for dysfluencies (i.e. self-repairs, false starts, reformulations etc. are removed). Breakdown fluency requires establishing how long a breakdown needs to be to constitute a pause. Clearly, measurements will differ depending on the pause length selected and there is no agreement about minimal pause length. Studies have varied enormously in how they operationalized a 'pause' – e.g. 1 second in Mehnert (1998) but only 0.25 in Kormos and Denes (2004). Some studies (e.g. Lambert *et al.*, 2017a) simply neglect to specify the minimal pause time they used. Length of run is often used as a measure of breakdown fluency (i.e. the greater the number of syllables between pauses, the more fluent the speech) but this measure would seem to tap into complexity as much as fluency and also is influenced by the use of formulaic expressions. Repair fluency can be measured generally (as in the measures shown in Table 7.4) or in terms of the frequency of use of different types of repair (self-repairs, reformulations, repetitions etc.) in relation to total words produced or to some unit of measurement such as AS-unit.

Lexis

Early research on tasks neglected lexis. Lexis can be seen as an aspect of both complexity and accuracy. That is, more complex language will likely include more difficult words, whereas more accurate language will contain fewer lexical errors. However, Skehan (2009) has argued that lexis needs to be measured separately. There are theoretical grounds for this. Levelt's (1989) model of speaking proposes that formulation involves lexical selection prior to grammatical encoding (i.e. distinct processes are involved).

There are three types of measurement:

(1) *Lexical diversity.* The most common measure is type-token ratio (i.e. the ratio of different words used to total words). The difficulty here is that it is influenced by text length; as text length increases, the type-token ratio decreases. Malvern and Richards (2002) however developed a formula for correcting for text length. This is available in the CLAN suite of programmes (MacWhinney, 2000) – http://talkbank.org/clan/.

(2) *Lexical variety.* Lexical diversity measures are text internal in the sense that they rely entirely on the texts being analysed. In contrast, lexical variety measures make use of an external source of reference, typically frequency word lists. Skehan (2009) described the procedure used to calculate LAMBDA which makes use of such lists. The text is first divided into 10-word chunks and then the number of infrequent words in each chunk is calculated. This results in a measure of the extent to which a speaker uses less frequent words. Meara and Bell (2001) provide a detailed description of how to calculate LAMBDA.

(3) *Lexical density.* This refers to the proportion of content words (i.e. nouns, verbs, adjectives and adverbs) in the total number of words of a text. The rationale for this measure is that a text with a high proportion of content words contains more information than a text with a high proportion of function words (i.e. prepositions, pronouns, articles, connectors and conjunctions).

Researchers have focused on lexical diversity and variety. A general finding is that choice of lexis is influenced more by the type of the task (e.g. whether the task involves narration or decision-making) than by how the task is implemented (e.g. whether time for pre-task planning is available).

Commentary

The psycholinguistic approach has proved enormously productive for investigating tasks. A typical study selects specific variables relating to the task type, task design features, or implementation conditions and then investigates these experimentally by examining their impact on CALF. Examples of such studies can be found in Skehan and Foster's (2012) synthesis of their own studies, in the collection of articles in Skehan (2014a) and in Robinson (2011a). These studies have noble aims. One is to provide information about task complexity that can be used in the preparation of task-based syllabuses. Another is to identify specific tasks and task conditions that lead to different aspects of language being prioritized. Such information can be used to design task-based programmes that can help learners to develop balanced proficiency (i.e. enable them to produce language that is complex, accurate and fluent).

There are both strong theoretical grounds and also consistent empirical findings to support the separateness of the different aspects. Skehan (2014b) staked out a theoretical basis for CAF by relating the different components of Levelt's (1989) model of speaking to the different aspects of language use (i.e. conceptualization $\rightarrow$ complexity; formulation $\rightarrow$ accuracy; articulation $\rightarrow$ fluency) but he also admitted that we are still a long way from an adequate theory of performance.[6] Empirical evidence of the separateness of the three constructs is available from factor analyses that test whether a mixed bag of measures load on different factors corresponding to the three aspects. Skehan and Foster (1997, 2005) reported the results of two factor analyses indicating that the various measures do effectively distinguish the different aspects. Interestingly, length of run loaded with measures of both fluency and a complexity, bearing out the point made earlier about this particular measure.

There are, however, considerable problems with research based on the psycholinguistic approach. The main one is that 'task' is a holistic construct and thus any single task will embody multiple features. It follows that findings about the effect that specific task variables have on performance are applicable only to the particular task(s) being investigated and cannot to be generalized to other tasks. Over time, after multiple studies investigating the same variables with different tasks, generalization may become more possible. Studies that have investigated pre-task planning, for example, are now sufficient in number to allow for generalization (see Ellis, 2009). But even here, as noted in Chapter 5, there is considerable variance in the results obtained. Some studies indicate that planning increases complexity but others show an effect for accuracy and a few on both complexity and accuracy. The explanation for the lack of consistency may be that the studies involved different learners in different contexts who responded in different ways to the opportunity to plan – as sociocultural theorists have claimed happens (see Chapter 2). Of course, the search for generalizations is clearly desirable. But to date, despite the insights that CALF studies have provided, there are few generalizations that can be readily used in the design of task-based courses.

A further problem is that different studies have operationalized the four aspects in different ways. For example, some studies have investigated complexity or accuracy using only global measures, whereas others have used finer-grained measures focusing on specific linguistic features. Similarly, some studies have used measures of breakdown fluency to investigate pausing in general, whereas others (more recent studies) have distinguished between within and end-of-clause pausing. In other words, complexity, accuracy and fluency can mean very different things in different studies making it difficult to compare results. It would help if consensus could be reached about which specific measures to use but although there has been progress towards this – in particular, in Skehan's work – we are still a long way from agreeing on the choice of the different measures.

There are also problems in coding learner texts for the different measures. A major issue is that learners (like native speakers) make use of formulaic chunks which can give the impression of fluency and also confound measures of complexity. Accuracy too is perhaps more likely to occur in ready-made chunks. The problem lies in the difficulty of distinguishing formulaic and creative speech. Most studies do not attempt to do so. A final problem is that the coding of CALF measures is extremely time-consuming. However, Bui and Skehan (2016) have developed an analytical tool called 'CALF'. This processes coded files and outputs results for a wide range of measures. 'CALF' is freely available at http://www.censpothk.com/calf/.

Personal Investment Approach

How a task is performed will depend in part on the task and the conditions of performance but also on the learners themselves. The approaches we have considered up to this point focus on the impact that the task has on performance. The personal investment approach takes account of both the task and the learners' subjective response to it. In line with the importance attached to learners' personal investment, the key performance construct is 'engagement' as the place where learning happens.

The term 'engagement' has been applied to LREs where it is used to refer to the 'quality of learners' meta-talk' (Storch, 2008: 99) but in recent studies it has come to mean much more than this and to cover a whole range of performance behaviours. Svalberg (2009) offers this definition:

> In the context of language learning and use, engagement with language (Engagement) is a cognitive, and/or affective, and/or social state and a process in which the learner is the agent and the language is the object (and sometimes vehicle). (2009: 247)

By characterizing engagement as a 'state', Svalberg emphasized the learner-internal factors that influence performance. By referring to it also as a 'process' she leads us back to the behavioural aspects of performance. Implicit in the notion of engagement is that there is a relationship between the state and behavioural aspects of performance, indicating the need to investigate how the two aspects are connected. The extent to which learners are engaged is, of course, a matter of degree – that is, as Svalberg noted, it can more or less.

Engagement as a state

Another construct very relevant to engagement-as-state is 'flow'. People are in a state of flow when they experience intense and focused concentration on the task at hand, a loss of self-consciousness, a sense of personal control over the activity, a sense that the activity is intrinsically rewarding, and their subjective experience of time is altered (Nakamura & Csíkszentmihályi, 2005: 90). Csikszentmihályi et al. (2005) proposed that a number of conditions must be met to achieve a state of flow: the activity must have a clear set of goals, there is clear and immediate feedback, and the task poses a reasonable level of challenge in relation to an individual's own perceived skills. The primary means of investigating flow is by means of a questionnaire asking individuals to identify definitions of flow and situations in which they say they have experienced it.

Egbert (2003) asked learners to perform a number of different tasks and evaluated the extent to which each task resulted in a state of flow by means of questionnaire. This differed from the kind of questionnaire used by Csikszentmihályi et al. (2005). It was of the Likert-scale type asking learners to respond on a scale of strongly disagree (1) to strongly agree (7) to 14 statements such as 'the task excited my curiosity' and 'the task allowed me to control what I was doing'. Egbert also interviewed the learners. On the basis of the learners' subjective responses to the tasks, Egbert distinguished those tasks that elicited 'high', 'moderate' and 'low' flow and concluded that 'we can, therefore, talk about tasks that support flow' (2005: 514). However, as the learners responded holistically to the tasks, she was not able to say which specific characteristics of the tasks were important for promoting flow.

To date, however, there has been little research investigating tasks in relation to 'flow'. Aubrey (2017) compared the flow resulting from the same tasks performed intra-culturally (i.e. in pairs of Japanese L2 learners) and inter-culturally (i.e. where the L2 learners interacted with international students from their university). Using a questionnaire based on Egbert's he found that intercultural contact had a significant positive effect on flow and also that that there was a significant positive correlation between and flow and the number of turns. More studies such as Aubrey's are needed to pinpoint what task factors promote flow and how flow is related to task behaviour.

Engagement as a process

Egbert also investigated learners' behaviours as they performed the tasks using a task observation chart designed to capture four dimensions of flow – control over the activity, the extent to which learners stayed focused, their level of interest, and the degree of challenge. She reported clear differences in these four dimensions. Interestingly, tasks that were high or low in task behaviours in particular tasks were uniformly high or low in all four dimensions.

Other researchers have followed a more standard approach to investigating engagement as a process. That is, they transcribed recordings of the performance of tasks and then looked for specific behaviours indicative of engagement. Philp and Duchesne (2016) adopted this approach. They distinguished four dimensions of engagement – behavioural,[7] cognitive, emotional and social. Definitions of these dimensions along with the indicators they suggested for each are shown in Table 7.5. It is clear that these four dimensions are intertwined, which Philp and Duchesne acknowledged. They suggested that each dimension could be 'mediated' by the other three dimensions, activating/strengthening engagement or conversely deactivating/inhibiting it, and showed how this might occur. For example, 'behavioural engagement' is more likely when learners' attention is focused (cognitive engagement), when they are keen to carry on with the task (emotional engagement) and when a cooperative task strengthens group cohesion (social engagement). In their article, Phil and Duchesne make no attempt to quantify indicators of the four dimensions. Instead, they illustrate each in qualitative discussions of extracts from task-based lessons.

Commentary

The study of learners' personal investment in the performance of tasks – as reflected in their engagement – offers a much more encompassing account of tasks and the language use they elicit than the other

Table 7.5 Measures of engagement (based on Philp & Duchesne, 2016)

Dimension	Definition	Measures
Behavioural	Behavioural engagement is being 'on task' and is reflected in terms of time on task or level of participation.	Number of minutes spent on and off task Number of words produced Number of turns Mean number of words per turn
Cognitive	Cognitive engagement occurs when there is sustained attention and mental effort.	Asking questions Completing another speaker's utterances Making evaluative comments Justifying an argument Making gestures and facial expressions Private speech
Emotional	Emotional engagement occurs when there is motivated involvement in a learning activity and a sense of purposefulness and autonomy.	Positive indicators: Interest Enthusiasm Enjoyment Feeling of connection with peers Negative indicators: Boredom Frustration
Social	Social engagement occurs when learners engage collaboratively in a task, i.e. there is equality and mutuality (Storch, 2002).	Listening to each other Drawing on each other's ideas and expertise Providing feedback to one another

approaches. It connects closely with a major line of research in education (Christenson *et al.*, 2013). It also resonates with how teachers are likely to view tasks. Teachers are more likely to ask whether a particular task engaged a learner than whether it resulted in a high level of negotiation of meaning or LREs or how it affected the complexity, accuracy and fluency of learners' production. Perhaps too engagement is important for initiating the cognitive processes (e.g. noticing; establishing form-meaning connections) that research has shown are important for language learning although that has yet to demonstrated.

However, because interest in engagement is relatively new, the task-based research is clearly programmatic. There is a danger in engagement becoming a catch-all term for a variety of somewhat ill-defined constructs. If the four dimensions of engagement are as interdependent as Philp and Duchesne suggest, one is left wondering if it actually makes much sense to distinguish them. What is useful, however, is distinguishing engagement-as-state and engagement-as-process as these involve quite distinct investigatory methods. Engagement-as-state is best investigated by means of self-report instruments (questionnaires and interviews). Egbert showed the way and provided us with some useful self-report tools. It might also be possible to identify behavioural indicators of engagement-as-state. Engagement-as-process involves examining the behaviours involved in performing a task and takes us closer to the other three approaches for investigating tasks, all of which involved examining behaviours.

If research on engagement is to progress it will be necessary to theorize exactly what behaviours are important – as happens in the other approaches. Simply listing behaviours that purport to reflect cognitive, emotional and social engagement (as in Table 7.4) constitutes a start but we need to know which engagement behaviours are important for both successful task performance and learning (and these may not be the same).We also need to know what relationships exist between engagement-as-state and engagement-as-process. Svalberg (2009) is helpful here as she distinguishes what she calls 'key characteristics of engagement' in terms of state and process at the cognitive, affective and social levels (see Table 4 on p. 255 in her article). One way forward might be to compare the behaviours evident in tasks where learners report a high level of engagement-as-state with those evident in tasks where they report a low level. Studies that examine engagement both as a state and as behaviours are also needed. Lambert *et al.* (2017b) report such a study, which showed that when learners are emotionally engaged in a task they are also demonstrate a higher level of participation.

Conclusion

The purpose of this chapter is to provide an overview of how task performance has been measured. The focus has been exclusively on oral production. I have not considered written task performance nor the receptive aspects of task performance. There is a substantial literature on the measurement of written task performance (e.g. Jiang, 2013) but to date little thought has been given to either theorizing or measuring learners' receptive response to tasks.[8] The focus on oral production, however, is justified given the centrality of this mode of communication in TBLT and in research on tasks.

The four approaches I have considered all tackle the measurement of learners' oral performance of tasks from a theoretical standpoint. Negotiation measures are based on theories that emphasize the role of interaction in triggering the internal mechanisms involved in acquisition. Language-related episodes provide a means of investigating the role of 'languaging', which sociocultural theory sees as central to the process of developing new linguistic features *in* interaction. CALF measures are used to investigate how learners' working memory and task variables jointly impact on conceptualization, formulation and articulation as in Levelt's (1989) model of speaking. Finally, drawing on educational theories, measures of engagement have been devised to examine learners' personal investment as reflected in their engagement with a task.

Table 7.5 compares the measures associated with the four approaches in terms of five factors. 'Mode' refers to whether the measurements are applicable to dialogic/and or monologic production. 'Scope' concerns the extent to which the measurements address a broad or narrow range of production features. 'Precision' considers whether the measures are clearly defined operationally and involve a relatively low level of inference or are fuzzier requiring a higher level of inference. 'Perspective' addresses whether the approach focuses only on external (process) aspects of production or also on the internal state of the learners. Finally, I consider to what extent the measures associated with each approach are developmental (e.g. can distinguish the behaviours of low- and high-proficiency learners). My aim is descriptive rather than evaluative. Although I recognize that the analysis presented in Table 7.6 is open to challenge I argue that it broadly reflects how the various measures have been utilized in the research to date. What emerges from this analysis is that each approach has its strengths and limitations. Although the four approaches have very different epistemological bases, they can be seen as complementary, each offering unique insights into how a task is performed. The psycholinguistic approach is arguably the most comprehensive although somewhat surprisingly little attention to date had been paid to learners' psychological states as they perform tasks in this approach. The personal investment approach is promising as it covers both learners' subjective response to

Table 7.6 Comparison of measures of task performance in the four approaches

Approach	Mode	Scope	Precision	Perspective	Development
Interactionist	Dialogic	Narrow – focused mainly on negotiation sequences.	Low inference	External processes[9]	To a limited extent – frequency of negotiation sequences varies according to proficiency.
Sociocultural	Dialogic	Narrow – focused on 'languaging' in interactional sequences.	Low inference	External processes	Unclear – 'languaging' potentially evident at all developmental levels.
Psycholinguistic	Monologic and dialogic	Broad – addresses oral production in its entirety but does not consider interactional features.	Low inference	External processes	CALF measures are developmentally sensitive but not in a linear fashion.
Personal investment	Dialogic	Broad – addresses a wide range of cognitive, affective and social behaviours.	High inference	External processes and internal state	Unclear – no reason to expect level of engagement to vary developmentally.

tasks (their internal state) and their behaviours (performance processes). However, work is needed to refine the measures that have been used and to establish which measures serve as the best indicators of engagement.

Research investigating tasks is more often than not decontextualized. A typical study selects tasks (e.g. tasks with loosely or tightly structured content) which are then performed by learners either under the same condition or in two or more different conditions (e.g. with and without opportunity for pre-task planning). The task performances are recorded, transcribed, coded to allow for measurements to be calculated and then compared quantitatively and/or qualitatively. Such studies attempt to establish the effect that task type, task design features or task conditions have on performance. The overall aim is to arrive at generalizations about the effect of these variables on performance. In such research little attention is paid to factors outside the task itself. Contextual factors, however, are important. Factors that are likely to impact on the performance of a task include individual learner factors such as their L2 proficiency, personality, language aptitude and motivation for learning the L2 and factors relating to the setting of the study (in particular, laboratory vs classroom and how pairs/groups of learners are composed). Nor can context be viewed just in structural terms. Context is dynamically constructed through the performance of task so that what happens at the start may be very different from what happens later on.[10] As Samuda (2015) noted, 'it is not the task as a tool that is relevant but how it is used to mediate learning and teaching' (2015: 274). She went on to comment 'a task has the capacity to open up a space for learning and teaching' (2015: 282). So what is needed are studies that adopt a more dynamic and context-sensitive approach to investigating tasks and measuring task performance.

Another limitation of the research that has employed these various measures of L2 production is that it has almost always been cross-sectional or short-term in design. There is a notable lack of longitudinal studies that plot how L2 learners' production changes over time. Such studies are sorely needed. Without longitudinal studies it will be difficult to test the claims of Dynamic Systems Theory regarding the extent to which L2 development involves unpredictable variability and troughs and peaks in the development of different aspects of language use, as reported by Larsen-Freeman (2006) or whether there are more consistent and predictable trajectories of development as Vercelotti (2017) found.

Notes

(1) The four approaches I have chosen to consider all involved quantitative measures of task performance. I have not considered approaches such as conversation analysis that involve the qualitative analysis of task-induced production. This would require a separate article.

(2) A somewhat similar construct to language-related episodes is form-focused episodes (FFEs) (Ellis *et al.*, 2001). Whereas LREs occur in dialogic talk resulting from pair or

group work, FFEs have been investigated in lock-step lessons where tasks are performed with the whole class.

(3) Loewen (2005) investigated the relationship between form-focused episodes (FFEs) – in task-based, whole-class interaction. He also reported a relationship between successfully resolved FFEs and scores in tests administered both immediately after the lessons and two weeks later.

(4) An alternative to quantitative measures of complexity (and of accuracy and fluency) is the use of a rating scale. This approach is more common in language testing studies. L2 researchers have preferred measures derived directly from learners' production.

(5) It is, however, not clear that an increase in linguistic complexity over time is indicative of L2 development. The complexity of linguistic texts is highly variable, influenced not just by processing conditions but also by genre, topic, addressee etc. Arguably what constitutes true development is the ability to vary the complexity of output in accordance with these variables.

(6) Skehan (2014b) also theorises how the three aspects of performance figure developmentally suggesting that there is an 'acquisitional dynamic' (2014b: 2) involving initially complexity (when change/development occurs) followed by accuracy (when there is a focus on greater control) and finally on fluency (when learners consolidate existing language). However, as Housen et al. (2012b) point out this developmental sequence is very 'speculative at best and probably simplistic' (2012b: 7).

(7) The choice of 'behavioural' for labelling one of the dimensions is unfortunate as in fact the measures of all four dimensions are behavioural. It would seem that by 'behavioural' Philp and Duchesne (2016) are referring to 'level of participation'.

(8) Receptive task performance involves at the least (1) learners' comprehension of input and (2) learners' attention to form in the input. One of way measuring (1) is by devising tasks so that the task outcome provides a measure of comprehension – see Chapter 3. (2) has been investigated by stimulated recall protocols that shed light on linguistic features learners report having noticed as they performed a task.

(9) Although the interactionist approach is primarily concerned with external processes, increasingly it has also attempted to examine internal states (such as attention) through stimulated recall protocols.

(10) Skehan and Foster (2005) reported a study that showed that differences in CALF measurements occur if they are based on the first five as opposed to second five minutes of a task performance. This study points to the importance of investigating how a task changes as it is performed.

Part 3

Task-based Language Pedagogy

In the previous section of this book I focused on research that has investigated tasks and task-based teaching. At the same time, however, I also addressed a number of pedagogic issues. In fact, all but the last of the chapters dealt with some aspects of task-based pedagogy – input-based tasks, focus-on-form, how to prepare learners to perform a task, and the role of explicit knowledge. My concern was what research has shown us about these issues. These issues will also figure in this section of the book. However, my focus has now shifted to pedagogical concerns although I will from time to time also refer to research. So the previous section and this section should be seen as two sides of the same coin with the emphasis on research or on pedagogy.

I start this section with a chapter where I address some common misconceptions about task-based teaching. Because TBLT is in many ways a quite radical approach it is not surprising that it has met with resistance from conservative forces. The critics are invariably those who wish to protect 'traditional' language teaching (i.e. teaching that itemizes the objects to be taught through presentation and practice). Tasks have a role in such teaching, of course, but only to provide a communicative flavour to an approach that emphasizes accuracy over fluency. A major problem with the criticisms that have been levelled at TBLT is the failure to recognize that TBLT is not monolithic but in fact is quite varied – it is an 'approach', not a 'method'. Another problem is the woeful lack of knowledge (or understanding) of the theory and research that underpins TBLT.

In this section of the book I draw heavily on Michael Long's work on TBLT. His work is seminal. It has shaped both pedagogy and the research that has investigated TBLT. However, Long promotes a particular version of TBLT and it is not the only one and not one that I entirely agree with. Long argues that a task-based course should be based on a needs analysis of target tasks; I argue that this is only appropriate in contexts where it is possible to determine the specific needs of learners and that in many contexts (e.g. EFL in Asian state schools) it makes no sense and so courses intended for such contexts should be built around 'pedagogic tasks' rather than 'real-life tasks'. Long is also dismissive of any role for *a priori* explicit instruction, while I believe that it can have a place in TBLT. Long evinces belief in the role that research can play in developing a framework for determining task complexity but I am much more sanguine about whether such research will pay dividends. Long is dismissive of my advocacy of consciousness-raising tasks but, while I certainly do not see these as appropriate for all learners, I argue that they do function as 'tasks' (in accordance with how I have defined a task) and double up in both helping learners develop explicit knowledge of problematic grammar points and facilitating general development through the talk they generate. It is of course no surprise to find points of disagreement such as these between advocates of TBLT. One point Long and I do agree on is that there are some real issues that need to be addressed if TBLT is to flourish. I take a look at these in Chapter 9.

In Chapter 10, I advance an argument for a modular curriculum, consisting of both a task-based module and structural module. The task-based module is the starting point and is primary throughout the curriculum. However, there is also a supplementary list of linguistic features, which research and experience shows learners are likely to fail to master. My idea is that once basic communicative fluency is established teachers can watch out for these problems and devise more explicit language lessons to address them. These lessons will be of the task-supported kind and will involve focused tasks. I discuss how to assemble a task-based syllabus and a structural check list.

In Chapter 11 I switch my focus to the methodology of a task-based lesson, drawing on and updating the relevant chapter in my 2003 book. I discuss how to design a task-based lesson in terms of a set of options for the three phases of such a lesson – the pre-task phase (involving task preparation activities of one kind or another), the main task phase, and the post-task phase. An options-based approach makes it clear that there is not just one way of teaching a task-based lesson but many possible ways. Again, then, it emphasizes the need to treat TBLT as an 'approach', not a 'method'.

During my time at the University of Auckland I taught a course on task-based language teaching and learning. The final chapter in this section draws on my experience of this course. I asked my students to first design a task and then carry out an evaluation of it by teaching it. Over the years I taught this course I accumulated a number of my students' micro-evaluations of their tasks. I present a number of these in this chapter along with my analysis of what they show. Teacher education is of enormous importance if task-based teaching is to flourish. Ideally, teacher education programmes should themselves be task-based and one way of achieving this is by asking teachers to design their own tasks and then evaluate them.

8 Task-based Language Teaching: Sorting Out the Misunderstandings

Introduction

Task-based language teaching (TBLT) has attracted increasing attention from researchers and teacher educators since Candlin and Murphy's (1987) seminal collection of papers. This approach to language teaching – it cannot be said to constitute a distinct 'method' – has drawn extensively on research into L2 acquisition (i.e. second language acquisition (SLA)), as reflected in books by Crookes and Gass (1993), Skehan (1998a), Ellis (2003), Samuda and Bygate (2008) and Long (2015). It is worthwhile noting, however, that it is not just SLA researchers who are its advocates; teacher educators such as Prabhu (1987), Estaire and Zanon (1994), Willis (1996), Nunan (1989, 2004) and Willis and Willis (2008) have also presented a strong case for it, drawing on both their own experience of language teaching and educational theories. Samuda and Bygate (2008) make this connection with educational theory quite explicit:

> Many of the principles underlying the design and use of what we now call 'tasks' in second language pedagogy owe their genealogy to development in general education over the last century. (2008: 18)

They showed how TBLT, with its emphasis on purposeful and functional language use, had its origins in Dewey's (1913) views about the importance of experience, relevance and 'intelligent effort' for effective learning. Long (2015) too emphasized the compatibility of TBLT and general principles of education. There are also documented examples of the practice of TBLT, starting with Prabhu's (1987) account of the Communicational Language Teaching Project, and, more recently in books reporting case studies of TBLT (e.g. Leaver & Willis, 2004; Edwards & Willis, 2005; Van den Branden, 2006a). TBLT has progressed well beyond theory into actual practice.

However, as is often the case when a 'new' approach receives the support of theorists and researchers in academe, resistance can set in. TBLT challenges mainstream views about language teaching in that it is based on the principle that language learning will progress most successfully if teaching aims to simply create contexts in which the learner's natural language learning capacity can be nurtured rather than through a systematic attempt to teach the language bit by bit (as in approaches based on a structural syllabus). Not surprisingly, therefore, TBLT has been subjected to criticism – often strident – by those teachers and educators who favour a more traditional approach. Foremost among these critics are Sheen (1994, 2003) and Swan (2005a, 2005b). Other critics include Seedhouse (1999, 2005), who has challenged TBLT on the grounds that 'task' does not constitute a valid construct around which to build a language teaching programme, and Widdowson (2003), who has argued that the criteria for defining tasks are overly loose and that TBLT over emphasizes 'authentic' language use.

TBLT has also been subjected to criticism on the basis of evaluations of its implementation in different instructional settings. In particular, questions have been raised by Li (1998), Carless (2004), Butler (2005) among others, as to whether TBLT is practical in Asian countries where teachers are likely to adhere to a philosophy of teaching that is radically different to that which underlies TBLT and where they also face practical problems such as students' limited second language proficiency and the washback from tests they need to prepare their students for.

In this chapter, I would like to mount a defence of TBLT. To this end I will address a number of criticisms. I will argue that many of these are based on misunderstandings of what advocates of TBLT actually propose. I will also examine, much more sympathetically, the problems of implementation identified in the evaluation studies of innovative TBLT projects. First, though, I need to provide a quick thumbnail sketch of what TBLT entails.

Background: Task-based Language Teaching is an 'Approach' not a 'Method'

TBLT, like other kinds of language teaching, entails both design and methodology. That is, decisions need to be taken regarding which type of tasks to include in a course, what the content of the tasks will be, and, crucially, how to sequence the tasks so as to best facilitate learning. Methodological decisions concern how to structure a task-based lesson and what type of participatory structure to employ. A task-based lesson can involve three phases (the pre-task phase, the main task phase and the post-task phase), although only one of these (the main task phase) is obligatory. Tasks can be performed in a whole-class context, in pairs, in groups, or by learners working individually.

Thus there is no single way of doing TBLT. Table 8.1 distinguishes three general approaches to TBLT – Long's (1985), Skehan's (1998a) and my own (Ellis, 2003). I have described these approaches in terms of five

Table 8.1 A comparison of three approaches to TBLT

Characteristic	Long (1985, 2015)	Skehan (1998a)	Ellis (2003)
Natural language use	yes	Yes	Yes
Learner-centredness	yes	Yes	Not necessarily
Focus on form	Yes – through corrective feedback	Yes – mainly through pre-task	Yes – in all phases of a TBLT lesson
Tasks	Yes – unfocused mainly	Yes – unfocused	Yes – unfocused and focused
Rejection of traditional approaches	Yes	Yes	No

characteristics: (1) the provision of opportunities for natural language use (what Widdowson (2003) refers to as 'authenticity'), (2) learner-centredness (as manifested in the centrality of small group work), (3) focus-on-form (whether the approach includes devices for focusing learners attention on form while they are communicating), (4) the kind of task (i.e. whether unfocused or focused) and (5) the rejection of traditional approaches to language teaching (e.g. presentation–practice–production (PPP)). The only characteristics that all three approaches share are (1) – they all emphasize the role of tasks in creating contexts for natural language use – and (3) focus-on-form. However, differences exist in how attention to form is to be achieved, with Long emphasizing corrective feedback, Skehan task-design and pre-task planning and myself a variety of ways in all three phases of a task-based lesson. Differences in the three approaches are evident with regard to (2) (i.e. I do not see group-work as an essential characteristic), (4) (i.e. Skehan favours just unfocused tasks whereas I also see a role for focused tasks) and (5) I, Long and Skehan view traditional structural teaching as theoretically indefensible whereas I see it as complementary to TBLT. As we will shortly see, many of the misunderstandings about TBLT derive in part from the tendency of its critics to view it as monolithic, rather than quite variable.

In other words, task-based language teaching is not a 'method' but an 'approach'. I use these terms in the same way as Richards and Rogers (2001) to distinguish a well-defined set of procedures informed by a single coherent theory (a method) from a more general orientation to teaching that is informed by a set of principles but can manifest itself in a number of different ways of teaching (an approach).

It is still important, however, to distinguish task-based and task-supported language teaching (see Chapters 1 and 6) depending on whether the task is preceded by explicit instruction. There is a difference between a 'task' and a 'situational grammar exercise'. In task-based language teaching the content of the instructional programme is specified in terms of the tasks to be completed as in Prabhu (1987). Task-supported language teaching is based on a structural syllabus and typically involves PPP, with the final stage taken up with what is often referred to as a 'task' but in fact is better described as a 'situational grammar exercise'. According to Widdowson (2003), task-supported language teaching is likely to result in 'encoded usage rather than realization as purposeful use' (2003: 119). However, as Widdowson went on to argue, such teaching is not to be dismissed if it can inspire 'engagement'. Contrivance and language display may have their place in language teaching as indeed I argue in Chapter 10. The critiques I will now turn to have focused on task-based language teaching. The motivation for the critiques appears to a desire to reaffirm the legitimacy of task-supported language teaching.

With this background to TBLT completed, I will now address a number of misunderstandings in the critiques of TBLT advanced by Sheen, Swan, Seedhouse and Widdowson.

Misunderstandings about TBLT

The misunderstandings I will consider have arisen for a number of reasons but two in particular derive from misrepresentations of the theoretical rationale for TBLT and from a failure to acknowledge the differences that exist among advocates of TBLT (as shown in Table 8.1).

I shall consider the following misunderstandings:

- the definition of a 'task' is not sufficiently clear to distinguish it from other kinds of instructional activities;
- tasks prioritize pragmatic meaning and neglect semantic meaning;
- the interaction that results from tasks is often impoverished and thus cannot constitute an adequate context for L2 acquisition;
- it is not possible to predict what kinds of language use will result from the performance of a task and thus it is not possible to ensure adequate coverage of the target language in a task-based course;
- because there is no underlying grammar syllabus TBLT cannot ensure adequate coverage of grammar;
- attention to form in TBLT is limited to corrective feedback in order to ensure minimal interruption of the performance of a task;
- attention to grammar in the post-task phase is limited to conscious-raising activities (i.e. there are no production practice activities);
- the theoretical rationale for TBLT addresses only grammar, ignoring vocabulary and pronunciation;
- TBLT emphasizes output and thus fails to ensure that learners are exposed to rich input;
- the role of the teacher in TBLT is limited to that of a 'manager' or 'facilitator' of communicative activities;
- TBLT is only suited to 'acquisition-rich' contexts;
- there is insufficient empirical support to support the theoretical rationale for TBLT or to show that TBLT is superior to traditional approaches.

The Definition of a 'Task'

Widdowson (2003) argued that:

The criteria that are proposed as defining features of tasks are ... so loosely formulated ... that they do not distinguish tasks from other more traditional classroom activities. (2003: 126)

He reached this conclusion on the basis of a discussion of the definition of a task provided by Skehan (1998b). Skehan identified four criteria:

- meaning is primary;
- there is a goal that needs to be worked towards;
- the activity is outcome-evaluated;
- there is a real-world relationship.

Widdowson's critique of these criteria is not without merit. He is right to point out that Skehan's use of the term 'meaning' is indeterminate as it does not distinguish semantic and pragmatic meaning, that it is not clear what Skehan means by 'goal' and that the nature of the 'real-world relationship' is not specified. However, his dismissal of the third criterion (relating to the outcome of the task) is less convincing. Widdowson argued that a successful outcome to a task may not result in any learning if only minimal language is involved. However, this misses the point, as Skehan's definition of a task is directed at specifying what a task is and by 'outcome-evaluated' he is referring to the communicative outcome of a task not to specific learning outcomes. Indeed, in TBLT it is generally not possible to pre-determine what learning will take place.

   The definition of a task has proved problematic, however. This is evident in the discussion of various definitions to be found in Bygate *et al.* (1991), Ellis (2003) and Samuda and Bygate (2008). But there are more precise definitions of 'task' than Skehan's available and if Widdowson wishes to claim that the defining criteria are 'loosely formulated' he should consider a range of definitions and not limit himself to one and then generalize from that. The definition I provided in Chapter 1 consisting of four criteria for a task is sufficiently tight to distinguish activities like 'completing a family tree' and 'agreeing to give advice to the writer of a letter to an agony aunt' (examples from Skehan, 1998a) from traditional language learning activities (what I have called 'exercises') such as 'filling the blanks in sentences' or even situational grammar activities. My definition emphasizes the importance of a 'gap' to motivate the 'goal' of a task and the need for learners to use their own linguistic resources (rather than simply manipulating texts they are provided with). It is these criteria that are important for distinguishing a task from an exercise. My definition too assumes that a 'focus on meaning' refers to both semantic and pragmatic meaning.

   Widdowson also seems to be guilty of a more fundamental misunderstanding of a task. He argued, quite correctly, that many of the tasks mentioned by Skehan are unlikely to figure in the real life of people. In so doing he appears to assume that a defining characteristic of a task is that it should be 'authentic' – a view also taken by Long (1985, 2015), who argued that a task-based curriculum should be based on a needs analysis of the 'target tasks' that particular learners need to master. However, as Bachman (1990) pointed out, we can distinguish two types of authenticity – situational authenticity and interactional authenticity. Widdowson and Long only had the former in mind but even a cursory reading of the task-based literature should make it clear that what is important for most advocates of task-based teaching is interactional authenticity. That is, some tasks may achieve situational authenticity (although, as Widdowson noted, given the exigencies of the classroom context this is unlikely) but *all* tasks are designed to instigate the same kind of interactional processes (such as the negotiation of meaning and form, scaffolding, inferencing and monitoring) that arise in naturally occurring language use.

Semantic vs Pragmatic Meaning

A second, related criticism of TBLT that Widdowson made is that tasks prioritize pragmatic meaning and neglect semantic meaning. The former refers to the way language is used in natural contexts of use; the latter refers to the notional and functional meanings encoded in the lexis and grammar of a language. To borrow Widdowson's example, the sentence:

I am walking to the door.

if said while the speaker walks to the door is pragmatically inappropriate (unless the intention is to infer some additional meaning such as 'Look, my hip's not so bad after all') but it successfully illustrates one of the semantic meanings of the present continuous tense. Widdowson's point is that what he referred to as structural-oral-situational teaching (and what I mean by 'traditional' teaching) make use of such sentences to teach the semantic meanings of the linguistic code and, as a consequence, fails to address pragmatic meaning. In contrast, TBLT, according to Widdowson, requires learners to process pragmatic meaning but fails to provide them with the situational clues needed to acquire semantic meaning.

Given that learners need to master both pragmatic and semantic meaning, it would seem that Widdowson was arguing for combining TBLT and traditional approaches such as the structural-oral-situational approach. Indeed, he stated that a 'preferable procedure is to give critical attention to the basic tenets of SOS and TBI to establish where they correspond and where they might complement each other' (Widdowson, 2003: 129). However, the general tenor of his essay is clearly dismissive of TBLT.

There are two weaknesses in Widdowson's argument. The first is the mistaken claim that TBLT fails to address semantic meaning. It is not difficult, for example, to think of a task that would create a context for the use of the present continuous tense to express ongoing activity. A spot-the-difference task that showed people performing different actions would require one participant to describe these actions in order to see if they were the same or different from the actions people were performing in his/her partner's picture. Such a task surely requires attention to both pragmatic and semantic meaning. The second problem lies in Widdowson's assumption that contriving contexts to teach specific grammatical structures such as the present continuous tense enables learners to acquire these structures. Widdowson provided no evidence that this is the case. The fundamental problem with a structural approach to language teaching of the kind implicit in the structural-oral-situational approach is that it does not take account of the learner's own built-in syllabus (Corder, 1967) and the processes of form-function mapping involved in the development of an interlanguage. TBLT was developed as a way of ensuring that instructional and acquisitional processes were properly matched (see Long & Crookes, 1992).

Impoverished Interaction

A common objection to TBLT is that learners' performance of tasks will result only in samples of impoverished language use that are of little acquisitional value. This was implicit in Widdowson's criticism regarding the failure of tasks to address semantic meaning. This criticism has been made more explicitly by Seedhouse (1999), who claimed that performing tasks results in indexicalized and pidginized language because of the limitations of learners' linguistic resources and their over-reliance on context. In support of this claim he cited the interaction from Lynch shown in Table 8.2, where the learners are engaged in performing an information-gap activity that requires them to describe simple diagrams to each other. Seedhouse argued that such interactions are likely to promote fossilization rather than acquisition.

There is no doubt that such tasks can result in the kind of interaction shown in Table 8.2. But this does not justify a dismissal of task-based

Table 8.2 An example of an impoverished task-based interaction

L1:   What?
L2:   Stop.
L3:   Dot?
L4:   Dot?
L5:   Point?
L6:   Dot?
LL: Point, point, yeh.
L1:   Point?
L5:   Small point.
L3:   Dot

Source: From Lynch (1989).

instruction for two reasons. First, if the learners are beginners then engaging in such interactions might in fact be beneficial, encouraging them to develop the capacity to make use of their limited resources and thus helping them to develop their strategic competence. Nor can the acquisitional potential of such interactions be dismissed. In Ellis (2003) I argued that the interaction in Table 8.1 manifests a number of the qualities of the 'progressive discourse' that Wells (1999) claimed were required for collaborative knowledge building. It is clear, for example, that the participants are working towards a 'common understanding' (i.e. the meaning of 'dot') and that they frame questions in ways that help them to expand their knowledge base (i.e. by proposing synonyms for 'dot'). As a result, they arrive at the collectively valid proposition that a 'dot' is a 'small point'). Thus, there would seem to be a clear 'knowledge artefact' that results from this interaction (i.e. the meaning of 'dot').

The second reason for rejecting Seedhouse's argument is simply that the nature of the interactions that take place in TBLT will depend on three factors – the proficiency level of the students, the design features of the task and the method of implementation. More advanced learners performing more complex tasks will engage in more linguistically rich interactions, especially if they are given the opportunity to engage in pre-task and online planning (Yuan & Ellis, 2003). There is plenty of evidence from the task-based literature to show that tasks can result in complex language use (see, for example, the studies of the effects of planning on task-based performance discussed in Chapter 5). One of the aims of TBLT is, in fact, to create contexts in which learners can experience what is means to communicate at different stages of their development – using whatever resources at their disposal. Inevitably, with beginners, the interactions will be limited but this does not mean that they are of no pedagogic value.

Task-as-Workplan vs Task-as-Process

An important and certainly valid distinction is that between the task-as-workplan and the task-as-process (Breen, 1989: Chap. 1). The relevance of this distinction for TBLT is that if there is no correspondence between the task-as-workplan and the task-as-process it will not be possible to predict what kinds of language use will result from the performance of tasks and thus not possible to ensure adequate coverage in a task-based course.

There is plenty of evidence to demonstrate that the task-as-workplan does not always result in the anticipated use of language. This is true of both unfocused and focused tasks. Coughlan and Duff (1994), drawing on the tenets of sociocultural theory, showed that the 'activity' that results from an unfocused 'task' varied from learner to learner and also from performance to performance of the task by the same learner. Seedhouse

(2005) argued that the discrepancy between the predicted and actual language use resulting from a task was so great that a task could only be defined in terms of the language processes that resulted from its performance and that therefore it was impossible to plan a language course based on tasks-as-workplans. The problem becomes even more acute with focused tasks as it is very difficult to design production tasks that make the use of a specific target feature 'essential' and not easy to design tasks that make them 'useful' so that at best all we can hope to make the use of the target feature 'natural' (Loschky & Bley-Vroman, 1993). Learners are adroit at using their strategic competence to get round having to use a linguistic feature they do not know or cannot access easily.

This is a serious problem. If Seedhouse is correct then it is clearly difficult if not impossible to use 'task' as the unit for designing courses. But Seedhouse is not correct. First, as I pointed out in Chapter 2, although the relationship between task-as-workplan and task-as-process is not isomorphic, it does exist. Skehan (2001) showed that both specific design features and implementation options affect the accuracy, complexity and fluency of the language that results. Table 8.3 summarizes his findings. It shows, for example, that if the information comprising the task-as-workplan has a well-defined structure then the resulting language is markedly more fluent than when the information in the task has a loose structure. If the task outcome is complex, the resulting language is also more complex. Foster and Skehan (1996), and others, also showed that implementation variables such as planning influence the way a task is performed in predictable ways. Skehan's work demonstrates convincingly that it is possible to design and implement tasks in ways that will lead learners to prioritize different aspects of language. Also, studies of focused tasks have shown that in at least some cases it is possible to design tasks that will result in the required use of the target structure (see Ellis, 2003: Chap. 5).

Seedhouse is also wrong for another reason. His claim about the unsuitability of 'task' as a unit for designing a course is based entirely on his analysis of output-prompting tasks. But tasks can also be input-providing (see Chapter 3). In this case, it is obviously much easier to ensure a close match between the target language to be selected for attention and

Table 8.3 Effects of task design features on fluency, complexity and accuracy

Task characteristic	Accuracy	Complexity	Fluency
Familiarity of information	No effect	No effect	Slightly greater
Dialogic vs monologic	Greater	Slightly greater	Lower
Degree of structure	No effect	No effect	Greater
Complexity of outcome	No effect	Greater	No effect
Transformations	No effect	Planned condition leads to greater	No effect

the language that learners actually process when they perform the task. Critics of TBLT frequently make the mistake of assuming that a task is invariably a speaking task. The problem that Seedhouse sees disappears once it is recognized that tasks can involve listening and reading.

Inadequate Coverage of Grammar

A common complaint – and indeed this is really what underlies Widdowson's critique considered earlier – is that a task-based syllabus affords inadequate coverage of grammar. Sheen (2003) claimed that in task-based language teaching there is 'no grammar syllabus' and went on argue that proponents of TBLT 'generally offer little more than a brief list of suggestions regarding the selection and presentation of new language'. In a similar vein, Swan (2005a) insisted that TBLT 'outlaws' the grammar syllabus. Strong words! To address this criticism it is important to make a distinction between a task-based *syllabus* and task-based *teaching*. But in neither case is it accurate to claim that grammar has no place.

In my version of TBLT, a task-based syllabus can comprised both unfocused and focused tasks. As promulgated by Long and Crookes (1992) the primary units are unfocused tasks. If the syllabus is entirely composed of unfocused tasks then, indeed, grammar has no explicit place. But if the syllabus also incorporates focused tasks then it will also be necessary to stipulate the linguistic content of these tasks and this, typically, involves specifying the grammar to be taught. It is, therefore possible to conceive of a 'pure' task-based syllabus consisting entirely of unfocused tasks (and this is what Sheen and Swan must have had in mind when they complained about the lack of grammar). It is also possible to conceive a grammar-oriented task-based syllabus consisting of focused tasks although this would run up against the same difficulty facing a structural syllabus, namely the learner's built-in syllabus. A third type of task-based syllabus is also possible – a hybrid one that consists of a mixture of focused and unfocused tasks. In each of these syllabuses, however, the primary unit will be 'task' as I have defined it in this book. Various arguments can be advanced for preferring a pure task-based syllabus, a grammar-oriented task syllabus or a hybrid task syllabus. It is true that some advocates of TBLT (e.g. Long & Crookes, 1992; Skehan, 1998; Willis, 1996) have generally opted for a pure task-based syllabus but others, such as myself (Ellis, 2003) and Samuda and Bygate (2008), have acknowledged that 'grammar' can have a place in a task-based syllabus. I develop an argument for a hybrid curriculum in Chapter 10.

'Teaching', of course, involves more than just a syllabus; it also includes methodology (i.e. the means by which the syllabus is implemented). When we look at the methodology of task-based teaching, the claim that there is no grammar is fundamentally mistaken. All advocates to TBLT see a role for grammar in the methodology of task-based teaching. Potentially, attention to form (including grammatical form) can figure in all three phases of a task-based lesson (i.e. the pre-task phase, the main task phase and the post-task phase), although differences exist among advocates as to what is the preferred approach. Willis (1996), for example, argued that attention to form should be restricted to the post-task phase, Long (2006) proposed that it is best incorporated into the main-task phase in the form of recasts, Ellis *et al.* (2001) showed that teachers engage in extensive focus on form in the main-task phase both pre-emptively and reactively using a variety of devices. Estaire and Zanon (1994) suggested that the pre-task phase can incorporate some teaching of grammar but arguably this results in task-supported language teaching. Furthermore, advocates of TBLT do not view attention to form as an optional element of TBLT but as necessary to ensure 'noticing', which Schmidt (1994) viewed as a requisite for acquisition to take place.

Thus, whether TBLT is viewed in terms of syllabus or methodology, it is clearly incorrect to claim that it 'outlaws grammar'. Grammar may not be central to TBLT but it has an important place within it.

Attention to Form

The term 'FonF' was coined by Long (1991) to stand in contrast to 'FonFs' (see Chapter 4). The latter refers to traditional language teaching based on a structural syllabus. 'FonF' refers to teaching where learners' attention is focused on form in the context of communicative activities (i.e. TBLT). Both approaches involve grammar. However, Long's early insistence that attention to form is instantiated through the negotiation of meaning has led to another criticism – namely, that 'the only grammar to be dealt with (in TBLT) is that which causes a problem in communication' (Sheen, 2003).

This criticism might be justified if the only version of TBLT was Long's but, as I have already pointed out, this is not the only version. Attention to form can occur in a variety of ways – not just through 'focus on form' as defined by Long. Nor is it correct to claim that 'focus on form' is restricted to occasions where there is a 'problem in communication' – i.e. to what Long has called the 'negotiation of meaning'. Attention to form can arise didactically as well as communicatively during a performance of a task, as illustrated by this example from a task-based lesson:

T: What were you doing?
S: I was in pub
     (2)
S: I was in pub
T: In the pub?
S: Yeh and I was drinking beer with my
     friend.
     (Ellis *et al.*, 2001)

It is clear that there is no communication problem here – the teacher understands what the student has said but nevertheless goes ahead with a partial recast ('In the pub?'). Ellis *et al.* (2001) provided evidence to suggest that in communicative adult ESL classes this kind of didactic focus on form occurs more frequently than what they called 'conversational' focus on form.

An excellent example of how teachers can switch from conversational to didactic focus on form can be found in Samuda's (2001) account of a task-based lesson, which I considered briefly in Chapter 6. To recap, the 'Things-in-Pocket' task that this lesson was based on asked students to speculate about the identity of a person when shown the contents of this person's pockets. This was a focused task designed to afford opportunities for the learners to use epistemic modals. Samuda documented how the teacher began the lesson by attempting to interweave the target structure into the talk the task aroused by means of recasts and when this failed, resorted to a more explicit and didactic treatment of the target structure. If Sheen had read Samuda's article it is difficult to see how he could continue to argue that the only grammar dealt with is that which causes a communication problem.

Consciousness-raising Tasks

Sheen (2003) also claimed that in TBLT any post-task grammar-work is supposed to take the form of grammar-problem solving tasks (i.e. consciousness-raising (CR) tasks). This criticism probably derives from my own advocacy of CR tasks – see Ellis (1991) and (1993). I contrasted CR activities with practice activities and argued that the former are more compatible with what is known about L2 acquisition in that they are directed at explicit rather than implicit knowledge and, as such, do not run up against the problem of trying the match the instruction to the learner's built-in syllabus, which only concerns implicit knowledge. I also argued that CR tasks double up as communicative tasks as 'grammar' becomes a topic to talk about. In this respect, then, they satisfy the criteria for defining a task.

However, although I would certainly see CR activities as an ideal way of providing post-task grammar work, especially for adults who have achieved intermediate proficiency in the L2, I certainly would not claim they are the only way of treating grammar in the post-task phase. In Ellis (2003) and in Chapter 11, I identify a number of ways in which grammar can be addressed in this phase of the lesson, including direct explicit instruction and traditional practice type exercises. Other supporters of TBLT (e.g. Willis, 1996) have likewise proposed a variety of options for the post-task phase.

Sheen is guilty of generalizing on the basis of one writer's views about the post-task phase (my own) and, even in this respect, has not accurately represented my position regarding how grammar can be dealt with in the post-task phase of a task-based lesson.

Vocabulary and Pronunciation

It has also been claimed that 'the theoretical rationale for TBLT is typically limited to the acquisition of grammar and that vocabulary and phonology are ignored (Swan, 2005a). This criticism seems to have arisen over a misunderstanding of the term 'focus on form', namely that 'form' refers exclusively to grammar. This, however, is not how researchers of TBLT have operationalized focus-on-form. Williams' (1999) study of learner-initiated focus on form in collaborative group work found that the type of form that the learners focused on was 'overwhelmingly lexical'. Ellis *et al.* (2001) reported that out of 429 focus-on-form episodes that they identified in some 12 hours of TBLT in two adult ESL classes, 159 of them addressed lexical problems and 76 pronunciation problems. There were 163 episodes related to grammar. Thus, in this study, the total focus on form episodes for vocabulary and pronunciation combined exceeded that for grammar. In a follow-up study, Loewen (2005) found an even greater emphasis on vocabulary and pronunciation in 12 adult ESL classes involving 32 hours of TBLT; 43% of the form-focused episodes addressed vocabulary and 22% pronunciation, while 33% addressed grammar.

Not only is Swan wrong in claiming that theorists of TBLT ignore vocabulary and pronunciation but he is himself guilty of ignoring the very substantial evidence from empirical studies of TBLT that vocabulary and, to a lesser extent, pronunciation receive frequent attention in task-based lessons, whether these are teacher-led or involve small group work.

Output- vs Input-based Task-based Language Teaching

One of the most astonishing criticisms levelled at TBLT is that it 'provides learners with substantially less new language than "traditional" approaches' (Swan, 2005a: 392). Swan went on to claim:

> In the tiny corpus of a year's task-based input, even some basic structures may not occur often, much core vocabulary is likely to be absent, and many other lexical items will appear only once or twice. (2005a: 393)

One wonders how Swan would measure the quantity of 'new language' that learners are exposed to in traditional and task-based approaches. Is he referring to the materials found in course books or to the interactions that occur in classrooms? And what exactly does he mean by 'new language'?

It would seem that Swan's criticism is predicated on the assumption that tasks must inevitably involve interaction and production. But, as I pointed out earlier, tasks can also be 'input-based' (i.e. involve listening or reading). In Chapter 3 I reviewed research that has investigated what I called 'non-reciprocal tasks' and showed how listen-and-do tasks can be enriched with 'new' vocabulary in ways that foster acquisition. I concluded that the research based on listen-and-do tasks has shown that such tasks are effective both for practising listening comprehension and as a means for presenting new linguistic material to students. Reading tasks also afford opportunities for exposing learners to rich input. Indeed, extensive reading activities can be viewed as tasks. Again, there is research to show, that incidental vocabulary acquisition occurs as a result of extensive reading (see, for example, Dupuy & Krashen, 1993). A brief study of popular 'traditional' course materials is likely to reveal the poverty of the input they provide – indeed, in many course books for low-level learners more space is given over to cosmetic pictures than to linguistic input! I would argue that, a task-based course is capable of providing much greater exposure to the target language, including 'new' language, than a traditional course.

The Role of the Teacher

According to Swan (2005a), task-based language teaching promotes learner-centredness at the expense of teacher-directed instruction. Swan commented 'the thrust of TBLT is to cast the teacher in the role of manager and facilitator of communicative activity rather than an important source of new language'. This criticism assumes, rightly in my view, that there is a place for teacher-centred activities in language teaching, helpful though small group work may be in creating contexts for the kinds of language use that will promote acquisition. In many instructional contexts, the teacher is the major source of input.

However, Swan is mistaken in assuming that the teacher is limited to managing and facilitating students' performance of tasks in TBLT. First, it should be noted that some versions of TBLT are in fact entirely teacher-centred. Prabhu (1987), for instance, distinguished between a pre-task, which was to be performed by the teacher in lock-step fashion with the whole class and the main task, which was to be performed by students individually. He argued that it was only the teacher who could ensure the 'good models' needed to promote interlanguage development and that 'sustained interaction between learners is likely to provide much less opportunity for system-revision' (1987: 81) and could result in pidginized use of the L2 and concomitant interlanguage fossilization. Prabhu described the kind of teacher-talk that took place in the Communicational Language Teaching project and was needed for interlanguage development:

> ... in the classroom, the teacher controlled the complexity of his or her language in more or less the same way as an adult does in speaking to a child – avoiding or paraphrasing what he or she felt might be too difficult,

repeating statements, and speaking slowly when there seemed to be difficulties of understanding. (1987: 57)

Clearly, this involves the teacher in much more than just managing tasks. Nor does it correspond to what Swan had in mind when he talked of the teacher as 'facilitator'. Rather it places the teacher in the role of skilled communicator – surely a necessary role for any kind of teaching and of particular importance in TBLT.

In just about all versions of TBLT, including those that prioritize group work, the teacher is much more than a manager and facilitator of tasks. The need to direct learners' attention to form during the performance of the task requires the teacher to engage in various types of pre-emptive and reactive focus on form (see Chapter 4). There is now a rich literature documenting how teachers respond to learner errors in TBLT, for example. This shows that they adopt both implicit and explicit corrective strategies, at times intervening very directly to 'teach' about some item of language as in Samuda's (2001) Things in Pocket lesson referred to above.

Swan's description of the teacher's role also ignores the fact that TBLT can include a pre-task and post-task phase, where opportunities can arise for the explicit teaching of language. Thus, although it is true that TBLT requires teachers to function as a manager and facilitator, it is also the case that it requires them to adopt other more 'teacherly' roles of the kind that Swan feels are needed. In this respect, TBLT is no different from any other instructional approach. Like other types of teaching, TBLT can be both learner- and teacher-centred.

Acquisition-rich versus Acquisition-poor Environments

A commonly held view – one voiced by Swan (2005a) – is that beginner learners need to be taught grammar because without it they will not be able to communicate and, in particular, they will fail to shift attention to code features in interaction because they know so little basic grammar that they cannot produce discourse to shift from. A corollary of this view is that TBLT is only suited to 'acquisition-rich' environments (e.g. where learners have access to the target language in the wider community) and is not suited to 'acquisition-poor' environments (such as many 'foreign' teaching contexts), where, Swan claims. a more structured approach is required to ensure that learners develop the grammatical resources for communicating.

There are a number of problems with this line of argument. First, it assumes that TBLT requires production right from the start – when learners are beginners. I have already pointed out that TBLT can be input-providing as well as output-prompting and clearly, with beginners the appropriate approach would be one that emphasizes listening and reading

tasks. There is plenty of evidence (e.g. see Ellis (1999) for a review of studies and Shintani's (2016) detailed report of her own input-based research)
to show that input-based approaches not only enable learners to develop
the ability to comprehend input but also the lexical and grammatical
resources they will need to speak and write.

A second problem lies in the assumption that learners need grammar
in order to be able to communicate. This is clearly wrong. The very early
stages of L2 acquisition (as evidenced in learner production) are agram-
matical. Klein and Perdue (1997) showed that the starting point is what
they call the 'pre-basic variety'. This is characterized by nominal utterance organization. Production at this stage involves scaffolded utterances
(i.e. utterances constructed over more than one turn) and is context-
dependent. Grammaticalization takes place only very gradually and so it
is some time before finite verb organization appears in what they term the
'post-basic variety'. In fact, everything that we know about how learners
acquire grammar is that it is a gradual and dynamic process. It is precisely
this that TBLT seeks to accommodate. From this perspective, teaching
grammar to beginners is of little use unless the aim is simply to develop
their explicit knowledge of grammatical rules.

It would follow from this argument that TBLT might in fact be better
suited to 'acquisition-poor' environments than to 'acquisition-rich ones'.
In situations where learners have access to communicative contexts outside the classroom there may be a case for teaching grammar as a way of
preventing the stabilization that often occurs in interlanguage development after learners have achieved a basic ability to communicate in everyday situations. In situations where such communicative opportunities are
not found (e.g. for learners of English in many European and Asian countries), there is an obvious need to provide them inside the classroom.
TBLT is a means for achieving this. If grammar teaching has a role in such
contexts it is arguably after learners have acquired a basic communicative
competence – a view I develop in Chapter 10.

In short, TBLT caters to what we know about the way that beginner
learners learn an L2. It aims to create a context in which grammar can be
acquired gradually and dynamically while at the same time fostering the
ability to use this grammar in communication. It is ideally suited to
'acquisition-poor' environments.

'Legislation by Hypothesis'

Both Sheen (2003) and Swan (2005a) argue that there is no empirical
evidence to support either the hypotheses that construct the theoretical
rationale for task-based teaching or to demonstrate that FonF is superior
to traditional FonFs. Swan claims that SLA researchers are guilty of 'legislation by hypothesis'. He lists four hypotheses that he claims underlie
TBLT and are not supported by research.

It is incorrect that there have been no comparative evaluations of TBLT. Neither Sheen nor Swan makes any reference to Prabhu (1987) and Beretta and Davies' (1985) evaluation of this project in India. Their evaluation sought to compare the learning that resulted from the Communicational Language Teaching Project and traditional language teaching (the 'structural-oral-situational approach' – a version of PPP). In the attempt to ensure that the evaluation was fair Beretta and Davies included tests that favoured each approach as well as method-neutral tests. The findings were as follows:

- in the tests favouring the traditional group, this group did best;
- in the tests favouring the task-based group, this group did best;
- in the neutral tests (e.g. a contextualized grammar test; dictation; listening/reading comprehension), the task-based group did best.

On balance, this evaluation suggests that TBLT is superior to traditional teaching. The task-based group demonstrated both that they had acquired some grammar and the capacity to utilize their linguistic knowledge communicatively. However, Beretta and Davies were careful to note that conducting a post-hoc evaluation of this kind was problematic. The difficulties of conducting global method comparisons are well-known (see Allwright, 1988) and it is perhaps wise not to attempt them. More recently, however, there have been a number of other well-designed comparative studies (e.g. Gonzalez-Lloret & Nielson, 2015; Shintani, 2016), which also point to the superiority of TBLT. Shintani's study is of particular interest because it investigated the process features of FonF and FonFs instruction showing how only the former enabled learners to carry out the form-function mapping that is essential for the learning of grammar.

There are also plenty of small-scale studies demonstrating that task-based learning does result in acquisition. For example, in an experimental study, Ellis *et al.* (1994) investigated the effects of Japanese learners' acquisition of English vocabulary in a listen-and-do task. They showed that even when focused primarily on meaning – as required by a task – they were able to acquire new words and maintain what they had learned over time. Other studies (e.g. Ellis *et al.*, 2006; Mackey, 1999) have shown that performing tasks can also assist the acquisition of grammar.

In order to refute Swan's claims about legislation by hypothesis I have listed the four hypotheses that he considered together with some of the research that has addressed each hypothesis (see Table 8.4). The Online Hypothesis states that acquisition is fostered when learners attend to form in the context of ongoing communication (i.e. when they are primarily focused on meaning). This has been demonstrated in a number of studies – for example, Mackey and Philp (1998), who showed that learners are able to attend to grammatical features in recasts providing they are developmentally ready to do so. The Noticing Hypothesis claims that noticing (i.e. paying conscious attention to linguistic form) is necessary for

Table 8.4 Research supporting four SLA hypotheses

Hypothesis	Research
The Online Hypothesis	Online attention to form does result in learning (Mackey & Philp, 1998; Mackey, 1999).
The Noticing Hypothesis	Learners do pay attention to linguistic form and this can result in learning (e.g. Mackey et al., 2000; Sheen, 2004).
The Teachability Hypothesis	There is a substantial body of research that shows that L2 acquisition involves both an order and sequence of acquisition (e.g. Bardovi Harlig, 2001; Ellis, 1994) and that this cannot be easily altered through instruction (e.g. Ellis, 1989).

acquisition to take place. A number of studies (e.g. Y. Sheen, Spada, N., 2004) have shown that learners frequently repair their errors following the teacher's corrective feedback, demonstrating that they must have noticed the correct form. The Teachability Hypothesis proposes that learners will only be able to acquire those features that they are developmentally ready for. A number of studies (e.g. Ellis, 1989; Pica, 1983) have shown that the natural order of acquisition cannot be subverted by instruction and that learners can only acquire those features they are developmentally ready for.[1] Swan is correct in claiming that these hypotheses provide a theoretical rationale for TBLT. He is incorrect in claiming that there is no empirical support for them.

There is clearly a need to demonstrate the efficacy of TBLT. SLA researchers have been able to show that incidental learning does occur as a result of performing tasks and have gone some way to identifying the conditions that facilitate this. Clearly, though, this research is still insufficient to convince doubters like Sheen and Swan. It probably always will be. It is worth noting, however, that the case for TBLT does not rest solely on SLA. As I noted in the introduction to this article, TBLT draws on a variety of theories, including those drawn from general education. Thus, even if Swan is right and SLA researchers are guilty of 'legislating by hypothesis', there is still a strong educational case for TBLT.

Problems in Implementing TBLT

The objections to TBLT considered in the previous sections were theoretical and empirical in nature. Widdowson, Seedhouse, Sheen and Swan have challenged the theoretical basis for TBLT and/or argued that there is insufficient empirical evidence to support it. Their criticisms are unjustified, as I have attempted to show. However, there are a number of practical difficulties that teachers face in implementing TBLT, as a number of evaluations and my own experience of working with teachers have shown. These practical problems are real and will need to be addressed if TBLT is to be made to work in actual classrooms. I will consider them in greater detail in Chapter 9. Here I will briefly examine two evaluation studies, one of which found that teachers largely failed to implement TBLT success-fully and the other reporting a more effective uptake of the approach.

Carless (2004) examined the implementation of TBLT in the context of the introduction of a 'target-oriented curriculum' in elementary schools in Hong Kong. He addressed two research questions: (1) What are the teachers' attitudes and understandings toward TBLT and (2) how are the teachers attempting to implement TBLT and what issues emerge from these attempts? He collected data by means of 17 classroom observations for each of three native-speaking Cantonese teachers, six semi-structured interviews, and an attitude scale. The data were analysed qualitatively and the results presented in terms of representative classroom episodes for each teacher. He concluded that overall the teachers demonstrated a poor under-standing of what a task was and that, as a result, the tasks they employed resulted in 'practice' rather than genuine communication. He noted three key issues in the implementation of the tasks: (1) wide use of the students' mother tongue, (2) discipline challenges (i.e. there was a tension between the need to get the students talking and the need to maintain class disci-pline, (3) many of the tasks resulted in non-linguistic activity, such as draw-ing, rather than use of the L2. It was clear that overall the task-based approach was not working effectively in this teaching context.

McDonough and Chaikitmongkol (2007) reported on an innovative task-based course for students at Chiang Mai University in Thailand. The course replaced a traditional FonFs course and was developed by the teachers involved in the programme. It included a learning-strategies com-ponent and, in addition to the self-made task-based materials, utilized a supplementary commercial text book. The evaluation addressed two research questions: (1) what were the teachers' and students' reactions to a task-based course? and (2) what concerns (if any) did the teachers have about the course? A variety of data were collected by means of open-ended questions about the tasks, a notebook kept by the students, obser-vation of the teachers, a final course evaluation consisting of open-ended questions, interviews with the students and teachers and field notes kept by one of the teachers participating in the course. McDonough and Chaikitmongkol considered both the teachers' and learners' reactions to the course, reporting that it resulted in (1) increased learner independence, (2) some concern among the teachers about the lack of grammar (but this dissipated as the course progressed) and (3) the students' recognition that the course was relevant to their academic needs but not to their real-world needs outside the academic context. McDonough and Chaikitmongkol also reported how the course designers attempted to address these con-cerns by (1) undertaking revisions to help both teachers and students adjust to the course, (2) providing learner support (e.g. developing supple-mentary materials to help students understand the task assignments) and (3) reducing the number of activities in the course. Overall, this task-based course was a success.

It is pertinent to ask why the Hong Kong elementary programme was relatively unsuccessful and the Chiang Mai course more successful. There are many possible reasons. The elementary students in the Hong Course had very limited English proficiency, whereas the university students had a substantial basis in English. The teachers in the Hong Kong course were not directly involved in developing the tasks they taught whereas the university teachers were. The Hong Kong teachers lacked a clear understanding of what a task was, whereas the university teachers clearly understood what constituted a task. There was no built-in opportunity for the Hong Kong teachers to revise the materials used in the course whereas there was for the university teachers.

These differences point to a number of principles that, if followed, may help to ameliorate the problems that arise in the implementation of TBLT. These principles are:

(1) Tasks must be tailored to the proficiency levels of the students (e.g. if the students have limited proficiency tasks should initially be of the input-providing rather than output-prompting kind).
(2) Tasks need to be trialled to ensure that they result in appropriate L2 use and then revised in the light of experience.
(3) For TBLT to work, teachers need a clear understanding of what a task is.
(4) Teachers and students need to be made aware of the purpose and rationale for performing tasks (e.g. they need to understand that tasks cater to incidental learning of the kind that will facilitate their communicative skills).
(5) Ideally, the teachers involved in teaching a task-based course must be involved in the development of the task materials.

Such principles, however, are arguably relevant not just to TBLT but to any form of teaching. They speak to the importance of teacher-involvement in course development and to teacher education. They underlie the successful implementation of any innovation in language teaching – see for example Ellis (1997) and Rea-Dickens and Germaine (2000).

There are, however, some serious structural impediments to TBLT that cannot be so easily addressed. Educational systems in many parts of the world place the emphasis on knowledge-learning rather than skill-development and a task-based approach to language teaching is not readily compatible with such a philosophy. A structural approach based on teaching discrete items of language accords more closely with such an educational philosophy. TBLT calls for the use of performance-based testing but in many educational contexts examinations test knowledge rather than skills and, understandably, teachers will feel the need to tailor their teaching to such examinations. Arguably too, TBLT is not easily implemented in large classes – a structural feature of many educational contexts. Solutions to these impediments to TBLT require a radical review of the educational philosophy and resources that underpin teachers' beliefs about language teaching. Such a review entails a shift in educational policy and is unlikely to be undertaken readily. Teachers are well aware of the problems they face in implementing TBLT. In Chapter 13 I consider ways in which they can be tackled.

Conclusion

In this article, I have attempted to address a number of criticisms of TBLT, arguing that they constitute misunderstandings and misrepresentations of both its theoretical rationale and its methodology. I shall conclude with what I see as the advantages of a task-based approach.

(1) TBLT offers the opportunity for 'natural' learning inside the classroom.
(2) It emphasizes meaning over form but can also cater to learning form.
(3) It affords learners a rich input of target language.
(4) It is intrinsically motivating.
(5) It is compatible with a learner-centred educational philosophy but also allows for teacher input and direction.
(6) It caters to the development of communicative fluency while not neglecting accuracy.
(7) It can be used alongside a more traditional approach – at least in my own version of TBLT.

I also identified a number of practical problems and advanced a set of principles that will go some way to ensuring the successful implementation of a task-based course. Finally, I acknowledged that there may be more serious structural difficulties relating to the nature of educational systems and that these cannot be so easily addressed.

It remains to acknowledge one final and more compelling objection to TBLT. Some language educators have advanced a social critique, arguing that there is no single approach to language teaching that should be adopted in all teaching contexts. Widdowson (1993), for example, cited an unpublished study by Scollon and Scollon suggesting that 'conversational methods' are antithetical to the Confucian emphasis on benevolence and respect between teacher and students in China. He views TBLT as implying a particular cultural context that may be in conflict with cultural contexts where learning is not seen as a collaborative and experiential activity. From this perspective, the classroom practices required by TBLT can be seen as culturally loaded, imposing the democratic, egalitarian discourses seen as desirable in the west. They could be seen as an example of what Pennycook (1994) calls cultural imperialism. Although these criticisms are overstated (i.e. TBLT, as I have pointed out, is not just a matter of 'conversational methods'), it must be accepted that there may cultural barriers to the uptake of TBLT. Clearly, no matter how convincing a case can be made for TBLT on psycholinguistic or educational grounds, social and cultural factors may make it difficult (perhaps impossible) to implement in some contexts.

Note

(1)   The existence of a natural route for the acquisition of an L2 grammar has been disputed. DeKeyser (1998), for example, drew on skill-learning theory to argue that it is possible to subvert the natural route through instruction although he acknowledged that this may only result in automatized explicit knowledge rather than true implicit knowledge. Spada and Lightbown (1999) conducted a study that showed that instruction can overcome the natural route to some extent at least. See Chapter 6 for further information about the effect that explicit instruction can have on learning.

9 Moving Task-based Language Teaching Forward

Introduction

In some respects, the advocacy of task-based language teaching (TBLT) has the characteristics of a movement and, is the case with such movements, it has aroused resistance from advocates of traditional, object-oriented teaching (Bruton, 2002; Sheen, 1994; Swan, 2005a). The critiques that have been levelled at TBLT are based on 'misunderstandings' about TBLT and concern 'non-issues' have already been addressed (see Chapter 8; Long, 2016). There are, however, a number of issues in need of discussion not least because advocates of TBLT do not always agree on what the 'real issues' are, and, if they do agree, they differ in how they can be best addressed. In this chapter, then, I want to build on the previous one by staking out my own position on these issues, pointing out where I differ from other advocates of TBLT and suggest a way of addressing fundamental disagreement about the merits of task-supported and task-based language teaching.

Real Issues

Table 9.1 lists the issues that I see as very 'real' for the design and implementation of TBLT programmes. In many cases, these issues concern different positions among advocates of TBLT, suggesting the need to debate them and, if possible, arrive at some consensus. Long (2016), in an issue of the *Annual Review of Applied Linguistics* devoted to TBLT, produced his own list of 'real issues' (only #3, 9 and 10 in Table 9.1) based on his particular view of what constitutes TBLT . My list is longer, reflecting my view that alternative versions of TBLT are possible and indeed are necessary to accommodate different instructional contexts.

Issue 1: What is a 'Task'?

The key question here is whether 'task' should be defined narrowly in terms of real-world activities or more generically in terms of activities that

Table 9.1 Some real issues in the design and implementation of TBLT courses

1. What is a 'task'?
2. What types of tasks should figure in a given type of a task-based course?
3. What makes a task complex and how can tasks be sequenced effectively?
4. What is the role of explicit instruction?
5. What types of focus-on-form are compatible with task-based teaching?
6. What types of corrective feedback are compatible with task-based teaching?
7. Should feedback be immediate or delayed until a task has been completed?
8. What kinds of participatory structure – group/pair work versus whole-class – are compatible with task-based teaching?
9. Are task-based abilities transferable?
10. How can teacher education programmes enable teachers to overcome the problems they face in task-based teaching?

are purely pedagogic in nature. Nunan (1989) first introduced the distinction between 'real-world tasks' and 'pedagogic tasks'. In a sense, any task carried out in a classroom ends up being 'pedagogic' but the distinction is useful because it encapsulates two kinds of authenticity – situational and interactional (Bachman & Palmer, 1996). Real-world tasks aim at situational authenticity as they are based on the target tasks performed in the outside world. An example might be a task where two students take on the roles of hotel receptionist and prospective guest where one has to make a booking for a room based on information provided by the latter. A pedagogic task lacks situational authenticity but aims at interactional authenticity (i.e. the kind of natural language processing found in communication in the world outside the classroom). An example is Spot the Difference. It is very unlikely that two people would engage in talk aimed at identifying the differences in two pictures in real life but this task can result in patterns of turn taking and repairs of misunderstandings that are typical of everyday talk and thus achieve interactional authenticity.

Long (1985, 2015, 2016) has consistently argued that the tasks in a course should be needs-based. He proposed that the starting point for establishing the content of a task-based syllabus should be the identification of those target tasks that a specific group of learners need in order to 'function adequately in a particular target domain' (Long, 1985: 91). There is an obvious advantage of such an approach as it helps to ensure content relevance. Long (2005) claimed that 'every language course should be considered a course for specific purposes, varying only (and considerably, to be sure) in the precision with which learner needs can be specified' (2005: 1).

There are, however, problems with such an approach. One problem is that learners have wants as well as needs and that good language teaching should go beyond addressing purely functional needs. Another problem concerns the procedures to be adopted in conducting a needs analysis. Long proposed first grouping specific target tasks into task types as the basis for designing pedagogic tasks and outlined the procedures to be followed (see Long, 2005, 2015) but this raises the thorny question as to how broad these task types should be. The main problem, however, is that it is difficult and perhaps impossible to identify target tasks for some groups of learners. In an instructional context where the target language plays no significant role in the wider society, identifying target tasks is clearly more problematic and can only be conducted on the basis of speculation about possible future uses of the target language. Cameron (2001), for example, argued that a needs-based syllabus is not feasible for young foreign language learners. Bachman (2002), in a discussion of task-based assessment also questioned whether tasks should be defined as target tasks for all L2 learners and argued that a needs-based approach is not always appropriate. He saw situational authenticity as not particularly relevant when the purpose is to assess the communicative abilities of general-purpose learners. For such learners, he argued, the aim should just be to achieve interactional authenticity in the assessment tasks. Whether tasks are to be defined as real-life tasks that have both situational and interactional authenticity or as pedagogic tasks that have interactional authenticity but no situational authenticity must surely depend on the instructional context.

Finally, clarification is needed as to whether a 'task' should be defined solely in terms of its design features or also in terms of how it is to be implemented. Skehan (2016) makes a clear distinction between design and implementation options. Robinson (2011b), however, conflates the two in his Cognition Hypothesis. For example, he includes +/− planning time in his list of variables that determine task complexity whereas Skehan treats planning as an implementation variable. My view is that a clear distinction should be made between design and implementation variables and that 'task' is a workplan and so should be specified solely in terms of its design features. The reasons for this will become clearer when I discuss issue #3 (task complexity and sequencing).

Issue 2: What Types of Tasks Should Figure in a Given Type of a Task-based Course?

Various typologies of task types have been proposed. These often consist of lists of the types of pedagogic tasks commonly found in task-based teaching (e.g. information/opinion gap, role-playing, personal, problem-solving, story-completion) – see, for example, Bruton (2002) and Willis (1996). What is lacking is a principled way of classifying such tasks. In Table 9.2 I distinguish two intersecting dimensions of tasks that constitute a more systematic way of classifying tasks and provide examples.

The distinction between input-based and output-tasks is an important one for a number of theoretical and practical reasons. Input-based tasks

Table 9.2 Types of tasks

	Unfocused – tasks involving general samples of language.	Focused – tasks designed to elicit the processing of specific, pre-determined linguistic features.
Input-based – tasks that do not require but do not prohibit production.	Written instructions about how to make a model airplane. Learners are required to read the instructions and assemble the model.	Oral descriptions of the location of animals in a zoo. The instructions are designed so that learners have to distinguish between singular and plural nouns. Learners place pictures of the animals in the correct locations. (Shintani, 2016)
Output-based – tasks that require speaking and/or writing to achieve the outcome.	Learners act as judges to decide what punishment to give to a number of offenders when given information about the crimes they had committed. (Foster & Skehan, 1996)	Things-in-pocket task (Samuda, 2001); learners shown the contexts of a person's pocket and asked to speculate who the person might be (target = epistemic models).

are needed for beginners, who lack the resources to produce in the L2; they provide learners with the comprehensible input that helps get them get started in learning an L2. Input-based tasks are also useful for introducing task-based teaching to learners who are accustomed to a more traditional, structural approach and who may be resistant to a mode of teaching that requires them to treat language as a tool rather than as an object. Input-based tasks are easily conducted with the whole class making them well-suited to large classes and to teachers more used to teaching in lockstep. Output-based tasks are needed to develop higher levels of proficiency (Swain, 1985). They provide greater opportunities for the negotiation of meaning (Long, 1996), the negotiation of form (Lyster, 2001) and 'languaging' (Swain, 2006), which have been shown to promote L2 acquisition.

Advocates of TBLT acknowledge that both input-based and output-based tasks have a role to play but, in fact, TBLT is nearly always discussed and researched in terms of output-based tasks. Willis and Willis (2007), for example, give scant attention to input-based tasks. All the studies in Robinson's (2011) book investigating the claims of the Cognition Hypothesis involve speaking tasks. Many of the misconceptions about TBLT have arisen because it is seen as necessarily involving speaking tasks (see Chapter 8). Given the importance attached to input in all theories of L2 acquisition, there is an obvious need to give greater attention to the role of input-based tasks in TBLT and to some extent this is now happening (e.g. Shintani, 2016).

The utility of focused – as opposed to unfocused tasks – is more controversial, as I have already noted. Both Long (2016) and Skehan (1998) see no need for them in TBLT. In Long's case this is because all tasks should be derived from target-tasks, thus allowing no place for tasks designed to focus on specific linguistic features. In Skehan's case, tasks are seen as the means for ensuring balanced development in terms of complexity, accuracy, fluency. In Ellis (2003), however, I argued that focused tasks have a place in both a language programme and in research designed to inform pedagogy. It is well-known that certain linguistic features (e.g. subject-verb agreement and complex structures such as hypothetical conditionals), constitute learning problems that continue even at advanced stages. However, I do not envisage a task-based programme composed entirely of focused tasks but rather their selective use when it becomes apparent that learners are attempting to use specific linguistic forms but cannot do so accurately. Focused tasks can be used to raise learners' awareness of the functional or semantic meanings of linguistic features as in Samuda's (2001) 'Things in Pocket' task. They allow for intensive corrective feedback directed at a target structure and, as is now well-established, such feedback is effective (Lyster *et al.*, 2012). In research, focused tasks make it possible to investigate whether the performance of tasks results in learning through pre- and post-testing, as for example in Mackey (1999) and the numerous corrective feedback studies. Measuring the learning that results from unfocused tasks is difficult and, in fact, has been rarely undertaken. A focused task, of course, must satisfy the same criteria as an unfocused task (see p. 12).

A particular type of focused task is a consciousness-raising task (Ellis, 1991). This makes a linguistic feature (typically grammatical or pragmatic) the topic of the task and aims to help learners achieve a metalinguistic understanding of a rule or regularity. Long (2016) dismisses consciousness-raising tasks on the grounds that they are 'components in the delivery of a traditional linguistic syllabus' (2016: 6). But this is to misunderstand the case I have made for them. Again, I do not envisage that such tasks should comprise a complete programme but see them as a means for developing explicit knowledge of specific features that are problematic to learners on the grounds that such knowledge might facilitate attention to these features in subsequent input and output and that aid acquisition. Furthermore, consciousness-raising tasks also provide opportunities for communicating if learners work together to 'solve' the linguistic problems they pose. It is in for this reason that they can still be called 'tasks'. After all, one can make language the topic of talk just like any other topic. Consciousness-raising tasks, however, clearly do not have a place in Long's version of TBLT where all tasks must address functional needs except perhaps in a task-based programme for linguists!

Issue 3: What Makes a Task Complex and How can Tasks be Sequenced Effectively?

The issue of task complexity is important for syllabus design if one accepts the basic premise that there should be a progression from 'simple' to 'complex'. The problem is how to define 'task complexity'. Long (2016) saw this as a 'real issue'. He noted that although 'much good work has been published on task complexity ... the overall yield has been disappointing' (2016: 27). He sees the solution as more research to 'help make findings cumulative, encourage replication studies, increase productivity, and generally speed up progress on this issue'. To my mind, however, little progress is likely until some fundamental issues have been addressed. These are considered below.

The problem, however, is perhaps less 'real' where input is concerned. There are established ways of determining the complexity of input. In the case of written input there are standard measures of readability, for example, the Dale-Chall (1948) formula. A limitation of these older measures is that they were based on vocabulary level and sentence length only. However, in more recent work (e.g. Pitler & Nenkova, 2008) measures that also take account of discourse factors such as cohesion and coherence have been developed. There is an enormous literature on readability and researchers interested in the design of task-based syllabuses would do well to refer to it. Readability measures may also be relevant for determining the listenability of oral texts as research has shown that the cognitive processes involved in reading and listening are not modality specific but rather draw on unimodal cortical regions of the brain (Jobard *et al.*, 2007). There is also research on foreigner-talk that points to the kinds of modifications that speakers intuitively make to facilitate communication. Also relevant is research showing that modification consisting of elaboration that makes the comprehension of the input easier by restructuring the propositional content more clearly is more effective than simplification (Long & Ross, 1993). Determining input complexity is relevant for all tasks that incorporate linguistic input in the task materials.

The main problem arises when it comes to determining the complexity of output tasks. The most developed framework for sequencing tasks from simple to complex – and the one that has attracted the most research – is Robinson's (2001, 2011b) Cognition Hypothesis, in particular those factors in his Triadic Componential Framework relating to Task Complexity, which he claims provide 'a parsimonious way to sequence L2 tasks in a programme of instruction' (2011b: 10). Robinson is concerned with how a given task can be varied to approximate ever more closely to the demands of a target task. For example, he proposes a task sequence that manipulates two task complexity factors ('simple' versus 'complex reasoning' and +/– 'planning'). The same basic reporting task is performed under different conditions that systematically enhance its complexity:

Pedagogic task 1: – reasoning/ + planning time.
Pedagogic task 2: – reasoning/ – planning time
Pedagogic task 3: + simple reasoning/ – planning time.
Pedagogic task 4: + complex reasoning/ – planning time

Such a proposal provides a predictive model that can be tested empirically. But there are some obvious problems with it and with the research based on it.

The first is that it cannot be assumed that a task designated as 'complex' actually entails a greater cognitive load. Current research such as Révész *et al.* (2016) is starting to address this by investigating how the specific design features of tasks affect the level of mental activity involved in performing the tasks. Sasayama (2016) used a dual task methodology, time-estimation, and learners' self-ratings to distinguish the cognitive load imposed by four narrative tasks predicted to vary in complexity. Her study showed that these tasks did indeed differ in the cognitive load they imposed. However, clear differences were only evident between the least and the most complex task in her study, suggesting that fine gradations may not impact on the actual complexity of tasks.

The second – and to my mind the more serious problem – is that tasks are holistic and thus involve conglomerates of factors. It is difficult to see how a task can be designed based solely on two of the many factors[1] that comprise the resource directing and resource-dispersion variables in Robinson's model. Sasayama's study found that there were task variables (such as code complexity) other than those she built into the design of her tasks that affected the cognitive load of the tasks. The question is, then, how do we take account of the clusters of design variables involved in any task in predicting the complexity of a given task? I can find no discussion of this is Robinson's or Sasayama's work.

The third problem is that the complexity of any single task will depend not just on the design of the task as workplan but also on how the workplan is implemented. Robinson's task sequence does in fact take this into account as it builds in +/− planning time – clearly an implementation variable – into the task sequence. But there are numerous other implementation variables that can affect the difficulty of performing a task – for example, asking the learners to perform a similar task first (Prabhu, 1987), asking learners to listen to a model performance of the task (Aston, 1982), brainstorming ideas relevant to the topic of the task (Skehan, 1996b), and, +/− pressure to perform the task rapidly (Yuan & Ellis, 2003). An inspection of Robinson's list of resource-directing and resource-dispersing variables reveals that apart from +/− planning there are no implementation variables. My point is this; if we want to investigate the effect of task complexity we must necessarily involve one or more implementation options. Sasayama's study, for example, incorporated two implementation variables – the learners did a 'practice' task before they started the sequence of four narrative tasks and they were given three seconds to look at the picture stories before they started to tell the stories. These implementation variables may have affected the cognitive load the learners experienced when performing the different tasks. Would the cognitive load of the different tasks have differed had they been given longer planning time, for example? In effect, the complexity of a task can never be considered separately from how the task is implemented. One might also ask what has the greatest impact on the complexity of a task and on cognitive load – the design features of the task or the conditions under which it is performed? Skehan (2016) is fairly clear on this. Although he does not reject the impact that design features can have on performance, he concludes that 'they do not generate consistency or robust generalizations' (2016: 37) and that 'putative manipulations of task complexity may not in reality produce different levels of complexity' (2016: 40) and then goes on to argue that studies that have investigated the effect of task conditions – such as pre-task planning – have produced more consistent results.[2]

In articulating these problems, however, I do not want to suggest that we should abandon the search for a model of task complexity. There is an obvious need for this as course designers and materials writers do need reliable criteria for determining task complexity. However, we do not currently have such criteria and we need not just a list of putative design variables but a theory of how the variables interact to determine complexity. Above all, we need to recognise that such a theory must also take account of the conditions under which a task is to be performed. Clearly, building such a theory is a major challenge.[3]

Finally, developing a task-based syllabus involves both the vertical and horizontal sequencing of tasks. By vertical sequencing I mean the order in which specific tasks (or task types) will figure in the syllabus. For example, if the starting point is the target tasks for a specific group of learners (as Long proposes) then decisions need to be taken about how to order these functionally oriented tasks. By horizontal sequencing I mean how different versions of the same task can be developed so that they lead incrementally to a simulation of the target task itself. Robinson's work on task complexity appears to be primarily concerned with horizontal sequencing but clearly we need to consider vertical sequencing as well.

These are all very real issues. It is not easy to see how they will be resolved and difficult to see how research will resolve them, at least in the short-term. In the meantime, perhaps, we need a practical way forward. In Ellis (2003) I suggested that designers of task-based courses will need to draw on both what research has shown about task complexity and on their own experience and intuitions about what constitutes the right type and level of task for a particular group of learners. From a practical standpoint intuition is needed and probably always will be.[4]

Issue 4: What is the Role of Explicit Instruction?

I addressed this question in Chapter 6. Here I offer some further thoughts about an issue that I see as central to thinking about task-based teaching.

In 'pure' TBLT – the kind that Long (2015) promotes – there is no room for explicit instruction preceding the performance of a task. Long argued that the default processes involved in L2 acquisition are those relating to incidental and implicit learning. He acknowledged, however, that these have 'reduced power' (2015: 40) in adults and that it is therefore necessary to facilitate intentional initial perception of new forms in the input. An obvious way to achieve this is through explicit instruction. However, Long rejects this on the grounds that it constitutes a return to FonFs, which he sees as incompatible with research that makes it clear that 'learners, not teachers, have most control over their development' (2015: 24). In Long's view explicit instruction followed by practice can only result in automatized declarative knowledge, not true implicit knowledge. Thus, Long argues for 'focus on form', where various pedagogic procedures are utilized to attract learners' attention to linguistic features *while* they are performing a task. In contrast, in task-supported language teaching (TSLT), specific linguistic forms are first taught explicitly and then practised in 'real operating conditions' using tasks (DeKeyser, 1998). TSLT is supported by skill-learning theory, which claims that practice enables declarative knowledge to be proceduralized and automatized.

In pitting 'focus on form' against 'focus on forms' some obvious questions need to be asked. One such question is whether FonFs instruction does or does not result in true implicit knowledge. This question is notoriously difficult to address given the difficulty in devising tests that afford separate measures of explicit and implicit knowledge. Some progress has been made (see, for example, Ellis, 2005), although problems still remain (see Suzuki & DeKeyser, 2015). What is clear, however, is that task-supported language teaching (TSLT) can, at least, result in the ability to deploy the target of instruction in unplanned language use. Long does not deny this but argues that it only occurs when massive practice of the target feature found such as that found in Day and Shapson (1991) and Harley (1989) is provided, which he suggests is not feasible if teachers need to cover all the linguistic features listed in the syllabus. This is a valid point but it is only a reason for rejecting TSLT as the basis for a complete course, not for the wholesale rejection of TSLT. TSLT might still have a place in helping learners acquire those linguistic features that are not learned 'naturally'. In fact, it was precisely this aim that motivated the studies by Day and Shapson and Harley, who investigated the effects of direct instruction on grammatical structures that previous research had shown immersion learners typically fail to acquire.

If we accept that both FonF and FonFs can result in the kind of L2 knowledge (implicit or automatized explicit knowledge) that enables learners to communicate fluently and accurately – and there is plenty of evidence to support this – then we still need to ask whether, in the long term, one approach is more effective or efficient than the other. Unfortunately, most of the studies that have sought to compare TBLT and TSLT (e.g. De la Fuente, 2006; Laufer, 2006; Sheen, 2006) have been short term and/or methodologically flawed. This question cannot be answered until we have well-designed, longitudinal comparative studies.

There is, however, another question that needs to be considered. Does prior explicit instruction affect how a task is performed – for example, by causing learners to focus on practising the target structure rather than trying to communicate? In other words, if learners are focused on trying to produce the target structure correctly, does the task still afford 'real operating conditions'? Again, there has been surprisingly little research that has addressed this question. I reviewed two studies that have examined the effect that explicit instruction has on the performance of a task in Chapter 6, noting that they produced different results. Mochizuki and Ortega (2008) reported that a group that received a hand-out providing explicit information about English relative clauses produced more than twice as many relative clauses when they performed the focused task than a group that did not receive the hand-out and that there was no difference in the global complexity and fluency of the production of the two groups. The second study, Li *et al.* (forthcoming), also found that learners who had received explicit instruction in the target structure (past passive) were more likely to try to use it when they performed the tasks than learners who did not receive this instruction. In this study, however, the explicit instruction did have an effect on global complexity, accuracy and fluency with the explicit instruction group producing language that was less complex and fluent and that also tended to be less accurate overall. Whether and to what extent explicit instruction 'interferes' in the way a task is performed is an important issue for TSLT. If it does interfere, then clearly tasks in TSLT are not functioning as they do in TBLT. Even if they result in better learning of the target structure, they will not provide the same opportunities for natural language use and thus, in the long term, may be less successful in developing all round proficiency in the L2. Clearly, though, this is an issue in need of further investigation.

Issue 5: What Types of Focus-on-Form are Compatible with Task-based Teaching?

Ellis *et al.* (2001) distinguished pre-emptive and reactive form-focused episodes (FFEs) that occurred in task-based lessons. In the former either a student or the teacher initiated a focus on a specific linguistic feature. In the latter a classroom participant (normally the teacher) drew attention to a particular linguistic form that was the source of a problem either because the meaning of an utterance was not clear or because an utterance contained a linguistic error. In the 448 FFEs Ellis *et al.* identified in 12 hours of teaching, 165 were student-initiated pre-emptive FFEs, 41 pre-emptive teacher-initiated FFEs and 223 reactive FFEs. This study shows that both pre-emptive and reactive FFEs can occur frequently in task-based teaching.

As I pointed out in Chapter 4, Long (2015) insists that focus-on-form should be reactive. He defines it as involving 'reactive use of a wide variety of pedagogic procedures to draw learners' attention to linguistic problems in context, as they arise in communication'. Thus, for Long focus on form is necessarily 'a *response* to a difficulty' (2015: 317; italics in original). He recognizes that there will be times when it is necessary for teachers to draw learners' attention to form explicitly but this too should occur as a response to what learners have said or written. Long does not discuss pre-emptive focus on form but it would seem that he has little time for it.

Research has concerned itself almost entirely with reactive focus on form (see, for example, the corrective feedback studies). There has been almost no research that has examined pre-emptive focus on form. Ellis *et al.* (2001) investigated the likelihood of successful uptake (defined as the correct repair of a linguistic feature or demonstrated understanding of an item) occurring in pre-emptive and reactive form-focused episodes (FFEs). They reported that successful uptake was more likely to occur in learner-initiated pre-emptive and in reactive FFEs than in teacher-initiated pre-emptive FFEs. Successful uptake, of course, cannot be equated with acquisition but in another study Loewen (2005) reported that successful uptake was the most significant variable predicting learning as measured in tailor-made tests of those linguistic forms that were addressed in class-room FFEs. Taken, together, these two studies suggest that, as Long claims, reactive focus on form facilitates learning, but also that pre-emptive focus on form, especially when initiated by students, is beneficial.

The issue here is how narrowly we are to define focus on form – as purely reactive or as also pre-emptive. Given that students (adult ones at least) tend to naturally topicalize problematic linguistic points during the performance of a task, it would seem unwise to dismiss pre-emptive focus on form. In Chapter 4 I argued for a broad definition of focus-on-form and also noted that it is best viewed as a set of procedures rather than an approach as the same procedures can occur in both TBLT and TSLT.

Issue 6: What Types of Corrective Feedback are Compatible with Task-based Teaching?

Reactive focus on form mainly consists of corrective feedback. The six types of corrective feedback that Lyster and Ranta (1997) identified in their study of immersion classrooms has informed the considerable body of experimental research that followed. This research was directed at investigating the effect that different types of corrective feedback have on acquisition. Some researchers (e.g. Ammar & Spada, 2006; Lyster, 2004) investigated the relative effects of input-providing feedback (e.g. recasts) versus output-prompting feedback (e.g. clarification requests, metalinguistic feedback and elicitation). Other researchers (e.g. Ellis *et al.*, 2006) investigated implicit feedback (i.e. recasts, clarification requests and repetitions) versus explicit feedback (i.e. explicit correction and metalinguistic feedback). These two dimensions of feedback intersect so each feedback strategy can be classified in terms of whether it is input-providing or output-prompting and implicit or explicit. For example, recasts (at least those that are 'conversational' in nature) can be classified as input-providing and implicit and metalinguistic feedback as output-prompting and explicit.

This typology of corrective feedback strategies has provided a basis for making and testing theory-based claims about the efficacy of different types of feedback. Lyster (2004) drew on skill-learning theory to argue that output-prompting feedback is more likely to be beneficial than input-providing feedback (recasts) on the grounds that learners more frequently repair their errors following the former. Long (2006), however, claimed that recasts are more likely to promote acquisition as they provide learners with positive input for 'new' features and disputed whether the uptake of feedback has any utility. Theoretical arguments can also be made for implicit and explicit feedback; implicit feedback caters to implicit learning whereas explicit feedback is more likely to result in the conscious attention to form that Schmidt (2001) saw as important for acquisition and lead to explicit learning. From a theoretical perspective, there is an obvious need to investigate the effects of these different corrective strategies. Goo and Mackey (2013), for example, argue for carefully designed studies that investigate the effects of narrowly prescribed types of corrective feedback.

However, there are several reasons for doubting the practical relevance of the research. First, the relative effects of different types of feedback are contextually constrained; thus one type may be more effective in one context and another in a different context. Second, teachers are likely to quite naturally employ a variety of strategies rather than stick to a single type – although research does suggest that recasts tend to predominate in the meaning-focused interactions that tasks elicit. Third, it is possible to combine different strategies when addressing a particular error – for example, in 'corrective recasts' (Doughty & Varela, 1998) errors are first corrected by means of a repetition (i.e. output-prompting) and then by means of a recast (i.e. input-providing) if the repetition did not result in successful uptake. Combining strategies in this way is likely to make the feedback explicit and therefore more salient to learners. Fourth, and perhaps most important, the research has typically investigated the effects of intensive feedback directed at a single linguistic feature (e.g. regular past tense) elicited by means of focused tasks. For obvious reasons, there has been very little experimental research that has investigated extensive feedback directed at a whole range of linguistic problems as these arise during the performance of unfocused tasks, which some advocates of TBLT (e.g. Long and Skehan) have argued should constitute the content of a task-based course. A more pedagogically relevant approach to investigating the effects of corrective feedback would involve longitudinal studies where the feedback is extensive rather than intensive but such research is currently lacking.

The theoretical controversies concerning the relative merits of input-providing versus output-prompting and implicit versus explicit feedback appear to be abating. Long's early commitment to recasts as an implicit form of feedback (see Long, 1996, 2006) is less evident in his later publications (Long, 2015) in part because he now sees feedback as catering to intentional learning as well as to incidental learning. He currently considers the provision of explicit grammar rules as legitimate so long as this occurs in response to problems that arise during communication. In other words, he advocates a variety of feedback strategies – a view echoed by Ellis (2009) and Lyster and Ranta (2013). Teachers do need to know, however, the potential benefits of the different strategies and to guard against over-utilizing a single type.

Issue 7: Should Feedback be Immediate or Delayed until after the Task has been Completed?

A common misconception about TBLT is that 'acquisition only takes place online during communication' (Swan, 2005a: 379). Long (2016) pointed out that that this is not the case but he also questioned whether metalinguistic knowledge acquired at one time can be used by the learner at another time – as Swan claimed can happen. What Long emphasizes is that focus on form must be reactive. At issue, however, is whether reactive focus on form needs to occur during the performance of a task or can delayed until the task has been completed. I considered this issue in Chapter 6 and so will just review the main points here.

There has been little discussion of this issue in TBLT circles and little research that has investigated it. From a psycholinguistic perspective, which emphasizes learning through interaction, immediate feedback is preferable. But a theoretical case can be made for delaying feedback – for example Preparatory Attention and Memory Theory, which proposes that learning is enhanced when complete attention is available rather than divided between multiple goals and that learners are more likely to pay attention to feedback when it is subsequently made available to them. Currently it is not really possible to decide between these two positions. The research that has taken place has reported mixed findings. McDonough and Mackey (2006) found that what they called 'primed repetition' of recasts (i.e. repetition that did not take place immediately following the recasts but within six turns) was associated with L2 development. Immediate repetition was not. However, it could be argued that the 'primed repetition' in this study was more of an immediate than a delayed response. Quinn (2014) found neither immediate nor delayed feedback produced better learning than a task only (i.e. no feedback) condition. Li *et al.* (2016), however, reported both the immediate and delayed feedback led to gains in accuracy whereas the no-feedback group did not. However, the benefits were only evident in a test measuring explicit knowledge, with immediate feedback showing some advantage over delayed feedback for those learners that had some prior knowledge of the target structure.

There is insufficient research to adjudicate on this issue. Quinn and Nakata (2017), in their review of the research investigating it concluded that 'the dearth and inconsistency of the findings in the research of CF timing clearly indicate the need for future research' (2017: 42) and hesitated to point out any pedagogical implications. It is clear, however, that the pedagogic advice that teachers should desist from correcting learners during fluency work has no warrant. In fact, teachers do focus on form during communicative tasks even when they believe they should not be doing so (Basturkmen *et al.*, 2004).

Issue 8: What Kinds of Participatory Structure – Group/Pair Work, Whole-Class – Are Compatible with Task-based Teaching?

In Chapter 8 I noted that tasks can be performed in a variety of participatory structures, including teacher-class – as is necessary with input-based tasks – and individually when learners work by themselves – as in Prabhu's (1987) Communicational Teaching Project. Teachers have a choice of participatory structures in TBLT. Even speaking tasks can be conducted through teacher-class interaction, as illustrated in Ellis *et al.* (2001) and Loewen (2005).

What is lacking is any discussion about what constitutes an appropriate participatory structure for different groups of students. The advantages of small group work are well-documented – see, for example, Long and Porter (1985). But there are also potential disadvantages. As I mentioned above, it is not reasonable to expect beginner-level learners to perform speaking tasks in groups as they lack the necessary proficiency and thus will resort to their L1 or else produce the kind of restricted, pidgin-like output that Seedhouse (1999) was critical of. I have also argued that using group work may not be the best way to introduce students to TBLT if their previous experience of classroom instruction consisted only of traditional, lockstep teaching. There is also the problem that focus on form may be limited in group work. Adams (2007) reviewed a number of studies that have examined whether and to what extent learners correct each other when performing tasks in groups, concluding that 'while learner–learner interactions may provide a site for feedback to occur, the restricted set of feedback types may not provide evidence appropriate to learner developmental needs' (2007: 33). Of course, much depends on the nature of the tasks the learners perform, with some tasks being more likely to lead to the negotiation of meaning and a focus on form than others. Adams' own study found that learners did provide each other with feedback when performing opinion-gap and information-gap tasks and that it resulted in both grammar and vocabulary learning. Swain's research (e.g. Swain, 1998) also provides convincing evidence that language-related episodes arise as learners perform tasks and that learning results especially if the problems that these episodes address are resolved successfully. However, often studies such as these were carried out in a laboratory setting and with intermediate or advanced level learners. More evidence is needed to show how far focus on form is common and facilitative of learning in different participatory structures with learners of different proficiency levels.

Issue 9: Are Task-based Abilities Transferable?

This is one of the 'real issues' that Long (2016) addressed. There are, in fact, two related issues here. One is whether the performance of one task (or one of a series of tasks) results in improved performance on subsequent new tasks. This is a fundamental issue for TBLT. TBLT advocates emphasize how tasks can promote effective learning but there is only limited evidence to show that there is transferability of whatever is learned to a new task. The second issue concerns assessment. How do we determine whether performing tasks results in learning?

Experimental studies have frequently used tasks as pre- and post-tests to measure the learning of specific linguistic forms that results from performing the treatment tasks. In cases where the performance of the treatment task involves some kind of intervention (for example, corrective feedback) there is clear evidence of learning. However, in cases where there is no such intervention, transferability to a new task may not be found (see Ellis, 2009). The clearest evidence of this can be found in task-repetition studies. In these studies, learners are asked to repeat the same task without any intervention between performances and then to perform a new task (typically of the same type). Complexity, accuracy and fluency improve when the task is repeated but this improvement does not seem to transfer to the performance of a new task. It is possible, however, that although transferability is not evident in these global measures, it may become evident in the use of specific linguistic features (see, for example, Shintani & Ellis, 2014). Also, task repetition studies that included some kind of intervention between performances of the task (e.g. an explicit focus on specific linguistic forms) have shown that transfer of learning to a new task can occur (e.g. Baleghizadeh & Derakhshesh, 2012; Hawkes, 2012). Much of the TBLT research has been premised on the assumption that by manipulating task design features and implementation options (such as pre-task planning) it is possible to prioritize the attention that learners pay to complexity, accuracy and fluency and over time this will help them to achieve a balanced proficiency. But research that focuses on the one-off performance of a task cannot show that development has taken place. Again, to establish transferability longitudinal studies are needed.

There is plenty of good work on assessing the outcomes of task-based instruction (see, for example, the special issues on task-based assessment in *Language Testing* in 2002). However, from my own experience teachers often ask how they can assess students in TBLT when there are no explicit linguistic targets (i.e. the tasks are unfocused). Norris (2016), in a review of work on task-based language assessment (TBLA), commented that 'designing, implementing and evaluating task-based language assessments are by no means simple tasks' and went on to list the issues involved:

> ... the extent to which tasks and associated language use contexts can be adequately simulated within controlled testing conditions, the authenticity of criteria for evaluating task performances, the reliability of raters in judging task performance, the comparability of tasks in terms of construct representation as well as difficulty, the generalizability and extrapolation limitations as a basis for assessment design, and the practicality and expense involved in creating and using task-based tests. (Norris, 2016: 239–240)

These problems are more acute with speaking assessment tasks. Input-based tasks can be assessed more easily in terms of whether learners achieve the outcome of the task (e.g. can correctly draw in the route described on a map). Whatever the difficulties, however, assessment of learning must be task-based. TBLT is directed at integrative, holistic learning and cannot be assessed through discrete-point tests, which if used are likely to have a negative wash-back effect on teaching.

Issue 10: How can Teacher Education Programmes Enable Teachers to Overcome the Problems they Face in Task-based Teaching?

This is another real issue that Long acknowledged. In many respects, it is the most serious problem. TBLT, with its emphasis on holistic teaching and learning-through-doing constitutes a major innovation for many teachers. Prabhu (1987) recognized this:

> A new perception of pedagogy, implying a different pattern of classroom activity, is an intruder into teachers' mental frames – an unsettling one, because there is a conflict of mismatch between the old and new perceptions and, more seriously a threat to prevailing routines and to the sense of security dependent on them. (1987: 105)

In Ellis (1997) I listed the key characteristics of successful innovation. These included the teacher's dissatisfaction his/her current practice, the feasibility of the new approach in the particular context in which the teacher works, the extent to which the new approach is seen as matching the needs of the students, how easy the principles and procedures of the new approach are to grasp, the extent to which teachers are required to demonstrate a high degree of originality in order to implement the innovation, and, perhaps, crucially, the extent to which teachers feel that they 'own' the innovation. It is easy to see how TBLT might run into problems and, indeed, evaluations of TBLT (e.g. Carless, 2004) have shown that in some contexts it was not successful. Teachers may lack confidence in their L2 proficiency and thus feel that they cannot use tasks (Butler, 2011). Students may be unconvinced that the incidental learning that TBLT caters to is the most efficient way of learning an L2. A particular problem noted by Carless (2004) is that teachers do not always have a clear idea of what a 'task' is. He found that the tasks used by primary school teachers in Hong Kong often ended up as 'language practice' rather than affording opportunities for genuine communication. Erlam (2016) found that the tasks she asked teachers to design in an in-service programme did not fully match up to a definition of a 'task'.[5] In particular, the teachers tended to design tasks that involved the prior presentation of language reflecting their pre-existing ideas of what an instructional activity should do.

These are real problems. They can only be addressed through carefully designed initial and in-service teacher training/education programmes that take account of the characteristics of successful innovations. An excellent model of how TBLT can be successfully introduced can be found in Van den Branden's (2006c) account of its implementation in Flanders (Belgium). This involved the development of task-based syllabuses, extensive teacher training, and ongoing research into the implementation of task-based programmes. However, to date, there has been very little research investigating the how effective teacher education/training programmes are in enabling teachers to implement TBLT.

Conclusion

Misconceptions about TBLT abound. In part these are the product of the kind of research that has investigated tasks – often laboratory-based and often focusing on the performance of single tasks. These misconceptions are likely to prevail until there are more accounts of full task-based courses. Doubts will also continue to exist until it can be shown that TBLT is effective – not just in developing communicative ability but also in achieving linguistic accuracy. Critics of TBLT are unlikely to be convinced until there are more studies like Shintani (2016), who produced evidence that TBLT is more effective than traditional, structural teaching.

But although it is clearly necessary to address the misconceptions, it is equally important to acknowledge and try to address the real problems of designing and implementing task-based courses. This has been the main focus of this article. I have discussed 10 issues and suggested ways in which they might be addressed.

I do not see TBLT as constituting a single, monolithic approach and this affects how I see the kinds of developments that are needed to move TBLT forward. Whereas Long's version of TBLT emphasizes the importance of needs-analysis to identify the target tasks relevant to a specific group of learners, I have argued such an approach is not feasible in contexts such as the state educational systems in East Asia that I am familiar with. Nor do I see task-based language teaching and task-supported language teaching involving explicit instruction and focused tasks as incompatible but rather as mutually supporting. There is plenty of evidence to show that explicit instruction involving focused tasks is effective (see Chapter 6). Not all linguistic features can be acquired incidentally and implicitly through task-based teaching. Redundant, non-salient and complex features, especially when these are 'blocked' by the learner's L1, are unlikely to be acquired even with the help of focus on form. For such features explicit instruction is necessary. It is for this reason that I argue for a hybrid syllabus consisting primarily of a task-based component but supported by a task-supported component to address recalcitrant linguistic problems when these become evident. Task-based and task-supported teaching draw on different psycho-linguistic rationales – as Long (2015) pointed out – but it does not follow that we should opt for just one of these. Successful L2 acquisition clearly does call for learning incidentally through task-based teaching but it can also benefit from the skill-development that task-supported teaching can provide. To my mind, then, the final 'real issue' that has to be addressed is how to design courses that are task-based but that also build in, where needed, opportunities for working on specific linguistic problems through task-supported teaching. I address this issue – to my mind the central one for task-oriented instruction – in the following chapter.

Notes

(1)   Robinson (2001, 2011b) provides a taxonomy of resource-directing and resource-dispersing factors. Examples of the former are +/− few elements, +/− here and now, +/− reasoning demands. Examples of the latter are +/− planning, +/− single task and +/− prior knowledge. His taxonomy does not exhaust all the possible features of a task.

(2)   A reviewer of this article also suggested another reason why the design of a task cannot be expected to have a predictable effect on complexity – learners can always use strategies to handle problems that they experience with tasks, for example, by breaking down propositions into sub-propositions or sharing out parts of the task dialogically.

(3)   Skehan (2016) suggests that the challenge of developing a theory that can inform how design and implementation variables impact on task performance might best be met by drawing on Levelt's (1989) model of speaking and has attempted to do this in his own research.

(4)   It is also possible that learners' engagement with a task will be more influenced by whether they find the tasks relevant or interesting than by task-complexity. See Chapter 7.

(5)   The tasks used in research on TBLT also do not always satisfy the definition of a task.

10 Towards a Modular Language Curriculum for Using Tasks

Introduction

Task-based language teaching (TBLT) and task-supported language teaching (TSLT) are often seen as incompatible as they draw on different theories of language learning and language teaching. The position I will develop in this chapter, however, is that both approaches are needed, especially in instructional contexts where 'pure' task-based teaching may be problematic for various reasons. I argue the case for a modular curriculum consisting of separate (i.e. non-integrated) task-based and structure-based components. I will discuss different curriculum models in the light of what is known about how a second language is learned. The model that I support assumes the importance of developing fluency first. It consists of a primary task-based module implemented with focus-on-form (Long, 1991) and, once a basic proficiency has been achieved, supported by a secondary structural module to provide for explicit accuracy-oriented work to counteract learned selective attention (N. Ellis, 2006), one of the main sources of persistent error.

I will also address the content and grading of the task-based and structural modules. I will consider the factors involved in the vertical and horizontal grading of tasks and argue that, for the time being, syllabus designers will have to draw on their experience and intuition as much as on theory and research to make decisions about how to sequence tasks. I suggest that the structural component is best used as a checklist rather than as a syllabus so as to allow teachers to address selectively those features that are found to be problematic for their students when they perform tasks.

Two Kinds of Syllabus

In the 1970s, the traditional structural syllabus, consisting typically of an inventory of grammatical items, was challenged when new models of language (Halliday, 1973; Hymes, 1971) emerged, resulting in proposals for a communicative syllabus based on a functional view of language. The notional syllabus proposed by Wilkins (1976) drew heavily on these models of language. It listed semantic and functional categories – such as possibility and requesting – along with the linguistic means for realising these in language use. Such a syllabus was deemed 'analytic' in the sense that it required the learner to induce the elements comprising the linguistic system from the holistic input provided. In this respect it was viewed as fundamentally different from the 'synthetic' structural syllabus, where linguistic (typically grammatical) elements are taught, leaving it to the learner to assemble them in order to communicate.

In a sense, however, the structural and notional syllabuses were not so different. They were both examples of what White (1988) called a Type A syllabus. That is, they both focused on *what* is to be learned – the grammatical features in the case of the structural syllabus and the linguistic exponents of notions and functions in the notional syllabus. Both were interventionist and other-directed; that is they sought to plot the course of learning for the learner. White argued that Type B syllabuses are fundamentally different in that they focus on *how* language is to be learned, are non-interventionist and involve no pre-selection of the elements to be learned. A Type B syllabus assumes that learners have their own internal syllabus and should be left to follow this without any attempt to impose a sequence of learning externally. Consequently, the content of a Type B syllabus is not framed in language terms but rather in terms of either subject matter as in immersion programmes and content-based language teaching or as 'tasks' in task-based language teaching.

Brumfit (1984) made a similar distinction to White's. He distinguished a product-based syllabus consisting of explicitly stated linguistic content catering to an 'accuracy' approach to teaching, where the primary focus is on language-as-usage, and a process-based syllabus consisting of subject content and/or problem-solving activities catering to a 'fluency' approach, where the focus is on the use of language for meaning-making. This distinction between an 'accuracy' and 'fluency' approach[1] rests on the intended mental set of the learner – in one case it involves requiring learners to demonstrate the ability to understand or produce specific linguistic features and in the other to engage in natural language use. Brumfit saw these two approaches as distinct but argued that both are needed in a language programme. He proposed an integrated curriculum with a variable emphasis on accuracy and fluency according to the learners' developmental stage. I will return to his integrated syllabus later.

Task-supported and Task-based Language Teaching

Task-supported language teaching (TSLT) and TBLT both make use of 'tasks' (i.e. workplans designed to provide opportunities for using language under real-operating conditions). However, tasks have very different functions in TSLT and TBLT. TSLT draws on a Type A syllabus, it is product-oriented, and it involves an accuracy-oriented approach. In contrast, TBLT draws on a Type B syllabus, is process-oriented, and constitutes a fluency-based approach although with attention to form built in through the design of tasks and by how they are implemented. In other words, tasks are simply methodological devices for practising specific structures in TSLT but serve as the means for defining the content of an instructional programme in TBLT.

The intended mental set created by a task differs markedly in TSLT and TBLT. In the former, a task aims to provide opportunities for learners to display correct use of explicitly taught target language features while trying to achieve a communicative outcome. In the latter, a task aims to provide opportunities for using language naturally in order to achieve a communicative outcome. In both cases it is anticipated that learners will pay attention to form but in TSLT students are *directed* to attend to a pre-determined form, whereas in TBLT attention to form arises *incidentally* while learners are performing the task.

For TSLT focused tasks are required – that is tasks that are designed in such a way as to create contexts for the use (receptively or productively) of pre-determined target features (i.e. those features that have been explicitly taught). Focused tasks can also figure in TBLT and indeed have been used in a large number of studies that have investigated tasks (e.g. Doughty & Varela, 1998; Lyster, 2004; Mackey, 1999). But when focused tasks are used in TBLT there is no *a priori* attempt to make learners aware of the linguistic feature targeted by the task. Focused tasks may or may not be successful in eliciting use of the target feature (Loschky & Bley-Vroman, 1993).[2] An important issue, then, is whether such tasks are more effective in eliciting use of the target feature when learners' attention is explicitly directed to it as in TSLT than when it is not as in TBLT. Another key issue is whether the general quality of language produced (i.e. its complexity, global accuracy and fluency) differs when a focused task is performed in TSLT (with *a priori* explicit instruction) and in TBLT (with no *a priori* explicit instruction).[3] In short, we need to know whether explicit instruction affects how focused tasks are performed.

Some advocates of TBLT, however, (e.g. Long, 2015; Skehan, 1998), reject what they call 'structure tapping tasks' and argue for the use of only unfocused tasks (i.e. tasks designed to elicit only general samples of language) supported by a well-established set of methodological procedures for drawing learners' attention to form as they perform the tasks. These involve 'focus on form', defined by Long (2015) as the 'reactive use of a wide variety of pedagogic procedures to draw learners' attention to linguistic problems in context, as they arise during communication' (2015: 317). Long sees such procedures as relating only to TBLT. However, as I argued in Chapter 4, the procedures that Long has in mind (e.g. corrective feedback strategies) are equally applicable to TSLT. At the discourse level, strategies for focusing attention on form are applicable and relevant to both types of teaching although it is an open question whether the learners' response to these procedures is the same in TSLT and TBLT.

TSLT and TBLT draw on very different theories of language learning. TSLT is based on skill-learning theory as this has been applied to language learning (DeKeyser, 1998). This theory claims that learning commences with a declarative representation of a linguistic feature, which is first proceduralized and then automatized through practice. DeKeyser (1998) distinguished two types of practice needed to effect the change from declarative to automatized procedural knowledge. In communicative drills learners can draw on 'declarative crutches' to assist proceduralization. More open-ended activities – i.e. tasks – facilitate automatization. This theory then lends support to presentation–practice–production (PPP), arguably the mainstream methodology in structural language teaching today and, in effect, the same as TSLT. DeKeyser, however, was careful to recognize the limitations of PPP. First, he acknowledged that the L2 knowledge that results may not be true implicit knowledge (i.e. the kind of knowledge that arises during first language acquisition) but rather automatized explicit knowledge. He considered that such knowledge is 'functionally equivalent' to implicit knowledge and so is sufficient for communicative purposes. More importantly he also suggested that skill-acquisition theory is 'most easily applicable' to 'the learning of simple structures' (DeKeyser, 2015: 101) and that only learners with a high aptitude for language learning are able to master complex structures (DeKeyser, 2000). Examples of simple structures are English plural –s and interrogative word order; examples of complex structures are English articles and subject–verb inversion after negative adverbials such as 'rarely'. The caveats that DeKeyser raises are important as they suggest that, although TSLT may serve to develop a basic L2 competence, for most learners it may not be effective for developing more advanced levels of competence.[4]

In contrast, TBLT draws on research-driven theories of L2 acquisition that emphasize the importance of social interaction, usage-based learning, and implicit or incidental acquisition. Research demonstrating that there is a natural order and sequence of acquisition for grammatical features (Ellis, 2008: Chap. 3) constitutes evidence for a built-in learner syllabus that cannot be easily subverted through form-focused instruction. In TBLT, L2 learning is incidental and implicit – 'the default learning mechanism' (Long, 2015) – with learners following their own learning path to the target grammar. The aim is to provide contexts for this mechanism to operate. However, even though 'incidental and implicit learning remain options for adult learners' (2015: 45) because there is a decrease in learners' ability to learn implicitly at puberty and beyond Long argued that instruction needs to make linguistic forms – especially those that learners fail to learn naturally – salient through the use of focus on form procedures. TBLT, then, aims to enhance natural learning processes through focus on form.

TSLT and TBLT are not just seen as alternative approaches to teaching an L2 but as incompatible. This is apparent in the critiques that have been levelled at TBLT by advocates of TSLT (e.g. Sheen, 1994; Swan, 2005a) and also by the position adopted by some advocates of TBLT (e.g. Long, 2015). Swan, for example, argued that those second language acquisition (SLA) researchers who promote TBLT 'legislate by hypothesis' and disputed the validity of the hypotheses he saw as underpinning TBLT (i.e. the Online, Noticing and Teachability Hypotheses) on the grounds that there was insufficient evidence to support them. Sheen (2006) claimed that there is no evidence that TBLT is more effective than TSLT and reported his own study, which he claimed showed the superiority of TSLT.[5] However, many of the points raised by Sheen and Swan display a misunderstanding of what TBLT is and an ignorance of the relevant research – see Chapter 8 and Long (2016) for refutations of their critiques. Long (2015), on the other side of this debate, claimed that TSLT and TBLT are incompatible because they are based on different psycholinguistic theories (as outlined above). He emphasized the fundamental difference between TSLT as 'synthetic' and TBLT as 'analytic' and dismissed the focused tasks used in TSLT as 'counterfeit' tasks – 'little more than activities and exercises relabelled as tasks' (2015: 6). Interestingly, however, he did acknowledge that TLST has its champions and, citing Shehadeh (2005), suggested that it might serve 'as a bridge between traditional synthetic syllabi and genuine task-based approaches' (2005: 7). However, he did not elaborate on how this bridge might be constructed.

To sum up this section, TSLT and TBLT constitute different ways of using tasks in language teaching. The former is synthetic and product-oriented, drawing on a structural syllabus and an accuracy-oriented methodology. The latter is analytic and process-oriented, drawing on a task-based syllabus and a fluency-oriented methodology. TSLT and TBLT are based on different learning theories, skill-learning theory in the case of TSLT and usage-based theories of implicit/incidental learning in the case of TBLT. In both TSLT and TBLT, however, the same set of focus-on-form procedures are needed. TSLT and TBLT are often presented in the literature as alternative ways of teaching and incompatible, each with its own advocates.

In the following section I want to challenge the view that TSLT and TBLT are incompatible. I will draw on both Brumfit's (1984) educational arguments for combining accuracy and fluency approaches and on my own theory of second language learning (Ellis, 1994) to argue the need for a curriculum that combines a product-based component realized through TSLT and a process-based component realized through TBLT. Later I will consider how these two components can be organized in a curriculum.

The Compatibility of Task-supported and Task-based Language Teaching

The educational case for adopting a curriculum that integrates task-supported and task-based language teaching was convincingly made by Brumfit (1984) some time ago. His starting point was:

> We seem to have two different types of information available to us for incorporation in a syllabus: that which is capable of systematization, and that which is not. (1984: 101)

Brumfit argued that a syllabus cannot be just 'a random joining together of elements with no particular cohesion or system' (1984: 98.) He argued that even if a structural syllabus does not accord with the learners' internal syllabus, this does not warrant discarding it and noted that 'insofar as we wish to make our language teaching coherent to either learners or teachers, we have little choice but to turn to the systems of linguists' (1984: 94).

Brumfit's case for a product syllabus, however, goes beyond the need for systematicity. He recognized that 'the key issue will be the expectations about the nature of learning ... which students bring to the school' (1984: 100) and argued that 'a syllabus will also have to operate in the real educational world' (1984: 117). This is a position more recently taken up by Littlewood (2014), who challenged the feasibility of task-based teaching in the Chinese context on the grounds that it is ill-suited to the traditional Chinese culture of learning, where 'education is conceived more as a process of knowledge accumulation than as a process of using knowledge for immediate purposes' (2014: 653). Littlewood listed a whole range of problems that he argued make the successful implementation of TBLT difficult and perhaps impossible in such a context – the problem of using TBLT in large classes, the excessive demands that TBLT makes on the language skills of teachers with limited communicative ability, the need for new organizational skills required for group work, the tendency of students to talk in the mother tongue when performing tasks, students' beliefs that language learning involves the item-by-item progression through a syllabus, and teachers' commitment to the traditional view of teaching as the transmission of knowledge.[6] Although Littlewood overstates the difficulties involved in introducing TBLT, many of the problems he mentions warrant serious attention. It was Littlewood's conviction that TBLT is impractical in contexts such as China that led him to argue in favour of TSLT.

Brumfit, however, did not reach the same conclusion as Littlewood:

> We have, then, a product-based syllabus in order to ensure that there are some controls on the activity that takes place in the classroom. But it is clear that the syllabus must also contain a process element. (1984: 117)

He saw the need for a 'delicate balance between a specification which is so unrealistic as to prevent change, and one which is so conventional as to reinforce the past and equally prevent change' (1984: 117). He acknowledged that 'language is best memorized when the learner is exposed to suggestion rather than to overt and self-conscious presentation of the system' (1984: 100) and discussed the Bangalore Project (subsequently called the Communicational Teaching Project – Prabhu, (1987)) at length as an example of a process-syllabus and a fluency-based approach.[7]

The key question, then, becomes how to combine product- and process-based approaches. Brumfit saw a linguistic syllabus as serving two purposes. It provides a structure for the initial teaching of linguistic tokens and it can be used as a checklist to enable teachers to check coverage and relevancy of material. He was less clear, however, about the process element of the curriculum and did not take on board Prabhu's task-based syllabus. Instead, he emphasized the role of projects to provide opportunities for fluency work. Project work was to be supported through the presentation of relevant linguistic tokens of the target language (but avoiding over-exact analyses of the language to be so taught), input material that is comprehensible, interesting and relevant, and corrective feedback. Brumfit also made the important point that a syllabus does not dictate the methodology to be employed, thus allowing for the possibility that lessons motivated by a linguistic syllabus could incorporate fluency work – which is, in fact, exactly what TSLT seeks to achieve in the free-production stage of a lesson. The integrated model that Brumfit proposed is shown schematically in Figure 10.1. Accuracy and fluency work occur from the start (Year 1) but the balance changes over time, with accuracy work based on a linguistic syllabus dominating initially before giving way increasingly to fluency work involving projects as proficiency increases.[8]

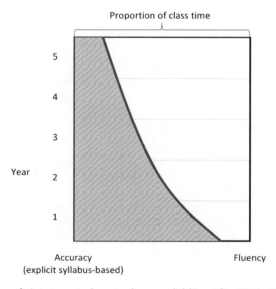

Figure 10.1 Brumfit's integrated curriculum model (Brumfit, 1984: 119)

Where Brumfit drew mainly on educational arguments in support of an integrated curriculum, R. Ellis (1993, 1994) drew on research in SLA to propose a theory of instructed language learning that lends support to both a task-based and a structural syllabus. Ellis' theory is founded on the distinction between implicit and explicit knowledge and, in particular, on the role that explicit knowledge plays in the development of implicit knowledge.

Ellis saw implicit knowledge as primary. The acquisition of grammatical features is a slow and gradual process, reflecting the psycholinguistic constraints that govern integration of new features into a learner's interlanguage system. In line with Schmidt's Noticing Hypothesis (Schmidt, 1990), he suggested that implicit learning is in part a conscious process as learners must notice new features in the input and also notice the gap between what they attend to in the input and their current interlanguage systems in order to learn. Implicit learning results in implicit knowledge, which is accessible via automatic processing and thus available for spontaneous, communicative language use. Explicit knowledge is secondary but still an important part of language proficiency as it is needed in some kinds of formal language work (e.g. academic writing). Ellis suggested that it is accessible mainly through controlled processing but can also be automated to some extent. It is typically learned through studying descriptions of grammatical rules or as a result of explicit instruction.

The development of L2 proficiency proceeds largely through the processes responsible for acquiring implicit knowledge (e.g. noticing, noticing-the-gap, and chunking). However, in Ellis' theory, explicit knowledge can contribute to this in a number of ways. In accordance with the weak-interface hypothesis, he argued:

(1) Explicit knowledge can be converted into implicit knowledge through practice in the case of those linguistic features that are not subject to developmental constraints (for example, copula 'be' in English).
(2) However, this is only possible for developmental features if the learner has reached the stage of readiness needed to acquire a specific feature in accordance with Pienemann's (1985) Teachability Hypothesis.
(3) Explicit knowledge can facilitate the processes of noticing and noticing-the-gap that lead to implicit knowledge. That is, learners are more likely to attend to features in the input and to the difference between the input and their current interlanguage if they have prior explicit knowledge of them.
(4) Explicit knowledge can be used to edit utterances constructed from implicit knowledge, which helps accuracy in language use and the automatization of explicit knowledge. In addition, monitored output serves as a source of auto-input for implicit learning.

In the case of (1) and (2) there is a direct relationship between explicit and implicit knowledge as claimed by skill-learning theory although for those features that are developmental this is constrained by the learner's readiness to acquire them. In the case of (3) and (4) explicit knowledge contributes indirectly to the acquisition of implicit knowledge by facilitating the processes involved in implicit learning. Subsequently, Ellis (2006) emphasized these indirect roles and downplayed (1) and (2), which he saw having little relevance to language teaching because there is insufficient information about which features are developmental and non-developmental and because of the impracticality of establishing whether individual learners are developmentally ready to benefit from explicit instruction. The application of his theory that I discuss below is therefore based on (3) and (4).

In Ellis (1993), the theory is applied to language pedagogy. He proposed a different role for the structural syllabus from its traditional role. Traditionally, a structural syllabus serves as a basis for developing implicit knowledge by means of TSLT. Ellis argued that this is problematic for the reasons that Long (1988) articulated so well – namely, the incompatibility of the external syllabus and the learner's built-in syllabus. Therefore, Ellis suggested that the function of a structural syllabus should be limited to developing learners' explicit knowledge and proposed this could be achieved through inductive consciousness-raising tasks aimed at helping learners to learn *about* specific linguistic features (i.e. develop explicit representations of how they function in the linguistic system). This more limited goal for a structural syllabus was justified on the grounds that explicit knowledge can subsequently facilitate the acquisition of implicit knowledge providing learners have on-going opportunities for incidental/implicit learning and is also available for monitoring.

Ellis' proposal – as Long (2015) has pointed out – can be seen as providing support for TSLT. Long rejected it precisely because of this, claiming that it represented a return to traditional language teaching. However, in so doing he ignored the details of Ellis' proposal. Ellis was not arguing in support of TSLT but for an approach aimed solely at developing learners' explicit representations of linguistic features through inductive consciousness-raising tasks. In other words, in Ellis' proposal there were no practice activities. The focus is not on trying to transform explicit knowledge into implicit knowledge through practice but rather on helping learners to discover how linguistic features work and then allowing them to make use of the explicit knowledge they gain in this way in their own time. Thus, in Ellis' theory a structural syllabus has a reduced purpose. It cannot serve as the basis for a complete language programme as it needs to be complemented by 'other kinds of syllabuses that are based on the provision of input hypothesized to promote implicit knowledge – a functional or task-based syllabus' (2015: 110).

Ellis (1993) acknowledged that the precise relationship between the structural component and the other component of the curriculum remained unspecified. The key issue here is the timing of the structural component. A number of options are possible.

(1) The structural and task-based components of the syllabus operate in parallel from the start to the end of the curriculum. In other words, work on developing learners' explicit and implicit knowledge takes place throughout the curriculum.
(2) The structural component precedes the task-based or project-based component. In other words, the aim is to develop the learners' explicit knowledge before the introduction of the fluency-oriented component.
(3) The task-based component precedes the accuracy-based structural component. In other words, the initial focus should be on fluency and the development of implicit knowledge and a focus on target-language accuracy introduced later.

In the next section I will examine the arguments for these different options. However, it will first be necessary to consider whether the curriculum I have in mind should be an integrated or modular one.

Designing a Language Curriculum

None of the three options listed above correspond to TSLT. TSLT draws on a structural syllabus, with tasks providing the real operating conditions for proceduralizing declarative (explicit) knowledge. The problem with such an approach is that it prioritises accuracy over fluency and assumes that implicit knowledge is mastered item by item, which as Long (2015) pointed out is not how an L2 is acquired. However, as I noted earlier, it is supported by skill-learning theory and there is certainly evidence to show that it can result in automatized knowledge that is functionally equivalent to implicit knowledge. Nevertheless, it is still difficult to see how a structural syllabus and TSLT can serve as the basis for a *complete* language programme as (1) grammar is complex and there will not be enough time to provide the in-depth practice needed for mastery of the full system (Krashen, 1982) and, in any case, as I have already noted, (2) TSLT may not work for complex grammatical features except perhaps for learners with a strong aptitude for language learning. Yalçin and Spada (2016), for example, reported a study that showed instruction was only effective in helping those learners with high grammatical inferencing ability to acquire a complex grammatical structure (English passives). Another reason is that explicit instruction may in fact distort how tasks are performed, reducing their effectiveness as tools for developing L2 proficiency in general (see Note 3 and Chapter 6). The curriculum that I wish to argue for, therefore, is not a structural one although, as will become clear, such a syllabus along with explicit language teaching can find a place in a modular curriculum.

The three options referred to above all assume a modular syllabus rather than a syllabus where the structure-based accuracy component and the task-based fluency component are integrated. In this respect, the proposal I want to advance differs from Brumfit's proposal. Brumfit quite clearly favours integration at the level of the syllabus. This lies at the centre of his accuracy/fluency distinction. Irrespective of whether the learning activities are based on the structural component or on the project component of the syllabus, he argued that *both* accuracy and fluency can and should be integrated throughout. In contrast, in the modular curriculum I am proposing, the structural and task-based components of the syllabus are kept separate. However, as I will shortly argue, this does not preclude the possibility of finding ways of integrating accuracy and fluency *methodologically* in the performance of specific activities. Before I consider how this can be achieved, however, I will discuss the four options for a modular syllabus.

In option 1, work on developing learners' explicit and implicit knowledge takes place contiguously and in parallel. As in Brumfit's model (see Figure 10.1), the proportion of class time allocated to the different components varies over the course of a language programme. However, this option differs from Brumfit's as at any stage there will be separate activities for developing explicit and implicit knowledge. In the case of the task-based component learners will perform unfocused tasks supported by focus on form. In the case of the structural component, they will experience TSLT or consciousness-raising tasks directed at developing explicit knowledge of target features. The model does not presuppose integration of the two components. The rationale for separation is that the integration of explicit and implicit knowledge is necessarily learner-driven and cannot be directed externally through instruction. Learners need to be left alone to make use of the knowledge they gain from the structural component of the curriculum in their own way and in their own time when they engage in activities derived from the task-based component. The advantage of this option is that, by encouraging learners to focus on accuracy from the start, it may help to prevent pidginization, which some commentators such as Seedhouse (1997) suggest occurs in a pure task-based approach. The problem with this model, however, is that learners may not be able to make effective use of the knowledge they gain from the structural component in the early stages of L2 acquisition because they are not developmentally ready to do so. As SLA research has shown, implicit learning is usage-based, involving the acquisition of chunks that are only slowly decomposed into rule-like constructions (N. Ellis, 1996; R. Ellis, 1984). Thus some development – in particular lexical – needs to take place before learners are ready and able to make use of their explicit knowledge.

The second option (shown schematically in Figure 10.2) runs up against the same objection but even more so. It is nevertheless the model that is favoured by advocates of an accuracy-first approach – see, for

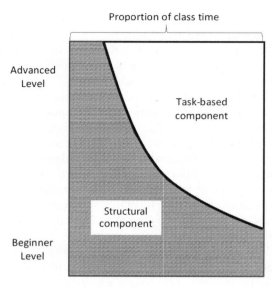

Figure 10.2 A modular curriculum (option 2)

example, Yalden (1986) – and by teachers who believe that learners cannot be expected to perform tasks until they have acquired some grammatical knowledge of the target language. However, as R. Ellis (2002) pointed out such a view does not accord with what is known about L2 acquisition. Immersion studies (e.g. Johnson & Swain, 1997) have shown that learners do not need grammatical instruction to acquire considerable grammatical competence. Basic word order and salient morphological features can be acquired incidentally without any formal instruction. If the early stages of L2 acquisition are lexical rather than grammatical (Lewis, 1993), there might be a case for an initial explicit component for teaching vocabulary but arguably, what is needed is an approach that initially prioritizes incidental acquisition through the performance of tasks. This would seem most obviously true for young language learners but is also preferable for older learners.

Option 3 (shown schematically in Figure 10.3) is more clearly compatible with how L2 proficiency develops naturally. As R. Ellis (2002) argued:

> If grammar teaching is to accord with how learners learn, then, it should not be directed at beginners. Rather, it should await the time when learners have developed a sufficiently varied lexis to provide a basis for the process of rule-extraction. In crude terms, this is likely to be at the intermediate stages of development. (2002: 23)

This option then reverses the traditional sequence of instruction. It calls for a task-based approach initially with the structural component kicking in at a later stage and continuing as long as learners provide evidence of

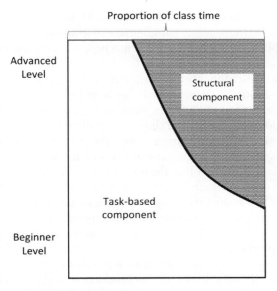

Figure 10.3 A modular curriculum (option 3)

the need for it. The task-based component, however, occupies the greater space in the model throughout. In other words, in this model priority is given to the incidental acquisition of implicit knowledge at all times in a language programme.

Although the curriculum framework I am proposing consists of separate components for task-based and structural work, as I noted above, there are opportunities for integrating a focus on form and on meaning-making *methodologically*. Brumfit proposed the explicit teaching of linguistic forms to assist the performance of project-based activities – as in TSLT. Long's advocacy of a task-based syllabus is premised on unfocused tasks derived from a needs analysis of the target tasks relevant to specific groups of learners. It also depends crucially on the use the of focus-on-form strategies that attract attention to those linguistic forms required to achieve the communicative outcome of a task and, thereby, help learners to approximate more closely to target language norms. Long's approach involves enhancing natural language learning by facilitating attention to form and so avoiding the danger of pidginization that can occur when there is nothing to push learners towards greater accuracy.[9] The problem with Brumfit's proposal is that learners may not be developmentally ready to benefit from explicit instruction in fluency-oriented work. The problem with Long's proposal, as Pica (1996) pointed out, is that focus-on-form (especially when it only consists of the negotiation of meaning) typically does not address some grammatical features such as morphological inflections and thus cannot guarantee their acquisition.[10] In other words, TBLT even with focus on form is unlikely to ensure that learners acquire high levels of grammatical accuracy. This is why an explicit structural component is needed to complement the task-based component.

Earlier I suggested that one way of implementing a structural syllabus is by using consciousness-raising tasks to help learners construct explicit mental representations of linguistic rules and regularities. Such tasks, however, have a double purpose and thus potentially integrate a focus on form and on a focus on communication within the same activity. In addition to developing awareness of linguistic forms they function as problem-solving tasks where 'language' becomes the topic to be talked about. They conform to the definition of a task; that is, they are meaning centred in the sense that the talk they elicit is directed at solving a linguistic problem, there is a gap (it can be an information or opinion gap depending on the design of the task), they elicit the use of learners' own linguistic resources as the task is performed, and there is a communicative outcome (a statement of the rule or regularity the task focuses on). It is important to understand that consciousness-raising tasks do not aim at production of the target feature and do not require it. They elicit general talk in the L2. For evidence of these claims see studies by Fotos and Ellis (1991) and Eckerth (2008b).[11]

To sum up, I have argued for a modular curriculum framework consisting of two separate components – a structural component and a task-based component – but with no attempt to integrate them at the level of syllabus. Of the three options for this framework, I have suggested that the one most compatible with what we know about L2 acquisition is option (3) where the task-based component is primary but – and it is in this respect the model I am proposing differs most clearly from Long (2015) – there is a structural component to address residual problems with specific grammatical features once basic L2 proficiency has been developed. Some integration of structural and task-based work can take place at the level of methodology in TSLT or through performing consciousness-raising tasks but the overall curriculum is modular with the emphasis on each component changing as a programme develops. Having presented the case for a modular curriculum, I will now turn to consider the content of the two components of the syllabus.

Determining the Content of the Task-based and Structural Modules of the Curriculum

The design of a syllabus requires two kinds of decisions to be made: (1) which content to include and (2) how to sequence of the content so that there is progression from simple to complex. In a modular syllabus, the content of the task-based component will consist of the tasks to be performed, whereas in the structural component it will consist of a list of grammatical structures. The principles and procedures for organizing the content of the two components are necessarily different.

Content in the task-based syllabus

In the case of specific purpose courses, the obvious way to ensure the relevancy of a task-based syllabus is to conduct a needs analysis to identify the target tasks that the learners need to be able to perform. Long (1985, 2015) suggested that specific target tasks can be grouped together into task types (for example, 'buying a railway ticket' and 'buying an airline ticket' could be grouped as 'buying a ticket') and then pedagogic tasks developed to ensure that the activities meet the requirements of a 'task'. However, as I noted in Chapter 8, other commentators have pointed out that it is not always possible or sensible to try to identify target-tasks. Also, there is the problem of determining just how 'general' the task-types have to be. Van Avermaet and Gysen (2006) questioned whether any transfer of learning from the performance of one task to another task of the same type can be expected. It does not follow, for example, that because learners can 'buy a railway ticket' then can also 'buy an airline ticket' even though both belong to the same task type. The central problem of Long's (1985, 2015) proposal, however, lies in whether language proficiency is best conceptualized as domain and task-specific or as a set of general abilities applicable across task types and situations. If the latter, then, arguably there is no reason for the content of the task-based component to be derived from a needs analysis of target tasks.

The alternative is to select tasks that have interactional authenticity without undue concern for their situational authenticity (see Bachman & Palmer, 1996). Interactional authenticity can be achieved by ensuring that the tasks meet the requirements for a task mentioned earlier. There is, however, still the important question of what topics the tasks should address. Ideally these should motivate learners' engagement with the tasks (Philp & Duchesne, 2016). However, there are dangers in syllabus designers basing the choice of topics on their own judgement of what will engage their students; ideally students should be consulted about what topics interest them. In the case of task-based courses based on academic subject content, as in immersion programmes, the choice of topics will be derived from the relevant subject syllabi.

The syllabus designer needs to decide whether the syllabus should specify the specific pedagogic tasks to be performed or just general types of tasks. Prabhu (1987) argued that if the syllabus is intended as a basis for teaching on a large scale (for example, in state school systems), the tasks are best specified in general terms. The examples he provided are task types specified in terms of (1) their topics (e.g. maps; school timetables) and (2) the particular operations a task stipulates (e.g. 'Finding, naming or describing specific locations on a given map'; 'Constructing class timetables from instructions/descriptions'). For each task type Prabhu proposed a number of different tasks that differed in the kinds of operations they involved.

Table 10.1 Horizontal and vertical dimensions of a task-based syllabus (based on Prabhu, 1987: 138–139)

Task types		Task operations		
Clock faces	Relating days to days of the week	Calculating durations from movement of a clock's hands	Stating the time on a twelve and a twenty-four hour clock	
Monthly calendars	Relating dates to days of the week	Calculating durations in days and week in the context of travel	Identifying relevant dates or days of the week in relation to cyclic activity	
School timetables	Constructing class timetable from instructions/ descriptions	Comparing such timetables to identify frequencies of lessons in different subjects	Constructing timetables for teachers of particular subjects from class timetables	

Prabhu's proposal for designing a general task-based syllabus remains one of the most practical to date. It provides a basis for both the vertical and horizontal grading of tasks in the syllabus. Vertical grading in Prabhu's syllabus is achieved by sequencing the different task types; horizontal grading is achieved by considering the difficulty of the operations involved in the particular tasks belonging to each task type. In Table 10.1 I have illustrated vertical and horizontal grading using examples taken from Prabhu's syllabus.

The construction of a general task syllabus should be undertaken in accordance with principles for determining both the vertical sequence of task types and the horizontal sequencing of task operations. Prabhu did not make explicit what principles should inform the sequencing of task types. An inspection of his syllabus, however, suggests that one general factor he considered was the potential familiarity of the topics of the tasks. Thus, for example, his early task types all involve topics that 11-year-old secondary students could be expected to be familiar with. Later task types (e.g. 'the postal system' and 'stories and dialogues') involve less familiar topics and imagination. Estaire and Zanon (1994) also proposed sequencing tasks in terms of how close or remote the topics are to the lives of the students and suggested this sequence:

the students themselves,
their homes,
their school,
the world around them and
fantasy/imagination.

There are also other factors that need to be considered in vertical sequencing. Prabhu advocated this general progression:

information gap → reasoning gap → opinion gap tasks.

I have suggested that the first task types should be input-based with closed outcomes with output-based tasks involving open outcomes introduced progressively at later stages.

Grading and sequencing for the horizontal dimension requires identifying the specific task characteristics that determine task complexity. Prabhu suggested a number of factors that need to be considered – the amount of information to be handled, the nature of the reasoning needed, the precision needed in interpreting information and reaching outcomes, and the degree of abstractness. These are very general characteristics, however. Subsequently, attempts have been made to identify more specific design features that determine complexity and then to investigate these empirically. Robinson (2011b) argued that a taxonomy of task characteristics is needed which can serve as 'a focus for concerted research into the effects of those characteristics on learning' (2011b: 17) and also as a basis for classifying and sequencing tasks. According to Robinson's Triadic Componential Framework (Robinson, 2010), the resource-directing characteristics of tasks (e.g. +/– few elements; +/– here-and-now; +/– no reasoning demands) determine task complexity and provide 'a parsimonious way to sequence L2 tasks in a programme of instruction' 2010: 10).[12] Tasks with the + features are presumed to be less complex than tasks with the – features. Resource-directing factors such as pre-task planning can be combined with resource-dispersing variables to reduce the processing load and thus assist automaticity, as in the example provided in Chapter 9 (see p. 182).

Robinson's framework provides a useful way of sequencing tasks horizontally but it is not without problems. Its strength is that it aims to provide an empirically supported basis for sequencing tasks according to their complexity. However, to date research based on his taxonomy has failed to support Robinson's central claim convincingly – namely, that more complex tasks result in L2 production that is both more complex and more accurate. Jackson and Suethanapornkul's (2012) meta-analysis of studies based on Robinson's taxonomy did not support this claim. As I noted in Chapter 9, the obvious problem with a taxonomic approach to determining task complexity is that tasks are holistic in nature and thus comprise clusters of features. Thus, there needs to be some metric for determining how combinations of different resource-directing and resource-dispersing features affect task complexity and L2 output but no such metric is currently available. Perhaps in the long-term research will be able to show which combinations of features are optimal for determining horizontal sequencing. Some progress in this direction has been made (see, for example, Sasayama, 2016) but there is still no agreement about specific features need to be investigated. Also, individual researchers do not operationalize the features that figure in Robinson's theory in a consistent manner so that results cannot easily be compared across studies. We are a long way from a convincing theory of task complexity and perhaps such a theory is not achievable given the nature of tasks.

It should be clear from the preceding comments that there is no algorithm for selecting tasks and sequencing them vertically and horizontally. All that is available are some common-sense notions (such as topic familiarity and learners' interests) supported by research that has identified specific design variables that affect task complexity. So, for the time being and probably for a long time, syllabus designers will have to draw on their experience and intuition, informed by taxonomies such as Robinson's and research such as Sasayama's, to decide how to sequence tasks. Designing a task syllabus must, for the time being at least, be as much an art as a science.

Structural content

The principles for selecting and grading the content of the grammatical content of a syllabus are well-established although not perhaps empirically motivated. They are reflected in the very considerable uniformity in the ordering of grammatical structures in structural syllabi. Yalden (1983), for example, found a remarkably similar order in four audiolingual textbooks. No substantial changes have taken place since except that textbook authors try to link the teaching of grammatical forms to particular situations, topics or themes as in Swan and Walter (1984) or Soars and Soars (2013). The limitations of the structural syllabus are well-established and have already been considered but, as Brumfit (1984) pointed out, a structural syllabus does at least provide a systematic basis for a language programme. In the modular curriculum I am proposing, however, the structural component takes the form of a *checklist* rather than a syllabus.

The essential difference between a syllabus and a checklist is that the former specifies both what is to be taught and the order of teaching whereas the latter consists only of a list of items with no expectation that teachers will follow the order in which the items are listed or, indeed, teach all of the items. In other words, if the structural content is presented as a checklist there is no need to address the thorny problem of how to grade and sequence structural items. There is, however, still the question of which items to include in the checklist. And guidance will be needed about when specific items listed in the syllabus should be addressed.

A checklist serves as a reference for observing whether learners have acquired specific linguistic features. That is, as previously noted, in the modular curriculum shown in Figure 10.3 learning progresses primarily incidentally/implicitly through performing tasks but a check is needed to see if learners have acquired specific grammatical features. Ideally, then the content of the checklist should reflect those grammatical structures that are known to be difficult for learners to acquire incidentally. We now have a fairly good idea of what these problem structures are – see, for example, Han's (2014) research on fossilized L2 forms. They include structures where entrenchment of non-target forms occurs due, in particular, to learned selective attention (N. Ellis, 2006) and the influence of the learners' first languages. Two processes interfere with the learners' ability to attend to new information in the input. Overshadowing occurs when there are two cues associated with an outcome and the more subjectively salient of the two cues overshadows the weaker. This results in blocking where the learner only attends to the more salient of the two cues. Also, L1 cues over-shadow L2 cues and thus block attention to the latter and prevent their acquisition. Other causes of learned selective inattention are the inherent saliency of one cue over another and the overgeneralization of an unmarked linguistic form. Examples of English structures that are subject to over-shadowing and blocking are morphological features such as past tense, third person-s, particular tense distinctions not found in the L1, epistemic modal verbs, the definite and indefinite articles, passive constructions, hypothetical conditionals and unusual or exceptional word orders (e.g. subject–verb inversion after a negative-meaning adverbial such as 'scarcely' or in embedded questions). The extensive work in error analysis on late-acquired linguistic features that has taken place over the years together with consultations with experienced teachers about the persistent errors that they have observed in their learners can provide a basis for selecting the grammatical forms to include in the structural checklist.

The purpose of the structural component of a modular curriculum, then, is to overcome the adverse effects of learned selective attention through explicit instruction – either through TSLT or consciousness-rais-ing tasks. However, the structural checklist is only suggestive of the prob-lems that particular groups of learners are likely to experience. It will be necessary for teachers to obtain evidence whether their learners are actu-ally experiencing difficulties with specific structures in the list. This can only be obtained by inspecting how they perform the tasks in the task-based component of the syllabus. If, for example, it becomes clear that learners are persistently failing to use past tense in narrative tasks, it would justify the direct teaching of past tense. The decision to intervene in this way calls for considerable skill on the part of the teacher. For exam-ple, a close inspection of learners' use of the past tense might reveal that the verb is not marked in contexts when there is an accompanying adverb but is marked when there is no adverbial expression. A well-designed checklist would provide guidance as to how linguistic context influences the likelihood of errors occurring.

Conclusion

Any curriculum must take account of how languages are learned. The primary rationale for a task-based curriculum is that it is learning-centred. It seeks to create communicative contexts that will allow learners' to grow their interlanguages in their own way while helping them to do so through focus-on-form. There is now clear evidence that a task-based curriculum is effective in enabling learners to develop both the linguistic and interactional competence needed to communicate in an L2 (De Ridder *et al.*, 2007; González-Lloret & Nielson, 2015; Shintani, 2016; Van den Branden, 2006c). However, a task-based curriculum may not succeed in enabling learners to achieve high levels of linguistic proficiency. Long (2015) acknowledged that some L2 forms are 'tricky, perhaps because of L1 influence' (2015: 28) and also that explicit attention to such forms might be needed. He argued, however, that this should be reactive and occur only within the context of the task-based lesson – 'sometimes just for a matter of seconds' – as focus-on-form. This should clearly be the first line of attack. However, experience suggests that it may not succeed in overcoming learned selective attention. It is for this reason that I have argued there is a need for a complementary strand in the curriculum where residual linguistic problems are addressed more intensively through TSLT or consciousness-raising tasks.

It could be argued, however, that these residual problems are not addressable – that once past the critical period for achieving a high level of proficiency (the onset of puberty in the case of grammar) L2 learners will be unable to master the full target language. This would be an argument for a pure task-based curriculum on the grounds that it is the best that can be achieved. However, there is plenty of evidence (e.g. Day & Shapson, 1991; Harley, 1989) that functional grammar teaching of the TSLT kind is effective in helping learners achieve higher levels of accuracy for problematic grammatical structures. Thus I have argued for a modular curriculum where the task-based component is primary, but supported by a language-related component consisting of a checklist of problematic linguistic features that can guide explicit language teaching in a way that is complementary to the task-based work. I have also argued that– contrary to Long's (2015) claim – the two approaches are not incompatible. TSLT may not result in implicit knowledge but it may lead to automatized explicit knowledge that is functionally equivalent to implicit knowledge – a useful substitute.

Consciousness-raising tasks can help develop the explicit knowledge of grammatical structures that will facilitate the processes involved in incidental/implicit learning.

I have acknowledged the difficulty of integrating explicit language instruction into a task-based curriculum and for this reason I have argued for separate modules. Finally, I reiterate the arguments advanced by Brumfit (1984) and Littlewood (2014) that cognizance must be taken of the constraints imposed by the educational context and that in some contexts it may be easier to implement a task-based if it is supported by a structural component.

Notes

(1) Brumfit's use of the terms 'accuracy' and 'fluency' differ from how these terms are used in task-based research. For Brumfit, they were not aspects of language use but methodological approaches for teaching language. For researchers such as Skehan (1998) they were aspects of language production.

(2) Focused tasks are sometimes successful in eliciting productive use of the target structure (e.g. in Mackey, 1999). Dictogloss tasks have proven effective in this respect.

(3) There is in fact very little research that has investigated what effect *a priori* explicit instruction has on the performance of a task. I reviewed this research in Chapter 6.

(4) The fact that TSLT (PPP) might not be effective for teaching complex structures does not necessarily mean that it is any less successful in this respect than TBLT as, arguably, such structures are resistant to learning no matter what the approach.

(5) Sheen's (2006) study is, however, methodologically flawed. A much better designed study – Shintani (2016) – reported that TBLT resulted in superior learning to TSLT for young beginner-level learners.

(6) Long (2016) also acknowledged that there may be problems in teachers' implementing TBLT but argued that this can be addressed through training programmes and cited the Belgian experience reported in Van den Branden (2006a).

(7) Long and Crookes (1992) viewed Prabhu's Communicational Language Teaching Project as a 'procedural syllabus' which they distinguished from a 'task-based syllabus' on the grounds that only the latter incorporates a focus-on-form.

(8) Brumfit's curriculum model incorporates what Yalden (1986) called a 'proportional syllabus', where the proportions of different components change over time.

(9) Long (2015) views focus-on-form as a purely reactive phenomenon – that is it should take place only in response to a linguistic of communicative problem. In Chapter 4, however, I advanced a much broader view of focus on form.

(10) It might be argued that there is a better chance of guaranteeing a high level of grammatical competence through task-based language teaching if the focus-on-form is not restricted to the negotiation of meaning but also includes the negotiation of form – as, in fact, Long (2015) recognized. Even so, certain non-salient grammatical features are still unlikely to be acquired.

(11) Long (2015) viewed consciousness-raising tasks as 'exercises'. This, however, is a misunderstanding. Long failed to recognize that when performed such tasks involve 'talk' (including the negotiation of meaning and form) in much the same as other types of tasks. See Chapter 9 for a full rebuttal of Long's criticism.

(12) Robinson did not explicitly limit his resource-directing characteristics to production tasks but it would seem that this is the case. The research based on his taxonomy has invariably concerned production tasks. Arguably a different set of criteria will be needed to grade input tasks. See Duran and Ramant (2006) for suggestions about this.

11 An Options-based Approach to Doing Task-based Language Teaching

Introduction

A task-based lesson can consist of three phases – a pre-task phase involving some kind of preparation for the performance of a task, the main task phase when the task is performed and a post-task phase involving follow-up activities. In an option-based approach to the design of task-based lessons described in this chapter, options for each of these three phases of a task-based lesson are outlined and illustrated. Options for the pre-task phase include both teacher-centred activities (e.g. modelling performance of the task and pre-teaching vocabulary and perhaps also grammar) and learner-centred activities (e.g. providing students with opportunities to plan before they perform the task). Options for the main-task phase include deciding whether to allow the students to see the input materials when they perform the task and whether to set a time-limit for completing the task. Also, there are online focus-on-form options for addressing communicative and linguistic problems as these arise when a task is performed. Options for the post-task phase are teacher-centred (e.g. asking students to repeat the task or reviewing learner errors) and also learner-centred (e.g. using consciousness-raising tasks to develop learners' explicit knowledge of aspects of language shown to be problematic when they performed the task). In this chapter I describe the various options involved in the three phases of a task-based lesson.

The Case for an Options-based Approach

In Chapter 8 I pointed out that TBLT is not a 'method' but an 'approach' that encapsulates a number of different possibilities. I pointed out, for example, that unlike Long and Skehan I do not reject the possibility of a modular curriculum that incorporates a more traditional component based on a structural syllabus. In Chapter 10 I spelled out my ideas of what such a modular syllabus might look like.

The fact that TBLT is not monolithic raises the question of how to present the methodology for doing TBLT. My solution is to adopt an options-based approach. That is, I propose to describe some of the key options available for each phase of a TBLT lesson. The idea behind this approach is that teachers can select those options that they consider best suited to their own students. An option-based approach allows for flexibility and in so doing acknowledges the importance of not viewing TBLT as a methodological straight jacket.

My starting point, however, is to revisit what is meant by a 'task' as this is central to all versions of TBLT. As evaluation studies have shown (e.g. Carless, 2004), teachers often lack a clear understanding of what a task is. Without a clear understanding, however, it will be impossible to implement TBLT effectively.

What is a 'Task'?

I repeat here the definition of task I offered in Chapter 1. For a language teaching activity to be considered a task it must satisfy the following four criteria:

(1) The primary focus should be on 'meaning', i.e. learners should be mainly concerned with processing the semantic and pragmatic meaning of utterances.
(2) There should be some kind of 'gap', i.e. a need to convey information, to express an opinion or to infer meaning.
(3) Learners should largely have to rely on their own resources – linguistic and non-linguistic – in order to complete the activity, i.e. the task materials do not dictate what linguistic forms are to be used.
(4) There is a clearly defined outcome other than the use of language, i.e. the language serves as the means for achieving the outcome, not as end in its own right.

These criteria effectively distinguish a 'task' from an 'exercise'. By way of example consider these two language teaching activities.

Activity 1: Dialogue
Students are given a script of a dialogue and put into pairs. Each student is allocated a part in the dialogue and asked to memorize the lines for this part. The students then act out the dialogue.

Activity 2: Spot the Difference
Students are placed in pairs. Each student is given a picture and told that the two pictures are basically the same but there are five small differences. Without looking at each other's picture, they talk together to locate and write down the five differences.

Table 11.1 Comparing an 'exercise' and a 'task'

Criteria	Dialogue	Spot the Difference
1. Primary focus on meaning	No	Yes
2. Gap	No	Yes (information)
3. Own linguistic resources	No	Yes
4. Communicative outcome	No	Yes

Table 11.1 describes these two activities in terms of the four criteria above. In 'Dialogue' the focus is not primarily on meaning as students can perform it without even having to understand what is being said. There is no gap because both students can see the whole dialogue. They do not have to use their own linguistic resources – just memorize and reproduce the text they are given. There is no communicative outcome – the only outcome is the performance of the dialogue – language practice for its own sake. In 'Spot the Difference', the focus is clearly on meaning (i.e. the students have to make themselves understood to each other), there is an information gap (i.e. each student has a different picture), they have to use their own linguistic resources (i.e. they are not given any language to use), and there is a communicative outcome (i.e. a list of the differences in the two pictures).

The type of discourse that arises from these two activities is likely to be very different. In the case of 'Dialogue', the language use is likely to be mechanical – focused on an accurate rendition of the script. In the case of 'Spot the Difference', the discourse is likely to be interactionally authentic. That is, it will resemble the kind of language use that occurs outside the classroom where the aim is to encode and decode real messages. For example, it is probable that communication problems will arise leading to attempts by the students to resolve them with the result that there is attention to form.

My purpose, however, it not to suggest that exercises such as 'Dialogue' are pedagogically worthless and tasks such as 'Spot the Difference' are worthy. Both may have a place in a language course as they cater to different aspects of language learning. However, a course that consists only of exercises is unlikely to develop the kinds of communicative skills that students need in order to cope with the exigencies of real-life communication outside the classroom. To achieve this, most of some of the teaching time will need to be based on tasks.

In previous chapters, we have seen that there are many different types of tasks and many ways of classifying them. Nunan (1989) distinguished 'real-world tasks', i.e. tasks that replicated situations that occur in the real-world, and 'pedagogic tasks', i.e. tasks that seek to achieve interactional authenticity but not situational authenticity. A second distinction of importance is that between input-based and production-based tasks. The former consists of oral or written input and require listening or reading on the part of the learner. Examples of oral input-based tasks can be found in Chapter 3. The latter require oral or written output from the learner. In a third distinction common in the TBLT literature, tasks are distinguished in terms of whether the gap involves information-providing or opinion-making. A fourth distinction is between unfocused and focused tasks. The difference here consists of whether the task has been designed to elicit language use in general or the use of some specific linguistic feature such as a grammatical structure. 'Spot the Difference' is a pedagogic task, it is production-based, it involves an information gap and it is unfocused. 'Candidates for a Job' (see Table 11.2) is also a pedagogic task (but perhaps for some learners could have elements of a real-world task), it is production-based, it involves an opinion-gap, and it is focused, i.e. it was designed to provide learners with the opportunity to practise their use of the present-perfect tense. Of course, there is no guarantee that learners will try to use this tense when they perform the task. Learners are adept at avoiding the use of grammatical structures that are difficult for them. It is extremely difficult to design tasks that might the production of a pre-determined grammatical structure 'essential' (Loschky & Bley-Vroman, 1993)[1] although, as we will see, it is possible to induce attention.to the target form methodologically (e.g. through focus-on-form techniques).

Drawing on previous proposals for TBLT (e.g. Estaire & Zannon, 1994; Lee, 2000; Willis, 1996) a task-based lesson can be seen as consisting of three distinct phases.

(1) The pre-task phase, i.e. the various activities that the teacher and students can undertake before they perform the task);
(2) The main-task phase, i.e. the actual performance of the task;
(3) The post-task phase, i.e. the various activities that the students and the teacher can undertake to follow-up on the performance of the task.

However, not all task-based lessons will include all three phases. The only essential phase is the main-task phase; the pre-task and the post-task phases are optional. Potentially, then, a lesson can consist of:

• just the main-task phase;
• the pre-task phase and the main-task phase;
• the main-task phase and the post-task phase;
• all three phases.

The design of a particular lesson will depend on a number of factors – the extent to which the teacher considers the students need some kind of preparation before they perform the task, the difficulty of the task itself, what aspect of language (accuracy, complexity, fluency) the teacher wants the learners to prioritize, and the extent to which linguistic problems emerge during the actual performance of the task. A number of different options are possible for each phase of the lesson. These are discussed below.

Table 11.2 'Candidates for a Job' task (based on Ur, 1988)

Candidates for a job
Imagine you are a student in a private language school. Consider the following four applications for a job as a teacher in your school. Which of the applicants would you hope would be chosen for the job? Discuss with the other students in your group.

▶ **JOCK, aged 30**

B.A. in social studies.

Has spent a year working his way round the world.

Has spent six years teaching economics in state school.

Has written a highly successful novel about teachers.

Has lived in a back-to-nature commune for two years.

Has been married twice – now divorced. Two children.

Has been running local youth group for three years.

▶ **BETTY, aged 45**

Has been married for 24 years, three children.

Has not worked most of that time.

Has done evening courses in youth guidance.

Has spent the last year teaching pupils privately for state exams – with good results.

Has been constantly active in local government – has been elected to local council twice.

▶ **ROBERT, aged 27**

Has never been married, no children.

Has served a term in prison – killed a man in a drunken fight; but has committed no further crimes since release two years ago.

Has recently become a Catholic, regularly goes to church.

Has been working in school for mentally retarded in poor area – has been recommended by principal of the school.

Has followed no course of formal study.

▶ **CLAIRE, aged 60**

Has been married, husband now dead, no children.

Has been a teacher for 35 years, mostly teaching English abroad.

Has lived many years in the Far East (husband was diplomat).

Has taught English in British Council school in Singapore and Hong Kong.

Has been Principal of British School for girls in Kuala Lumpur.

Husband died two years ago; since then has been in this country, doing voluntary youth work; has recently completed Diploma in Youth Counselling.

Pre-Task Phase Options

The research that has investigated different pre-task options was considered in Chapter 5. In this chapter my focus is more on the available pedagogic strategies. These really divide into two types; (1) teacher-centred options and (2) student-centred options.

Teacher-centred options

These involve a number of different activities that the teacher carries out with the whole class. Learners need to have a clear understanding of the contribution that performing tasks can make to their language learning. That is, they need to recognize that performing tasks will not only help them to develop greater communicative fluency but also to acquire new language, albeit 'incidentally' rather 'intentionally'. This is especially important if the students are used to a more traditional approach to language teaching based on exercises. Such students may treat tasks as 'games' to have fun with rather than as serious activities that will help them to learn (Foster, 1998). How the students orientate to task-based teaching will determine what they gain from it.

Teachers also need to 'frame' the task for the students. This can involve suggesting how they might undertake the task, letting them know what they are required to do, and specifying the nature of the outcome they should arrive at (Lee, 2000). For example, the students might be told prior to performing 'Candidates for a Job' that they should first make a list of the criteria they would use to evaluate the four teachers and then systematically apply these to each applicant. Motivating students to perform the task is also of obvious importance. Dörnyei (2001) emphasized the importance whetting students' appetite to perform a task. One way that this might be achieved could be by choosing students to be each of the candidates and then having the rest of the class fire questions at them that they have to answer in character.

Other teacher-centred options involve modelling the performance of the task for the students. One way of achieving this is by the teacher performing a similar task with the whole class. For example, the teacher could devise another similar 'Candidates for a Job' task with information about four different applicants and then guide the students through this by helping them to see the strengths and limitations of each candidate before setting them to work in groups on the 'Candidates for Jobs' task. The advantage of this option is that it allows the teacher to scaffold the students into using the language they will need when they perform the task by themselves. In terms of sociocultural theory, it constitutes an attempt to provide 'other-regulation' in order to facilitate the 'self-regulation' students will need when working independently. Prabhu (1987) adopted a similar approach to this in the Communicational Teaching Project. Students first completed a 'pre-task' with the teacher. They then worked independently on a task of the same kind and with similar content. Another way of modelling the task for the students might be to ask them to listen to a performance of the task by native speakers (or other learners) or watch a video of the task being performed. In this case they can be provided with a transcript of the interaction to help them follow what is said. As Willis (1996) noted, observing others performing a task can make it easier for students to perform the task themselves. Following the transcript will help with the language they will need.

Another possibility is to pre-teach the vocabulary and structures that will be useful for performing the task. For example, the teacher might select lexical items that the students are unlikely to know, e.g. for 'Candidates for a Job' these items might be chosen: *back-to-nature commune, mentally retarded, voluntary*, and devise exercises to practice their use. Or the teacher might revise the present-perfect tense (the grammatical focus of this task). However, as we saw in Chapter 6, there are potential dangers in this option. Students may feel that they have to use the linguistic forms that have been pre-taught when performing the task and, as a result, fail to use or limit the use of their own linguistic resources. As we saw in Chapter 6 when students are focused on the structure they have been taught, their language may become less globally complex, accurate and fluent when they perform the task. If this happens there is a real danger of the task losing its 'taskness' and becoming an exercise. This danger is perhaps less acute when the pre-teaching focuses on vocabulary rather than grammar.

Student-centred options

Learner-centred options centre on providing students with an opportunity to plan the performance of a task before they undertake it. Pre-task planning has been shown to assist learners both cognitively and affectively. It helps the retrieval and rehearsal of language from long-term memory, it can promote attention to form, and it can foster automatization of linguistic knowledge. It also reduces the anxiety that many learners feel when asked to speak spontaneously in the L2. It is especially helpful with learners who lack oral competence or are reluctant to risk speaking in the L2. As we saw in Chapter 6, there is now a rich body of research that has investigated pre-task planning.

Pre-task planning can be implemented in a number of ways. The time set for the planning can be varied. In research studies, learners are often given 10 minutes. But there is also evidence that different planning times have different effects on performance. For example, Mehnert's (1998) study showed that accuracy benefits most with just one minute of planning time! Perhaps then teachers should vary the time they allocate for planning and investigate the effects of different planning times on their own students.

There are also options about how the students carry out the planning. They could be asked to simply think about the task and plan silently in their heads. Alternatively, and probably more helpful, is to give them a piece of paper and let them make notes as they plan. The danger here is that they will not just jot down ideas and useful words and phrases but try to write out full sentences. For this reason, it is probably advisable to collect in the notes they have made before they start to perform the task.

Table 11.3 Types of pre-task planning

Type of pre-task planning	Example
Unguided planning	Students are given the materials for the task and told they have ten minutes to plan what they want to say about each applicant when they get into their groups.
Guided planning – content focus	Students are given the materials for the task and asked to think of the criteria they would use to evaluate the applicants. They then consider each applicant in terms of the criteria and rate their suitability.
Guided planning – language focus	Students are asked to look carefully at the information about each applicant and pay attention to the verb tense that is used. They then work out sentences they can say to give their opinion about who should get the job and who should not get the job and think of reasons for their opinions using the information about the applicants.

Pre-task planning can be unguided or guided. In guided planning the focus can be placed on either language or content or on both. Table 11.3 gives examples of these different types of pre-task planning for the 'Candidates for a Job' task.

These options apply to task materials that are given to the learners. However, another option is to ask the learners to generate their own materials. For example, for a Describe and Draw task, instead of giving the learners the picture or diagram they have to describe, they could be asked to generate their own pictures. They could be given a blank piece of paper and asked to think of something that happened to them and then draw a picture of it. Drawing the picture will help them to conceptualize what they will say when they describe their picture and, because it involves a personal experience, is likely to be more motivating than describing a picture given to them.[2] There is evidence to suggest that learner-generated content results in a higher level of engagement when learners perform a task. Lambert *et al.* (2017b), for example, compared Japanese learners' levels of engagement in a narrative task where the content was provided and a narrative task where they were asked to fill in their own story content in four empty picture frames. The learners who generated their own content spent more time on task, produced more words and elaborative clauses, negotiated for meaning more and back-channelled more.

Main-Task Phase Options

Two kinds of options are available in the main-task phase; task-performance options (i.e. options that teachers can consider when planning a task-based lesson) and process options (i.e. the online choices available to the teacher and the students as the task is being performed).

Task performance options

A key decision concerns the participatory structure of the during-task phase. There are three possibilities. The first is a teacher-class participatory structure where the teacher performs the task with the whole class. If the task is of the input-based type (e.g. involves students listening to descriptions of instructions and demonstrating comprehension of the input by performing some action as in the listen-and-do tasks discussed in Chapter 3), a teacher-class participatory structure is required. It is also possible with some production-based tasks. For example, a Spot the Difference task can be performed in a whole class setting if the teacher holds one of the pictures and all the students the other picture. One advantage of a teacher-class participatory structure is that it enables the teacher to monitor students' performance online – i.e. it provides a context for the kind of focus-on-form features described later. The second possibility is the one most commonly associated with TBLT – pair-work or small group work. The advantages of this are well-established (see, for example, Long and Porter 1985) but there are also dangers, including the possibility that students will overuse their first language (L1) or are become so outcome-oriented that they make little effort to utilize their full L2 resources and their speech becomes pidgin-like. The third possibility is the one exploited by Prabhu (1987) – students perform the task individually. This, of course, is only possible if the task does not involve speaking or listening and the outcome is written or requires reading.

In Ellis (2003) I described three other task-performance options. The first concerns deciding whether to set a time limit for performing the task (as suggested by Lee, 2000) or to allow the students whatever time they need to complete it. This option determines the extent to which the learners are able to undertake online planning. If students are not pressured to complete the task rapidly they will have time to access their linguistic resources and also to monitor and reformulate their utterances for correctness. Yuan and Ellis (2003) reported that when students were given unlimited time to perform a narrative task their language was both more complex and more accurate than when they had to perform the task under time pressure – a finding that has been replicated in subsequent studies (see Chapter 5). However, a case can also be made for setting a time limit for a task. Students need to get used to communicating under pressure as this is what they will often be faced with outside the classroom. The case for setting a time limit is perhaps stronger if students have had time for pre-task planning as the fact that they are already familiar with what they want to say and how to say it will enable them to cope with the need to speak rapidly.

The second task-performance option involves deciding whether to allow learners access to the input-data while they perform a task. For example, the teacher could allow students to keep the information about the four applicants in the 'Candidates for a Job' task or could take it from them once they had had a chance for pre-task planning. The issue here is whether the teacher wants to encourage 'verbatim' or 'generated' use of the L2 (Joe, 1998). If the students continue to have access to the input-data they are likely to 'borrow' from it when performing the task, e.g. by reading chunks from the data out aloud. However, if the information is removed, they are thrown back on having to generate their own utterances. There are pros and cons regarding this option. The input-data can be viewed as a form of 'scaffolding', assisting learners to perform utterances that would be beyond them without it. Seen from this perspective, 'borrowing' supports participation in the task and fosters learning. However, there is always a danger of 'borrowing' becoming a very mechanical process, obviating the need for students to engage in the struggle that generated use of the L2 entails. Deciding whether to let the students keep the task materials or to remove them can affect the complexity of a task. Robinson (2001) proposed that what he calls a 'there-and-then task' (i.e. the students do not have access to the task materials) is more complex than a 'here-and-now task' (i.e. the students keep the task materials). Thus the decision about whether to allow students access to input-data will involve consideration of the students' proficiency level. If the task is likely to be demanding on learners' processing capacity, then the opportunity to borrow from the input will be beneficial but if the task is viewed as easy for the students, then it would be preferable to encourage generated language use by removing the input-data.

The third option consists of introducing a surprise-element into the task (Skehan & Foster, 1997). For example, halfway through the 'Candidates for a Job' task the teacher could introduce some new information in the form of references for each applicant (see Table 11.4 for some suggestions), thus forcing the students to review their opinions of them. One obvious advantage of selecting this option is that it can prolong the talking time. It might also prompt the learners to produce more complex language. For example, the surprise information for the 'Candidates for a Job' task might encourage them to mitigate their opinions by using expressions of concession (e.g. 'Well, I know Claire has had a lot of teaching experience *but* I think her perfectionist tendencies will cause problems for the school.') and in this way increase utterance complexity.

A final possibility – also one investigated by Skehan and Foster – is to tell the students that after they have completed the task they will have to report their conclusion publicly to the whole class. The thinking behind this option is that knowing a public performance will be required of them later will encourage the students to pay greater attention to the accuracy of their language *while* they are doing the task as they will want to be able to perform at their best later on. There is some evidence that this is the case.

Table 11.4 Introducing a surprise element in the 'Candidates for a Job' task

Now consider the following information about each applicant that has been provided by their referees. Do you want to revise your opinion about who should be offered the job?

▶ **JOCK, aged 30**

'Jock has matured considerably in the last few years. In his twenties he had difficulty in accepting authority and responsibility for his family. But he is clearly a changed man now and is looking to settle down into a regular job.'

▶ **BETTY, aged 45**

'Betty has shown herself to be a born leader. She will contribute enormously to your school, both in the energy she puts into her teaching and in improving organizational systems in the school. She is an activist by nature.'

▶ **ROBERT, aged 27**

'Although lacking a university degree, Robert is a highly educated man. He is widely read. He is also highly committed to anything he chooses to take on. In the last year, however, he has been struggling with depression largely as a result of guilt over killing a man.'

▶ **CLAIRE, aged 60**

'Claire is very young for her age. She has demonstrated enormous energy and is able to channel this effectively into any task she takes on. She is, however, something of a perfectionist and is easily frustrated if decisions do not go the way she wants them to.'

Process options

The goal of TBLT is not just to provide learners with the opportunity to communicate using their existing linguistic resources and thereby to improve their fluency but also to help them acquire new linguistic resources. In other words, TBLT seeks to be both 'skill-using' and 'skill-developing' (Rivers & Temperley, 1978). However, unlike more traditional approaches to teaching, TBLT does not distinguish skill-using from skill-developing activities. Rather, it combines them by asking students to perform tasks that involve them using their own linguistic resources in such a way as to afford opportunities for the acquisition of new language. How then can teachers help students (or students help each other) to acquire new language through performing tasks that, by definition, require a primary focus on meaning?

One way is by ensuring that the discourse that results from the performance of the task has 'interactional authenticity' – that is, it resembles the way in which language is used for social interaction in the real world. Classroom discourse is typically dominated by initiate-response-feedback (IRF) exchanges, where the teacher initiates an exchange, typically by asking a question, the student responds, and the teacher then indicates whether the response is the one required and, if it is not, corrects it. IRF exchanges have their role to play in teaching but they do not usually occur in the real world and thus are not the ideal way of preparing students to use language communicatively. One of the purposes of TBLT is to create a discourse context where students have a chance to initiate, where teachers ask open rather than closed questions (i.e. questions that have no predetermined answers) and crucially where students have the opportunity to perform long as well as short turns when they speak and to use a variety of language functions (requesting, apologising, expressing agreement and disagreement, hypothesising, explaining etc.). This will not happen if learners are restricted to responding to the teacher's closed questions. Ultimately, then, for TBLT to be successful the teacher needs to relinquish some degree of control of the discourse to the students.

We saw in Chapter 4, the importance of focus-on-form in TBLT. We noted that there are various ways of inducing learners to attend to form, including pre-task planning. The principal way, however, remains the way that Long (1991) initially envisaged – namely strategies for overtly or covertly drawing students' attention to linguistic elements as they engage in performing tasks.[3] Ellis *et al*. (2002) described various ways in which focus-on-form can be accomplished (see Table 11.5). A basic distinction is drawn between 'reactive focus-on-form', where attention to form arises out of some problem in a participant's utterance, and 'pre-emptive focus on form', where the participants make a particular linguistic form the topic of the conversation even though no actual problem has arisen. These can be viewed as options for managing this key process aspect of TBLT.

Table 11.5 Doing focus-on-form (Ellis *et al.*, 2002)

Options	Description
A. Reactive focus-on-form	The teacher or another student responds to an error that a student makes in the context of a communicative activity.
1. Negotiation a. Conversational	The response to the error is triggered by a failure to understand what the student meant. It involves 'negotiation of meaning'.
b. Didactic	The response occurs even though no breakdown in communication has taken place; it constitutes a 'time-out' from communicating. It involves 'negotiation of form'.
2. Feedback a. Implicit feedback	The teacher or another student responds to a student's error without directly indicating an error has been made, e.g. by means of a recast.
b. Explicit feedback	The teacher or another student responds to a student's error by directly indicating that an error has been made, e.g. by formally correcting the error or by using metalanguage to draw attention to it.
B. Pre-emptive focus-on-form	The teacher or a student makes a linguistic form the topic of the discourse even though no error has been committed.
1. Student initiated	A student asks a question about a linguistic form.
2. Teacher-initiated	The teacher gives advice about a linguistic form he/she thinks might be problematic or asks the students a question about the form.

The strategies that Ellis *et al.* described can occur in both teacher-class lessons when the teacher performs a task with the students or in small group work when the learners deploy them. However, the research casts some doubt on whether students engage extensively in focus on form when performing a task in groups (see, for example, Williams, 1999). This is one reason for adopting a teacher-class participatory structure where students are given the opportunity to initiate pre-emptive focus on form and the teacher takes up opportunities for reactive focus on form. A study by Ellis *et al.* (2001) reported a total of 448 focus-on-form episodes (FFEs) in 12 hours of adult ESL task-based lessons – a rate of one FFE every 1.6 minutes. Other studies (e.g. Loewen, 2005) have provided evidence that such focus on form results in learning. Doing focus on form, whether in lockstep task-based lessons or in group work is a key process feature of the during-task phase.

Finally, teachers need to consider what constitutes appropriate use of the L1 by students. Overuse of the L1 is a commonly cited problem (see Chapter 8). It is important to recognise, however, that the L1 does have a place in TBLT. For a start it is likely (and probably) advantageous if learners make use of their L1 in pre-task planning. Also when performing the task learners have been found to use their L1 effectively, for example to agree on what they have to do and working out how best to set about doing it. Also, the L1 has a place in language-related episodes (see Chapter 7) as it can help learners to arrive at successful solutions to the linguistic problems they experience. What is important is to ensure that the task outcome is worked out and presented in the L2.

Post-Task Phase Options

Post-task activities also afford an opportunity to focus learners' attention on form – this time quite explicitly. Given that tasks aim to induce primary attention to form, it is always possible that learners will neglect to attend to form, especially if the task is performed in pairs or groups. Given the importance of 'noticing' in L2 acquisition (Schmidt, 1994), the failure to attend to form may have deleterious effects on their learning. Thus, post-task activities need to shift the emphasis from 'fluency' to 'accuracy'. There are a number of ways in which this can be achieved.

Task repetition

If students are told they will have to repeat the task, then the first performance effectively becomes a pre-task option (i.e. a preparation for performing the task a second time). However, if they are not forewarned then repeating the task becomes a post-task option. We noted in Chapter 5 that to date there is no research that has compared these two ways of handling task repetition and that in general task-repetition is seen as a post-task option.

Research (e.g. Bygate, 2001; Lynch & Mclean, 2000) has shown that when students are given an opportunity to repeat a task, their production improves in a number of ways – complexity increases and propositions are expressed more clearly. The first performance of a task enables the learners to formulate 'what' they want to say; the second performance allows for greater attention to be paid to the selection of linguistic forms for encoding the already-established propositions. Task repetition can be carried out under the same conditions as the original performance or under different conditions. For example, if the first performance was unpressured, the second could be pressured. Or, if the first performance involved group work, the second could call for individual student performances. In Chapter 5, I also noted that there is evidence to suggest that some kind of intervention between performances of the task can add to the benefits that repetition has on accuracy in particular. Thus the teacher might want to use some of the options described in the next section to draw learners' attention to the linguistic problems they manifested in performing the task the first time before asking them to repeat it.

Being asked to repeat a task might not appeal to all students. Aubrey (2015), for example found that when university-level Japanese students responded negatively when they were asked to repeat a task even with a new Japanese partner. In contrast, these students did not object to repeating it with an international student from their university (i.e. someone with whom they were not familiar and who was a fluent speaker of English). Aubrey's study suggests that teachers might need to give thought to the choice of partners or group members when asking students to repeat a task. If there is an opportunity to bring people in from outside the students' class they might be more motivated to repeat the task. Asking young students to repeat tasks is, however, much less problematic. Shintani (2016), for example, repeated the same listen-and-do tasks with six-year-old children nine times. She found that the children remained motivated throughout, in part because the task-as-process changed with each performance. In other words, while the task-as-workplan stayed the same, the way in which it was enacted evolved over time.

Addressing linguistic problems directly

Various options exist for dealing directly with the linguistic problems that became evident during the performance of the task. These can be teacher-centred or student-centred.

1. Teacher-centred options

The most obvious way of addressing the students' linguistic problems is for the teacher to closely observe the students performing the task and make notes of both any errors they make and cases of avoidance, i.e. failure to use a particular form that would have been 'natural' in the context created by the task. The teacher can then undertake a review of these problem areas with the whole class. I noted in Chapter 6 that Rolin-Ianziti (2010) identified two approaches that teachers of L2 French used when providing delayed feedback following a role-play task. In both cases the teachers initiated correction but in the first approach they provided the correction themselves while in the second they attempted to elicit correction from the students. However, I also noted that at the moment we do not know which approach is more effective, so teachers may like to experiment with both.

It would also be possible for the teacher to devise a traditional language lesson involving presentation and controlled practice. The feature targeted in such a lesson would be one that constituted a problem for the students when they performed the task. In effect, then, the traditional sequence of present–practice–produce (PPP) has been modified with the main task providing an initial opportunity for free production and the presentation and practice occurring in the post-task stage. This makes good sense as it ensures that the explicit instruction is directed at attested linguistic problems as opposed to presumed ones. This is what Johnson (1982) had in mind when he proposed his 'deep-end strategy' (see Chapter 1).

2. Learner-centred options

Consciousness-raising tasks (Ellis, 1991, 2003) are a special type of task. They involve presenting students with some data related to a particular linguistic feature, e.g. the use of the prepositions *in, on* and *at* in expressions of time, guiding the analysis of the data to help them discover the underlying rules, and then asking students to state the rules explicitly. Consciousness-raising tasks constitute a kind of discovery-based grammar activity.

Such tasks can be used in the during-task phase of the lesson (see, for example, Eckerth, 2008a) although this is controversial as some advocates of TBLT such as Long dismiss them on the grounds that they are really grammar exercises. See Chapter 9 for a discussion of Long's objection. I argued that grammar can become a topic for a task just like any other topic. Consciousness-raising tasks do not require students to produce the target structure. They require them to work out the rule and this can lead to talking freely about what the rule is and how best to express it.

Irrespective of whether consciousness-raising tasks have a role to play in the during-task phase of a lesson, they clearly have a place in the post-task phase. They provide a means of focusing students' attention on how to address a linguistic error in this phase. When used for this purpose the data for the task could be usefully taken from the students' performance of the main task and include examples of both correct and incorrect language.

Another way of raising students' consciousness about their use of language when they performed the task is through 'proof listening'

(Lynch, 2001). The students play a recording of the task and attempt to edit their own performance. Other students can also be asked to listen to the recording and comment, correct or ask questions. Lynch also suggests asking the students to make a transcript of an extract of their task performance (Lynch, 2001) and then to edit it. I considered Lynch's ideas and the research they have generated in Chapter 6.

Conclusion

There is general acceptance that tasks provide learners with valuable opportunities for developing their fluency but some critics of TBLT have expressed scepticism that tasks are the most effective way to promote linguistic development. Commentators such as Sheen (2003) have claimed that there is 'no grammar syllabus' in task-based language teaching and that proponents of TBLT 'generally offer little more than a brief list of suggestions regarding the selection and presentation of new language'. Swan (2005a) insisted that TBLT 'outlaws' the grammar syllabus. I addressed these misconceptions about TBLT in detail in Chapter 8. In this chapter, I have attempted to show that TBLT is in fact much more versatile than Sheen and Swan claim. It offers plentiful opportunities for teaching and learning grammar – through the use of focused tasks such as 'Candidates for a Job' and through a range of options in all three phases of a lesson. An options-based approach to TBLT of the kind I have presented in this chapter allows teachers to select options that prioritise fluency but also to ensure that learners' attention is focused on form as they communicate. It demonstrates that TBLT is not a prescriptive method but an approach affording teachers a range of choices about how to plan a lesson around a task.

Notes

(1) The difficulty in making the processing of a pre-determined grammatical structure essential is much less in the case of input-based tasks where the input is structured in such a way that learners will only be able to comprehend it if they successfully process the target structure. See Chapter 3.
(2) Phung (2017) provides examples of other learner-generated tasks in her EdD dissertation. In one task, the students were asked to find pictures of three artefacts that were representative of American culture. They then worked in a group of three to select three out of the nine artefacts that they considered most typical. In a teacher-generated version of this task the students were given the pictures of nine American artefacts.
(3) As pointed out in Chapter 4, Long's position about the role of negotiation in inducing attention to form has changed over the years. Whereas initially he emphasized the negotiation that arises when there is a communication breakdown (i.e. the negotiation of meaning) in his 2015 book he appears to acknowledge that negotiation of form is also relevant.

12 Teachers Evaluating Tasks

Introduction

Pica (1997) pointed out that 'task' was a construct of equal interest to researchers and teachers and afforded a basis for a 'relationship of compatibility' between them:

> As classroom activities, communication tasks can provide a context for meaningful, purposeful L2 learning and use ... As data collection instruments they can be used in a variety of ways: to generate input, feedback, and output conditions to assist researchers in their study of L2 learning. (1997: 61)

Pica's claim of a relationship of compatibility, however, is challengeable on two fronts. First, researchers have frequently resorted to using tasks in laboratory contexts rather than in actual classrooms, raising the question as to whether laboratory-based studies of tasks have much relevance to classrooms. Second, and perhaps more important, the kinds of questions that researchers and teachers ask about tasks are often not the same.

A number of studies have investigated the effects of setting on task performance (Eckerth, 2008b; Foster, 1998; Gass *et al.*, 2005; Slimani-Rolls, 2005). Only Gass *et al.* reported a direct comparison of task performance in laboratory and classroom settings. They asked students enrolled in a third semester university Spanish course to perform three tasks (two information-gap tasks and one opinion-gap task) in dyads in a laboratory setting with the researcher present and in their normal classroom setting. They reported no statistically significant differences in three aspects of interaction (negotiation of meaning, language-related episodes, and recasts) in the two settings. They argued that the results of their study demonstrated that laboratory-based research findings could be cautiously generalized to classroom settings. However, Eckerth (2008b) cast doubt on whether Gass *et al.*'s classroom really functioned as a classroom. He noted that the students were asked to complete the three tasks in an uninterrupted succession and that the three tasks were all completed in nearly the same time. He concluded 'while the classroom may have looked like a classroom, it may not have been perceived as such by the students'. Evidence from two recent meta-analyses (Li, 2010; Mackey & Goo, 2007) suggests that tasks may function in markedly different ways in laboratory and classroom settings. That is, they found that the interactions that resulted from performing tasks had a greater effect on learning when they occurred in laboratory settings. Also, irrespective of what researchers have found regarding the similarity and difference in the way tasks are performed in the laboratory and the classroom, it is surely the case that teachers will have greater confidence in the results of research on tasks conducted in real-life classrooms.

Researchers interest in tasks – as the quotation from Pica shows – lies in their value in collecting data that can be used to address theoretical questions of importance to second language acquisition research. These questions address such issues as the effect that task design and implementation variables have on the fluency, complexity and accuracy of learners' production (Foster & Skehan, 1996), on the negotiation of meaning (Pica *et al.*, 1993), or on the 'activity' that arises when a task is performed (Coughlan & Duff, 1994). Although these questions may be of relevance to language pedagogy, they are not the kinds of questions that teachers themselves typically ask about tasks. Teachers' questions centre on 'task investigations in action, all in normal classroom conditions' (Willis, 2005: 1). They address such issues as the motivational value of using tasks (Loumpourdi, 2005), how to incorporate tasks into lessons based on traditional text-book materials (Muller, 2005), the extent to which it is possible to predict the language that will be needed to perform specific tasks (Cox, 2005), the effect of asking students to report the outcome of a task publicly on the quality of their language output (Johnston, 2005), and the effect of training students to use meaning-negotiation skills on task performance (Lee, 2005).[1] While the questions that teachers ask may draw on the theories that inform task-based research they reflect the specific problems that teachers have identified in their own classrooms and are action-oriented rather than theory-based.

The vast bulk of the research on tasks has been published in academic journals (*Applied Linguistics, Language Learning, Modern Language Journal, Studies in Second Language Acquisition, Language Teaching Research, TESOL Quarterly*) or in collections of articles in books edited by researchers. There have been relatively few publications of studies of tasks by practising teachers. The collection of articles in Van den Branden *et al.* (2009) *Task-Based Language Teaching: A Reader* contains not a single chapter by a teacher-researcher. This is, of course, not surprising, given the importance that is attached to satisfying the academic conventions and standards of publishable research both of which are hard to achieve in practitioner research. Nevertheless, there is a case for examining what teachers make of tasks when they research their use in their own classrooms. After all, most task-based research is directed at informing language pedagogy and such a goal is surely best met not just through formal research but through the insights provided in practitioner research. There is a need for reports of studies written by teachers and for teachers – such as those in Edwards and Willis (2005). How then can teachers research tasks? I will first consider two ways in which practitioner research has been conducted before moving on to my own proposal for the micro-evaluation of tasks.

Practitioner Research

Practitioner research comes in various guises. A popular form is action research, defined by Carr and Kemmis (1986) as 'a form of self-reflective enquiry undertaken by participants in social situations to improve the rationality and justice of their own practices, and the situations in which those practices are carried out' (1986: 162). The model for conducting action research for teachers emphasizes a number of features: (1) it is context-specific, (2) it is practical, (3) it is systematic, (4) it is reflective and (5) it is cyclical. Conducting action research is, however, not without its problems. The precise specification of a problem is not something that teachers always find easy (Nunan, 1990). Also, the requirement that it is cyclical places an enormous burden on teachers. Like, more formal research it is also technicist (i.e. it requires technical skills required to design the research and to collect and analyse the data).

Responding to these problems, Allwright (2003, 2005) proposed 'exploratory research'. He argued that teacher research needs to be feasible as teachers will not engage in it if they see it as too demanding. Exploratory practice is not directed at solving problems but at developing an understanding of some aspect of 'the quality of life in a specific classroom by integrating enquiry into actual classroom practice'. It is focused on investigating 'puzzles' rather than 'problems'. Allwright (2005) lists the general principles (along with two practical suggestions) that provide the ethical and epistemological basis of exploratory practice. These are shown in Table 12.1.

There is much to be said for exploratory practice, not least because it leads teachers to examine issues that are central to an understanding of how their classrooms work and what makes them work (or not work). It

Table 12.1 Exploratory practice in six principles plus two practical suggestions

Principle 1	Put 'quality of life' first.
Principle 2	Work primarily to understand language classroom life.
Principle 3	Involve everybody.
Principle 4	Work to bring people together.
Principle 5	Work also for mutual development.
Principle 6	Make the work a continuous enterprise.
Suggestion 1	Minimize the extra effort of all sorts for all concerned.
Suggestion 2	Integrate the 'work for understanding' into the existing working life of the classroom.

is, however, not so easy to see how it can be utilized in teachers' investigation of tasks where the starting point is not some general aspect of 'life in the classroom' – such as why tensions arise among the participants in a classroom as in Bloom (2007) – but rather the workplan of some specific task. Perhaps, though, it might be possible to talk about the 'life of a task' if the goal of a task evaluation is not just investigating whether the task 'works' but understanding the quality of the teaching and learning experience that the task affords. I will argue that the kind of micro-evaluation of tasks I will now discuss can achieve just this – they can tell us about the 'life of a task' – and that this is what has been missing from much of the research with and on tasks.

Micro-evaluation of Tasks

My own proposal for investigating tasks through practitioner research is 'micro-evaluation'. To date, this has entailed collecting data to examine whether a particular task 'works' (see Ellis, 1997, 1998, 2011) and involves what Allwright (2005) would consider (and perhaps dismiss) as a 'technicist' approach to practitioner research. I see merit in technically executed micro-evaluations of tasks and will provide examples to support my view. However, I can also see their limitations and the value of looking 'downwards' (i.e. 'for deep understanding') in order to understand more about the nature of the teacher's and learners' engagement with the task in the particular context in which it was performed. Here, however, I will simply outline the technicist approach I and my postgraduate students have employed, reserving the challenge of examining how the 'life of a task' can be more fully understood till later in the chapter.

Investigating whether a task 'works'

The starting point for such an evaluation is determining what is meant by 'works'. In fact, this can mean very different things. One obvious criterion that is likely to be attractive to many teachers is whether students enjoyed doing the task and found it useful. This constitutes the motivational criterion. Another criterion is the extent to which the task results in the type of learner behaviour that the teacher had in mind when selecting or designing the task. This constitutes the performance criterion. A third criterion is whether the task contributes to the students' acquisition of the L2. This is the development criterion. Each criterion requires a different approach to the micro-evaluation and different data collection instruments, as shown in Table 12.2.

In Ellis (1997) I distinguished three general approaches for conducting a micro-evaluation of a task; student-based, response-based and learner-based. These approaches correspond to the three evaluation criteria, as shown in Table 12.2. A student-based evaluation is the easiest to carry out as it does not involve any interruption to the normal conduct of the task. It can be conducted by inviting learners to self-report by means of a rating-slip (McGrath, 2002), questionnaire, interview or written commentary after they have completed the task. A response-based evaluation can also be relatively undemanding if it only involves collecting documentary evidence of the task outcome (e.g. a written list of differences for a Spot the Difference task). However, it becomes more demanding if the aim is to examine how students actually performed the task. This requires specially designed check lists or alternatively recording and transcribing the interactions that result from performing the task. The most demanding type of micro-evaluation is when the teacher wishes to investigate whether any learning takes place as a result of performing the task. This can be undertaken in two ways. One involves the design of a test that is administered before and after the task performance. The other draws on a sociocultural view of learning (Lantolf, 2000) and involves a careful examination of a transcript of the complete performance of a task to ascertain whether there is any evidence of 'learning in-flight' (i.e. of the students' ability to use a specific feature with interactional support and then subsequently independently).

In their discussion of programme evaluation, Weir and Roberts (1994) distinguish what they call 'accountability evaluation' and 'development evaluation'. The former aims to establish to what extent the programme is efficient in meeting its goals. The latter is concerned with ways in which the programme can be improved. This distinction is also useful for the micro-evaluation of tasks. Teachers want to know whether a specific task has achieved the aims they set for it. But they also want to discover flaws in the design of the task or problems relating to the particular implementation procedures they chose. Both 'accountability' and 'development' need to be investigated when evaluating a task. Interestingly, this is where

Table 12.2 Three approaches for conducting micro-evaluation of tasks

Criterion for evaluating the task	Approach	Data collection
Motivation ('Were the students motivated when performing the task?')	Student-based	Self-report – rating slips; questionnaire; interviews; post-task written commentary.
Performance ('Do the students perform the task in a manner intended by the design of the task and its manner of implementation?'; 'Are they successful in achieving the task outcome?'	Response-based	Transcriptions of audio and video recordings of students performing the task; observation check lists; documentary record of task outcome.
Development ('Is there any evidence that learners have acquired some new language or achieved greater control over their existing L2 resources?'	Learning-based	Uptake-charts (Slimani, 1989); pre- and post-tests; transcriptions of audio and video-recordings examined over the duration of the task.

formal research on tasks differs from teacher-led micro-evaluations of a task. Researchers are interested in accountability (i.e. they want to know if a task is successful in enabling them to achieve the aims of their research) but they are not really concerned with 'development' although they may sometimes point to problems with the task in the 'limitations' section of their report of a study. I cannot recall any published study of a task that concludes with suggestions for how the task itself might be improved. In contrast, as we will see, teacher evaluators frequently point to ways in a task might be further developed as a result of their micro-evaluations.

Not all micro-evaluations are directed at evaluating whether a task 'works' in the general sense discussed above. Teachers may elect to focus on some specific design feature of a task or an implementation procedure. This kind of micro-evaluation can usefully draw on the findings of more formal research and on the theoretical premises that inform task-based teaching. For example, teachers may elect to investigate whether a particular type of task (e.g. a narrative task) elicits the use of past tense forms or they may want to find out whether giving learners opportunity to plan before they perform the task enhances fluency, complexity and accuracy when they perform it. Directed task evaluation of this kind becomes especially appropriate in the case of focused tasks (i.e. tasks that have been designed to elicit the use of a pre-determined linguistic feature). It requires a response-based evaluation to discover how the task is performed and it also allows for a learning-based evaluation as the teacher-researcher can focus analysis on whether any learning of the feature that is targeted in the task has occurred.

Table 12.3 outlines a procedure that can be used to plan a systematic evaluation of a task. Here I should make it clear that it is the 'task-as-workplan' that is being evaluated, not the 'task-as-process'. That is, the aim of a task evaluation is to determine to what extent the task materials and pre-determined implementation procedures work in the way they were intended to.

The first step, therefore, is to provide a clear description of the task materials and implementation procedures. In Ellis (2003) I provided a framework for describing tasks (see Table 12.4). In effect, this requires

Table 12.3 Procedure for conducting a systematic evaluation of a task

Step 1	Describe the task materials and the specific implementation procedures for teaching the task.
Step 2	Determine the aim of the micro-evaluation by formulating a research question.
Step 3	Determine how to collect data for the evaluation and locate or design any data collection instruments needed.
Step 4	Draw up an evaluation plan indicating whether data are to be collected before the performance of the task, while the task is being performed, or after students have completed it.
Step 5	Analyse the data using appropriate qualitative and/or quantitative methods.
Step 6	Prepare a report of the findings of the evaluation.

Table 12.4 A framework for describing a task

Design feature	Description
1. Goal	The general purpose of the task (e.g. to practise the ability to describe objects concisely; to provide an opportunity for the use of relative clauses).
2. Input	The verbal or non-verbal information supplied by the task (e.g. pictures; a map; written text).
3. Conditions	The way in which the information is presented (e.g. split vs shared information) or the way in which it is to be used (e.g. converging vs diverging).
4. Procedures	The methodological procedures to be followed when performing the task (e.g. group vs pair work; planning time vs no planning time).
5. Predicted outcomes:	
a. Product outcomes	The 'product' that results from completing the task (e.g. a completed table; a route drawn in on a map; a list of differences between two pictures). The predicted product can be 'open' (i.e. allow for several possibilities) or 'closed' (i.e. allow for only one 'correct' solution).
b. Process outcomes	The discoursal, linguistic and cognitive processes the task is predicted to generate.

teachers to first select the task they wish to evaluate and then decide the procedures for teaching it. In other words, they need to draw up a teaching plan. This plan will minimally specify how the task it to be performed but, depending on the aim of the micro-evaluation it can also include a specification of the pre-task activity (e.g. pre-task planning). In guiding my own MA students' plans, however, I recommend they do not attempt to evaluate the entire lesson but just focus on the main task.

The second step is to determine the aim of the micro-evaluation. Where the aim is to determine whether the task 'works', teachers will need to decide if they intend to investigate this with reference to the motivation criterion ('Did the students find the task enjoyable and useful?'), the performance criterion ('Did the students perform the task in way predicted?') or the development criterion ('Did the students learn anything as a result of performing the task?'). Often, it is helpful to formulate a more precise question directed at some specific design feature or implementation procedure. For example, 'Were the students able to identify the five differences in the Spot the Difference task?' or 'Did the task elicit any negotiation of meaning?' If the task is a focused one, it is possible to ask whether the task was successful in eliciting the targeted feature. Micro-evaluations of tasks are likely to be more insightful if the aim is stated in a precise way. Ultimately, though it is for the teacher to decide for him/herself what is to be evaluated.

In the next (step 3), teachers decide what data are needed to carry out the evaluation. At this stage, therefore, they will need to establish what approach (or approaches) to evaluation they will use (i.e. student-based, response-based or learning-based). The aim of the evaluation will dictate the approach(es) required. Table 12.2 lists some of the main methods relating to each approach. Where data collection instruments (e.g. a check list or a student questionnaire) are needed, teachers will need to locate an existing instrument or, as if often the case, design their own.

Step 4 follows on. It involves drawing up an evaluation plan that specifies what data for evaluation will be collected and when (i.e. before, during or after the performance of the task). One way of doing this is to indicate at what points in the lesson plan for the task the data will be collected.

The analysis of the data (Step 5) can involve both qualitative and quantitative methods. In response-based evaluations, it is often necessary to first transcribe the interactions – in all or in part – that arose when the task was performed. If the task involves pair or group work, teachers will probably not be able to transcribe all the interactions and will need to select the interactions of one or two pairs/groups for analysis. Willis (2005) clearly favours qualitative analysis on the grounds that the aim of a task evaluation is 'simply to shed light on and deepen our understanding of what happens in TBL in our specific context' (2005: 8). Although this is broadly true of micro-evaluations of tasks, quantitative analysis can also be informative. For example, if the aim of the evaluation is to investigate the process features in a task performance, it is often helpful to count the frequency with which specific processes (such as negotiation of meaning) occur. However, this runs the danger of the evaluation becoming 'technicist' – the problem that led Allwright to reject action research as a model for teacher-led research.

In the final step (Step 6) teachers prepare a report of their evaluation. This will need to include a rationale for conducting the evaluation, an account of the instructional context, a description of the task being evaluated, a method section that details the aim of the evaluation, the instruments and procedures used to collect data and the methods used to carry out the analysis, a results section, and a discussion of what the evaluation has revealed about the task. The report can take different forms – a conventional written account of the evaluation, power-point slides or an oral presentation.

Some Examples of Micro-evaluations

The micro-evaluations I will present were all undertaken by students enrolled in a course in the *MA in Language Teaching and Learning* at the University of Auckland. The students in this course come from very mixed backgrounds. Some are working in private language schools in Auckland, some in the public school system and many from schools and universities in Asia (China, Japan, Korea, Malaysia). They are also varied in their experience of teaching, some with more than twenty years in different instructional contexts, some with just two or three years in a single setting and some with none.

The course – called 'Task-based Language Learning and Teaching' – had the following aims:

- to review research which has investigated task-based language learning;

- to examine pedagogical proposals for a task-based approach to teaching English as a foreign/second language;
- to provide an opportunity for the participants in the seminar to undertake a micro-evaluation of a task.

In other words, the course aimed to create an interface between the theory and research that informs task-based teaching and the actual use of tasks with L2 learners. This was reflected in the assignments set for this course. The first assignment asked the students to design a task for a particular group of learners with whom they were familiar, prepare a lesson plan for teaching the task and then provide a rationale for the design and implementation features of the task by drawing on relevant literature. The students worked in small groups to design the task and prepare the lesson plan but they wrote up their assignments individually. They then used the feedback on their first assignments to make changes to the task.

For assignment 2, they were asked to plan an evaluation of the task and then actually carry it out by teaching the task to a group of L2 learners. The task was taught by one member of the group with other members sitting in as observers. The group also collaborated in analysing the data that had been collected but the report of the evaluation was written up individually. The micro-evaluations that I will now present are based on these reports.

Jennifer Freeman

Jennifer investigated a dictogloss task performed by a group of three upper-level ESL students in an intensive ESL programme in a local tertiary institution. The students were asked to listen to a text nine sentences long three times. Each student was given a worksheet to guide their listening. In the first listening they were asked to answer a general comprehension question, in the second to note down key content words and in the third to focus on a specific grammatical form (i.e. a different form for each student). The three grammatical structures targeted in this way were relative clauses, passives and transition signals. The students then worked collaboratively to reconstruct the text. This task, then, is an example of what I have called a 'focused task' (Ellis, 2003).

Specific aims for the task were identified: (1) to promote discourse competency by drawing attention to the macro-structure of the text, (2) to promote noticing of the target forms and thereby to increase linguistic accuracy and (3) to promote interaction to facilitate L2 acquisition.

The evaluation was intended to be both objectives-based and provide information that could be used to improve the design and implementation of the task – that is, it was directed at both accountability and development. It involved both a student-based evaluation (i.e. a student questionnaire was administered after the task had been completed and a response-based evaluation (i.e. the students' worksheets were collected, the observers took notes, the group discussion was audio-recorded and transcribed, and the reconstructed text was examined). The transcript of the group discussion was analysed in terms of Form Focused Episodes (Ellis *et al.*, 2001) according to whether the focus was on the three target features or other features (i.e. non-target features or lexis). The reconstructed text was analysed for use of the three target structures.

Both quantitative and qualitative results were presented. These showed that the students were successful in noticing all the incidences of the three target structures when they listened to the text and that they made an attempt to use these forms (although not always correctly) in the reconstructed text. The analysis of the reconstructed text also showed that the students were able to successfully reproduce its rhetorical structure. The task generated a high level of interaction but only from two of the students. One student participated quite minimally. Interestingly, the questionnaire showed that this student found the task more difficult than the other two students and also that this student viewed the task as involving grammar practice whereas the other two thought it was a communicative activity. Jennifer concluded that the task was successful in contributing to the students' discourse competence and in inducing noticing of the target forms but only partially successful in generating talk that led to accurate use of the target features.

Jennifer identified a number of problems with the implementation of the task. She noted that it would have been better to have assigned the job of scribe of the reconstructed text to the weakest of the three students and also that she should have prevented students from sharing their notes during the reconstruction phase as she felt this removed the need for them to interact and led to the students' utterances being typically quite short.

Juanita Watts

Juanita investigated six upper intermediate-level adult students in an intensive ESL programme in a private language school. The task she evaluated was an interesting variant on Spot the Difference. She obtained two photos of the same location in Auckland taken 100 years apart. She asked the students to not just identify the differences but to determine what changes had taken place in this time period. The students worked in pairs with one of the photos given to student A and the other to student B. Thus, this was a two-way information-gap task – the kind of task that Pica *et al.* (1993) considered likely to generate plentiful negotiation of meaning.

The evaluation was intended to investigate both accountability and contribute to the development of the task. It was both student-based and response-based. A learning preferences questionnaire was administered to the six students prior to the performance of the task. The observers kept notes as the task was performed to establish to what extent each student was engaged with the task. The performance of all three pairs was recorded and a transcript prepared. The students' lists of changes (the task outcome) were collected. After completing the task, the students completed a questionnaire to determine whether they had enjoyed it and found it useful and what difficulties they had experienced.

Both qualitative and quantitative results were presented. The task outcome was only partially achieved as the students listed 'differences' in their photos rather than 'changes'. The students demonstrated positive attitudes while performing the task (e.g. they were smiling and laughing and focused their gaze on the task sheet and their partners). The task generated considerable negotiation of meaning but there were marked differences in the three pairs of students. The post-task questionnaire revealed a number of problems with the task. Although the students were generally positive, they reported that they found the task difficult due to lack of vocabulary and also indicated that they would have liked some pre-task grammar instruction.

Juanita concluded that the task instructions needed clarifying to make it clear to the students that they needed to focus on 'changes'. She also suggested that it would have been better to have used pictures of the exact same location. Juanita did not agree with the students' request for some pre-task grammar work but felt that some focus on form was needed and that this could have best provided in a post-task activity. Finally – and perhaps most importantly – conducting the task evaluation helped Juanita to appreciate the fact that individual learners will inevitably respond differently to the same task.

Vanessa Marlow

Vanessa conducted an evaluation of an input-based task with nine intermediate-level adult students enrolled in a university-level ESL course. The task focused on prepositions of movement (e.g. 'towards', 'through' and 'across'). It involved the students listening to directions based on a floor plan of an apartment. They had to write in numbers in the plan to show where various objects mentioned in the directions were located and also draw in arrows to show the direction in which they were walking through the apartment. Thus, this was a non-reciprocal task (Ellis, 2001) but the students were allowed to 'negotiate' if they did not understand a direction.

As in the other task evaluations, the evaluation of this task focused on both accountability and development and was both response-based and student-based. The task was audio recorded and a transcription prepared in order to investigate to what extent the students engaged in negotiation. The students' completed floor plans were collected and analysed to find out which of the prepositions the students had processed correctly when locating the different objects and drawing in arrows to show direction. The questionnaire administered after the task had been completed asked the students to indicate what words they thought they had learned when performing the task (a technique used in Slimani, 1989), whether they had asked any questions, and whether they had found the task easy or difficult.

Vanessa reported that the students varied enormously in their ability to process the prepositions in the input. Scores varied from one to nine out ten. She found that in general the students failed to negotiate if they did not understand a direction. The students varied greatly in their views about the task. Some found it very easy but four out of nine rated the task as very difficult. Nevertheless, the students reported that they had succeeded in learning some of the prepositions. For example, seven learners indicated they had learned 'against', which had occurred in a direction that had elicited negotiation.

Vanessa concluded that simply incorporating unfamiliar words in the input of a task is no guarantee that learners will attend to them even though they might need to do so in order to carry out the task. She felt that what she had learned most from the evaluation was the importance of sequencing activities. She suggested that the task might have worked more effectively if she had included a pre-task activity where the students were trained to use clarification requests in order to negotiate and then given practice in doing so.

Daniel Willcocks

The students in this task evaluation were 10 intermediate-level learners in an intensive ESL programme. They completed the task in three small groups. The task was an opinion-gap task that required the students to reach agreement about which member of a family had stolen a pavlova from the kitchen. They were given pictures of the family members, a house plan, two sets of cards giving different information about each family member (one set was given out at the beginning of the task and the other half way through) and a probability cline where the students could write the names of the suspects according to how likely it was they had committed the crime. The task was designed to elicit expressions of probability and thus can be considered an example of a focused task.

To evaluate task accountability and ways of improving it, Daniel carried out both a student-based and response-based evaluation. Data were collected by audio recording the group discussions, an observation chart to measure the extent to which the students engaged with the task, a reflection questionnaire completed by the teacher and the observers and a student questionnaire to elicit the learners' perspective on the task.

The main finding was that there was considerable variation in the amount of talk by the individual students, both in terms of total turns and number of words. Two learners, for example, completed more than double the number of turns of any of the other students. The groups also differed in the amount of off-task talk that occurred. The three groups did not approach the task in the same way as they exploited the various artefacts that were part of the task workplan very differently. Two groups relied principally on the information and language provided on the cards. The other group, however, behaved in a more self-regulated way by drawing more extensively on their own linguistic resources. Overall, the groups differed markedly in the extent to which their members demonstrated mutuality and equality (Storch, 2002) and this was reflected in the extent to which negotiation of meaning occurred. The students made little use of expressions of probability, even when encouraged to do so by the teacher. The responses to the student questionnaire indicated that although the students liked the task. they disliked the fact that there was no correct outcome (i.e. the information provided did not allow students to deduce who was the thief).

It is perhaps unfair to say that this task was unsuccessful but clearly there were problems with it, as Daniel recognized. He suggested that the task would have been effective if it had been designed with a closed rather than open outcome. He recognized that it probably went on too long and that it would have been better to reshuffle the groups when the second set of cards was given out. Above all he noted that need to constitute groups more carefully to ensure greater mutuality and equality among their members.

Issues in the Micro-evaluation of Tasks

These four micro-evaluations raise a number of issues, some of which have to do with the design and implementation of tasks and others to do with the methodology of such evaluations.

Choosing and developing the tasks

Teachers choose tasks for different reasons. This is very evident in the case of the four micro-evaluations. Jennifer Freeman chose a dictogloss task because she saw it as relevant to the needs of her students and because it was focused (i.e. provided a means of investigating specific linguistic features). Juanita Watts was interested in developing her students' oral ability and so chose a task-type (Spot the Difference) that research has shown is likely to promote negotiation of meaning. Vanessa Marlow used an input-based task to meet the listening assessment requirement of the course she was teaching. However, she was also clearly influenced by the Noticing Hypothesis and by my own research involving listen-and-do tasks. Daniel Willcocks was interested in learners' 'engagement' with a task and thus chose a topic for his opinion-gap task that he thought would be interesting to the learners. Thus, we can see that the choice of task was motivated by (1) student needs, (2) course aims, (3) the teachers' understanding of the research findings and (4) a desire to engage the learners.

Teachers also approach the development of a task differently. Johnson (2000) reported a study in which he investigated how a group of experienced and less experienced teachers set about designing a task. He distinguished three general ways in which the teachers viewed tasks – in terms of task function (e.g. 'describing a person'), task genre (e.g. information-gap) or task frame involving a cluster of factors (e.g. participatory organization, skills to be practiced and teacher roles). He reported that the less experienced teachers used task frame as a starting point for designing a task whereas the more experienced teachers opted mainly for task genre or task function. He also noted that the teachers varied in terms of whether they opted for a 'language-oriented' or 'task-oriented' approach. These different approaches are also evident in the tasks the four teachers developed. The teachers were all experienced and appear to have based their choices on genre and/or function. Their tasks varied in terms of whether they were 'language-oriented' (i.e. focused) or 'task-oriented' (i.e. unfocused). Johnson did not find that the teachers he investigated drew on research involving tasks. However, the four teachers did make use of the research-based knowledge they had acquired on their MA course.

Task sequencing

Tasks are not performed in a vacuum. They are part of whole lessons that can consist of a pre-task and post-task phase as well as the main-task phase – see Chapter 11. It is interesting to note, however, that, with the notable exception of work on strategic planning in the pre-task phase of a lesson (see, for example, Ellis, 2005), researchers have tended to focus their attention only on the main task phase (i.e. on the performance of a single, discrete task). I also asked the students conducting the micro-evaluations to focus on the main task and not on any pre- or post-task activities they had included in their lesson.[2] In fact, though, the evaluations pointed to the important role played by the pre- and post-task activities.

Manalo, in particular, pointed to the importance of sequencing activities in order to ensure that a task works effectively. She found that students failed to negotiate for meaning in the main task when they did not understand a command and suggested that this was because she had not included a 'facilitating task' in the pre-task phase to prime learners to make use of such strategies for requesting clarification, checking understanding, clarifying something and interrupting. She commented:

> The selection of tasks and/or sequencing of tasks in a way that prepares learners for the main task phase can have a significant influence on learners' ability to modify the verbal input.

Watts also felt that her task needed to be supplemented to include a focus on form. In their comments on the task, the students indicated that they would have liked some pre-task focus on form. However, Watts felt that this need was best catered for in a post-task activity rather than a pre-task activity as to have started with a focus on form would have run the risk of turning the task into a practice activity (see Ellis, 2003).

Teachers, unlike some researchers, then, are very aware that tasks have a context and that this can influence both how the task is performed and what is learned as a result. Ultimately, tasks cannot be properly understood without reference to their instructional contexts.[3]

Task vs activity

A task is a workplan, i.e. a set of materials. When the task is implemented it results in 'activity', which may or may not be that envisaged by the designer of the task. This is because the same task can result in very different kinds of activity (Coughlan & Duff, 1994). One of the main purposes of a micro-evaluation is to investigate whether the activity that results from the performance of the task was that expected by the designers of the task.

One of the clearest findings from the micro-evaluations is that a task does not result in the same 'activity' when it is performed by different students. Juanita Watts' micro-evaluation, for example, showed that an information-gap task resulted in marked differences in the negotiation of meaning that took place in different pairs of students. One pair engaged much more extensively in negotiation than the other. This pair worked harder to resolve the communication problems that arose and was more successful in doing so. There was also a difference in how they negotiated. The pair that negotiated extensively did so by means of clarification requests whereas the other pair employed confirmation checks. The two examples below illustrate these differences. In Example 1 the two students persist until they successfully resolve their communication problem with S2 repeatedly requesting clarification. In Example 2, S4 uses a confirmation check to address a vocabulary problem but even though S3 indicates that S4 has not understood no further attempt is made to resolve the problem. S1 and 2 worked hard as equals to help each other but S3 assumed a dominant role and S4 a more passive role, reflecting differences in their English proficiency. Clearly, this 'task' resulted in very different interactional processes for these two pairs of students. The micro-evaluations invariably focused on how individual learners responded to a task.

Example 1:

S1:   on the left, I can see um lam – post. Lam-post.
S2:   wh-pardon? What? (=clarification request)
S1:   lam-sorry. Lam post.
S2:   name post? (=clarification request)
S1:   /leim/post/laem/post post
S2:   L – A? (=clarification request)
S1:   L-A-M lam
S2:   Ah, lamp. Ah lamp post (successfully resolved)

Example 2:

S3: And ... can you see the, can you say, electronic lines
S4: road? (=confirmation check)
S3: no, no
S4: no (not resolved)

Students also vary in their perceptions of the purpose of the task they have been asked to perform. In sociocultural terms, they have very different motives for the 'actions' they carry out. Jennifer Freeman, for example, found that one of three students (Student C) working on the dictogloss task thought it was really a grammar practice activity whereas the other two viewed it as a communicative activity. This was reflected in how the task was performed. Student C participated relatively little in the interaction except in the form-focused episodes that centred on the specific target form he had been asked to attend to. Freeman suggested that student C demonstrated little interactional involvement because it was 'superfluous' to the activity he was performing.

Daniel Willcocks also reported that the three groups of students he investigated performed the task in very different ways. Drawing on sociocultural theory, he suggested that two of the groups were 'object regulated' in that they relied extensively on the input provided, whereas the other group was more 'self-regulated' in that they drew on their own linguistic resources. Their main reference point was not the cards that provided them with input but the pictures of the family members. This group also engaged in less 'off task' talk.

The difference between 'task' and 'activity' has led some researchers to argue that there is little real merit in investigating 'tasks' and that attention should be focused only on the activity that arises. Seedhouse (2005) wrote:

> a secure basis for 'task' as research construct and for the quantification of discoursal data is attainable only by switching the conceptual and methodological focus to task-in-process. (2005: 533)

Seedhouse, however, was talking from the perspective of the researcher. From the perspective of the teacher, 'task' remains a crucial pedagogic unit because it serves as the basis for planning a task-based curriculum and individual lessons. What is important for teaching is the relationship between 'task' and 'activity'. The fact that the same task results in different activity is not problematic for teaching (it is true of any kind of material a teacher uses). What is important is that teachers develop an understanding of what factors are responsible for the differences that arise in how a task is performed. This is exactly what these micro-evaluations helped to show.

Process and product

The evaluation of a task involves examining both the 'process' (i.e. what transpires when the task is being performed) and the 'product' (i.e. whether the learners' are successful in achieving the outcome of the task). The evaluation of both process and product are part of a response-based approach; that is, it addresses whether a task achieves what was predicted of it. Evaluating the learners' response to a task lies at the heart of a micro-evaluation. All four micro-evaluations employed a response-based approach.

The product of a task varies in terms of how 'closed' or 'open' the outcome is. This is reflected in the four tasks my MA students chose to evaluate. The most open was Willcocks' opinion-gap task and the most closed was Marlow's input-based task. Freeman's task was relatively open (in that there was no one way to reproduce the dictogloss passage) while Watt's task was relatively closed (but not completely in that there was not a finite number of 'changes' in the two locations for the students to identify nor a single way of expressing these changes).

OPEN   Willocks   Freeman   Watts   Marlow   CLOSED

It is clearly easier to evaluate the product of a task if the task is closed. Marlow, for example, was able to inspect the students' plans to see if they had located the various objects correctly. Watts found that her students were not entirely successful in achieving the outcome of the task as they interpreted it as requiring them to identify 'differences' rather than 'changes'. Freeman reported partial success. The students successfully reproduced the rhetorical structure of the task but were less successful in using the target grammatical structures. Willocks was not able to evaluate the product of his task as it was completely open. He concluded that the task would have been more effective if it had been designed with a closed outcome. These evaluations suggest that there is merit in teachers' employing closed tasks – not just because they facilitate micro-evaluation but because they allow teachers a quick and easy method of determining whether a task has 'worked'. A closed outcome also allows the students to see whether they have been successful or not, and, as Willocks discovered, students want this.

Ultimately, however, it is not the outcome of a task that matters but the processes that arise out of it. It is not a matter of whether the learners are successful in achieving the outcome but whether they engage in language use that fosters L2 development. It is 'process' that is all-important and what teachers need are ways of evaluating the process. This requires asking first 'What aspects of the process should be examined?' The four micro-evaluations chose to look at the following aspects of process:

- accurate processing of target-forms (Freeman; Manalo);
- engagement with the task (Freeman; Watts; Willcocks);
- negotiation of meaning (Freeman; Watts; Manalo);
- language-related episodes (Freeman; Watts; Manalo);
- participation in group/pair work (Freeman; Watts; Willcocks).

The first of these – accurate processing of target forms – can only be investigated if the task is a focused one. In the case of an input-based task, it can be determined relatively easily by inspecting the task outcome (e.g. the floor plans in Manalo's study). In the case of production-based tasks, it requires recording the interactions that take place and then analysing them to check whether individual students used the target forms and if so whether they did so correctly or not. This is a painstaking process. So too is investigating negotiation of meaning, language-related episodes and students' participation – all aspects of task-based interactions that figure prominently in formal task-based research. The reports of the micro-evaluations are full of tables showing the frequency of negotiation sequences, triggers, uptake and the number of turns/words produced by each student etc. These quantitative analyses certainly help to document the kinds of processes that took place when the tasks were performed[4] and they certainly enabled the student-evaluators to demonstrate that they had read and understood the literature on task-based research!

Three of the studies also employed 'observation' and 'reflection' to examine the qualitative aspects of the task processes. Willcocks, for example, designed an observation chart to record those student behaviours that were indicative of motivation, enjoyment, and task fatigue. He also included a 'reflection questionnaire' which the teacher and the observers completed after the lesson. This included questions such as 'What do you think the students learned from the lesson?' and 'To what extent were students motivated by the activity?' Willcocks presented his results in the form of descriptive comments about each group, focusing on the differences both between and within the groups. These descriptions about the level of the learners' engagement and the nature of students' participation were often more illuminating than the quantitative analyses borrowed from the research literature. They provided confirmatory evidence of Storch's (2002) finding about the importance of mutuality and equality in small group work. The use of observation and reflection and the qualitative analyses they afford are also, arguably, more compatible with what teachers might be able to undertake as part and parcel of their normal teaching.

Students' perceptions

All the micro-evaluations adopted a student-based approach by asking the learners to complete a questionnaire after they had completed the task. The questionnaire elicited responses about the learners' perception of the purpose of the task, whether they had found the instructions clear, whether they found the task enjoyable and useful, whether they felt they had learned anything and their views about the level of difficulty. Overall, the students indicated they liked the tasks and found them enjoyable but perhaps they just wished to please the teachers! They were less certain about whether they had learned anything. This is not surprising as the essence of a task is that there is no specification of what learners are supposed to learn. But some of the learners who completed the focused tasks (Freeman and

Marlow) were able to identify specific linguistic features they had noticed. The learners' individual responses to the task differed in two main respects – how they viewed the purpose of the task (i.e. as practising language or communication) and how difficult they found the task.

Collecting data on students' perceptions of a task is on obvious strategy in an evaluation. In contrast, it is rare to find a research study collecting such data. These micro-evaluations suggest that it would be useful to do so because clearly how learners orientate to a task affects how they perform it. From the teacher's standpoint, it is even more important to elicit students' comments on a task and not just rely on their own perceptions of how it was performed. Also, asking students to complete a short questionnaire about a task involves little preparation and can be viewed as part and parcel of the pedagogy of task-based teaching (i.e. as a legitimate post-task activity).

Conclusion

The purpose of this chapter is twofold. First, I wanted to investigate a particular type of practitioner research – the micro-evaluation of tasks. I was interested in whether this constitutes a viable form of this kind of research. Second, I was interested in what insights could be obtained from the findings of such evaluations and whether these findings had any value for researchers of tasks.

The purpose of a micro-evaluation of a task, to slightly adapt Weir and Roberts (1994), is 'to collect information systematically in order to indicate the worth or merit of a task' (1994: 4). It seems to me that the micro-evaluations I have discussed have achieved this. Information was collected systematically about the tasks and this was used by the teachers to determine whether the tasks had worth or merit, and, also to identify ways in which they could be improved for future use. It depends, of course, on how 'worth' and 'merit' are defined. All four evaluations were student- and response based. That is, they tried to establish the worth of a task in terms of the value that the students attached to it and whether it resulted in the kinds of language use that, on the basis of established theory, could be hypothesized to promote learning. None of the evaluations were learning-based (i.e. no attempt was made to establish whether the tasks actually resulted in any learning). Arguably, this would provide the truest measure of 'worth'. But it is also extremely difficult to determine what learning results from performing a single task unless, perhaps, one adopts a sociocultural perspective and measures learning simply in terms of the scaffolded production of language within a learner's zone of proximal development – see Markee (1994) for an example of such an approach.

The teachers who conducted these micro-evaluations most certainly found them of value. In their reflective comments they all indicated that the evaluations had increased their understanding of task-based teaching. In this respect, the micro-evaluations achieved the main goal of the MA course – they enabled my students to make the link between theory/ research and the practice of task-based teaching. However, these students also commented that the micro-evaluations were time-consuming and that they were unlikely to undertake them in their day-to-day teaching. As one student put it:

> ... micro-based task-evaluation is a good introspective opportunity for evaluating teaching techniques and materials. There's only one disadvantage: it takes a lot of time to carry out. Therefore, it may not fit some busy teachers' schedule. But I had a lot of fun. (Chan, 1995)

Are micro-evaluations therefore as impractical as action research – 'parasitical' on teachers' 'normal working lives and the lives of their learners' (Allwright, 2005: 355). Will they simply lead to burn-out? I think the answer is almost certainly 'yes', at least if the micro-evaluations are carried out as thoroughly as those by the four teachers discussed in this paper. Perhaps then I need a set of general principles that can guide such micro-evaluations – analogous to the Six Principles that Allwright (2005) proposed for exploratory practice. Table 12.5 contains a list of the general principles I would like to propose.

I am not sure that the evaluations my students carried out conformed to these seven principles. For example, I did not suggest to them that they should report the results of their reflections on the evaluation to their students. Also, the data was not always collected in a way that was practical and that was of mutual benefit to the students. This is probably the aspect of these micro-evaluations that needs reconsidering the most. A response-based evaluation need not require audio or video recording and laborious transcribing. It can be conducted quite effectively through the

Table 12.5 General principles for guiding the micro-evaluations of tasks

Principle 1: Choice of task	The task to be evaluated should be chosen by the teacher with due regard to the specific instructional context in which he/she works.
Principle 2: Purpose of the evaluation	The task should be evaluated to discover whether it 'works' and also how it might be improved.
Principle 3: The evaluators	Whenever possible, the teacher should collaborate with other teachers to carry out the evaluation.
Principle 4: Focus of the evaluation	Focus should be on the evaluation on the main task but account should be taken of the activities that precede and follow the task.
Principle 5: Method of evaluation	Data should be collected in a way that is practical and that enhances the pedagogic value of the task; the evaluation should be seen as a mutual enterprise.
Principle 6: Reflect on the evaluation	The teacher should reflect on both what he/she has discovered about the task as performed by the students and on the evaluation itself.
Principle 7: Sharing the findings	The findings of the teacher's reflections should be shared with the students.

use of observation charts. A student-based evaluation is easily carried out by means of a short questionnaire and does meet the requirement of integrating the 'work for understanding' into the 'existing working life of the classroom' (Allwright, 2005: 360). If the task is a closed one, it is also easy to evaluate how successful the learners were in achieving the outcome.

My second purpose was to consider whether the micro-evaluation of tasks has anything to offer the SLA researcher. I think they do. Researchers have used tasks to collect data in order to test or build theory (e.g. Mackey, 1999) or they have investigated the effects of specific design features and implementation procedures on learners' comprehension, production or L2 acquisition (Foster & Skehan, 1996; Loschky, 1994). Reading reports of such classroom-based studies one is struck by the fact that tasks are treated as discrete devices that can be investigated without reference to the context in which they are performed. But as I noted earlier, a task is not performed in a vacuum. It is part of a lesson, with activities that precede and follow it, and the lesson is likely to be part of sequence of lessons. Also, research reports rarely include any information about the students' own perceptions of a task or of the teachers' reflections about its performance. What these micro-evaluations have shown is that it is necessary to investigate the life of a task by treating a classroom as 'a culture in its own right' (Wright, 1992: 192). This involves taking an ecological view of a task in order to understand why it was developed and performed in the way in which it was. This is what the micro-evaluations I have discussed have done. They have much to offer research with and into tasks because they shed insight about the life of a task.

Notes

(1) I have extracted these issues from the collection of practitioner research studies reported by teachers in Edwards and Willis (2005).

(2) The reason for asking students to focus on evaluating only the main task was to try to limit the data they would need to collect and thus to make the evaluation more manageable.

(3) Teacher educators such as Willis (1996) have shown awareness of the importance of task-sequencing and the importance of creating an appropriate context for the performance of a task.

(4) One interesting finding was that students made almost no use of comprehension-checks when negotiating. Negotiating triggers were almost invariably of the responsive kind (e.g. recasts or classification requests).

Part 4
Conclusion

In the chapter in this final part of the book I look back at the chapters in the previous three parts of the book to consider the interface between research and pedagogy in the development of task-based language teaching. There is now a substantial body of research that has investigated tasks and also a number of commentaries about the pedagogy of task-based teaching. Pica (1997) emphasized the compatibility between the fields of research and language teaching as both were concerned with tasks. Clearly, research has had an impact on pedagogy. However, to a considerable extent there has been a disconnection, with much of the research focusing narrowly on tasks and pedagogy concerned more broadly with complete task-based lessons and courses.

This suggests a need for an applied research agenda in the future – one that is driven less by the need to test or build a theory of task performance and more by how best to address the practical issues that teachers face when introducing task-based language teaching (TBLT) into their classrooms – including how to handle 'grammar'. In other words, rather than taking 'task' as the starting point for research, I propose a research programme built on identifying key issues relating to the implementation of task-based teaching. I argue, too, that more thought needs to be given to the design of teacher-education programmes and to investigating whether such programmes are effective in supporting teachers when they introduce TBLT into their classrooms.

13 Key Issues in Task-based Research and Pedagogy

Looking Back

In Chapter 1 I pointed out that task-based language teaching has quite a short history. It grew out of the communicative language teaching movement of the 1970s but did not really establish itself as a distinctive approach until the 1990s. It would, however, be wrong to suggest that tasks did not figure in language pedagogy before that. In the 1960s I was an English teacher in a new rural secondary school in Zambia. Although much of what I and other teachers at the school did was based on a structural approach, we also made frequent use of what I would now call 'tasks'. For example, we would invite a student to pretend to be a character in a story book and ask the other students to fire questions at him/her which had to be answered in character. We would design reading comprehension activities where students had to complete a map showing the route described in the text. We would make use of situational composition exercises, where students had to write a report based on the minutes of meetings. I would definitely call these activities 'tasks' as they clearly satisfied my four criteria for a task (see Chapter 1). However, although we included tasks in our teaching, we did not build our whole programme around tasks. We just made eclectic use of 'tasks' in some of our lessons. I am sure that most teachers have always done this.

What is innovative about task-based language teaching, then, is not 'tasks' but rather the idea that a language course can consist of nothing but tasks – that there is no need to teach the language directly because learners do better if they acquire it incidentally by performing tasks supported by focus-on-form. For many teachers this is a radical way of going about teaching. It requires them to abandon long-held views about what language is and their beliefs about the importance of directing what learners should learn and when they should learn it. As we saw in Chapter 8, task-based language teaching (TBLT) has met with some resistance and problems have arisen in introducing it in some instructional contexts. As an approach it constitutes an innovation and as such will be subject to the factors that influence whether innovations are successfully implemented.

In this concluding chapter of the book I would like to take a look at what I see as the key issues that need to be addressed to drive task-based teaching (as an approach) forward. In line with how this book has been organized, I will first examine the contribution that research has made. I will argue that while the research to date has certainly contributed to the development of TBLT, it is also limited in a number of respects and I will suggest that a more profitable way forward might be evaluation studies that investigate complete programmes in specific teaching contexts. In the following section I will consider a number of practical issues that my work with teachers has shown me are of concern to them in implementing TBLT. Then I will point to the importance of teacher training/education to ensure the effective implementation of TBLT and consider a few studies that have investigated training programmes. To conclude, I consider what needs to be done to ensure the future of TBLT.

Researching Task-based Language Teaching

The task-based research that has been undertaken to date might be described in one of several ways:

- it has been largely driven by theoretical issues rather than by the practical concerns of teachers;
- it has been highly technicist, involving data collection procedures and methods of data analysis that are largely inaccessible to teachers;
- it has focused on the performance of discrete tasks rather than task-based lessons – often in laboratory-based studies rather than actual classrooms;
- there has been almost no research of complete task-based courses;
- it has been overly focused on oral production tasks to the neglect of listening, reading and writing tasks;
- it has emphasized task performance at the expense of the learning that results from the performance; that is, it has often failed to demonstrate how the performance of tasks leads to learning;
- it has pointed to the factors that affect task complexity but to date there are no clear and practical guidelines for the design of task-based syllabuses derived from the research;
- it has mainly investigated intermediate-level learners to the neglect of beginners and advanced-level learners.
- it has paid little attention to learners' subjective responses to tasks and how these can affect the performance of tasks;
- there are very few studies that have investigated the effectiveness of teacher training/education programmes for TBLT.

Framed in this way, this list can be construed as enumerating the limitations of the research to date. There are, of course, good reasons for these limitations. The focus on theoretical issues is inherent in any research and, in any case, as Kurt Lewin (1951) pointed out, 'there is nothing so practical as a good theory' (1951: 169). The technicist nature of the research can be seen as both inevitable and desirable given the goals of research. The fact that most research has investigated individual tasks has been driven by the need to understand the design and implementation factors that affect the performance of tasks and, perhaps, by the lack of time and resources needed to investigate whole courses. The emphasis on oral production tasks reflects both the primacy of 'speaking' in most models of language and the origins of task-based teaching in communicative language teaching where the same emphasis existed. The focus on task-performance at the expense of investigating learning is really a product of the focus on discrete tasks because it is extremely difficult to demonstrate the learning that takes place as a result of performing a single task. It could be argued that the lack of clear guidelines for designing task-based courses is not because researchers have not addressed the thorny issue of task complexity but because they have only just started to tackle it. Also, it is important to acknowledge the achievements of the TBLT research.

Achievements of TBLT Research

Research has undoubtedly been a major driver of TBLT and has influenced its development in several ways.

- There is a solid theoretical foundation for TBLT in second language acquisition research and in educational principles that emphasize learning-by-doing. Second language acquisition theories emphasize the importance of incidental acquisition and the need to acknowledge that L2 development is organic and controlled by the learner rather than externally by the teacher. Educational principles that emphasize *l'èducation integrale*, individual freedom, rationality, emancipation, learner-centredness, egalitarian teacher–student relationships, participatory democracy and cooperation (see Long, 2015) underscore TBLT. If there is a single reason responsible for the growing interest in TBLT it is the strength of its theoretical foundations.
- There has been substantial development in theory-grounded tools needed to analyse the language that results from the performance of tasks. In Chapter 7 I discussed four approaches to investigating task-induced oral production (the cognitive-interactionist, the sociocultural, the psycholinguistic and personal investment approaches) and the measurement tools based on them.
- The research has contributed to our understanding of the nature of a task and to developing empirically based typologies of task types, design features and implementation options. Pedagogic accounts of tasks are based superficially on the operations they

involve (e.g. listing, ordering and sorting, comparing, sharing personal experiences etc.) as in Willis (1996). Task-based research has led to classifying tasks in terms of factors that impact on how they are performed (e.g. input-based versus output-based tasks; information-gap versus opinion-gap tasks; focused versus unfocused tasks) and to identifying key design features such as tight versus loose structure and implementation options such as strategic and within-task planning. Research has undoubtedly had a major impact on how tasks are conceptualized and classified.

- The research has also grappled with some of the contentious issues in TBLT. In Chapter 6, for example, I considered research that has investigated the role of explicit instruction in TBLT. Although this research cannot be said to have resolved this issue as yet, it has pointed to some of the advantages and possible disadvantages of pre-teaching grammatical features prior to the performance of a task and, therefore, informs the debate that centres on this crucial issue.

- The research has also addressed issues where the opinions of TBLT theorists and practitioners are divided – to my mind one of the main purposes of applied research. It suggests, for example, that contrary to what some popular teacher guides suggest, teachers can usefully focus on form in the main-task phase of a lesson as well as in the post-task phase.

- The research has identified practical ways of doing focus-on-form – an essential element of TBLT. In Chapter 4 I spelt out the procedures and techniques available to teachers for drawing learners' attention to form in all stages of a task-based lesson. In Chapter 5 I focused on research that has investigated ways of preparing learners to perform a task. This is perhaps where the symbiosis of research and pedagogy has been most clearly evident.

- There is one line of research at least that has moved beyond just examining task performance to investigating the learning that takes place. There is now a large number of studies that point to the effectiveness of corrective feedback in helping learners improve their accuracy in the production of grammatical features targeted in focused tasks. This research provides a basis for evaluating the advice given to teachers in popular teacher guides. See Ellis and Shintani (2014) for such an evaluation.

- While it is certainly the case that researchers have largely neglected learners' subjective responses to tasks and how individual learner factors influence task performance, there are at least a few programmatic studies that have attempted to investigate these important aspects of TBLT. Research on task engagement has investigated both learners' performance of tasks and their personal responses to them and looked for how the latter influences the former (see Chapter 7). There is also growing interest in how differences in working memory affect the performance of tasks (e.g. Révész, 2012). This research is, however, in its infancy and, to date, there has been little attempt to suggest how it can be applied in practice.[1]

These are notable contributions of the research to TBLT but, still, in a number of respects the research is quite limited.

Limitations of the TBLT research

Technicist constructs such as complexity, accuracy and fluency, so dominant in the research to date, are not likely to appeal to teachers. They clearly have strong construct validity for research but no obvious face validity for teachers, who are more likely to relate to 'engagement' as a performance goal.

The absence of research on full task-based courses is understandable but the continuing focus on the performance of discrete tasks at the expense of complete lessons is surprising. Tasks are not performed in a vacuum but in the context of what happens in the pre-task, main-task and the post-task stages of a lesson. Investigating what transpires in the whole lesson is the most useful way of advancing TBLT. More studies such as Samuda (2001) are needed. I have referred repeatedly to this study throughout the book. Its importance lies in the fact that Samuda documented how a teacher responded *in situ* to problems that arose when learners performed the Things-in-Pocket Task. As Samuda (2015) noted in another article, teachers are concerned with the role a task plays in a sequence of instruction. She emphasized that when task is viewed as a 'pedagogical tool' it can be variously interpreted and reshaped as the teacher implements it and thus what is important is the mediating role of the teacher: 'Hence it is not the task as a tool that is relevant but how it is used to mediate learning and teaching' (2015: 274). Researchers, however, have been hooked on task-as-a-tool.

I have questioned too whether the current drive to investigate the design factors that determine task-complexity will lead to any concrete proposals about how to construct a task-based syllabus (see Chapter 9). Quite apart from the problems of isolating design factors from the composite of variables that comprise a task, there is a danger that this research will ignore the fact that task complexity cannot be just considered in terms of individual tasks but must take account of the sequence of activities in which a task is embedded – Samuda's point again. Also, like Skehan (2016), I see greater value for TBLT in research that investigates implementation conditions, such as planning, than in research on task design variables.

The main limitation in the mainstream work on tasks, however, is the absence of research that have investigated whole task-based courses. Research, by definition, is directed at theory-building or theory-testing. The studies I will now consider have focused on evaluation and these have addressed complete courses. Such studies, I suggest, have greater practical value.

Evaluation studies of TBLT

Evaluation studies are carried out to establish to what extent a programme/project is effective and efficient in meeting its goals and to identify how it might be improved. The advantage of such studies is that they provide information about the factors that promote or impede the success of attempts to introduce TBLT in specific instructional contexts. Given the newness of TBLT, evaluation studies typically address TBLT as an innovation *in situ*.

There is a large literature on innovation in education and other fields. Rogers (2003) describes five stages involved in the 'innovation-decision process'. The first stage is the Knowledge Stage, where participants in the innovation learn about the what, how and why of the innovation. The next stage, the Persuasion Stage, concerns the extent to which the participants are persuaded that the innovation is worthwhile and thus develop a positive attitude to it. In the third stage, the Decision Stage, the participants choose to adopt or reject the innovation. Rogers noted that adoption is more likely to occur if there is an opportunity to experience the innovation on a partial trial basis. In the Implementation Stage the innovation is put into practice. Uncertainty is likely at this stage unless technical assistance is available to the implementers. Modifications in the innovation are also common in this stage. In the final stage, the Confirmation Stage, the participants' acceptance of the innovation is established or discontinuance occurs involving either partial replacement or its complete rejection.

Evaluation studies address the diffusion of TBLT as an innovation. I considered two such studies in Chapter 8. In one of these (Carless, 2004), problems were evident in the Knowledge Stage of Roger's model – that is, some teachers had very uncertain ideas of what a 'task' consisted of – and also in the Implementation Stage the elementary school teachers lacked the technical assistance they needed to help them implement TBLT effectively. In the other evaluation study (McDonough & Chaikitmongkol, 2007), the innovation was more successful but quite substantial modifications occurred in the Implementation Stage before it was finally accepted by the teachers. These two studies provide valuable information about the factors that affect the diffusion of TBLT in particular contexts and also suggest that Rogers' model can provide a basis for investigating TBLT programmes.

There are now a substantial number of evaluation studies (see Ellis *et al.*, forthcoming). Norris (2016) noted 'the diverse purposes to which an evaluation can and should be put' (2016: 50). He emphasized that evaluations of TBLT programmes are important in 'enabling a better understanding of how they work' – and, I would add, a better understanding of the problems that sometimes prevent them from working. As an example, of what such studies can tell us, I will consider Watson-Todd's (2006) evaluation of a TBLT course developed for university students in

Thailand. This evaluation is of particular interest as it reported on the continuation of a task-based programme over a number of years using data collected from course documentation and interviews with the teachers. Watson-Todd documented several changes that were made to the programme over time: (1) the number of tasks was reduced by either removing tasks or combining two tasks into one, (2) greater emphasis was placed on explicit teaching of linguistic objectives both in separate lessons and in pre-task work and (3) greater weighting was given to examinations rather than continuous assessment. Watson-Tod commented that 'these changes can be viewed as a move away from a "pure" version of task-based learning towards a more mixed methodology' (Watson-Todd, 2006: 9). He suggested that they occurred largely as a response to practical constraints. For example, the move away from continuous assessment was motivated by the need to accommodate increased numbers of students and the hiring of adjunct teachers unfamiliar with this kind of assessment. This study points to the importance of investigating the Confirmation Stage of Roger's model to establish whether confirmation takes place and to what extent discontinuation occurs.

Evaluation studies, such as those mentioned above, have pointed to a number of problems facing the successful diffusion of TBLT as an innovation. The problems can be grouped according to whether they concern the teacher, the students or structural issues within the education system. It is important to note, however, that many of these problems are not specific to TBLT but will be evident whatever approach to teaching is adopted. Table 13.1 lists these problems, many of which I have discussed in previous chapters. These are 'real' problems in the sense that they were attested in studies investigating attempts to introduce TBLT. There is a danger that listing them in this way over-emphasizes the barriers to the uptake of TBLT but if TBLT is to flourish it is important to address them. The structural problems are especially troublesome as they impose conditions on learners that make 'pure' TBLT very difficult (perhaps impossible) to implement. Solutions to the problems involving teachers and learners are easier to address and I have attempted to do so in previous chapters (see, in particular, Chapters 8 and 9). In some cases (e.g. learners' use of the L1 to overcome communication problems) these problems are, arguably, not really problems at all. These problems concerning teachers and students point to the need for teacher education.

Final comment

In this section, I have taken a critical look at the research that has investigated tasks and task-based teaching. I have pointed to ways in which research has informed the development of TBLT over the last three decades. But I have also suggested that, from the perspective of advancing the *practice* of TBLT, the research has been limited in a number of ways, in particular in its focus on discrete tasks and it relative failure to investigate complete lessons and programmes. In this respect, I have argued that evaluation studies are more helpful. These draw on diffusion-of-innovations models to examine the extent to which complete task-based programmes are successfully implemented or modified and the problems that arise.

One of the findings of the evaluation studies was that teachers involved in a task-based programme often felt the need to modify their initial approach by introducing elements of more traditional ways of teaching (i.e. explicit language teaching). This raises the question of whether TBLT is too idealistic and ambitious for some teaching contexts, as claimed by Littleood (2014), and whether concessions need to be made. I will return to this point in the concluding section of this chapter. First, though, I will consider the practical issues that teachers themselves have raised about TBLT.

Task-based Language Pedagogy: Questions Teachers Ask

In the third part of this book I focused on the pedagogy of task-based teaching, looking first at some common misconceptions about TBLT, then on the design of a task-based curriculum and methodological options, and finally on how teachers themselves can become researchers of tasks. In this final chapter, I will address task-based pedagogy in terms of a series of questions that teachers have asked me in the various seminars on TBLT I have conducted. By and large, these questions reflect the problems identi-fied in the evaluation studies and listed in Table 13.1. I will also suggest solutions to the problems the question raise.

Is the task-based approach suitable for beginners?

This question is often motivated by teachers' belief that learners need to be taught some language before they can perform tasks. It stems from a lack of understanding of how languages are acquired. In addressing this question, I begin then by pointing out three key aspects of the beginning stages of acquiring a language.

(1) Learning begins with vocabulary and short phrases – not with gram-mar, which comes later.
(2) Learning is initially receptive – it occurs incidentally when learners hear and understand what is said to them. Speaking follows later.
(3) Learning requires input that is comprehensible and provides multiple exposures to the same words and phrases.

This explains the importance of input-based tasks for beginners. I point out that such tasks can be performed in a whole-class participatory structure and emphasize that although such tasks do not require production on the

Table 13.1 Problems with implementing TBLT

Problems involving teachers	Problems involving learners	Structural problems
TBLT requires teachers to abandon the traditional roles of 'knower' and 'transmitter of knowledge' and take on the roles of 'participator' and 'co-learner'. This can be seen as an imposition of Western educational values on educational systems that are not culturally suited to them such as those in Asia.	Students used to treating language as an object rather than as a tool may fail to see the point of performing tasks as these cater to incidental rather than intentional language learning.	Teachers may be required to teach to a syllabus consisting of lists of words and grammatical structures. As a result, they prefer to base their teaching directly on the items listed in the syllabus rather than on tasks that have only an indirect relationship to the linguistic content of the syllabus.
Teachers may lack the necessary proficiency in English (or lack confidence in their proficiency) to conduct lessons in English.	Students cannot perform tasks unless they have already developed the English proficiency needed to communicate (i.e. TBLT is inappropriate for beginner-level learners).	Countries that have mandated the use of TBLT continue to assess learning by means of tests that measure learners' linguistic accuracy in ways that encourage the use of explicit rather than implicit L2 knowledge. As a result, teachers feel the need to focus on accuracy and encourage students to develop an explicit understanding of grammatical rules. This leads to resistance to using tasks.
Teachers are unclear about what constitutes a 'task'. It has been suggested that this is in part because the concept of 'task' remains fuzzy in the TBLT literature. Littlewood (2007), for example, argues that the distinction between 'task' and 'exercise' constitutes a continuum rather than a dichotomy.	When faced with communication problems that they cannot solve in English, learners will resort to the use of their L1. This can result in overuse of the L1 in TBLT classrooms.	
Teachers experience problems in managing task-based lessons, especially in large classes when the students work in small groups.	If students focus only on achieving the outcomes of tasks, they may fail to exploit their full L2 resources and thus the task will not result in the kinds of language use known to promote learning.	

Table 13.2 An example of an interaction based on input-based task for beginners (from Shintani, 2011)

In this extract, the teacher instructs the learners to find the picture cards representing different animals and to take them to the zoo (depicted in a frieze on the wall of the classroom).

T:	okay the next. okay, listen listen listen. please take the squirrels, squirrels to the zoo. Squirrels.
S2:	doubutsuen [the zoo]?
T:	zoo, that's right.
S5:	green? blue?
S1:	white?
T:	no, no, no, not white. not green. not blue. brown (pointing to a brown item in the Classroom
S2:	brown
S3:	(showing 'two' with his fingers) two?
T:	two, yes. three (.) two (.) one (.) go
Ss:	(all the students showing the correct cards)
T:	yes everyone is correct.

part of the learners, they do not prohibit it and that some learners will automatically imitate what the teacher says.[2] I emphasize that it can be helpful to repeat input-based tasks especially with younger learners. The task-as-process invariably changes when a task is repeated. Sometime later, simple reading tasks that require the learners to draw or make things can be introduced and, usefully, performed in pairs. I suggest that although the teacher should mainly speak English, occasional use of the L1 will be helpful, and learners should not be prevented from using their L1. I sometimes perform a simple task in a language the teachers do not know to demonstrate that it is possible for them to understand and to pick up words. I show them an example of the kind of interaction that can take place when a teacher performs an input-based task with near beginners (see Table 13.2).

I recommend that teacher should only introduce speaking tasks when it is clear that the students are able to comprehend simple input and when at least some students have started to try to speak. A good way is to first perform a listening task with the whole class and then ask the students to do the same or similar task in pairs. In this way teachers can make the move from input-based to output-based tasks.

How should I set about designing a task?

Obviously, the starting point is a clear grasp of what a task is. This requires an understanding of the definition of a task. I show them my own definition consisting of the four criteria However, as Erlam (2016) found, teachers are not always able to apply these criteria to the design of a task. To address this teachers can use the criteria to decide whether specific workplans constitute 'tasks' or 'exercises' (for an example see Ellis, 2010). What emerges from this is that many activities have elements of 'taskness' without fully satisfying the four criteria. Thus, teachers become aware that 'task' is a somewhat fuzzy construct and leads to a consideration of what is the fundamental feature of a task – namely, that learners are engaged in text-creation (receptively or productively) rather than text-manipulation.

I then suggest a step-by-step procedure that teachers can follow when they design a task.

(1) Choose the topic area (e.g. food; animals; family; a problem).
(2) Decide the kind of task (e.g. input-providing or output prompting; open versus closed; teacher-generated or learner-generated content).
(3) Decide what kind of gap to build into the task (i.e. information-gap; opinion-gap; reasoning-gap). The type of task chosen may require a particular kind of gap (e.g. input-providing tasks will require an information-gap).
(4) Decide what the outcome of the task is to be. The outcome will be non-verbal in the case of an input-based task (e.g. drawing a picture; completing a map; making a model) but can be non-verbal or verbal in an output-based task.
(5) Prepare the materials for the task. The materials may be non-verbal (e.g. the outline of a map; a set of pictures) and/or verbal (e.g. oral or written information) or a mixture of both.
(6) Check the outcome of the task by stating clearly what the intended product of the task will be, making sure that the product is not just the display of correct language.
(7) Write the rubrics for the task.

When making decisions at each step, teachers need to bear in mind the particular learners the task is intended for. I emphasize that designing a task is ultimately both a rational and creative process – an art rather than a manufacturing process. As Johnson (2000) showed, it involves expertise that is mainly built up from experience.

How can I use tasks in a mixed ability class?

Individualizing instruction by setting up work-stations where groups of students work on different tasks is one way of catering to mixed ability students. It would also be possible for the work stations to cater to different language skills by means of tasks that focus on listening, speaking, reading or writing. However, organizing work stations is demanding on teachers' skills and time especially as the necessary task-based materials are unlikely to be available and it will be logistically very difficult to organize in large classes I do not see it as a practical solution for classrooms in state schools in Asia, for example.

The difficulty of catering to students with mixed ability is, of course, a problem in any approach. Arguably, however, it is less of a problem with task-based teaching than with traditional, structural approaches. Tasks by their nature do not dictate the language that students need to use but rather allow them to use whatever resources they have available. Thus the same task can be performed in very different ways by different learners in accordance with their L2 proficiency.

The main way of addressing this problem is through scaffolding learners' performance of a task. The extent of the scaffolding will depend on the ability of individual students. In the case of input-based tasks, for example, students can be encouraged to request clarification if they do not understand, enabling the teacher to modify the input to assist comprehension. In Chapter 3 I looked at research that has shown the value of such interactionally modified input. Use of the L1 by both students and teacher, as illustrated in the teacher–student interaction in Table 13.2, can also assist weaker students.

When students are working in pairs on information-gap tasks, thought needs to be given to how to set up the pairs of students. Research helps here. Yule and McDonald (1990) found that tasks were performed more successfully if a more proficient student was paired with a less proficient one and if the information to be exchanged was given to the less rather than the more proficient student. This was because the more proficient students were more likely to push the less proficient to resolve any referential conflicts that arose. If the information was given to the less proficient student such conflicts were either ignored or not resolved due to a lack of proficiency. With opinion-gap tasks performed in small groups, the job of 'reporter' of the groups' views should also be given to a lower-proficiency student.

Finally, teachers should consider repeating a task including, if necessary, some linguistic assistance between performances. A task that is too difficult the first time becomes easier the second for less able students. For more able students repeating a task can help to develop their fluency.

What can we do to ensure balanced language development in students?

What seems to underlie this question is teachers' fear that students will fail to develop the linguistic knowledge needed for traditional, discrete-point tests. In other words, there is a concern that accuracy will be sacrificed in favour of communicative fluency as some critics of TBLT have suggested will happen.

To achieve balanced development, it is necessary to ensure that tasks promote complexity, accuracy and fluency. We are still a long way from designing task-based courses to guarantee this but we do have some useful ideas about what kinds of tasks will lead to learners prioritising specific aspects of language. Tasks involving information familiar to students, for example, foster fluency and accuracy; tasks with a loose information structure foster complexity; tasks with a clear and tight information structure promote accuracy. Course-designers and teachers need to vary the tasks they use by taking into consideration the design features that have been shown to impact on the kind of language produced.

Again, though, this might not be of much practical help to teachers who are unlikely to be sufficiently familiar with the research to select tasks in a principled way that will promote balanced development. A more practical way is through task implementation. In particular, teachers can vary planning options. Providing time for strategic (pre-task) planning assists complexity and fluency. Performing a task without any time pressure leads to greater accuracy as learners have the opportunity to monitor their output. Allowing learners to keep possession of the task materials as they perform a task (i.e. the here-and-now condition) assists fluency; taking away the task materials (i.e. the there-and-then condition) forces learners to rely on their own linguistic resources and leads to prioritizing accuracy and complexity.

Finally, the post-task stage offers teachers opportunities to focus explicitly on linguistic accuracy if the learners' performance of a task has shown this is needed.

How can we ensure that learners focus on grammar when they perform a focused task?

This question, like the former, is motivated by teachers' concern for accuracy – in particular, grammatical accuracy. It also reflects a worry – supported by research studies – that focused tasks may not result in students attempting to use the target structure. The answer to this question again lies in the methodology of task-based teaching – in particular, the use of various pre-emptive and reactive focus-on-form techniques (see Chapter 4) to draw learners' attention to the target form, provide them with the correct form, and push them to use it correctly. Corrective recasts (Doughty & Varela, 1998) are ideal as they combine prompting learners to self-correct by repeating a student's erroneous utterance with recasting the utterance for them if they fail to correct.

Students working in small groups make use of focus-on-form techniques in the language-related episodes that focused tasks can give rise to but the responsibility for ensuring that learners do focus on form rests ultimately with the teacher. The teacher can visit groups as they perform a task and, when opportunities arise, provide focus-on-form. But a more effective way might be to always include a 'public performance' stage in a lesson. That is, after students have completed their group work, they present the outcome of the task to the whole class. This gives the teacher opportunity to focus attention on the target structure when students avoid the use of the target structure or use it incorrectly. As we saw in Samuda (2001), it may sometimes be necessary to stop the public performance to provide explicit instruction.

How do we teach grammar in task-based language teaching?

This question addresses the over-riding concern that teachers have about the place of grammar in task-based teaching. It reflects the view that TBLT neglects grammar. It is motivated by teachers' fear that it will not prepare their students for the kinds of high-stake examinations that exist in many instructional contexts. It represents, however, a misconception about TBLT, as I pointed out in Chapter 8.

There is plenty of grammar in TBLT:

- in guided strategic (pre-task) planning when learners are shown how to use of specific structures;
- by means of focused tasks;
- through focus-on-form techniques as a task is performed;
- through explicit instruction in the post-task stage of a lesson if performance of the task shows this is needed.

Advocates of TBLT differ in whether or not they see a case for hybrid curriculum (i.e. a curriculum containing both a task-based and a structural component). Whereas Long (2015) argued for 'pure' TBLT, I have made the case for a modular curriculum, where the task-based component is primary but a structure-based component can be drawn on remedially (see Chapter 10). Grammar does not constitute the foundation of a task-based course, but it is everywhere in TBLT.

How can I ensure that every group member is engaged in a task?

Off-task behaviour is not just a problem with tasks and arguably it is less of a problem as tasks are likely to be more intrinsically motivating than exercises for most students. If students are interested in an activity they will be engaged. But there are ways to promote engagement. One way is to make it clear to students that there will be a public performance of the outcome of the task and that all members of a group must participate in this. Knowing this will encourage students to remain on-task. Another way is to include a written outcome for a task. For example, in a Spot the Difference task the teacher can require the students to prepare and submit a written list of the differences in the pictures. If students know the teacher will check their written outcome – and perhaps award marks – they are more likely to put effort into the task.

How can I do task-based teaching in a class of fifty?

Again, the management of large classes is a major problem irrespective of the teaching approach (Coleman, 1989). The solution often suggested is small group work but this can be difficult to organize, especially in classrooms where desks are arranged in traditional rows and the groups cannot be easily monitored by the teacher. However, as I have already pointed out, it is possible to conduct tasks in lockstep with the whole class. In the case of input-based tasks this is required. But it is also possible with output-based information-gap tasks if the information is split between the students and the teacher. For example, in a Spot the Difference task, the teacher could hold one picture and the students the other. In Prabhu's Communicational Language Teaching Project, the teacher first performed a task with the whole class before asking the students to perform a similar task individually. This approach was adopted partly because of its suitability for large classes.[3]

Teachers might also benefit from using closed (as opposed to open) tasks as it is much easier to see if a task has been successfully accomplished and students can get feedback on how well they performed it. This has merit in any class, but can be particularly beneficial in large classes.

Can you recommend a task-based course book?

I am often asked this question and always find it difficult to answer. This is because there are still very few published task-based textbooks. Skehan (2011) pointed out that publishers are not typically concerned with ensuring that there is a solid research-base for the course books they publish. Rather they are more concerned to ensure their books are well-received by teachers and therefore sell well. Teachers understandably prefer course books based on an approach they are familiar with and are likely to reject materials that are radically different. Hence, major publishers stick to the tried and tested structurally or notionally organized courses.

Some course books do claim to be 'task-based' but an inspection of them indicates that they are, at best, task supported. *Cutting Edge* (Cunningham & Moor, 2008), for example, is presented as a task-based course in the online promotional material but clearly it is not. Rather, as stated, it aims to provide models which prepare learners to do tasks. Two course books, both designed for university-level students in Japan, that can claim to be task-based are *Widgets* (Benevides & Valvona, 2008) and *Welcome to Kyushu* (Cutrone & Beh, 2014).

In most instructional context, teachers will be thrown back on their own resources. They will need to devise their own tasks and/or adapt existing text book materials. Most contemporary course books (such as *Cutting Edge*) do include tasks. Thus teachers could use these without first doing the preparatory exercise-type activities. In accordance with Johnson's (1982) deep-end strategy they could then make use of the exercises in the post-task stage of the lesson but only if the students demonstrated a need for linguistically-focused practice. Adapting existing materials will involve 'taskifying' activities. This can be achieved by introducing a gap where none exists in the course book activity and ensuring that there is a clear communicative outcome for the activity. Willis (2006) provides some helpful guidelines for adapting materials.

Final comment

Several points emerge from this list of questions. One is that several of the questions raise problems that are not specific to TBLT but rather address issues (such as teaching in large classes) that are very general in nature. Another is that teachers are concerned with both the design of tasks/task-based courses and with the methodology of using tasks. A third is that concern over the place of grammar in TBLT is very prominent. A fourth is that some of the issues the teachers raised have not been addressed by research, pointing again to the gap between the concerns of researchers and teachers. This suggests the need for a research agenda that focuses on practical issues facing teachers – such as how to use tasks with mixed ability students and the best way to go about adapting existing textbook materials.

The questions point to the importance of teacher education. Studies are needed that investigate to what extent training programmes are successful in developing both a clear understanding of TBLT principles and the practical knowledge and skills required in TBLT.

Teacher Education Studies

Perhaps the most conspicuous lacuna in the research to date is the lack of studies that have investigated teacher training/education programmes. Long (2016) included 'in-service teacher education' in his discussion of the 'real issues' facing TBLT, noting that the skills required of a teacher in TBLT are greater than those in focus-on-forms or presentation–practice–production (PPP). Lai (2015), in a discussion of TBLT in the Asian context, noted that effective teacher training was critical and drew on research to suggest the key characteristics of successful training programmes (e.g. giving teachers a sense of ownership, engaging teachers in task design, giving the teachers opportunities for initiative, help in translating the training into actual practice through follow-up visits, access to supportive partners, and access to suitable teaching materials).

There have, however, been very few studies of actual teacher-education programmes for TBLT. Van den Branden (2006c) reviewed a number of in-service training programmes that accompanied the introduction of TBLT into state schools in Flemish-speaking Belgium. He described a programme where the training took place alongside the introduction of task-based syllabuses that 'were ready to be tried out in classrooms' (2006c: 226). He also pointed to the effectiveness of a training approach that involved 'practice-oriented coaching'. A key element of this approach was that the training was linked to tasks that teachers could actually perform in their classrooms. This encouraged teachers to reflect on their practice and also enabled the trainers to address the practical issues that concerned them (e.g. how much time to allocate to different phases of a lesson). Classroom observation and feedback was a key training method used in the programme to help the teachers 'discover their own truth' (2006c: 240). The trainers only gave explicit suggestions if a teacher requested it. In the conclusion to his chapter, Van den Branden emphasizes the importance of the various personnel involved in the introduction of TBLT (e.g. school counsellors, syllabus designers, school inspectors and the trainers) operating in accordance with an agreed set of general principles.

Other studies of training programmes have been much smaller-scale than the Flanders project. As part of an undergraduate programme in a Japanese university, Jackson (2012) conducted a training module designed to introduce English majors to planning a task-based lesson, conducting a teaching demonstration, observing lessons, and carrying out a debriefing session following observation. The training module was itself task-based. It was evaluated by eliciting retrospective comments on each training task, analysing the discourse of the debriefing sessions, and a questionnaire, the last of which was also completed by a group of students that did not receive the training. The trainee students reported knowledge gains relating to classroom techniques and practices, learning from others, and making, using and adapting lesson plans. The debriefing activity helped them to elaborate, synthesise and critique the practical knowledge gained from the tasks. However, responses to the questionnaire revealed no statistically significant differences in their trainee group's and a comparative group's beliefs about language teaching, suggesting that the training may not have achieved the fundamental goal of changing teachers' beliefs.

Hall (2015) reported on an ambitious project aimed at introducing TBLT into Malaysia primary and secondary schools. The training methodology used in this project involved motivating change through the teachers experiencing tasks in their training sessions in a loop approach. Hall used interviews with both the teacher educators and teachers to evaluate the effectiveness of the training. The teachers appreciated the interactive approach, commenting that they had not previously experienced this and felt that they could apply what they had learned about tasks in their own classrooms. The teacher educators were likewise positive about the activity-based approach. They felt that it provided the teachers with transferable tasks that increased acceptance of the task-based approach. Hall also noted that the teacher educators gained acceptance because they were prepared to use the teachers' local language, which led him to challenge the 'English only' policy of the Malaysian Ministry of Education and to emphasize the need for a plurilingual approach by both teachers and teacher educators.

Erlam (2016) reported on a year-long professional development course for in-service teachers of foreign languages in New Zealand. In her article she focused on one goal of the course – to enable the teachers to design their own tasks by satisfying the four criteria for a task in Ellis (2003). She found that the tasks the teachers developed had a primary focus on meaning (criterion 1) and a gap (criterion 2) and (largely) incorporated a clearly defined communicative outcome (criterion 4). However, that they did not always require learners to rely on their own linguistic and non-linguistic resources (criterion 3) – arguably the fundamental criterion. Erlam then went on to suggest how she might make changes to her course to help teachers develop a clearer understanding of what a task is, for example by emphasizing the need to make teachers aware that they can address learners' linguistic needs through scaffolding the performance of task.

These studies – along with the rich literature on general teacher-education programmes – point to ways of ensuring that TBLT training is effective.

- Training needs to be accompanied with actual tasks that teachers can use in their classrooms.
- Teachers also need to be actively involved in designing and performing tasks as part of their training.
- The training approach adopted in these studies should itself be task-based.
- Training in the form of observations of actual teaching followed by feedback provide a means for encouraging reflection by teachers and of addressing practical issues that concern teachers.

Training programmes are discontinuous – at some point they come to an end. An important question is what happens then. Do teachers continue with TBLT or do they return to well-established traditional ways of teaching? There is an urgent need for more studies of TBLT training programmes including follow-up studies of what happens when the training ends.

Conclusion

Long (2015), in the concluding chapter to his book, was quite sanguine about the feasibility of TBLT as an innovation, suggesting that adoption and continuation of TBLT in situations where students are homogeneous and large enough to justify the expense involved, financial resources and institutional support are available, local expertise exists or can be brought in, teachers have an adequate command of the L2, and the teaching staff are permanent and, ideally, full time. Such conditions do not prevail in the situations I am familiar with in Africa, Asia or, indeed, Europe. They are perhaps more likely to be found in language-for-specific purpose contexts such as the programme developed for US Border Patrol agents by Gonzalez-Lloret and Nielson (2015). Should then attempts to introduce TBLT into unfavourable situations be abandoned or replaced by task-supported language teaching as Littlewood (2014) proposed? This seems too defeatist to my mind. Students in general English courses such as those found in state educational systems in countries like China (which, of course, has the greatest number of language learners anywhere) still have a need for functional ability in a language, and TBLT remains the most likely way of achieving this.

In this chapter I have tried to look critically at the contribution that research has made to TBLT and what is needed to bring about the successful introduction of TBLT in different instructional contexts. I suggest the following is needed:

(1) Research directed at developing an understanding of what constitutes effective task-based teaching. Long (2015) emphasizes the need for research directed at 'improved criteria for classifying and sequencing pedagogic tasks' to assist in developing task syllabi. I have expressed doubts about the value of such a research agenda and instead propose that efforts are directed at investigating how teachers mediate tasks in complete lessons and identifying the characteristics of successful TBLT programmes. This will require refocusing research away from the design issues of discrete tasks to how tasks are implemented *in situ*. Evaluation studies – both of macro kind considered in this chapter and the micro kind discussed in Chapter 12 – may prove more informative than theory-driven research.

(2) An increased focus on practitioners of TBLT. This will involve addressing the issues and problems that teachers have indicated they have with TBLT. I have attempted to do this in this chapter. There is, however, a need to go beyond armchair solutions of the kind I have proffered to investigating possible solutions in actual classrooms. Practitioner research has a role here but, given that the problems are often common to many instructional settings, it would be helpful to institute a formal research agenda. For example, what can be done to help teachers with limited oral L2 proficiency?[4]

(3) Materials development projects. TBLT is unlikely to flourish unless teachers have access to suitable materials and these are not currently available. Hard-pressed teachers are unlikely to have the time (and perhaps the skills) to develop their own materials.

(4) The development of both pre-service and in-service teacher education/training programmes, drawing on research that has identified the characteristics of successful programmes. The effectiveness of these programmes needs to be investigated through research. It is noteworthy that teacher-education for TBLT has received very little attention in the published books on TBLT (including Ellis, 2003). An exception is Van den Branden (2006c).

Finally, I want to return to a core issue – whether TBLT needs to be 'pure' or can be modified to allow for explicit instruction – as in task-supported instruction. The case for pure TBLT is a strong one as it constitutes the approach that aligns most closely with second language acquisition theory and research and also with sound educational principles. But, as this chapter has shown, such an approach can conflict with teachers' and learners' beliefs about language, leading at best to doubts and at worst to rejection of TBLT. Structural constraints (see Table 13.2) and teachers' concerns about how to cope with them (see the questions teachers ask section of this chapter) point to the need for a curriculum that includes a structural component. My own proposal is for a modular syllabus that gives primacy to pure TBLT throughout but allows for the inclusion of explicit instruction once basic competence has been established as a means of helping learners overcome persistent learning problems. Such a proposal, I have argued, can help to address teachers' practical concerns and is also validated by second language acquisition theory and research.

Notes

(1) Suggestions have been made that research on individual learner factors can be applied through learner-instruction matching (Robinson, 2007). However, I do not see how the classroom contexts I am familiar with can achieve this. It is an example of how theory does not mesh with practice.

(2) Voluntary imitation of the teacher is very different from repetition demanded of students. Imitation is a natural phenomenon; repetition is a mechanical process.

(3) Prabhu's main reason for avoiding group work, however, was his belief in the importance of the 'good models' that only the teacher could provide.

(4) One suggestion for helping teachers with limited oral proficiency is to provide them with scripts for performing a task. Such scripts can help with input-based tasks in particular and can foster teachers' confidence in speaking and performing tasks.

References

Abbs, B. and Freebairn, I. (1982) *Opening Strategies*. Harlow: Longman.

Adams, R. (2007) Do second language learners benefit from interacting with each other? In A. Mackey (ed.) *Conversational Interaction in Second Language Learning.* (pp. 29–51). Oxford: Oxford University Press.

Ahangari, S. and Abdi, M. (2011) The effect of pre-task planning on the accuracy and complexity of Iranian EFL learners' oral performance. *Procedia – Social and Behavioral Sciences* 29, 1950–1959.

Ahmadian, M. (2011) The effects of guided careful online planning on complexity, accuracy and fluency in intermediate EFL learners' oral production: The case of English articles. *Language Teaching Research* 16, 129–149.

Ahmadian, M. (2012) The relationship between working memory capacity and L2 oral performance under task-based careful online planning condition. *TESOL Quarterly* 46, 165–175.

Ahmadian, M. and Tavakoli, M. (2010) The effects of simultaneous use of careful online planning and task repetition on accuracy, complexity and fluency of EFL learners' oral production. *Language Teaching Research* 15, 35–59.

Ahmadian, M., Tavokoli, M. and Dastjerdi, H. (2015) The combined effects of online planning and task structure on the complexity, accuracy and fluency of L2 speech. *Language Learning Journal* 43, 41–56.

Alanen, R. (1995) Input enhancement and rule presentation in second language acquisition. In R. Schmidt (ed.) *Attention and Awareness in Foreign Language Learning* (pp. 259–299). Honolulu: University of Hawai'I Press.

Aljaafreh, A. and Lantolf, J. (1994) Negative feedback as regulation and second language learning in the Zone of Proximal Development. *The Modern Language Journal* 78, 465–483.

Allwright, D. (1988) *Observation in the Language Classroom*. London: Longman.

Allwright, D. (2003) Exploratory practice: Rethinking practitioner research in language teaching. *Language Teaching Research* 7, 113–141.

Allwright, D. (2005) Developing principles for practitioner research: The case for exploratory practice. *Modern Language Journal* 89, 353–366.

Ammar, A. and Spada, N. (2006) One size fits all? Recasts, prompts, and L2 learning. *Studies in Second Language Acquisition* 28, 543–574.

Anderson, A. and Lynch, T. (1988) *Listening*. Oxford: Oxford University Press.

Andringa, S., de Glopper, K. and Haquebord, H. (2011) Effect of explicit and implicit instruction on free written response task performance. *Language Learning* 61, 868–903.

Appel, C. and Gilabert, R. (2002) Motivation and task performance in a task-based web-based tandem project. *ReCAL* 14, 16–31.

Appel, G. and Lantolf, J. (1994) Speaking as mediation: A study of L1 and L2 text recall tasks. *Modern Language Journal* 78, 437–452.

Aston, G. (1982) Trouble-shooting in interaction with learners: The more the merrier. *Applied Linguistics* 7, 128–143.

Aubrey, S. (2015) Effect of inter-cultural contact on L2 motivation and L2 learning: A process product study. Unpublished PhD Thesis, Auckland, New Zealand, University of Auckland.

Aubrey, S. (2017) Intercultural contact and flow in a task-based Japanese EFL classroom. *Language Teaching Research* 21 (6), 717–734.

Bachman, L. (1990) *Fundamental Considerations in Language Testing*. Oxford: Oxford University Press.

Bachman, L. (2002) Some reflections on task-based language performance assessment. *Language Testing* 19, 453–476.

Bachman, L. and Palmer, A. (1996) *Language Testing in Practice*. Oxford: Oxford University Press.

Bardovi-Harlig, K. (2001) Evaluating the empirical evidence: Grounds for instruction in pragmatics? In K. Rose and G. Kasper (eds) *Pragmatics in Language Teaching* (pp. 13–32). Cambridge: Cambridge University Press.

Bax, S. (1997) Roles for a teacher educator in context-sensitive teacher education. *English Language Teaching Journal* 51 (3), 232–241.

Basturkmen, H., Loewen, S. and Ellis, R. (2004) Teachers' stated beliefs about incidental focus on form and their classroom practices. *Applied Linguistics* 25, 243–272.

Baleghizadeh, S. and Derakhshesh, A. (2012) The effect of task repetition and noticing on EFL learners' oral output. *International Journal of Instruction* 5, 141–152.

Bax, S. (2003) The end of CLT: A context approach to language teaching. *ELT Journal* 57 (3), 278–287.

Benevides, M. and Valvona, C. (2008) *Widgets: A task-based Course in Practical English*. Hong Kong: Pearson Education.

Beretta, A. and Davies, A. (1985) Evaluation of the Bangalore Project. *ELT Journal* 39, 121–127.

Bialystok, E. and Sharwood-Smith, M. (1985) Interlanguage is not a state of mind: An evaluation of the construct for second language acquisition. *Applied Linguistics* 6, 101–117.

Bloom, M. (2007) Tensions in a non-traditional classroom. *Language Teaching Research* 11, 85–102.

Bohlke, D. (2014) Fluency-oriented second language teaching. In M. Celce-Murcia, D. Brinton and M. Snow (eds) *Teaching English as a Second or Foreign Language* (4th edn; pp. 121–135). Boston, MA.: Heinle Cengage.

Boston, J. (2010) Pre-task syntactic priming and focused task design. *ELT Journal* 64, 165–174.

Breen, M. (1989) The evaluation cycle for language learning tasks. In R.K. Johnson and M. Swain (eds) *The Second Language Curriculum* (pp. 187–2007). Cambridge: Cambridge University Press.

Brooks, F.B. and Donato, R. (1994). Vygotskyan approaches to understanding foreign language learner discourse during communication tasks. *Hispania* 77, 262–274.

Brown, G. (1995) *Speaker, Listeners and Communication*. Cambridge: Cambridge University Press.

Brumfit, C. (1984) *Communicative Methodology in Language Teaching*. Cambridge: Cambridge University Press.

Bruner, J.S. (1960) *The Process of Education*. Cambridge, MA: Harvard University Press.

Bruton, A. (2002) From tasking purposes to purposing tasks. *ELT Journal* 56, 280–288.

Bui, G. and Skehan, P. (2016) CALF: An automatic analytic tool for complexity, accuracy, lexis and fluency. Available at http://www.censpothk.com/calf/

Bui, H. (2014) Task readiness: Theoretical framework and empirical evidence from topic familiarity, strategic planning and proficiency levels. In P. Skehan (ed.) *Processing Perspectives on Task Performance* (pp. 63–93). Amsterdam: John Benjamins.

Bulté, B. and Housen, A. (2012) Defining and operationalising L2 complexity. In A. Housen, F. Kuiken and I. Vedder (eds) *Dimensions of L2 Performance and Proficiency* (pp. 21–46). Amsterdam: John Benjamins.

Butler, Y. (2005) Comparative perspectives towards communicative activities among elementary school teachers in South Korea, Japan and Taiwan. *Language Teaching Research* 9, 423–446.

Butler, Y. (2011) The Implementation of communicative and task-based language teaching in the Asia-Pacific region. *Annual Review of Applied Linguistics* 31, 36–57.

Bygate, M. (1996) Effects of task repetition: Appraising the developing language of learners. In D. Willis and J. Willis (eds) *Challenge and Change in Language Teaching* (pp. 136–146). Oxford: Heinemann.

Bygate, M. (2001) Effects of task repetition on the structure and control of oral language. In M. Bygate, P. Skehan and M. Swain (eds) *Researching Pedagogic Tasks, Second Language Learning, Teaching and Testing* (pp. 23–48). Harlow: Longman.

Bygate, M., Skehan, P. and Swain, M. (eds) (2001a) *Researching Pedagogic Tasks, Second Language Learning, Teaching and Testing.* Harlow: Longman.

Bygate, M., Skehan, P. and Swain, M. (eds) (2001b) Introduction. In M. Bygate *et al.* (eds) *Researching Pedagogic Tasks, Second Language Learning, Teaching and Testing.* Harlow: Longman.

Cameron, L. (2001) *Teaching Languages to Young Children.* Cambridge: Cambridge University Press.

Cancino, H., Rosansky, E. and Schumann, J. (1978) The acquisition of English negatives and interrogatives by native Spanish speakers. In E. Hatch (ed.) *Second Language Acquisition* (pp. 207–230). Rowley, MA: Newbury House.

Candlin, C. (1987) Towards task-based language learning. In C. Candlin and D. Murphy (eds) *Language Learning Tasks* (pp. 23–46). Englewood Cliffs N.J.: Prentice Hall International.

Candlin, C. and Murphy, D. (1987) *Language Learning Tasks.* Englewood Cliffs N.J.: Prentice Hall International.

Carless, D. (2004) Issues in teachers' reinterpretation of a task-based innovation in primary schools. *TESOL Quarterly* 38, 639–662.

Carr, W. and Kemmis, S. (1986) *Becoming Critical: Education, Knowledge and Action Research.* London: The Falmer Press.

Chan, S.H. (1995) A micro-evaluation-based task evaluation. Unpublished MA paper, Temple University, Philadelphia.

Chaudron, C. (1977) A descriptive model of discourse in the corrective treatment of learners' errors. *Language Learning* 27, 29–46.

Chaudron, C. (1982) Vocabulary elaboration in teachers' speech to L2 learners. *Studies in Second Language Acquisition* 4, 170–180.

Christenson, S., Reschly, A. and Wylie, C. (2013) *Handbook of Research on Student Engagement.* New York: NY: Springer.

Cintron-Valentin, M. and Ellis, N. (2015) Exploring the interface: Explicit focus-on-form and learned attentional biases in L2 Latin. *Studies in Second Language Acquisition* 37, 197–235.

Cleermans, A. and Jimenez, L. (2002) Implicit learning and consciousness: A graded, dynamic perspective. In R. French and A. Cleermans (eds) *Implicit Learning and Consciousness: An Empirical and Philosophical Consensus in the Making* (pp. 1–40). Hove: Psychology Press.

Coleman, H. (1989) *Learning and Teaching in Large Classes: A Bibliography. Project Report No. 1.* Distributed by ERIC http://www.eric.ed.gov/contentdelivery/servlet/ERICServlet?accno=ED335911

Corder, S.P. (1967) The significance of learners' errors. *International Review of Applied Linguistics* 5, 161–169.

Corder, S.P. (1980) Second language acquisition research and the teaching of grammar. *BAAL Newsletter* 10.

Corder, S.P. (1981) *Error Analysis and Interlanguage*. Oxford: Oxford University Press.

Coughlan, P. and Duff, P. (1994) Same task, different activities: Analysis of a SLA task from an activity theory perspective. In J. Lantolf and G. Appel (ed.) *Vygotskian Approaches to Second Language Research* (pp. 173–194). Norwood, NJ: Ablex.

Council of Europe (2011) *Common European Framework of Reference for Learning, Teaching, Assessment*. Strasburg: Council of Europe.

Cox, D. (2005) Can we predict language items for open tasks? In C. Edwards and J. Willis (eds) *Teachers Exploring tasks in English Language Teaching* (pp. 171–186). Basingstoke: Palgrave Macmillan.

Crookes, G. (1989) Planning and interlanguage variation. *Studies in Second Language Acquisition* 11, 367–383.

Crookes, G. and Gass, S. (eds) (1993) *Tasks and Language Learning: Integrating Theory and Practice*. Clevedon: Multilingual Matters.

Csikszentmihályi, M., Abuhamdeh, S. and Nakamura, J. (2005) Flow. In A. Elliot (ed.) *Handbook of Competence and Cotivation* (pp. 598–698). New York: The Guilford Press.

Cunningham, S. and Moor, P. (2008) *Cutting Edge*. Harlow: Longman

Cutrone, P. and Beh, S. (2014) *Welcome to Kysuhsu: A Task-based Approach to EFL Learning using Auathentic Dialogues*. Tokyo: Shohakusha.

Dale, E. and Chall, J. (1948) A formula for predicting readability: instructions. *Educational Research Bulletin* 27, 37–54.

Day, E. and Shapson, S. (1991) Integrating formal and functional approaches to language teaching in French immersion: An experimental study. *Language Learning* 41, 25–58.

De Jong, N. and Perfetti, C.A. (2011) Fluency training in the ESL classroom: An experimental study of fluency development and proceduralization. *Language Learning* 61 (2), 533–568.

De la Fuente, M. (2006) Classroom L2 vocabulary acquisition: Investigating the role of pedagogical tasks and form-focused instruction. *Language Teaching Research* 10, 263–295.

De Ridder, I., Vangehuchten, L. and Sesena Gomaz, M. (2007) Enhancing automaticity through task-based language learning. *Applied Linguistics* 28, 309–315.

DeKeyser, R. (1998) Beyond focus on form: Cognitive perspectives on learning and practicing second language grammar. In C. Doughty and J. Williams (eds) *Focus-on-Form in Classroom Second Language Acquisition* (pp. 42–63). Cambridge: Cambridge University Press.

DeKeyser, R. (2000) The robustness of critical period effects in second language acquisition. *Studies in Second Language Acquisition* 22, 499–533.

DeKeyser, R. (2015) Skill acquisition theory. In B. VanPatten and J. Williams (eds) *Theories of Second Language Acquisition* (2nd edn; pp. 91–112). New York: Routledge.

Dewey, J. (1913) *Interest and Effort in Education*. Arcturus Books.

Dewey, J. (1938) *Experience and Education*. New York: Collier Books.

Donato, R. (1994) Collective scaffolding in second language learning. In J. Lantolf and G. Appel (eds) *Vygotskian Approaches to Second Language Research* (pp. 33–56). Norwood, NJ: Ablex.

Dörnyei, Z. (2001) *Motivational Strategies in the Classroom*. Cambridge: CUP.

Doughty, C. (2001) Cognitive underpinnings of focus on form. In P. Robinson (ed.) *Cognition and Second Language Instruction* (pp. 206–257). Cambridge: Cambridge University Press.

Doughty, C. and Varela, E. (1998) Communicative focus-on-form. In C. Doughty and J. Williams (eds) *Focus-on-form in Classroom Second Language Acquisition* (pp. 114–138). Cambridge: Cambridge University Press.

Doughty, C. and Williams, J. (eds) (1998a) *Focus-on-form in Classroom Second Language Acquisition.* Cambridge: Cambridge University Press.

Doughty, C. and Williams, J. (1998b) Issues and terminology. In C. Doughty and J. Williams (eds) *Focus-on-form in Classroom Second Language Acquisition* (pp. 1–11). Cambridge: Cambridge University Press.

Doughty, C. and Williams, J. (1998c) Pedagogical choices in focus on form. In C. Doughty and J. Williams (eds) *Focus-on-form in Classroom Second Language Acquisition* (pp. 197–261). Cambridge: Cambridge University Press.

Douglas, D. (2000) *Assessing Languages for Specific Purposes.* Cambridge: Cambridge University Press.

Dulay, H. and Burt, M. (1973) Should we teach children syntax?' *Language Learning* 23, 245–258.

Dupuy, B. and Krashen, S. (1993) Incidental vocabulary acquisition in French as a foreign language. *Applied Language Learning* 4, 55–63.

Duran, G. and Ramaut, G. (2006) Tasks for absolute beginners and beyond: Developing and sequencing tasks at basic proficiency levels. In Van den Branden (ed.) *Task-based Language Education: From Theory to Practice* (pp. 47–75). Cambridge: Cambridge University Press.

Eckerth, J. (2008a) Task-based language learning and teaching – old wine in new bottles? In J. Eckerth and S. Sickmann (eds) *Task-based Language Learning and Teaching: Theoretical, Methodological, and Pedagogical Perspectives* (pp. 13–46). Frankfurt am Main: Peter Lang.

Eckerth, J. (2008b) Task-based learner interaction: Investigating learning opportunities, learning processes, and learning outcomes. In J. Eckerth and S. Siekman (eds) *Task-based Language Learning and Teaching: Theoretical, Methodological, and Pedagogical Perspectives.* Frankfurt am Main: Peter Lang.

Edwards, C. and Willis, J. (eds) (2005) *Teachers Exploring tasks in English Language Teaching.* Basingstoke, Palgrave Macmillan.

Egbert, J. (2003) A study of flow theory in the foreign language classroom. *Modern Language Journal* 87, 499–518.

Egi, T. (2007) Interpreting recasts as linguistic evidence: the roles of linguistic target, length, and degree of change. *Studies in Second Language Acquisition* 29, 511–537.

Ehrlich, S., Avery, P. and C. Yorio, C. (1989) Discourse structure and the negotiation of comprehensible input. *Studies in Second Language Acquisition* 11, 397–414.

Ellis, N. (1994) Introduction: Implicit and explicit language learning – an overview. In N. Ellis (ed.) *Implicit and Explicit Learning of Languages.* San Diego: Academic Press.

Ellis, N. (1996) Sequencing in SLA: phonological memory, chunking, and points of order. *Studies in Second Language Acquisition* 18, 91–126.

Ellis, N.C. (2005) At the interface: Dynamic interactions of explicit and implicit language knowledge. *Studies in Second Language Acquisition* 27, 305–352.

Ellis, N. (2006) Selective attention and transfer phenomena in SLA: Contingency, cue competition, salience, interference, overshadowing, blocking and perceptual learning. *Applied Linguistics* 27, 164–194.

Ellis, R. (1984) Formulaic speech in early classroom second language development. In J. Handscombe, R. Orem and B. Taylor (eds) *On TESOL'83: The Question of Context* (pp. 53–66). Washington D.C.: TESOL.

Ellis, R. (1987) Interlanguage variability in narrative discourse: Style shifting in the use of the past tense. *Studies in Second Language Acquisition* 9 (1), 1–20.

Ellis, R. (1989) Are classroom and naturalistic acquisition the same? A study of the classroom acquisition of German word order rules. *Studies in Second Language Acquisition* 11, 305–328.

Ellis, R. (1991) Grammar teaching – practice or consciousness-raising. In R. Ellis (ed.) *Second Language Acquisition and Second Language Pedagogy* (pp. 232–241). Clevedon: Multilingual Matters.

Ellis, R. (1993) Second language acquisition and the structural syllabus. *TESOL Quarterly* 27, 91–113.

Ellis, R. (1994) A theory of instructed second language acquisition. In N. Ellis (ed.) *Implicit and Explicit Learning of Languages* (pp. 79–104). San Diego: Academic Press.

Ellis, R. (1994) *The Study of Second Language Acquisition*. Oxford: Oxford University Press.

Ellis, R. (1995) Modified input and the acquisition of word meanings. *Applied Linguistics* 16, 409–441.

Ellis, R. (1997a) *SLA Research and Language Teaching*. Oxford: Oxford University Press.

Ellis, R. (1997b) The empirical evaluation of language teaching materials. *ELT Journal,* 51, 36–42.

Ellis, R. (1998) The evaluation of communicative tasks. In B. Tomlinson (ed.) *Materials Development in Language Teaching* (pp. 217–238). Cambridge: Cambridge University Press.

Ellis, R. (1999) Input-based approaches to teaching grammar: A review of classroom-oriented research. *Annual Review of Applied Linguistics* 19, 64–80.

Ellis, R. (2000) Task-based research and language pedagogy. *Language Teaching Research* 4 (3), 193–220.

Ellis, R. (2002) The place of grammar instruction in the second/foreign language curriculum. In E. Hinkel and S. Fotos (eds) *New Perspectives on Grammar Teaching in Second Language Classrooms* (pp. 14–34). Routledge: London.

Ellis, R. (2003) *Task-based Language Learning and Teaching*. Oxford: Oxford University Press.

Ellis, R. (ed.) (2005a) *Planning and Task Performance in a Second Language*. Amsterdam: John Benjamins.

Ellis, R. (2005b) Planning and task-based performance: Theory and research. In R. Ellis (ed.) *Planning and Task Performance in a Second Language*. (pp. 3–34). Amsterdam: John Benjamins.

Ellis, R. (2005c) Measuring implicit and explicit knowledge of a second language: A psychometric study. *Studies in Second Language Acquisition* 27 (2), 141–172.

Ellis, R. (2006) Current issues in the teaching of grammar. *TESOL Quarterly,* 40, 83–107.

Ellis, R. (2008) *The Study of Second Language Acquisition* (2nd edn). Oxford: Oxford University Press.

Ellis R. (2009) The differential effects of three types of task planning on the fluency, complexity and accuracy in L2 oral production. *Applied Linguistics* 30, 474–509.

Ellis, R. (2009) Task-based language teaching: Sorting out the misunderstandings. *International Journal of Applied Linguistics* 19, 221–246.

Ellis, R. (2010) Second language acquisition research and language teaching. In N. Harwood (ed.) *English Language Teaching Materials: Theory and Practice* (pp. 33–57). Cambridge: Cambridge University Press.

Ellis, R. (2011) Macro- and micro-evaluations of task-based teaching. In B. Tomlinson (ed.) *Materials Development in Language Teaching* (2nd edn; pp. 212–235). Cambridge: Cambridge University Press.

Ellis, R. (2012) *Second Language Classroom Research and Language Pedagogy*. Malden, USA: Wiley-Blackwell.

Ellis, R. (2015) *Understanding Second Language Acquisition* (2nd edn). Oxford: Oxford University Press.

Ellis, R. (2016) Focus on form: A critical review. *Language Teaching Research* 20, 405–428.

Ellis, R. and Barkhuizen, G. (2003) *Analyzing Learner Language*. Oxford: Oxford University Press.

Ellis, R., Basturkmen, H. and Loewen, S. (2001) Learner uptake in communicative ESL lessons. *Language Learning* 51, 281–318.

Ellis, R., Basturkmen, H. and Loewen, S. (2002) Doing focus on form. *System* 30, 419–432.

Ellis, R. and He, X. (1999) The roles of modified input and output in the incidental acquisition of word meanings. *Studies in Second Language Acquisition* 21, 285–310.

Ellis, R. and Heimbach, R. (1997) Bugs and birds: Children's acquisition of second language vocabulary through interaction. *System* 25, 247–259.

Ellis, R., Loewen, S. and Erlam, R. (2006) Implicit and explicit corrective feedback and the acquisition of L2 grammar. *Studies in Second Language Acquisition* 28, 339–368.

Ellis, R. and Sheen, Y. (2006) Re-examining the role of recasts in SLA. *Studies in Second Language Acquisition* 28, 575–600.

Ellis, R. and Shintani, N. (2014) *Exploring Language Pedagogy Through Second Language Acquisition Research*. London: Routledge.

Ellis, R., Skehan, P., Li, S., Shintani, N. and Lambert, C. (forthcoming) *Theory and Practice of Task-based Language Teaching: Multiple Perspectives*. Cambridge: Cambridge University Press.

Ellis, R. Tanaka, Y. and Yamazaki, A. (1994) Classroom interaction, comprehension and the acquisition of word meanings. *Language* 44, 449–491.

Ellis, R. and Yuan, F. (2004) The effects of planning on fluency, complexity, and accuracy in second language narrative writing. *Studies in Second Language Acquisition* 26 (1), 59–84.

Erlam, R. (2016) I'm still not sure what a task is: Teachers designing language tasks. *Language Teaching Research* 20, 279–299.

Estaire, S. and Zanon, J. (1994) *Planning Classwork: A Task based Approach*. Oxford: Heinemann.

Faerch, C. and Kasper, G. (1986) The role of comprehension in second language acquisition. *Applied Linguistics* 7, 257–274.

Foster, P. (1998) A Classroom perspective on the negotiation of meaning. *Applied Linguistics* 19, 1–23

Foster, P. and Skehan, P. (1996) The influence of planning on performance in task-based learning. *Studies in Second Language Acquisition* 18, 299–324.

Foster, P., Tonkyn, A. and Wigglesworth, G. (2000) Measuring spoken language: A unit for all reasons. *Applied Linguistics* 21, 354–375.

Foster, P. and Wigglesworth, G. (2016) Capturing accuracy in second language performance: The case for a weighted clause ratio. *Annual Review of Applied Linguistics* 36, 98–116.

Fotos, S. (1998) Shifting the focus from forms to form in the EFL classroom. *ELT Journal* 52 (4), 301–307.

Fotos, S. and Ellis, R. (1991) Communicating about grammar: a task-based approach. *TESOL Quarterly* 25, 605–628.

Fukuta, J. (2016) Effects of task repetition on learners' attention orientation in L2 oral production. *Language Teaching Research* 20, 321–340.

Galperin, P. (1989) Organization of mental activity and the effectiveness of learning. *Soviet Psychology* 27 (3), 65–82.

Gass, S. and Mackey, A. (2007) Input, interactions, and output in second language acquisition. In B. VanPatten and J. Williams (eds) *Theories in Second Language Acquisition: An Introduction* (pp. 175–200). Mahwah, NJ: Lawrence Erlbaum.

Gass, S., Mackey, A., Alvarez-Torres, M.J. and Fernandez-Garcia, M. (1999) The effects of task repetition on linguistic output. *Language Learning* 49 (4), 549–581.

Gass, S. and Madden, C. (eds) (1985) *Input in Second Language Acquisition*. Rowley, MA: Newbury House.

Gilabert, R., Baron, J. and Llanes, A. (2009) Manipulating cognitive complexity across task types and its impact on learners' interaction during oral performance. *IRAL* 47, 367–395.

Gonzalez, M. and Nielson, K. (2015) Evaluating TBLT: The case of a task-based Spanish program. *Language Teaching Research* 19 (5), 525–549.

González-Lloret, M. and Ortega, L. (eds) (2014) *Technology-mediated TBLT*. Amsterdam: John Benjamins.

Goo, J. and Mackey, A. (2013) The case against the case against recasts. *Studies in Second Language Acquisition* 35, 127–165.

Grice, P. (1975) Logic and conversation. In P. Cole and J. Morgan (eds) *Syntax and Semantics. 3: Speech Acts* (pp. 41–58). New York: Academic Press.

Guará-Tavares, M. (2008) Pre-task planning, working memory capacity and L2 speech performance. Unpublished doctoral thesis. Universidade Federal de Santa Catarina, Brazil.

Hall, S. (2015) Gaining acceptance of task-based teaching during Malaysian rural in-service teacher training. In M. Thomas and H. Reinders (eds) *Contemporary Task-based Language Teaching in Asia* (pp. 156–169). London: Bloomsbury Academic.

Halliday, M. (1973) *Explorations in the Functions of Language*. London: Edward Arnold.

Han, Z.H. (2014) From Julie to Wes to Alberto: Revisiting the construct of fossilization. In Z.-H. Han and E. Tarone (eds) *Interlanguage: Forty Years Later* (pp. 347–374). Amsterdam: John Benjamins.

Harley, B. (1989) Functional grammar in French immersion: A classroom experiment. *Applied Linguistics* 19, 331–359.

Harrison, C. (1980) *Readability in the Classroom*. Cambridge: Cambridge University Press.

Hatch, E. (1978) Apply with caution. *Studies in Second Language Acquisition* 2, 123–143.

Hawkes, M. (2012) Using task repetition to direct learner attention and focus on form. *ELT Journal* 66 (3), 327–336.

Hedge, T. (2000) *Teaching and Learning in the Language Classroom*. Oxford: Oxford University Press.

Henzl, V. (1979) Foreigner talk in the classroom. *International Review of Applied Linguistics* 17, 159–165.

Housen, A. and Kuiken, F. (2009) Complexity, accuracy, and fluency in second language acquisition. *Applied Linguistics* 30 (4), 461–473.

Housen, A., Kuiken, F. and Vedder, I. (eds) (2012a) *Dimensions of L2 Performance and Proficiency*. Amsterdam: John Benjamins.

Housen, A., Kuiken, F. and Vedder, I. (2012b) Complexity, accuracy and fluency: Definitions, measurement and research. In A. Housen, F. Kuiken and I. Vedder (eds) *Dimensions of L2 Performance and Proficiency* (pp. 1–20). Amsterdam: John Benjamins.

Howatt, A. (1984) *A History of English Language Teaching*. Oxford: Oxford University Press.

Hsu, H. (2012) Investigating the effects of planning on L2 chat performance. *Calico Journal* 26, 619–638.

Hsu, H. (2017) The effect of task planning on L2 performance in text-based synchronous computer-mediated communication. *Applied Linguistics* 38 (3), 359–385.

Hymes, D. (1971) *On Communicative Competence*. Philadelphia, PA: University of Pennsylvania Press.

Jackson, D. (2012) Task-based language teacher education in an undergraduate program in Japan. In A. Shehadeh and C. Coombe (eds) *Task-based Language Teaching in Foreign Language Contexts* (pp. 267–285). Amsterdam: John Benjamins.

Jackson, D. and Suethanapornkul, S. (2012) The cognition hypothesis: A synthesis and meta-analysis of research on second language task complexity. *Language Learning* 63, 330–367.

Jiang, W. (2013) Measurements of development in L2 written production: The case of L2 Chinese. *Applied Linguistics* 34 (1), 1–24.

Jobard, G., Vigneau, M., Mazoyer, B. and Tzourio-Mazoyer, N. (2007) Impact of modality and linguistic complexity during reading and listening tasks. *Neuroimage* 34, 784–800.

Joe, A. (1998) What effects do text-based tasks promoting generation have on incidental vocabulary acquisition. *Applied Linguistics* 19, 357–377.

Johnson, K. (1982) *Communicative Syllabus Design and Methodology*. Oxford: Pergamon.

Johnson, K. (1988) Mistake correction. *English Language Teaching Journal* 42, 89–96.

Johnson, K. (2000) What task designers do. *Language Teaching Research* 4, 301–321.

Johnson, R.K. and Swain, M. (1997) *Immersion Education: International Perspectives*. Cambridge: Cambridge University Press.

Johnston, C. (2005) Fighting fossilization: Language at different stages in the task cycle. In C. Edwards and J. Willis (eds) *Teachers Exploring Tasks in English Language Teaching*. Basingstoke: Palgrave Macmillan.

Kartchava, E. and Ammar, A. (2014) The noticeability and effectiveness of corrective feedback in relation to target type. *Language Teaching Research* 18, 428–452.

Kawauchi, C. (2005) The effects of strategic planning on the oral narratives of learners with low and high intermediate L2 proficiency. In R. Ellis (ed.) *Planning and Task Performance in a Second Language* (pp. 143–164). Amsterdam: John Benjamins.

Kim, J. (2012) Effects of pre-task modelling on attention to form and question development. *TESOL Quarterly* 47, 8–25.

Kim, Y. (2009) The effects of task complexity on learner-learner interactions. *System* 37, 254–268.

Kim, Y. (2013) Promoting attention to form through task repetition in a Korean EFL context. In K. McDonough and A. Mackey (eds) *Second Language Interaction in Diverse Educational Settings* (pp. 3–24). Amsterdam: John Benjamins.

Kim, Y. and Tracy-Ventura, N. (2013) The role of task repetition in L2 performance development: What needs to be repeated during task-based interaction? *System* 41, 829–840.

Klein, W. and Perdue, C. (1997) The basic variety (or: Couldn't natural languages be much simpler?). *Second Language Research* 13, 301–348.

Klippel, F. (1984) *Keep Talking*. Cambridge: Cambridge University Press.

Kormos, J. and Dénes, M. (2004) Exploring measures and perceptions of fluency in the speech of second language learners. *System* 32, 145–164.

Kowal, M. and Swain, M. (1997) From semantic to syntactic processing: How can we promote metalinguistic awareness in the French immersion classroom? In R. Johnson and M. Swain (eds) *Immersion Education: International Perspectives* (pp. 284–309). Cambridge: Cambridge University Press.

Krashen, S. (1981) *Second Language Acquisition and Second Language Learning*. Oxford: Pergamon.

Krashen, S. (1982) *Principles and Practice in Second Language Acquisition*. Oxford: Pergamon.

Krashen, S. (1985) *The Input Hypothesis: Issues and Implications*. London: Longman.

Krashen, S. (1994) The input hypothesis and its rivals. In N. Ellis (ed.) *Implicit and Explicit Learning of Languages* (pp. 45–77). London: Academic Press.

Krashen, S. and Terrell, T. (1983) *The Natural Approach: Language Acquisition in the Classroom*. Oxford: Pergamon.

Lai, C. (2015) Task-based language teaching in the Asian context: Where are we going now? In M. Thomas and H. Reinders (eds) *Contemporary Task-based Language Teaching in Asia* (pp. 12–29). London: Bloomsbury Academic.

Lai, C. and Li, G. (2011) Technology and task-based teaching: A critical review. *Calico Journal* 28, 498–521.

Lambert, C., Kormos, J. and Minn, D. (2017a) Task repetition and second language speech processing. *Studies in Second Language Acquisition* 39, 167–196.

Lambert, C., Philp, J. and Nakamura, S. (2017b) Learner-generated content and engagement in second language task performance. *Language Teaching Research* 21 (6), 665–680.

Lantolf, J. (1996) Second language acquisition theory-building: 'Letting all the flowers bloom!' *Language Learning* 46, 713–749.

Lantolf, J. (ed.) (2000a) *Socio-cultural Theory and Second Language Learning*. Oxford: Oxford University Press.

Lantolf, J. (2000b) Introducing sociocultural theory. In J. Lantolf (ed.) *Socio-cultural Theory and Second Language Learning*. Oxford: Oxford University Press.

Lantolf, J. and Appel, G. (1994) *Vygotskian Approaches to Second Language Research*. Norwood, NJ: Ablex.

Lantolf, J. and Thorne, S. (2006) *Sociocultural Theory and the Genesis of Second Language Development*. Oxford: Oxford University Press.

Lantolf, J.P. and Poehner, M.E. (2014) *Sociocultural Theory and the Pedagogical Imperative in L2 Education. Vygotskian Praxis and the Theory/Practice Divide*. New York: Routledge.

Larsen-Freeman, D. (2006) The emergence of complexity, fluency and accuracy on the oral and written production of five Chinese learners of English. *Applied Linguistics* 27, 590–619.

Laufer, B. (2006) Comparing focus on form and focus on forms in second-language vocabulary learning. *Canadian Modern Language Review* 63, 149–166.

Leaver, B. and Willis, J. (2004) *Task-Based Instruction in Foreign Language Education*. Washington DC: Georgetown University Press.

Lee, J. (2000) *Tasks and Communicating in Language Classrooms*. Boston: McGraw-Hill.

Lee, S. and Huang, S. (2008) Visual input enhancement and grammar learning. A meta-analytic review. *Studies in Second Language Acquisition* 30, 307–331.

Leont'ev, A. (1981) *Psychology and the Language Learning Process*. Oxford: Pergamon.

Levelt, W. (1989) *Speaking: From Intention to Articulation*. Cambridge MA: The MIT Press.

Lewin, K. (1951) Problems of research in social psychology. In D. Cartwright (ed.) *Field Theory in Social Science: Selected Theoretical Papers* (pp. 155–169). New York: Harper and Row.

Lewis, M. (1993) *The Lexical Approach*. Hove: Language Teaching Publications.

Li, D. (1998) It's always more difficult than you planned. Teachers' perceived difficulties in introducing the communicative approach in South Korea. *TESOL Quarterly* 32, 677–703.

Li, L., Chen, J. and Sun, L. (2015) The effects of different lengths of pre-task planning time on L2 learners' oral test performance. *TESOL Quarterly* 49, 38–66.

Li, S. (2010) The effectiveness of corrective feedback in SLA: A meta-analysis. *Language Learning* 60, 309–365.

Li, S., Ellis, R. and Zhu, Y. (forthcoming) The influence of pre-task explicit grammar instruction on task performance and L2 learning: A process-product study.

Li, S., Ellis, R. and Zhu, Y. (2016) Task-based versus task-supported language instruction: An experimental study. *Annual Review of Applied Linguistics* 36, 205–229.

Li, S., Zhu, Y. and Ellis, R. (2016) The effects of the timing of corrective feedback on the acquisition of a new linguistic structure. *Modern Language Journal* 100, 276–295.

Lightbown, P. (2008) Transfer appropriate processing as a model for classroom second language acquisition. In Z. Han (ed.) *Understanding Second Language Process* (pp. 27–44). Clevedon: Multilingual Matters.

Littlewood, W. (2007) Communicative and task-based language teaching in East Asian classrooms. *Language Teaching* 40, 243–249.

Littlewood, W. (2014) Communication-oriented teaching: Where are we now? Where do we go from here?' *Language Teaching* 47, 249–362.

Loewen, S. (2003) Variation in the frequency and focus of incidental focus on form. *Language Teaching Research* 7, 315–345.

Loewen, S. (2005) Incidental focus on form and second language learning. *Studies in Second Language Acquisitio* 27, 361–386.

Loewen, S. and Philp. J. (2006) Recasts in the adult English L2 classroom: Characteristics, explicitness, and effectiveness. *Modern Language Journal* 90, 536–556.

Long, M. (1981) Input, interaction and second language acquisition. In H. Winitz (ed.) *Native Language and Foreign Language Acquisition* (pp. 259–178). Annals of the New York Academy of Sciences 379.

Long, M. (1983) Native-speaker/non-native speaker conversation and the negotiation of comprehensible input. *Applied Linguistics* 4, 126–141.

Long, M. (1985) A role for instruction in second language acquisition: Task-based language teaching. In K. Hyltenstam and M. Pienemann (eds) *Modelling and Assessing Second Language Acquisition* (pp. 77–100). Clevedon: Multilingual Matters.

Long, M. (1988) Instructed interlanguage development. In L. Beebe (ed.) *Issues in Second Language Acquisition: Multiple perspectives* (pp. 115–141). Rowley, Mass: Newbury House.

Long, M. (1989) Task, group, and task-group interactions. *University of Hawaii Working Papers in ESL* 8, 1–26.

Long, M. (1991) Focus on form: A design feature in language teaching methodology. In K.d. Bot, R. Ginsberg and C. Kramsch (eds) *Foreign Language Research in Cross-cultural Perspective* (pp. 39–52). Amsterdam: John Benjamins.

Long, M. (1996) The role of the linguistic environment in second language acquisition. In W. Ritchie and T. Bhatia (eds) *Handbook of Second Language Acquisition* (pp. 121–158). San Diego: Academic Press.

Long, M. (1997) Focus on form in task-based teaching. McGraw Hill. Available at http://change.c4835149.myzen.co.uk/wp-content/uploads/2013/12/Focus-on-form-in-Task-Based-teaching.pdf

Long, M. (2005) Methodological issues in learner needs analysis. In M. Long (ed.) *Second Language Needs Analysis* (pp. 19–76). Cambridge: Cambridge University Press.

Long, M. (2006) *Problems in SLA*. Mahwah, N.J.: Lawrence Erlbaum.

Long, M. (2015) *Second Language Acquisition and Task-based Language Teaching*. Malden, MA: Wiley Blackwell.

Long, M.H. (2016) In defence of tasks and TBLT: Nonissues and real issues. *Annual Review of Applied Linguistics* 36, 5–33.

Long, M. and Crookes, G. (1987) Intervention points in second language classroom processes. In B. Das (ed.) *Communication and Learning in the Classroom Community*. Singapore: SEAMEO.

Long, M. and Crookes, G. (1992) Three approaches to task-based syllabus design. *TESOL Quarterly* 26, 27–56.

Long, M. and Porter, P. (1985) Group work, interlanguage talk, and second language acquisition. *TESOL Quarterly* 19, 207–228.

Long, M. and Norris, J. (2000) Task-based teaching and assessment. In M. Byram (ed.) *Encyclopedia of Language Teaching* (pp. 597–603). London: Routledge.

Long, M. and Robinson, P. (1998) Focus on form: Theory, research, and practice. In C. Doughty and J. Williams (eds) *Focus on Form in Classroom Second Language Acquisition* (pp. 15–63). Cambridge: Cambridge University Press.

Long, M. and Ross, S. (1993) Modifications that preserve language and content. In M. Tickoo (ed.) *Simplification: Theory and Application* (pp. 29–52). Singapore: SEAMEO Regional Language Centre.

Loschky, L. (1994) Comprehensible input and second language acquisition: What is the relationship? *Studies in Second Language Acquisition* 16, 303–323.

Loschky, L. and Bley-Vroman, R. (1993) Grammar and task-based methodology. In G. Crookes and S. Gass (eds) *Tasks and Language Learning: Integrating Theory and Practice* (pp. 123–167). Clevedon: Multilingual Matters.

Loumpourdi, L. (2005) Developing from PPP to TBL: A focused grammar task. In C. Edwards and J. Willis (eds) *Teachers Exploring Tasks in English Language Teaching*. Basingstoke, Palgrave Macmillan.

Lynch, T. (1989) Researching teachers: Behaviour and belief. In C. Brumfit and R. Mitchell (eds) *Research in the Language Classroom* (pp. 117–127). London: Modern English Publications and the British Council.

Lynch, T. (2001) Seeing what they meant: Transcribing as a route to noticing. *ELT Journal* 55, 124–132.

Lynch, T. (2007) Learning from the transcripts of an oral communication task. *ELT Journal* 61, 311–320.

Lynch, T. and Maclean, J. (2000): Exploring the benefits of task repetition and recyling for classroom language learning. *Language Teaching Research* 4, 221–250.

Lyster, R. (1998) Recasts, repetition and ambiguity in L2 classroom discourse. *Studies in Second Language Acquisition* 20, 51–81.

Lyster, R. (2001) Negotiation of form, recasts, and explicit correction in relation to error types and learner repair in immersion classrooms. *Language Learning* 51, (Suppl. 1), 265–301.

Lyster, R. (2004) Differential effects of prompts and recasts in form-focused instruction. *Studies in Second Language Acquisition* 26 (3), 399–432.

Lyster, R. and Ranta, L. (1997) Corrective feedback and learner uptake. *Studies in Second Language Acquisition* 19, 37–66.

Lyster, R. and Saito, K. (2010) Oral feedback in classroom SLA: A meta-analysis. *Studies in Second Language Acquisition* 32, 265–302.

Lyster, R., Saito, K. and Sato, M. (2013) Oral corrective feedback in second language classrooms. *Language Teaching* 46 (1), 1–40.

Mackey, A. (1999) Input, interaction and second language development: An empirical study of question formation in ESL. *Studies in Second Language Acquisition* 21, 557–587.

Mackey, A. (2006) Feedback, noticing and second language learning. *Applied Linguistics* 27 (3), 405–430.

Mackey, A., Gass, S. and McDonough, K. (2000) How do learners perceive interactional feedback. *Studies in Second Language Acquisition* 22 (4), 471–497.

Mackey, A. and Goo, J.M. (2007) Interaction research in SLA: A meta-analysis and research synthesis. In A. Mackey (ed.) *Input, Interaction and Corrective Feedback in L2 Learning* (pp. 379–452). Oxford: Oxford University Press.

Mackey, A. and Philp, J. (1998) Conversational interaction and second language development: Recasts, responses and red herrings. *The Modern Language Journal* 82, 338–356.

MacWhinney, B. (2000) *The CHILDES Project: Tools for Analyzing Talk* (3rd edn). Mahwah, NJ: Lawrence Erlbaum Associates.

Maehr, M. (1984) Meaning and motivation: Toward a theory of personal investment. In R. Ames and C. Ames (eds) *Motivation in Education: Student Motivation, Vol. 1* (pp. 115–144). San Diego: Academic Press.

Malvern, D. and Richards, B. (2002) Investigating accommodation in language proficiency interviews using a new measure of lexical diversity. *Language Testing* 19, 85–104.

Markee, N. and Kunitz, S. (2013) Doing planning and task performance in second language acquisition: An ethnomethodological respecification. *Language Learning* 63, 629–664.

Markee, N. (1994) Towards and ethnomethodological respecification of second language acquisition studies. In E. Tarone, S. Gass and A. Cohen (eds) *Research Methodology in Second Language Acquisition* (pp. 89–106). Mahwah, N.J.: Lawrence Erlbaum.

McDonough, K. (2004) Learner-learner interaction during pair and small group activities in a Thai EFL context. *System* 32, 2007–2034.

McDonough, K. and Chaikitmongkol, W. (2007) Teachers' and learners' reactions to a task based EFL course in Thailand. *TESOL Quarterly* 41, 107–132.

McDonough, K. and Mackey, A. (2006) Responses to recasts: Repetitions, primed production and linguistic development. *Language Learning* 56, 693–720.

McGrath, I. (2002) *Materials Evaluation and Design for Language Teaching*. Edinburgh: Edinburgh University Press.

Meara, P. (1980) Vocabulary acquisition: A neglected aspect of language learning. *Language Teaching and Linguistics: Abstracts* 13, 221–246.

Meara, P. and Bell, H. (2001) P Lex: A simple and effective way of describing the lexical characteristics of short L2 texts. *Prospect* 16, 5–15.

Mehnert, U. (1998) The effects of different lengths of time for planning on second language performance. *Studies in Second Language Acquisition* 20, 52–83.

Mehrang, F. and Rahimpour, M. (2010) The impact of task structure and planning conditions on oral performance of EFL learners. *Procedia Social and Behavioral Sciences* 2, 3678–3686.

Mennim, P. (2012) Learner negotiation of L2 form in transcription exercises. *ELT Journal* 66, 52–61.

Mochizuki, N. (2017) Contingent need analysis for task implementation: An activity systems analysis of group writing conferences. *TESOL Quarterly* 51, 607–631.

Mochizuki, N. and Ortega, L. (2008) Balancing communication and grammar in beginning-level foreign language classrooms: A study of guided planning and relativization. *Language Teaching Research* 12, 11–37.

Morgan-Short, K., Faretta-Stutenberg, M., Brill, K.A., Carpenter, H. and Wong, P. (2014) Declarative and procedural memory as individual differences in second language acquisition. *Bilingualism: Language and Cognition* 17 (1), 56–72.

Morgan-Short, K., Deng, Z., Brill-Schuetz, K.A., Faretta-Stutenberg, M., Wong, P.C.M. and Wong, F.C.K. (2015) A view of the neural representation of second language syntax through artificial language learning under implicit contexts of exposure. *Studies in Second Language Acquisition* 27 (2), 383–419.

Müller, T. (2005) Adding tasks to text books for beginning learners. In C. Edwards and J. Willis (eds) *Teachers Exploring Tasks in English Language Teaching* (pp. 69–77). Basingstoke, Palgrave Macmillan.

Murunoi, H. (2000) Focus on form through interaction enhancement. *Language Learning* 50, 617–673.

Nakakubo, T. (2011) The effects of planning on second language oral performance in Japanese: Processes and production. Unpublished doctoral dissertation, University of Iowa. http:// ir.uiowa.edu/cgi/viewcontent.cgi?article=2423andcontext=etd

Nakamura, J. and Csikszentmihályi, M. (2001) Flow theory and research. In C.R. Snyder, E. Wright and Shane J. Lopez (eds) *Handbook of Positive Psychology* (pp. 195–206). Oxford: Oxford University Press.

Nakatsukasa, K. and Loewen, L. (2015) A teacher's first language use in form-focused episodes in Spanish as a foreign language classroom. *Language Teaching Research* 19, 133–149.

Nassaji, H. (2010) The occurrence and effectiveness of spontaneous focus on form in adult ESL classrooms. *Canadian Modern Language Review* 66, 907–933.

Nassaji, H. (2011) Immediate learner repair and its relationship with learning targeted forms in dyadic interaction. *System* 39, 17–29.

Nassaji, H. (2013) Participation structure and incidental focus on form in adult EFL classrooms. *Language Learning* 63, 835–869.

Nassaji, H. and Fotos, S. (2010) *Teaching Grammar in Second Language Classrooms: Integrating Form-focused Instruction in Communicative Context*. London: Routledge.

Nation, P. (1990) *Teaching and Learning Vocabulary*. New York: Newbury House/ Harper Row.

Newmark, L. (1966) How not to interfere with language learning. *International Journal of American Linguistics* 32, 77–83.

Newton, J. (1991) Negotiation: Negotiating what? Paper given at SEAMEO Conference on Language Acquisition and the Second/Foreign Language Classroom, RELC, Singapore.

Newton, J. (1995) Task-based interaction and incidental vocabulary learning: A case study. *Second Language Research* 11, 159–177.

Nicholas, H., Lightbown, P. and Spada, N. (2001) Recasts as feedback to language learners. *Language Learning* 51, 719–758.

Nielson, K. (2014) Can planning time compensate for individual differences in working memory capacity? *Language Teaching Research* 18, 272–293.

Nobuyoshi, J. and Ellis, R. (1993) Focussed communication tasks. *English Language Teaching Journal* 47, 203–210.

Norris, J.M. (2016) Current issues for task-based language assessment. *Annual Review of Applied Linguistics* 36, 230–244.

Norris, J. and Ortega, L. (2000) Effectiveness of L2 instruction: A research synthesis and quantitative meta-analysis. *Language Learning* 50, 417–528.

Norris, J.M. and Ortega, L. (2009) Towards an organic approach to investigating CAF in instructed SLA: The case of complexity. *Applied Linguistics* 30, 555–578.

Norris, J., Brown, J.D., Hudson, T. and Yoshioka, Y. (1998) *Designing Second LANGUAGE Performance Assessments* (Vol. SLTCC Technical Report #18). Honolulu: Second Language Teaching and Curriculum Center, University of Hawaii at Manoa.

Nunan, D. (1989) *Designing Tasks for the Communicative Classroom*. Cambridge: Cambridge University Press.

Nunan, D. (1990) The teacher as researcher. In C. Brumfit and R. Mitchell (eds) *Research in the Language Classroom. ELT Documents 133* (pp. 16–32). Modern English Publications.

Nunan, D. (2003) The impact of English as a global language on educational policies and practices in the Asia-Pacific region. *TESOL Quarterly* 37, 589–613.

Nunan, D. (2004) *Task-based Language Teaching*. Cambridge: Cambridge University Press.

Ochs, E. (1979) Planned and unplanned discourse. In T. Givon (ed.) *Syntax and Semantics Vol 12: Discourse and Semantics* (pp. 51–80). New York NT: Academic Press.

Ortega, L. (1999) Planning and focus on form in L2 oral performance. *Studies in Second Language Acquisition* 21, 109–148.

Ortega, L. (2005) What do learners plan? Learner-driven attention to form during pre-task planning. In R. Ellis (ed.) *Planning and Task Performance in a Second Language* (pp. 77–109). Amsterdam: John Benjamins.

Pang, F. and Skehan, P. (2014) Self-reported planning behaviour and second language performance in narrative retelling. In P. Skehan (ed.) *Processing Perspectives on Task Performance* (pp. 95–127). Amsterdam: John Benjamins.

Pattansorn, C. (2010) Effects of procedural content and task repetition on accuracy and fluency in an EFL context. Unpublished PhD Dissertation, Northern Arizona University.

Patterson, C. and Kister, M. (1981) The development of listener skills for referential communication. In W. Dickson (ed.) *Children's Oral Communication Skills*. New York: Academic Press.

Pennycook, A. (1994) *The Cultural Politics of English as an International Language*. London: Longman.

Philp, J. and Duchesne, S. (2016) Exploring engagement in tasks in the language classroom. *Annual Review of Applied Linguistics* 36, 50–72.

Phung, L. (2017) Task preference, task engagement, and learners' subjective responses to tasks in a US university context. Unpublished EdD Thesis, Anaheim University. Anaheim, California.

Pica, T. (1983) Adult acquisition of English as a second language under different conditions of exposure. *Language Learning* 33, 465–497.

Pica, T. (1984) Methods of morpheme quantification: Their effect on the interpretation of second language data. *Studies in Second Language Acquisition* 6, 69–78.

Pica, T. (1992) The textual outcomes of native speaker-non-native~ speaker negotiation. In C. Kramsch and S. McConnell-Ginet (eds) *Text and Context: Cross-disciplinary Perspectives on Language Study* (pp. 198–237). Lexington, MA: D.C. Heath and Co.

Pica, T. (1996) Second language learning through interaction: Multiple perspectives. *Working Papers in Educational Linguistic* 12 (1), 1–22.

Pica, T. (1997) Second language teaching and research relationships: A North American view. *Language Teaching Research* 1, 48–72.

Pica, T., Kanagy, R. and Falodun, J. (1993) Choosing and using communication tasks for second language instruction. In G. Crookes and S. Gass (eds) *Tasks and Language Learning: Integrating Theory and Practice* (pp. 9–34). Clevendon, England: Multilingual Matters.

Pica, T., Young, R. and Doughty, C. (1987) The impact of interaction on comprehension. *TESOL Quarterly* 21, 737–758.

Pienemann, M. (1985) Learnability and syllabus construction. In K. Hyltenstam and M. Pienemann (eds) *Modelling and Assessing Second Language Acquisition* (pp. 23–75). Clevedon: Multilingual Matters.

Pitler, E. and Nenkova, A. (2008) Revisiting readability: A unified framework for predicting text quality. *Proceedings of the 2008 Conference on Empirical Methods in Natural Language Processing*. Honolulu: Association for Computational Linguistics, 86–195.

Platt, E. and Brooks, F. (1994) The 'acquisition-rich environment' revisited. *Modern Language Journal* 78, 497–511.

Porte, G. (ed.) (2012) *Replication Research in Applied Linguistics*. Cambridge: Cambridge University Press.

Prabhu, N.S. (1987) *Second Language Pedagogy*. Oxford: Oxford University Press.

Quinn, P. (2014) Delayed versus immediate corrective feedback on orally produced passive errors in English. Unpublished PhD thesis, University of Toronto.

Quinn, P. and Nakata, T. (2017) The timing of oral corrective feedback. In H. Nassaji and E. Kartchava (eds) *Corrective Feedback in Second Language Teaching and Learning: Research, Theory, Applications, Implications* (pp. 35–47). New York: Routledge.

Rea-Dickens, P. and Germaine, K. (eds) (2000) *Managing Evaluation and Innovation in Language teaching*. Harlow: Longman.

Reber, P. and Squire, L. (1998) Encapsulation of implicit and explicit memory in sequence learning. *Journal of Cognitive Neuroscience* 10 (2), 248–263.

Révész, A. (2012) Working memory and the observed effectiveness of recasts on different L2 outcome measures. *Language Learning* 62, 93–132.

Révész, A., Michel, M. and Gilabert, R. (2016) Measuring cognitive task demands using dual task methodology, subjective self-ratings, and expert judgments: A validation study. *Studies in Second Language Acquisition* DOI: http://dx.doi.org/10.1017/S0272263115000339

Richards, J. (1984) Language curriculum development. *RELC Journal* 15, 1–29.

Richards, J. and Rogers, T. (1986) *Approaches and Methods in Language Teaching*. Cambridge: Cambridge University Press.

Richards, J. and Rogers, T. (2001) *Approaches and Methods in Language Teaching* (2nd edn). Cambridge: Cambridge University Press.

Richards, J. and Rogers, T. (2014) *Approaches and Methods in Language Teaching* (3rd edn). Cambridge: Cambridge University Press.

Rivers, W. and Temperley, M. (1978) *A Practical Guide to the Teaching of English as a Second or Foreign Language*. New York: OUP.

Robinson, P. (1995a) Attention, memory, and the 'noticing' hypothesis. *Language Learning* 45, 283–331.

Robinson, P. (1995b) Task complexity and second language narrative discourse. *Language Learning* 45, 99–140.

Robinson, P. (2001) Task complexity, cognitive resources, and syllabus design: A triadic framework for examining task influences on SLA. In P. Robinson (ed.) *Cognition and Second Language Instruction* (pp. 285–318). Cambridge: Cambridge University Press.

Robinson, P. (2007) Aptitudes, abilities, contexts, and practice. In R.M. DeKeyser (ed.) *Practice in Second Language: Perspectives from Applied Linguistics and Cognitive Psychology* (pp. 256–286). New York/Cambridge: Cambridge University Press.

Robinson, P. (2010) Task-based language teaching: A review of the issues. *Language Learning* 61, 1–36.

Robinson, P. (ed.) (2011a) *Second Language Task Complexity: Researching the Cognition Hypothesis of Language Learning and Performance*. Amsterdam: John Benjamins.

Robinson, P. (2011b) Second language task complexity, the Cognition Hypothesis, language learning, and performance. In P. Robinson (ed.) *Second Language Task Complexity: Researching the Cognition Hypothesis of Language Learning and Performance* (pp. 3–38). Amsterdam: John Benjamins.

Robinson, P., Ting, S. and Unwin, J. (1996) Investigating second language task complexity. *RELC Journal* 26, 62–79.

Rogers, E. (2003) *Diffusion of Innovations* (5th edn). New York: Free Press.

Rolin-Ianziti, J. (2010) The organization of delayed second language correction. *Language Teaching Research* 14 (2), 183–206.

Rosch, E. (1975) Cognitive representations of semantic categories. *Journal of Experimental Psychology: General* 104, 192–233.

Russell, J. and Spada, N. (2006) The effectiveness of corrective feedback for the acquisition of L2 Grammar: A meta-Analysis of the research. In J. Norris and L. Ortega (eds) *Synthesizing Research on Language Learning and Teaching* (pp. 133–164). Amsterdam: John Benjamins.

Saeedi, M. (2015) Unguided planning, task structure and L2 oral performance: Focusing on complexity, accuracy and fluency. *Journal of Applied Linguistics and Language Research* 2, 263–274.

Samuda, V. (2001) Guiding relationships between form and meaning during task performance: The role of the teacher. In M. Bygate, P. Skehan and M. Swain (eds) *Researching Pedagogic Tasks, Second Language Learning, Teaching and Testing* (pp. 119–114). Harlow: Longman.

Samuda, V. (2015) Tasks, design, and the architecture of pedagogical spaces. In M. Bygate (ed.) *Domains and Directions in the Development of TBLT* (pp. 271–301). Amsterdam: John Benjamins.

Samuda, V. and Bygate, M. (2008) *Tasks in Second Language Learning*. Basingstoke: Palgrave MacMillan.

Sanchez, D. and Reber, P. (2013) Explicit pre-training instruction does not improve implicit perceptual motor sequence learning. *Cognition* 126 (3), 341–351.

Sanz, C. and Morgan-Short, K. (2004) Positive evidence vs. explicit rule presentation and explicit negative feedback: A computer-assisted study. *Language Learning* 54 (1), 35–78.

Sasayama, S. (2016) Is a 'complex' task really complex? Validating the assumption of task complexity. *Modern Language Journal* 100, 231–254.

Scarcella, R. and Higa, C. (1981) Input, negotiation and age differences in second language acquisition. *Language Learning* 31, 409–307.

Schmidt, R. (1990) The role of consciousness in second language learning. *Applied Linguistics* 11, 129–158.

Schmidt, R. (1994) Deconstructing consciousness in search of useful definitions for applied linguistics. *AILA Review* 11, 11–26.

Schmidt, R. (2001) Attention. In P. Robinson (ed.) *Cognition and Second Language Instruction* (pp. 3–32). Cambridge: Cambridge University Press.

Schmidt, R.W. and Frota, S. (1986) Developing basic conversational ability in a second language: A case – study of an adult learner. In R. Day (ed.) *Talking to Learn* (pp. 237–326). Rowley, Mass: Newbury House.

Scrivener, J. (2005) *Learning Teaching: A Guidebook for English Language Teachers.* Oxford: MacMillan Education.

Seedhouse, P. (1997) The case of the missing 'no'; the relationship between pedagogy and interaction'. *Language Learning* 47, 547–583.

Seedhouse, P. (1999) Task-based interaction. *ELT Journal* 53, 149–156.

Seedhouse, P. (2005) 'Task' as research construct. *Language Learning* 55, 533–570.

Shanks, D.R. (2005) Implicit learning. In K. Lamberts and R. Goldstone (eds) *Handbook of Cognition* (pp. 202–220). London, UK: Sage.

Sharwood Smith, M. (1986) Comprehension vs. acquisition: Two ways of processing input. *Applied Linguistics* 7, 239–256.

Sheen, R. (1994) A critical analysis of the advocacy of the task-based syllabus. *TESOL Quarterly* 28, 127–157.

Sheen, R. (2003) Focus on form—a myth in the making? *ELT Journal* 57 (3), 225–233.

Sheen, R. (2006) Focus on forms as a means of improving accurate oral production. In A. Housen and M. Pierrard (eds) *Investigations in Instructed Second Language Acquisition* (pp. 271–310). Berlin: Mouton de Gruyter.

Sheen, Y. (2004) Corrective feedback and learner uptake in communicative classrooms across instructional settings. *Language Teaching Research* 8, 263–300.

Sheen, Y. (2006) Exploring the relationship between characteristics of recasts and learner uptake. *Language Teaching Research* 10, 361–392.

Shehadeh, A. (2005) Task-based language learning and teaching: Theories and applications. In C. Edwards and J. Willis (eds) *Teachers Exploring Tasks in English language Teaching* (pp. 13–30). New York, NY: Palgrave Macmillan.

Sheppard, C. (2006) The effects of instruction directed at the gaps second language learners noticed in their oral production. Unpublished PhD thesis, University of Auckland.

Sheppard, C. and Ellis, R. (2018) The effects of awareness-raising through stimulated recall on the performance of on the same task and a new task of the same type. In M. Bygate (ed.) *Learning Language Through Task Repetition.* Amsterdam: John Benjamins.

Shintani, N. (2011) A comparison of the effects of comprehension-based and production-based instruction on the acquisition of vocabulary and grammar by young Japanese learners of English. Unpublished PhD thesis, University of Auckland, New Zealand.

Shintani, N. (2015) The incidental grammar acquisition in focus on form and focus on forms instruction for young beginner learners. *TESOL Quarterly* 49 (1), 115–140.

Shintani, N. (2016) *Input-based Tasks in Foreign Language Instruction for Young Learners.* Amsterdam, Netherlands.

Shintani, N. (2018) The roles of explicit instruction and guided production practice in the proceduralization of a complex grammatical structure. In R. DeKeyser and G. Prieto Botana (eds) *(Doing) SLA Research with Implications for the Classroom: Reconciling Methodological Demands and Pedagogical Applicability.* Amsterdam: John Benjamins.

Shintani, N. and Ellis, R. (2014) Tracking learning behaviours in the incidental acquisition of two dimensional adjectives by beginner learners of L2 English. *Language Teaching Research* 18, 521–542.

Shook, D. (1999) What foreign language reading recalls reveal about the input-to-intake phenomenon. *Applied Language Learning* 10, 39–76.

Skehan, P. (1996a) Second language acquisition research and task-based instruction. In J. Willis and D. Willis (eds) *Challenge and Change in Language Teaching.* Oxford: Heinemann.

Skehan, P. (1996b) A framework for the implementation of task-based instruction. *Applied Linguistics* 17 (1), 38–62.

Skehan, P. (1998a) *A Cognitive Approach to Language Learning.* Oxford, UK: Oxford University Press.

Skehan, P. (1998b) Task-based instruction. *Annual Review of Applied Linguistics* 18. 268–286.

Skehan, P. (2001) Tasks and language performance assessment. In M. Bygate, P. Skehan and M. Swain (eds) *Researching Pedagogic Tasks, Second Language Learning, Teaching and Testing* (pp. 167–185). Harlow: Longman.

Skehan, P. (2003) Focus on form, tasks and technology. *Computer Assisted Language Learning* 16, 391–411.

Skehan, P. (2007) Task research and language teaching: Reciprocal relationships. In S. Fotos and H. Nassaji (eds) *Form-meaning Relationships in Language Pedagogy: Essays in Honour of Rod Ellis* (pp. 289–301). Oxford: OUP.

Skehan, P. (2009) Modelling second language performance: Integrating complexity, accuracy, fluency and lexis. *Applied Linguistics* 30, 510–532.

Skehan, P. (2009) Models of speaking and the assessment of second language proficiency. In A. Benati (ed.) *Issues in Second Language Proficiency* (pp. 202–215). London: Continuum.

Skehan, P. (2011) *Researching Tasks: Performance, Assessment and Pedagogy.* Shanghai: Shanghai Foreign Language Education Press.

Skehan, P. (ed.) (2014a) *Processing Perspectives on Task Performance.* Amsterdam: John Benjamins.

Skehan, P. (2014b) The context for researching a processing perspective on task performance. In P. Skehan (ed.) *Processing Perspectives on Task Performance* (pp. 1–26). Amsterdam: John Benjamins.

Skehan, P. (2014c) Limited attentional capacity, second language performance, and task-based pedagogy. In P. Skehan (ed.) *Processing Perspectives on Task Performance* (pp. 211–260). Amsterdam: John Benjamins.

Skehan, P. (2016) Tasks versus conditions: Two perspectives on task research and their implications for language pedagogy. *Annual Review of Applied Linguistics* 36, 34–49.

Skehan, P. and Foster, P. (1997) Task type and task processing conditions as influences on foreign language performance. *Language Teaching Research* 1, 185–211.

Skehan, P. and Foster, P. (1999) The influence of task structure and processing conditions on narrative retellings. *Language Learning* 49 (1), 93–120.

Skehan, P. and Foster, P. (2001) Cognition and tasks. In R. Robinson (ed.) *Cognition and Second Language Instruction* (pp. 183–205). New York: Cambridge University Press.

Skehan, P. and Foster, P. (2005) Strategic and online planning: The influence of surprise information and task time on second language performance. In R. Ellis (ed.) *Planning and Task Performance in a Second Language* (pp. 193–218). John Benjamins B.V.

Skehan, P. and Foster, P. (2012) Complexity, accuracy, fluency and lexis in task-based performance: A synthesis of the Ealing research. In A. Housen, F. Kuiken and I. Vedder (eds) *Dimensions of L2 Performance and Proficiency: Complexity, Accuracy, and Fluency in SLA* (pp. 199–220). Amsterdam: John Benjamins.

Skehan, P., Foster, P. and Mehnert, U. (1998) Assessing and using tasks. In W. Renandya and G. Jacobs (eds) *Learners and Language Learning.* Singapore: Seameo.

Slimani, A. (1989) The role of topicalization in classroom language learning. *System* 17, 223–234.

Slimani-Rolls, A. (2005) Rethinking task-based language learning: What we can learn from the learners. *Language Teaching Research* 9, 195–218.

Soars, L. and Soars, J. (2013) *New Headway*. Oxford: Oxford University Press.

Spada, N., Jessop, L., Suzuki, W., Tomita, Y. and Valeo, A. (2014) Isolated and integrated form-focused instruction: Effects on different types of L2 knowledge. *Language Teaching Research* 18, 453–443.

Spada, N. and Lightbown, P.M. (1999) Instruction, L1 influence and developmental readiness in second language acquisition. *Modern Language Journal* 83, 1–22.

Spada, N. and Lightbown, P. (2008) Form-focused instruction: Isolated or intergated? *TESOL Quarterly* 42, 181–207.

Spada, N. and Tomita, Y. (2010) Interactions between type of instruction and type of language feature: A meta-analysis. *Language Learning* 60 (2), 263–308.

Stenhouse, L. (1975) *An Introduction to Curriculum Research and Development*. London: Heinemann.

Storch, N. (2002) Patterns of interaction in ESL pair work. *Language Learning* 52 (1), 119–158.

Storch, N. (2008) Metatalk in a pair work activity: Level of engagement and implications for language development. *Language Awareness* 17 (2), 95–114.

Storch, N. and Wigglesworth, G. (2003) Is there a role for the use of the L1 in an L2 setting? *TESOL Quarterly* 37, 760–770.

Storch, N. (2017) Sociocultural theory in the L2 classroom. In S. Loewen and M. Sato (eds) *The Routledge Handbook of Instructed Second Language Acquisition* (pp. 69–83). New York: Routledge.

Suzuki, Y. and DeKeyser, R. (2015) Comparing elicited imitation and word monitoring as measures of implicit knowledge. *Language Learning* 65, 860–895.

Svalberg, A. (2009) Engagement with language: Developing a construct. *Language Awareness* 18, 242–258.

Swain, M. (1985) Communicative competence: Some roles of comprehensible input and comprehensible output in its development. In S. Gass and C. Madden (eds) *Input in Second Language Acquisition* (pp. 235–253). Rowley, Mass.: Newbury House.

Swain, M. (1995) Three functions of output in second language learning. In G. Cook and B. Seidhofer (eds) *For H.G. Widdowson: Principles and Practice in the Study of Language*. Oxford: Oxford University Press.

Swain, M. (1998) Focus on form through conscious reflection. In C. Doughty and J. Williams (eds) *Focus-on-form in Classroom Second Language Acquisition* (pp. 64–81). Cambridge: Cambridge University Press.

Swain, M. (2000) The output hypothesis and beyond: Mediating acquisition through collaborative dialogue. In J. Lantolf (ed.) *Socio-cultural Theory and Second Language Learning* (pp. 97–114). Oxford: Oxford University Press.

Swain, M. (2006) Languaging, agency and collaboration in advanced second language learning. In H. Byrnes (ed.) *Advanced Language Learning: The Contributions of Halliday and Vygotsky* (pp. 95–108). London: Continuum.

Swain, M. and Lapkin, S. (1998) Interaction and second language learning: Two adolescent French immersion students working together. *Modern Language Journal* 82, 320–337.

Swain, M. and Lapkin, S. (2001) Focus on form through collaborative dialogue: Exploring task effects. In M. Bygate, P. Skehan and M. Swain (eds) *Researching Pedagogic Tasks, Second Language Learning, Teaching and Testing* (pp. 119–149). Harlow: Longman.

Swales, J. (1987) Communicative language teaching in ESP contexts. *Annual Review of Applied Linguistics* 8, 48–57.

Swan, M. (1994) Design criteria for pedagogic language rules. In M. Bygate, A. Tonkyn and E. Williams (eds) *Grammar and the Language Teacher* (pp. 45–55). New York: Prentice Hall.

Swan, M. (2005a) Legislating by hypothesis: The case of task-based instruction. *Applied Linguistics* 26, 376–401.

Swan, M. (2005b) Review of Rod Ellis' Task-based Language Learning and Teaching. *International Journal of Applied Linguistics* 15, 251–256.

Swan, M. and Walter, C. (1984) *The Cambridge English Course*. Cambridge: Cambridge University Press.

Taguchi, N. and Kim, Y. (2016) Collaborative dialogue in learning pragmatics: Pragmatic-related episodes as an opportunity for learning request-making. *Applied Linguistics* 37, 416–437.

Tavakoli, P. and Foster, P. (2011) Task design and second language performance: The effect of narrative type on learner output. *Language Learning* 61 (s1), 37–72.

Tavakoli, P. and Skehan, P. (2005) Strategic planning, task structure, and performance testing. In R. Ellis (ed.) *Planning and Task Performance in a Second Language*. (pp. 239–273). Amsterdam: John Benjamins.

Tavakoli, P., Campbell, C. and McCormack, J. (2016) Development of speech fluency over a short period of time: Effects of pedagogic intervention. *TESOL Quarterly* 50, 447–471.

Thai, C. and Boers, F. (2016) Repeating a monologue under increasing time pressure: Effects on fluency, complexity, and accuracy. *TESOL Quarterly,* 50, 369–393.

Thomas, M. and Reinders, H. (eds) (2015) *Contemporary Task-based Teaching in Asia*. London: Continuum.

Thomas, M. and Reinders, H. (eds) (2010) *Task-based Learning and Teaching with Technology*. London: Continuum.

Tomlin, R. and Villa, V. (1994) Attention in cognitive science and second language acquisition. *Studies in Second Language Acquisition* 16, 183–203.

Ur, P. (1988) *Grammar Practice Activities*. Cambridge: CUP.

Ur, P. (1996) *A Course in Language Teaching: Practice and Theory*. Cambridge University Press, Cambridge.

Valdebenito, M.S. (2015) Developing the metacognitive skill of noticing the gap through self-transcribing: The case of students enrolled in an ELT education program in Chile. *Colombian Applied Linguistics Journal* 17, 260–275.

Van Avermaet, P. and Gysen, S. (2006) From needs to tasks: Language learning needs in a task-based perspective. In K. Van den Branden (ed.) *Task-based Language Education* (pp. 17–46). Cambridge: Cambridge University Press.

Van de Guchte, M., Braaksma, M., Rijlaarsdam, G. and Bimmel, P. (2016) Focus on form through repetition in TBLT. *Language Teaching Research* 20, 300–320.

Van den Branden, K. (ed.) (2006a) *Task-based Language Education: From Theory to Practice*. Cambridge: Cambridge University Press.

Van den Branden, K. (2006b) Introduction: Task-based language teaching in a nutshell. In K. Van den Branden (ed.) *Task-based Language Education: From Theory to Practice* (pp. 1–16). Cambridge: Cambridge University Press.

Van den Branden, K. (2006c) Training teachers: Task-based as well? In K. Van den Branden (eds) *Task-based Language Education: From Theory to Practice* (pp. 217–248). Cambridge: Cambridge University Press.

Van Lier, L. (1991) Inside the classroom: Learning processes and teaching procedures. *Applied Language Learning* 2, 29–69.

Van Lier, L. (1996) *Interaction in the Language Curriculum*. London: Longman.

VanPatten, B. (1989) Can learners attend to form and content while processing input? *Hispania* 72, 409–417.

VanPatten, B. (1990) Attending to form and content in the input. *Studies in Second Language Acquisition* 12, 287–301.

VanPatten, B. (1996) *Input Processing and Grammar Instruction in Second Language Acquisition*. Norwood, N.J.: Ablex.

Varonis, E. and Gass S. (1985) Non-native/non-native conversations: A model for negotiation of meaning. *Applied Linguistics* 6, 71–90.

Vercelotti, M. (2017) The development of complexity, accuracy, and fluency in second language performance: A longitudinal study. *Applied Linguistics* 38, 90–111.

Vygotsky, L. (1978) *Mind and Society: The Development of Higher Psychological Processes*. Cambridge, MA: Harvard University Press.

Wang, Q. (2007) The national curriculum changes and their effects on English language teaching in the People's Republic of China. In J. Cummins and C. Davison (eds) *International Handbook of English Language Teaching in the People's Republic of China* (pp. 87–106). Springer.

Wang, Z. (2014) On time pressure manipulations: L2 speaking performance under five types of planning and repetition conditions. In P. Skehan (ed.) *Processing Perspectives on Task Performance* (pp. 27–61). Amsterdam: John Benjamins.

Watson-Todd, R. (2006) Continuing change after innovation. *System* 34, 1–14.

Weir, C. and Roberts, J. (1994) *Evaluation in ELT*. Oxford: Blackwell.

Wells, G. (1999) *Dialogic Enquiry*. Cambridge: Cambridge University Press.

Wen, Z. (2015) Working memory in second language acquisition and processing: The phonological/executive model. In Z. Wen, M. Mota and A. McNeill (eds) *Working Memory in Second Language Acquisition and Processing* (pp. 41–62). Bristol: Multilingual Matters.

Wen, Z. (2016) Phonological and executive working memory in task-based speech planning and performance. *Language Learning Journal* 44, 418–435.

White, L. (1987) Against comprehensible input: The input hypothesis and the development of second language competence. *Applied Linguistics* 8, 95–110.

White, R. (1988) *The ELT Curriculum, Design, Innovation and Management*. Oxford: Basil Blackwell.

Widdowson, H. (1978) *Teaching Language as Communication*. Oxford: Oxford University Press.

Widdowson, H. (1998a) Skills, abilities, and contexts of reality. *Annual Review of Applied Linguistics* 18, 323–333.

Widdowson, H. (1998b) Context, community and authentic language. *TESOL Quarterly* 32, 705–716.

Widdowson, H. (2003) *Defining Issues in English Language Teaching* (Chapter 9 – Pedagogic Design). Oxford: Oxford University Press.

Wilkins, D. (1976) *Notional Syllabuses*. Oxford: Oxford University Press.

Williams, J. and Evans, J. (1998) What kind of focus and on which forms? In C. Doughty and J. Williams (eds) *Focus-on-form in Classroom Second Language Acquisition* (pp. 139–155). Cambridge: Cambridge University Press.

Williams, J. (1999) Learner-generated attention to form. *Language Learning* 49, 583–625.

Williams, J. (2001) The effectiveness of spontaneous attention to form. *System* 29, 325–340.

Williams, J. (2009) Implicit learning in second language acquisition. In W. Ritchie and T. Bhatia (eds) *The New Handbook of Second Language Acquisition* (pp. 319–344). Bingley, UK: Emerald Publishing.

Willis, J. (1996) *A Framework for Task-based Learning*. Harlow: Longman.

Willis, J. (2005) Aims and explorations into tasks and task-based teaching. In C. Edwards and J. Willis (eds) *Teachers Exploring Tasks in English Language Teaching* (pp. 1–12). Basingstoke, Palgrave Macmillan.

Willis, J. (2008) Adapting your text book for task-based teaching. Harrogate: IATEFL Conference. http://willis-elt.co.uk/wp-content/uploads/2015/03/IATEFL_JW.pdf

Willis, D. and Willis, J. (2007) *Doing Task-based Teaching.* Oxford: Oxford University Press.

Wood, D., Bruner, J. and Ross, G. (1976) The role of tutoring in problem solving. *Journal of Child Psychology and Psychiatry* 17, 89–100.

Yalçin, S. and Spada, N. (2016) Language aptitude and grammatical difficulty. *Studies in Second Language Acquisition* 38, 239–263.

Yalden, J. (1983) *The Communicative Syllabus: Evolution, Design and Implementation.* Oxford: Pergamon.

Yalden, J. (1986) An interactive approach to syllabus design: the frameworks project. In C. Brumfit (ed.) *The Practice of Communicative Teaching: EKT Documents 124* (pp. 25–38). Oxford: Pergamon and the British Council.

Yilmaz, Y. (2012) The relative effects of explicit correction and recasts on two target structures via two communication modes. *Language Learning* 62 (4), 1134–1169.

Yalçin, S. and Spada, N. (2016) Language aptitude and grammatical difficulty: An EFL classroom-based study. *Studies in Second Language Acquisition* 38, 239–263.

Yalden, J. (1983) *The Communicative Syllabus: Evolution, Design, and Implementation.* Oxford: Pergamon.

Yuan, F. and Ellis, R. (2003) The effects of pre-task and on-line planning on fluency, complexity and accuracy in L2 monologic oral production. *Applied Linguistics* 24, 1–27.

Yule, G. (1997) *Referential Communication Tasks.* Mahwah, NJ: Lawrence Erlbaum.

Yule, G. and McDonald, D. (1990) Resolving referential conflicts in L2 interaction: The effect of proficiency and interactive role. *Language Learning* 40, 539–556.

Yule, G. and Powers, M. (1994) Investigating the communicative outcomes of task-based interaction. *System* 22, 81–91.

Yule, G., Powers, M. and McDonald, D. (1992) The variable effects of some task-based learning procedures on L2 communicative effectiveness. *Language Learning* 42, 249–277.

Index